Peckinpah: The Western Films

A Reconsideration

Paul Seydor

PECKINPAH
The Western Films

A Reconsideration

Foreword by David Weddle

UNIVERSITY OF ILLINOIS PRESS

Urbana and Chicago

© 1980, 1997 by the Board of Trustees of the University of Illinois
Manufactured in the United States of America
C 5 4 3 2 1

This book is printed on acid-free paper.

Library of Congress Cataloging-in-Publication Data

Seydor, Paul, 1947–
    Peckinpah : the Western films : a reconsideration / Paul Seydor ;
foreword by David Weddle.
        p.   cm.
    Includes bibliographical references and index.
    ISBN 0-252-02268-8 (cloth)
    1. Peckinpah, Sam, 1925–1984—Criticism and interpretation.
I. Title.
PN1998.3.P43S48   1997
791.43'028'092—dc20   96-4521
                                                                        CIP

To David Morrell,
who knows what this is all about

and Alexander C. Kern,
who stood me then in good stead

No scorn of the refined, no condescension of sophisticated critics toward the vagaries of romance, can keep us from feeling the pull: the American, or at least the American artist, cherishes in his innermost being the impulse to reject completely the gospel of civilization, in order to guard with resolution the savagery of his heart.

—Perry Miller

Contents

Illustrations

Foreword

David Weddle

I've noticed something about the books that have had a profound impact on my life. When I pull them off the shelf and open them again, see the fading ink and touch the slowly decaying pages, memories come rushing back to me.

I remember reading Paul Seydor's book—particularly the chapter on *The Wild Bunch*—in my living room in Sylmar, California, in the fall of 1980. My left leg was sprawled over the back of a flower-print couch, my head propped up by throw pillows. The wind rushed down through a pass in the San Gabriel Mountains and through the swamp cooler in the ceiling, which moaned like a mud-stuck cow. As I turned the pages, the outside world dropped away; soon I was reading with the all-consuming focus that great books demand.

A decade earlier, my father had taken me to see my first Sam Peckinpah movie: *The Wild Bunch*. As we stepped onto the plush red carpet of Edward's Cinema in Costa Mesa, a gush of refrigerated air and the salt-oil scent of fresh popcorn greeted us. The movie mesmerized me, and I went to every Peckinpah film that came out thereafter.

For the first time I was being drawn into the theater by a director instead of by a star. For the first time it occurred to me that the actors weren't making up their lines as they went along. For the first time I realized that a movie could be the product of an individual imagination.

I came of age, in a way, watching Peckinpah pictures.

Peckinpah: The Western Films played an important role in that maturation process. It taught me how to *look* at movies. Seemingly random scenes and atmospheric details in a picture like *The Wild Bunch* became strands in a complex and elegant thematic web spun by the director. Like the dots of a pointillist painting, they seem individually inconsequential, but in relation to each other they form a grand design.

My admiration for Seydor's book has grown since those afternoons on the flower-print couch in Sylmar. His remains the most penetrating study of Peckinpah, as well as one of the finest pieces of film criticism ever written. Seydor applies his keen analytical eye to Peckinpah's films and then, with breathtaking assurance and precision, traces the literary, cultural, and social forces that shaped the director's artistic vision.

Many earlier critics wrote about Peckinpah, and wrote well. Jim Kitses, Robert Culp, Pauline Kael, Stephen Farber, Stanley Kauffmann, Philip French, Cordell Strug, William S. Pechter—all wrote incisive reviews of Peckinpah's films and undoubtedly were strong influences on Seydor. But an equal number misinterpreted Peckinpah's "revisionist Westerns" as the works of a nihilist determined to demolish the romantic mythology of the American frontier. One cannot really fault them for this; the visceral power of Peckinpah's filmmaking and his savage sense of irony left most viewers shell-shocked in the late sixties and early seventies. Another decade would pass before audiences would begin to fully assimilate this extraordinary artist's work.

Seydor was the first to understand (or at least fully to articulate) that Peckinpah was not a nihilist but a desperate romantic at war with his own disillusionment; that Peckinpah deconstructed the Western myth, only to reassemble and reclaim it; that *Ride the High Country, The Wild Bunch,* and *Pat Garrett and Billy the Kid* are intricately constructed tragedies dominated by one obsessive theme: redemption. To put it in the simplest terms, *The Wild Bunch* is about a band of killers who find in death a meaning and a state of grace that eluded them in life.

"Every time I watch *The Wild Bunch,* I walk out of the theater feeling profoundly exhilarated," says Seydor. "I don't feel that I've seen a work about how disgusting and horrible humanity is. To me, it's exactly the opposite. I leave completely energized."

The author Ken Kesey has observed that "at the end of *Moby-Dick,* everybody's dead, the whale has killed everybody. But you don't feel bad about it. Now that's art! To take you to the bottom of the sea and still make you feel better about the world and the human being and the writer, and the primal force of evil, even. You feel better about it. It expands you. . . . That's hard to learn. That's the real essential trick of any kind of art. Picasso could create *Guernica,* which shows the horror of war, but when you look at *Guernica* you are ennobled and uplifted."

Seydor shows us how Peckinpah performs this sleight of hand with all the dexterity of Melville or Picasso.

I went to see *The Wild Bunch* at a revival theater in 1980, a few months after reading Seydor's book. I'd seen it a half-dozen times before, and this print was faded and scratched and full of bad splices. But for the first time I broke down at the end, sobbing uncontrollably. The value of great criticism lies in its ability to expand your understanding of a work and to heighten your response to it.

Initially, *Peckinpah: The Western Films* made little impact on public opinion. The 2,500 copies were distributed largely through independent bookstores; the large chains ignored it. Hard-core Peckinpah fans—the ones who gathered in the darkness of tattered revival houses—eventually gobbled up every available copy. But when the book first appeared, Peckinpah's reputation was at low ebb. The nihilist streak that he had fought so fiercely up to the brink of middle age finally overwhelmed him in the late 1970s. The earlier triumphs of *Ride the High Country, Noon Wine, The Wild Bunch,* and *Junior Bonner* had faded from public memory; most critics greeted his later films with comments like "another mindless bloodbath from the super-macho director Sam Peckinpah."

Seydor's assertion that this drunken delinquent was one of the most important American artists of the mid-twentieth century received a mixed reaction. Frank McConnell, who reviewed Seydor's book for the *Quarterly Review of Film Studies,* compared it to such classic texts of American studies as *Virgin Land* and *Machine in the Garden.* Ernest Callenbach of *Film Quarterly* and Michael Sragow of the Los Angeles *Herald-Examiner* both wrote glowing reviews, but *Library Journal* called the book "pedantic."

Meanwhile, in the early 1980s, Peckinpah struggled to pull together the pieces of his shattered career. I met him for the first time during preproduction for *The Osterman Weekend,* a modestly budgeted feature. We spent a couple of hours in his office at the old Columbia Studios on Sunset and Gower, talking about Tennessee Williams, James Gould Cozzens, and B. Traven. Toward the end he vented his frustrations about *Osterman:* the producers had saddled him with an incomprehensible script and refused to let him rewrite it.

As I got up to leave, I gestured at the production memos that littered his desk: "I hope all of this hard work won't be in vain."

His mouth twisted up in a bitter grimace-grin: "It always is!"

The picture opened to lukewarm reviews and box office, and his career stalled out again.

His final job involved directing a couple of music videos for Julian Lennon. Shortly before he died, he muttered to his wife, Begonia Palacios, "My last movie was only two minutes long."

"Entertainment Tonight" devoted only fifteen seconds to his passing.

But eventually a funny thing happened: Peckinpah's work endured. As the painful memories of his last years receded, his films emerged from the shadow of his personal reputation. They gripped a whole new generation of cineastes on campuses and in revival theaters. I have met these young converts at colleges across the country. As they talk about the films, with their voices excited and eyes aflame, they invariably pull copies of *Peckinpah: The Western Films* from their backpacks. The margins are often filled with scribbled notes, for Seydor's work invites dialogue. As they flip through the pages to talk about *The Losers* or "Miss Jenny," I can see that Seydor has ignited the same fire in them that he once lit in me. These fans track down every television episode, every piece of film Peckinpah shot, hoping to reconstruct the entire mosaic of this singular American artist.

By the early 1990s the Peckinpah revival had gathered irresistible momentum. The BBC produced a ninety-minute documentary on his life. Retrospectives of his work were staged at Lincoln Center in New York, at the Amiens Film Festival, at the Cinemathèque in Paris, at the University of Missouri in Columbia, and at London's National Film Theatre. *Film Comment* and *Sight and Sound* published major reappraisals.

In March 1995 Warner Brothers released fully restored 70mm prints of Peckinpah's cut of *The Wild Bunch* to American theaters. Without Seydor's efforts, that restoration might never have come to pass. For more than a decade he lobbied filmmakers, distributors, and the studio. Once the ponderous gears ground into motion, he donated his time to the project as a consultant.

A quarter-century after its original release, *The Wild Bunch* played to sellout crowds in New York, Los Angeles, and San Francisco. *The Today Show,* National Public Radio, CNN, and *Entertainment Tonight* all aired segments on the restoration of Peckinpah's masterpiece—with *ET* devoting a full six minutes to Peckinpah this time. The picture received rave reviews from the *New York Times, Los Angeles Times, New Yorker, Time, Newsweek, Rolling Stone,* and dozens of other publications. At last most critics recognized Seydor's claim of fifteen years earlier: that *The Wild Bunch* was a landmark American film, perhaps the most important since *Citizen Kane.* And most also recognized it as a romantic tragedy focused on the theme of redemption.

Now Seydor gives us an expanded new edition of *Peckinpah: The Western Films* in which he reconsiders both Peckinpah's work and his own earlier interpretations of it. He adds a great wealth of biographical detail that has surfaced since the director's death. He packs his new text with never-before-published details about Peckinpah's child-hood, marriages, and professional life. He includes a new chapter on *Noon Wine*, the pivotal work that carried Peckinpah across the threshold to artistic maturity.

Peckinpah: The Western Films stands as a shining example of how a single book from a small publisher can have a profound and lasting impact on our culture. It also demonstrates the value of literary and film criticism. Just as Malcolm Cowley rescued William Faulkner from obscurity, as James Agee helped us rediscover Buster Keaton and Harry Langdon, and as Philip Young enriched our appreciation of Ernest Hemingway, Paul Seydor has kept Peckinpah's work alive and relevant for us. For that we have owed him—and now owe him anew—a great deal.

Introduction

Despair is the only unforgivable sin, and it's always
reaching for us.
—Sam Peckinpah

I

When Sam Peckinpah died, from heart failure on the morning of 28
December 1984, reaction in the media and the popular press was
almost nonexistent. *Variety* ran an obituary, and some entertainment
reporters on television noted the occasion (when they took any notice at all) with a remark or two about the "maverick" Hollywood
director who had a "flair" for violence. But there were no obituaries
of substance and little commentary that gave any sense of the artist
who had just passed away or the seminal importance of his best work.
Even most movie reviewers and film critics paid little or no mind. A
few notable exceptions were Michael Sragow, Kathleen Murphy, and
Steve Vineberg, all of whom contributed thoughtful appreciations
that were less obituaries than impassioned eulogies. Sragow in particular spoke for a generation of filmgoers when he wrote:

> Sam Peckinpah is the man who made me want to write about mov-
> ies. When *The Wild Bunch* opened sixteen years ago, I saw it six times
> in two weeks; I can't count the number of times I've seen it since.
> To this day, I can't think of another film that's had such a near-hyp-
> notic holding power. It puts you in touch with the spirit of a man
> who's tearing himself apart on screen, expressing whatever is in
> him. After seeing that film I had to write and persuade others that
> it isn't just an essay in violence or even a magnificent Western. It is
> a great original work of art.[1]

But just as the Academy of Motion Picture Arts and Sciences ignored his greatest film in life, so it neglected the artist himself in
death. The Academy Awards ceremony the following spring featured
a tribute to François Truffaut, who had also died, but not one word
about Sam Peckinpah. Yet it is unlikely there was in the audience so

much as one film director under the age of sixty who had not been
influenced by Peckinpah's work. Worse, what Peckinpah said in
1972—that none of his best films was available in anything like the
form he'd made them in—was still substantially true (and continued
to be true for over a decade, until Warner Brothers restored *The Wild
Bunch* in 1995). Some of his films, like *Cross of Iron*, weren't, still aren't,
available at all, nor was (is) the television work, except in crude copies of copies taped by private collectors from syndicated broadcasts.
Later attempts to set things right often came out halfhearted and
careless. New World Video released a laserdisc of *The Deadly Companions*, but not in the widescreen format. When Metro-Goldwyn-Mayer, in response to countless requests, finally issued a laserdisc of *Ride
the High Country* in the early nineties, the format was widescreen but
the transfer cropped off the far edges of the image and the print was
disappointingly faded.

   Kathleen Murphy prefaced her obituary with a quote from
Melville's famous letter to Hawthorne: "He says No! in thunder; but
the Devil himself cannot make him say *yes*. For all men who say *yes*,
lie."[2] This is fitting. Peckinpah ruthlessly scorned the fatuous certainties and the pious hypocrisies rampant in our official culture, and he
undermined every absolute he came across. When he cursed the
human race, he was sweeping about it, but he always included himself. He did these things with an obsessiveness so wanton in its disregard for his own well-being and a fearlessness so breathtaking that it
was impossible not to recognize in him the wounded romantic, the
tragic idealist, the agonized believer. Which may be another way of
saying that Peckinpah also said his own forms of yes. But his optimism
was hard won and transitory—he had to fight the battles over and
over. Virtue in his films is so intimately entwined with vice that his
affirmations are less clarion calls than insistent voices whispering from
some almost forgotten recesses in the heart. His compromised heroes, especially the westerners, usually achieve some form of redemption, but the cost is high, the material rewards nonexistent (though
money is frequently the temptation that kicks off the adventure), and
the struggle violent. The beauty in his films is extravagant and pierc-
es the sublime; but it is felt most keenly in the way his style brings
everything it touches richly, vibrantly, thrillingly to life. "Recklessly
high on beauty and excess," wrote Pauline Kael in a wonderful description of his Western films.[3]

   But he is also capable of a sweet and lovely lyricism, and a gentle-
ness so tender it cleanses and heals. Then we realize that deep inside
his crusty exterior, way down there mixed in with all that irony, an-

ger, and rage, is also a generosity that sometimes embraced the world. The violence in his films feels by turns like purgations of his own worst impulses or the intoxicated revelings of a prodigiously Dionysian aestheticism. Yet the lasting impression is often of a man who is trying to get to the most decent places in himself. Like Mark Twain, Peckinpah may have hated the damned human race, but he loved people, the more colorful the better. Unlike Twain, he didn't wind up a total cynic, nor did he succumb to hopelessness.

Those of us who really love his films and return to them as we do to favorite paintings or pieces of music or literature know that much of his work is suffused with a deep and expansive love: for the tarnished valor of his flawed, corrupt heroes who discover in themselves an almost vestigial sense of honor they were unaware they possessed until all that's left is to die protecting it; for the unruly verve and vigor of his two-bit, rednecked peckerwoods, prospectors, bounty hunters, saddletramps, cowboys, low-rent miners, bums, and assorted other lowlifes and hangers-on in all their rude, feisty glory; for his wised-up prostitutes and dance hall girls who have courage enough to endure violence, grace enough to walk away from vengeance, and innocence enough to believe there is another way; for the intransigence, at once ornery and noble, of all his losers, loners, drifters, and misfits who assert themselves in a world doing its damndest to run them off, out, or over; for the rugged magnificence of his parched landscapes through which sometimes shines a bleak splendor; for the high country of his youth, with its clear, cool lakes and its soaring mountain ranges eloquent enough to ratify the passing of those who manage to enter their houses justified. Asked how he'd like his own passing to be marked, Peckinpah answered, "I suppose the fact that I never stopped searching."

The despair he feared so much almost caught up with him in the late seventies and early eighties. After the alcohol of his whole adult life, the cocaine he started using on *The Killer Elite,* and the heart attack of 1979 (which necessitated a pacemaker), Peckinpah found himself in probably the saddest, most abject and lonely place of his life. The industry was afraid to hire him, there was no family life to speak of, and he had alienated many friends, not because he abused or took advantage of them—their loyalty and forbearance had long ago passed those tests—but because they just couldn't stand to see him go on destroying himself with drugs and booze.

Yet somewhere he found reserves of sheer will and strength that enabled him, fitfully and inconsistently, to pull something good out of those last years. One thing was a reconciliation with his son, Matthew. ("For the first time in the ten years that I've known them," Garner Simmons said, "Sam and Matthew had a real relationship.")[4] He also repaid a debt to the man who gave him his first break in features, Don Siegel ("my *patron*,"), by second-unit directing an action sequence on *Jinxed,* a film Siegel was making with Bette Midler. Everybody was pleased with the results—ecstatic more accurately describes the reactions—and the job served its purpose. Demonstrating that he could still work productively, responsibly, and well, it landed him his last film. *The Osterman Weekend* began as an impossibly convoluted script. The plot, which concerns espionage, betrayal, and corruption among three friends and their families, seemed hardly worth the effort of figuring out what it was about. Peckinpah wanted to do a rewrite, the moneymen said no. When asked how it was going, he snapped, "How the fuck do you think it's going? It's a piece-of-shit script of some fifth-rate Robert Ludlum novel that I'm just trying to put some life into!"[5]

The finished product, released in November 1983, was a desultory affair, and, as a Peckinpah film, a disappointing one. There were the usual charges of studio interference, but Peckinpah soft-pedaled them this time. The truth, he knew, is that there is little difference between his preview (shown once in a shopping mall in Orange County) and the version eventually released. Told that the plot actually seemed to make a bit more sense in the studio cut, Peckinpah replied, "Do you really think so?"—by which he meant that the more apparent sense it made, the stupider it got.[6] Still, in the work with actors, in the probing of character (however ludicrous the context), in any of several scenes of domestic discord that many considered beyond his range of sympathies, and in a nightmarish action sequence under water in a burning swimming pool, there are flashes of the old brilliance. The genius in eclipse was a genius still.

The next year his health worsened steadily, but he never lost his passion for making films. Two months before he died he directed a pair of MTV videos for the singer Julian Lennon. It was the only work he could get at the time. The one called "Too Late for Goodbyes" is almost ground breaking in its utter simplicity. In stark contrast to the frenetic cutting, the acrobatic camerawork, and the overwrought lighting of most music videos, Peckinpah's three cameras just observe, from various angles, a single lonely musician seated at a piano trying to make music in a big, empty studio while someone looks on from the control booth. The angles dissolve one into another, the effect is smooth and melancholy, and as the song plays out we become aware that we've just seen a quiet meditation upon the relationship of art and technology in a commercial medium. Peckinpah's style here is subdued, and a bad cold laid him really low the first day of production. But oh, say his colleagues, once the shooting started, did he ever spring to life!

II

Critics are not judges, but one of the tasks of criticism is evaluation, if only because selecting a subject is implicitly to assign it some worth. From here it is but a short step to assess its place in history, and a shorter one still to project the assessment into the future. When the first edition of this book appeared, in 1980, all of Peckinpah's films except *The Osterman Weekend* and the two Julian Lennon videos had been made. Noting how the director, beginning more or less with *Bring Me the Head of Alfredo Garcia,* seemed to be reevaluating the central themes and preoccupations of his earlier films, the introduction concluded: "Whether this represents a transition, a digression, or a wholly new direction in his career remains to be seen." Now that all the evidence *has* been seen, the question still cannot be answered, because Peckinpah's career didn't really come to a close. It just sort of disintegrated for awhile and then stopped, or, rather, was stopped. It does not inscribe the lofty classical arc of Ford's or Kurosawa's; it does not comprise an *oeuvre* in the way of Renoir's or Satyajit Ray's; it doesn't even provide the satisfying finish of John Huston's, which at least allowed for some sentimental rhapsodizing about the recrudescence of youthful energy (*Prizzi's Honor*) or the ripe wisdom of old age (*The Dead*).

Like Orson Welles, Peckinpah was blessed in becoming a legend early on and damned by having to live up to it the rest of his life. The years of being blacklisted from features, between *The Cincinnati Kid* and *The Wild Bunch,* so traumatized him that later in his career he was saying yes to dreary projects just because he was afraid the last would be *his* last (and also because making films was always the strongest narcotic). Add to this the problems he had getting his films made and released in versions he approved, and it's a wonder the career makes any sense at all. Yet part of it does describe one beautifully shaped trajectory that travels straight and true from the early television work up through the first four films to *The Ballad of Cable Hogue;* then, after some swings and roundabouts, it comes back on course and target in *Pat Garrett and Billy the Kid,* his last Western. There are other ways to divide his work than between the Western and the non-Western films. But the considerable achievements of the latter not-

withstanding, it is doubtful they can be grouped together as cogent-
ly or as coherently as the Westerns.

That duly noted, we may now attempt a view from the vantage
point of future memory: Peckinpah made in *The Wild Bunch* one of
the great artworks of our century; he made a couple more great
films, some excellent and very good ones, and some mixed successes
and failures; he also made three or four fine short films for television, including a superb adaptation. (Individual titles are not here
assigned to these categories, excepting the first, so as to preclude
arguments that might obscure the claims.) His influence on subsequent films and filmmakers is ubiquitous, and some of his stylistic
innovations are now part of basic film vocabulary the world over. If
there were any doubts before Peckinpah that great art was possible
in the genre of the Western—and rightly or wrongly, there were—
after him there was none. He inflected it with a seriousness of purpose, an intensity of emotion, and a beauty that almost singlehandedly transformed it. Thus, then, his legacy: this is such stuff as
immortalities are made on.

III

The purpose of this book is the same as before: to study one self-
contained group of Peckinpah's films. The organization remains
chronological—beginning with his television work and concluding
with his last Western film, *Pat Garrett and Billy the Kid*—which enables
us to trace his progress as a filmmaking storyteller, what he always
insisted he was, first and foremost. The detailed analyses of the individual films are likewise pretty much as they were, though in many
places they have been augmented, in a few places trimmed. Of necessity factual errors have been corrected, and throughout changes
in tense and wording reflect the fact of the deaths of Peckinpah and
several of his colleagues. More subjectively, some passages have
benefited from the usual sort of mending and amending a writer will
do in the course of polishing up an early work for republication. As
for the large changes, perhaps the best way to indicate their size and
nature is chapter by chapter, which will serve to telescope the study
itself.

Chapter 1 originally considered Peckinpah's early television work
and his first two features, but it discussed only the pilot and the five
episodes he directed for *The Westerner*, the series he created and produced. When all fourteen episodes (counting the pilot) subsequently became available and were seen together, several gaps in his de-

velopment were filled and the meaning of his work at large was otherwise enriched. Thus, it seemed desirable to review them all and see
them whole, which was done. This expansion, together with the original treatment of *The Deadly Companions,* required that the long section on *Ride the High Country* be detached and given a chapter all its
own. The film always should have had one, anyhow; now that it does,
it can be fleshed out with valuable background material. *Major Dundee*
and the television shows immediately preceding it occupy chapter 3,
with new information on production and editing. *Noon Wine* received
only scant attention in the first edition because, the negatives destroyed, just three prints are known to exist; and none of them and
the critic were ever in the same place long enough to view, let alone
study, the film. This difficulty has long since been surmounted, and
the result is chapter 4, the only totally new one, which shows how this
short film occupies a key position in Peckinpah's development, bringing his television work to a fitting resolution and preparing the way
for *The Wild Bunch. Noon Wine* is also a remarkably autobiographical
work, as a short account of his parents' marriage and his relationship
to them demonstrates. Chapters 5 and 6, on *The Wild Bunch* and *The
Ballad of Cable Hogue,* respectively, continue to be companion pieces,
as the films themselves are. The treatment of *The Wild Bunch* now
includes a more detailed and accurate account of the studio interference both preceding and following the premiere, the story of how
an NC-17 by the Motion Picture Association of America almost killed
the 1995 restoration of the director's final cut, and a new section (III)
that explores the film's sources in terms of its personal significance
to Peckinpah. The analysis of *Pat Garrett and Billy the Kid,* here chapter 7, now has an epilogue that clarifies the several versions (at least
four) in circulation at one time or another and suggests why the so-
called "director's cut," now widely available on the home-video market, is misleadingly labeled.

  Chapters 8 and 9 (6 and 7 the first time around) are also companion pieces. Chapter 8, largely unchanged, relates this group of films
and Peckinpah's work as a whole to a continuing tradition in American art and expression of which his films are an extension and development. This essay does not argue that there are not other traditions in which his films can be placed; but it does argue that the more
closely his films are studied, the more apparent it becomes that they
deal with themes, ideas, and forces that have shaped, inspired, and
preoccupied American artists since the time of Cooper, if not before.
Chapter 9, substantially rewritten, deepens this argument, identifying specific influences on and sources of Peckinpah's art, including

his personal history and that of his family, toward the end of unearthing some fundamental patterns that touch off uniquely American rumblings. The original title of this chapter, "An American Artist and His Traditions," is here subordinate to a new one: "World of Our Fathers," which more closely suggests the theme of the argument and the locus of this particular artist's myths and obsessions.

Peckinpah: The Western Films

A Reconsideration

I created *The Westerner* because of anger; anger at never-miss sheriffs, always right marshals, white-washed gunfighters—all of the mistakeless "redwoods" who dominate the Western field today; anger at TV's quick-draw tin gods who stand behind a tin star or ten cents' worth of righteous anger and justify their skill and slaughter with a self-conscious grin or a minute's worth of bad philosophy.

—Sam Peckinpah

1
Westerners

I was trying to learn to write, commencing with the
simplest things.
—Ernest Hemingway

I

Sam Peckinpah himself provided the clearest picture of what life in
the world of his Western films is often like. In *The Wild Bunch* an introspective Deke Thornton, perhaps recalling his capture by the law
and subsequent conscription by the railroad or ranging back over his
days with Pike Bishop and Old Sykes, is riding slightly ahead of the
posse of gutter-trash bounty hunters he is forced to lead in pursuit
of the Bunch as the condition of his release from prison. One of the
posse suddenly slaps his holster, raises his hand, the fingers formed
like a pistol aimed at Thornton's back, and exclaims, "Bang! Got
him!" Shaken from his reminiscences, Thornton swivels abruptly,
reaching for his gun, only to be greeted by a burst of derisive laughter. He pulls up his horse and lets the posse pass in front of him.

Barely a minute in length, this little scene tells us many things. It
tells us why Thornton, as opposed to Pike, was caught: he is too slow
on the recoil, too given to spells of brooding or fits of nervousness,
perhaps even too trusting. It tells us something about how some people in this world treat firearms, as playthings that go bang, and how
they value life itself, as furnishing more targets for the playthings.
Most of all it tells us that the world occupying the film's space is dangerous and threatening, that injury or death is liable to come from
anywhere at any time, even from one's own companions, often when
least expected. Of course this time it is only a joke, but that is hardly
the point: some other time, some other place, it might not and probably won't be played for laughs, and then a man can't afford to be
caught off his guard.

Peckinpah adumbrated this world in much of his early television
work, now lost in studio vaults or available piecemeal only in syndication. In 1955 Don Siegel, a director on some of whose pictures

Peckinpah had served variously as gopher, bit player, dialogue pol-
isher, and assistant, was asked to produce *Gunsmoke,* then a new television series that had already enjoyed great popularity as a radio series. When Siegel declined the offer, the job fell to Charles Marquis
Warren, who knew Peckinpah slightly and, since Siegel spoke highly
of him, told him he could adapt one of the radio scripts, but only
without pay unless it went into production. Called "The Queue" and
first televised as the thirteenth *Gunsmoke* episode, on 3 December
1955, it tells of a Chinese immigrant victimized by racial prejudice
and violence ("I don't hold with killing people," a Dodge City citizen says; but, reminds a friend, "Killing Chinamen ain't really the
same as killing people").* Although an adaptation, "The Queue" is
branded clearly enough with Peckinpah's characteristic concerns. He
saw it again shortly after he had completed *The Wild Bunch* and "was
astonished how simply and how well it was done. Even then we were
dealing in terms of minorities and outsiders."[1]

This first effort, however modest, didn't come easily: "It took me
five months of day and night writing to get the first one finished."[2]
Soon enough he was able to knock out a *Gunsmoke* script in about
eight hours, "that is, after twenty straight hours of lying awake getting all of my ideas together."[3] Peckinpah would eventually elaborate
those ideas into the complex thematic structures that inform his films,
but for the time being it was enough to begin with the simplest things,
these terse half-hour television shows, several of which involve violence and death. In "How to Die for Nothing" Peckinpah dealt for
the first time with revenge, a theme to which he would return again
and again throughout his career. Marshal Matt Dillon, the main character of the series, is forced to kill a man who draws on him; later,
the man's brother shows up and tries to ambush Dillon, who must
shoot him too. "Now that man died for no reason at all," the mar-
shall remarks to his deputy; and the clear point is that both men died
pretty needlessly. In "How to Kill a Woman" the victim is a minor
character whose death occurs offscreen, a stray bullet piercing her
heart during a stage robbery. The theme is the same, to which Peckinpah added another: the victims of violence are often the uninvolved
and innocent. In "Yorky" he returned to the racial outsider; the title
character is a fourteen-year-old white boy who has been raised by
Indians; in the climax of the story, he kills a man to save Matt's life.

**Gunsmoke was created by John Meston, who had also written the radio version of
"The Queue." When the series was sold to television, Warren turned to other writers
because he was afraid Meston, so used to writing for radio, could not adjust to a visual medium.

And in "Cooter" violence is again crossed with innocence: Cooter, a retarded man (played by Strother Martin in the first of several collaborations with Peckinpah) kills a gambler who has tricked him.

An even clearer indication of the shape of things to come is "The Roundup." Scores of cowboys are descending upon Dodge City to celebrate the end of a long, hard cattle drive. Everybody expects trouble; Dillon is worried, even a little rattled, as the coming night will be too much for one man to handle, and his regular deputy, Chester, is laid up with an injury. An old friend of the marshal's, who had heard about the impending trouble, shows up and volunteers as a temporary deputy. That night a venial saloon owner (who wants to control the town himself) and several of his henchmen draw on Dillon. Guns are fired, bodies drop. By the time the smoke clears, the saloon owner and a few of his men are dead. So too is the new deputy. He had come to his friend's aid through a side door, behind the marshal, without announcing himself, just as the shooting started. Amid all the confusion, Dillon had whirled and shot at what he believed was another gunman. The marshal carries his friend's body back to the jail. Then, even though most everybody else is behaving within the law—just blowing off steam having a good time—he takes a shotgun and in a cold rage forces saloon after saloon to close down for the night until the entire town is deserted. Early in the story, Chester had remarked that any man who has to notch his gun to get his courage up is scarcely more than a coward. The show ends with Dillon burying his old friend, then cutting a single notch into the handle of his own gun so that he will always carry a visible mark of his mistake and his guilt.

Here is more than a little of the irony—and also the psychological probing and the treatment of conventions and character types in unconventional and atypical ways—that will distinguish Peckinpah's later films. Here too is the telling use of Western history: the deputy's death is surely based on the incident from Wild Bill Hickock's life when, surrounded by too many adversaries to think as clearly and shoot as straight as he would have wished or willed, Hickock whirled and mistakenly shot his own deputy who had come up behind him. And the hero himself emerges less as hero than as protagonist. Although Peckinpah did not create Matt Dillon, almost without exception the episodes he wrote depict a considerably darker, more troubled character than was the norm for the series, easily recognizable as a precursor of the all too humanly fallible men of action, plagued by doubt, burdened with guilt, of the Western films to come.

The look of these early shows is rather crude, with blocking that is often merely expedient and pacing that is frequently sluggish. Yet there is a freshness and vitality in the best of Peckinpah's writing that manages to shine through the defects of direction and the paucity of even minimal production values. In sum, his contributions to *Gunsmoke* totaled eleven scripts adapted from the radio plays (which were televised) and one original (which was not). Years later Warren summarized Pekinpah's work for the series:

> Goddamn, it was well written. I'd been getting scripts from all these guys who prided themselves on being authentic Western writers. . . . They'd try to write in dialect, "Howday padna!" God they were awful. But Sam's dialogue was crisp and clean and filled with little phrases. And he knew so much about the Old West, little details like the kind of carpenter's tools they used in those days. . . . He gave his scripts a real authentic feel. He learned fast. I never had to teach him twice, and sometimes he taught me.[4]

During these years Peckinpah also wrote for several other series, including *Have Gun—Will Travel, Trackdown, Tombstone Territory, Tales of Wells Fargo,* and *Broken Arrow.* By 1958 he had written his fourth script for *Broken Arrow* when the producer Elliott Arnold asked him if he would like to direct one: "Christ, they knew I was dying to direct. They didn't have to ask me a second time."[5] As he later pointed out, they had nothing to lose as the series was going off the air and the episode to which Peckinpah was assigned and which he also wrote was the last entry. Titled "The Transfer," it marks the first time the credit "directed by Sam Peckinpah" appears on film. The story has the enlightened Indian agent Tom Jeffords reassigned to a new territory, replaced by a benighted old bureaucrat determined to do things strictly "by the book." After getting several soldiers and Indians killed and a war nearly started, the old fool is relieved of his post. But Jeffords's reassignment stands, his eventual replacement is never introduced, and the series is left to end ambiguously: Jeffords and the Indian chief Cochise say farewell, pledging their undying loyalty to one other as blood brothers, while the fate of the Chiricahua tribe before an implacably advancing white America is left hanging.

This refusal to simplify issues falsely is just about the only glimpse "The Transfer" affords of the artist Peckinpah was to become. The craft is otherwise strictly neophyte. "It really went to my head," Peckinpah recalled. "There was one scene I must have photographed from at least eighteen angles. I was never so frightened in my life. Don't let anyone kid you, it's bloody murder learning how to direct."[6] But the experience was a good one, giving him the confidence to rewrite his original *Gunsmoke* script that had been rejected and take it over to Dick Powell at Four Star Productions. Powell read it, liked it, and bought it, though he assigned it to another director, Arnold Laven. It was televised in 1958 as part of *Dick Powell's Zane Grey Theatre,* an anthology series Powell often used to introduce shows with series potential. Titled "The Sharpshooter," it introduced a character named Lucas McCain and became the pilot for *The Rifleman.*

In Peckinpah's original script McCain is a stranger come to a town where he enters a shooting contest. He is soon recognized as a well-known marksman by some townspeople who bet their money on him. But the owner of the saloon threatens McCain with his life if he wins the contest over his own gunman, and he has a gang of several other gunmen on hand to back up the threat. Obviously unable to beat them all, McCain throws the contest and leaves the town in disgrace.

This was typical of the sort of downbeat story Peckinpah wrote in his pursuit of a truer, more realistic depiction of the Old West than was common in those days. "We loved the writing," Arnold Laven later told David Weddle, "but the ending, you just couldn't get that sponsored in 1958. I don't know if you could get it sponsored today, to tell you the truth—a guy who doesn't have the courage of the West, to stand up for what is right."[7] Laven suggested that the McCain character have both a son and a reason for entering the contest: he needs the prize money for a down payment on a ranch that will be their new home. Then, Laven said, "if the threat is made against the boy's life instead of the Rifleman's, I dare anybody in television to say that he should risk his son's life in the interest of putting the bad guys in place." The revised episode ends with McCain going to the saloon and defeating the villains, almost singlehandedly.

Peckinpah jumped at the idea of the son, doubtless because it struck some personal chords, as did the plot device of purchasing a new homestead. There are several references and allusions to Peckinpah's home and family, the most revealing of which is the name of the property McCain buys: the Dunlap ranch, also the name of his maternal grandparents' ranch in the foothills of the Sierra (the "for sale" sign advertises 4,100 acres, exactly the size of the real ranch by the time his grandfather died). Young Sam spent most summers there with his older brother, Denny, and their father and grandfather. Many years later his mother sold the ranch. By having McCain dispatch the bad guys and thus get the money that is rightfully his, Peckinpah got to entertain the fantasy of buying back the beloved ranch of his youth. "And," as Weddle points out, "this time the troubling presence of a woman who might one day sell the ranch is expunged": Peckinpah jumped at the idea of a son, but he made the father a widower.

The premise for the series became thus an old one: a man gains a reputation as a skillful gunman, and although he is essentially a man of peace, he lives in a violent world and his reputation stalks him through it. But this initial compromise seems to have bothered Peckinpah relatively little, as he must have realized that the real theme he had come upon here was not violence as such but redemption: of shedding a past identity and trying to begin a new life. This is the theme that obsessed him more than any other, and two of the better *Rifleman* episodes he both wrote and directed are early treatments of it. In one, called "The Boarding House," Katy Jurado plays a former madam who has come to North Fork to escape her past and start anew; one day her former pimp shows up and tries to force her to return to him by telling the townspeople what she used to be. In the other, "The Marshal," Paul Fix appears as a drunken ex-marshal named Micah Torrance who has been on the bum for several years. He is discovered by a pair of brothers with a score to settle (they anticipate the Hammonds from *Ride the High Country,* one of them even played by Warren Oates, the first time he was cast by Peckinpah). The episode boasts a fairly tough-minded treatment of alcoholism, an illness Peckinpah knew only too well. At one point Micah asks to borrow some money, promising to pay it back. "No you won't," Lucas tells him, "you're a drunk." With Lucas's help, the old man eventually reforms, dispatches the brothers, and becomes a marshal once again (and a series regular).

Both episodes suggest what Peckinpah might have done had he continued with the series. He had begun to conceive it as "the story of a boy who grows to manhood learning what it's all about."[8] For example, Mark, Lucas's son, is at first put off by his father's gruff treatment of the marshal, but soon learns that an alcoholic has no principles beyond the next bottle. When Micah complains that he needs a drink, Mark suggests he'd be better off finishing his supper. Peckinpah's episodes were serious and sometimes pretty rough. The pimp in "The Boarding House," for example, evokes a seedy world where cruelty and threats of violence are the norm. The people in charge of the series, in particular the producer, Jules Levy, preferred a show angled more toward children. Peckinpah stayed on for a while longer—in all he directed and/or wrote six episodes, counting the pilot—but eventually left in frustration and dismay.

Peckinpah's plans for *The Rifleman,* thwarted though they were, have more than passing interest. The conception of the series rein-

forces the parallels between Peckinpah and Hemingway that a number of critics have noted. Whether consciously or not Peckinpah here
conceived a theme and a structure for *The Rifleman*—each episode
built upon previous episodes, unified through the boy's experiences
and constituting his initiation into a violent, confused, and confusing world—that are strikingly similar to what is found in Hemingway's
Nick Adams stories, in particular his first important book, *In Our Time*.
More significant, however, is the personal investment Peckinpah
made in the series. Whatever their manifest plots, most of the episodes he had a hand in return to one underlying story, which develops a kind of idealized father-son relationship between Lucas and
Mark. Lucas is a wise, upstanding, and benevolent father, strict but
kind and loving. Set in stark contrast against him are several dark
father figures who are severe, absolutist, and cruel. In "The Baby Sitter," for example, a sadistic religious zealot who wields a bullwhip tells
Mark, "We wasn't put in this world to have fun." In the pilot episode
the competing gunman is an orphaned young man named Vernon
(played by a startlingly callow Dennis Hopper), under the influence
of his bad uncle and the much worse saloon owner, both of whom
can be seen as surrogate fathers. Vernon becomes friends with Mark,
is unaware of the threat against the boy when he wins the shooting
contest, and eventually helps Lucas defeat the saloon owner and his
gunmen. The significance of these contrasting father figures in Peckinpah's work will become evident soon enough, but they start here
in the first series he created.

When his plans for *The Rifleman* fell through, Peckinpah directed
and helped write two shows for *Dick Powell's Zane Grey Theatre*: "Miss
Jenny" and "Lonesome Road," neither of which is without its signs
of inexperience, yet both stake claims to territory he would explore
throughout his career. The former reveals the director's continuing
interest in the relationship between violence and innocence, and
marks his first substantial treatment of a subject that would occupy
him again and again in his television work: women in the West, their
place on the frontier, how they survive, and how they are victimized
or otherwise made to suffer by men and because of limited masculine attitudes. The situation in this story is classically Oedipal: a young
man tries to take a married woman—the title character (played by
Vera Miles)—from her husband. He means her no harm. On the
contrary, lonely, without much experience of women, hardly out of
his teens, he proposes a woodland idyll that seems at first wholly sex-
less. But any sign of hesitation or resistance from Miss Jenny is met
with subtle threats of physical violence, the boy's hand never far from

his gun even as he quietly, almost supplicatingly pledges his devotion, assuring her how gently he will ease her into her new marriage. When both Miss Jenny and her husband protest, the boy, obviously psychotic, declares, "Women ain't built to know what they want. They need a strong man to teach them." By the end he has wounded the husband in a gunfight, and Miss Jenny, both to save her husband's life and to prevent her own kidnapping, has had to kill him.

The point is clear enough: it isn't women but men and the frontier itself that ain't built to know what women want. A nice irony gives the husband a drinking problem and makes him otherwise not particularly sympathetic or attractive, and the marriage is obviously a troubled one. But out in the wilderness, against a mutual foe, she is forced to rely on him for protection, and that role in turn is ironized, as she winds up protecting herself and saving his life. The most powerful moment comes in the penultimate shot: a tight closeup of Jenny, almost in tears, tending to her husband and telling him the boy was lonely, that's all, he just went about getting the things he wanted in the wrong way, the expression on her face making it clear that, as much as for the boy whose life she was forced to take, she is grieving for her own loneliness and a future of increasing isolation in a loveless marriage.

"Lonesome Road" is equally interesting for its conception and its ambitions, although its script is bad and its direction clumsy (the actors mostly squint, grimace, and furrow their brows, visibly registering changes in expression in front of the camera). A marshal (played by Edmond O'Brien, later to be cast in *The Wild Bunch*) has spent five years cleaning up a tough town, in the process becoming corrupted by the job. He has taken to killing people before they've broken any laws and has acquired a reputation as "the most famous killer alive today." In a half hour Peckinpah tries to depict the marshal's psychotic disintegration from professionalism through various stages of abnormal cautiousness into utter paranoia, to portray the psychology of a cold-blooded killer, and to show how a man's reputation can engulf and ultimately destroy him. The climax is at once fitting, silly, and a little hysterical. The marshal is shot to death simultaneously by four persons, each of whom has a personal score to settle with him. One of them is a dance hall girl whose lover, a big Swede, the marshal had killed a few years earlier because, she says, "he was so big I think you just wanted to see what he would look like falling down, kicking in the dust." It hardly needs to be pointed out that the single most famous recurring visual motif in Peckinpah's later films is how, seen with the help of high-speed cinematography, men look in slow motion falling down and kicking in the dust.

II

In February 1959, before his involvement with *The Rifleman*, Peckinpah had written and directed a show for *Dick Powell's Zane Grey
Theatre* called "The Trouble at Tres Cruces," which introduced a
young drifter named Dave Blassingame (played by Brian Keith), who
carries a specially modified Winchester rifle, rides an Appaloosa, and
travels with a dog named Brown (who had played Disney's Old Yell-
er). The name is a combination of Peckinpah's father's—David, also
his own first name—and that of a family of ranchers he knew from
his childhood. The character was based on several old cowboys and
cattlemen Peckinpah had known growing up (including his father)
and also, he added, on "Brian Keith and me."[9]

Powell had actually commissioned the show as a pilot, but he found
no immediate takers. In the meantime, Peckinpah wrote and directed the pilot of *Klondike* for NBC and got to know a producer-execu-
tive there named David Levy. When Powell approached him with the
new series, Levy, already familiar with Peckinpah's work, bought it and
signed Brian Keith as the star and Peckinpah as the producer solely
in charge of production. Originally the series was to be called *Winchester*, after Blassingame's rifle; when someone discovered that Four
Star didn't own the rights to the title, it was changed to what was in
any event a more appropriate one, *The Westerner*.

Pauline Kael once called Peckinpah "a great 'personal' filmmaker."[10] That he surely is, but his vision begins small and for all practical purposes starts with *The Westerner*, where it consists in a fairly realistic look at the Old West through the adventures of an ordinary,
easy-going cowboy. About this he was explicit: "I wanted to create a
truly realistic saddle bum of the West. I wanted to make him as honest and real as I could do it. I drew him unlettered—most of these
guys couldn't read or write. Not too bright. Certainly unheroic. . . .
That's what David Blassingame is—a saddletramp."[11]

The world Dave Blassingame occupies is a masculine world, governed by codes and rules of conduct that are often spoken, but that
just as often go unspoken. He knows what most of these are, but this
knowledge is not enough to keep him out of trouble, for he is in many
ways still callow and without great experience of the world. Though
necessary, these rules and codes are not always reliable, are not adequate to cover all situations, and sometimes change or come into
conflict with one another. This is mostly because people are complicated and unpredictable. They are bruised or hurt or mean or igno-
rant or just plain crazy; they have axes to grind and scores to settle;

and they are proud and have ideals, dreams, and desires, most of which conflict with one another, sometimes even with themselves. Get enough people together—sometimes just two are enough—and there will be trouble. Trouble usually brings violence, and violence usually brings death.

The drifter who unifies a series of otherwise disparate people, places, and situations again recalls the model of Hemingway's *In Our Time*. A drifter of sorts himself, Nick Adams also moves through a violent world, and the meaning of his stories is the effect of his experiences upon his moral and psychological development. This is not to suggest that *The Westerner* is the equal of Hemingway's first important book—Peckinpah's mature work will stand easy comparison to the best of Hemingway, but we are not there just yet—only to recall that all of this was on the writer-director's mind during his thwarted development of *The Rifleman* scarcely a year earlier. While his work is not autobiographical with anything like the directness (sometimes even the literalness) that Hemingway's is, the more control Peckinpah was given over the selection and realization of his material, the more he would draw upon his life and his family and the more he would shape the material toward expressing his feelings and emotions, sometimes with an extraordinary intimacy.

The Westerner was part of Four Star's fall lineup for the 1960 season. Although Peckinpah himself directed only five and received screenplay credit for only four scripts of the thirteen completed episodes (fourteen, counting the pilot), they can all be seen as workings out of his ideas for the series, and that is the way they will be treated in the commentary that follows. This is in no sense to minimize the considerable contributions of other writers and directors, who will be noted as necessary.* It is, rather, to recognize that Peckinpah produced all the episodes, selected all the scripts, closely supervised all the rewriting, and on most of them did a lot of rewriting himself. (It was in these days that he acquired his reputation as the "best rewrite man around.") They have much of the characteristic Peckinpah look, feel, and vitality; and the small handful of the best of them are marked by a thematic density, psychological depth, and visual sophistication that suggest small films rather than television shows.

In the spring of 1960, with ten episodes in the can, Peckinpah

---

*One who won't be but deserves mention is Jack Gariss, the first-rate story editor Peckinpah met in graduate school. Gariss's criticisms improved scripts time and again, and Peckinpah often used his suggestions.

chose the one called "Jeff" to open the series. The reasons for the
selection are not hard to find. For one thing, Peckinpah himself had
directed and coscripted the episode. For another, he sensed that it
was substantially better than anything he had done before, a judgment that has since stood the test of time: in retrospect it was his
favorite of *The Westerner* episodes and, except for the adaptation of
Noon Wine, is generally the most highly esteemed of all his television
work. Perhaps the deciding reason was that Peckinpah himself had
a small personal involvement in the raw materials of the story. Several years earlier on a hunting trip in the Nevada mountains, he had
stopped at a bar called The Big Four, which offered the services of
prostitutes:

> I walked in on a Sunday morning, around twelve o'clock . . . and
> there was a woman sweeping up. In a jumper suit. Which didn't
> quite figure out, since she was seventy-two years old. As I walked
> in she smiled at me and said, Would you like to turn a trick, hon-
> ey? And I said, No, I'd like a beer though. Her name was Mae and
> we started talking. She told me she'd been working there . . . twenty-
> two . . . twenty-five . . . fifty . . . since she was eighteen years old.
> That's got to be better than fifty-three years. And I said, Did you
> ever want to leave? This is now about five o'clock, and we're on
> double shots of beer by that time. She laughed and said, A young
> fellow got to fall in love with me once. He'd take me out. I loved
> him. And he loved me. He whipped everybody. And I started to go,
> and then I said, No. And he said, Why? And I said, Because I like
> it here. So I stayed.[12]

Toward midnight Peckinpah finally left The Big Four but got
caught in a snowstorm that forced him to hole up in a bunkhouse
several miles up the road. He awakened two cowboys, a young fellow
and an old timer, took out a bottle of brandy, and started drinking
with them. "By God, this old timer told me the same story. It was his
fight. And he said, No, she wouldn't come." Peckinpah considered
it "a pretty good story," so he got together with Robert Heverly and
they wrote a script. (Two years or so after the episode was televised,
Peckinpah went back to see Mae and tell her he had done her story.
"What are you going to pay me?" she asked. "Well, Mae, what do you
want?" "I guess I'll have a beer," she said.)

As Heverly and Peckinpah retell it, Mae becomes Jeff, a young
prostitute who is a friend and perhaps a sweetheart from Blassingame's childhood. He finds her in a cheap bar hustling drinks and
whoring for an Englishman named Denny, an ex-boxer, now a pimp

and saloon owner, who keeps her in line with threats of violence and who won't let her go without a fight. Blassingame wins the fight by punching below the belt ("That's outside the rules," Denny cries; "This ain't a game!" Blassingame shouts back), but when he asks Jeff to come home with him to marry and settle on his ranch, she refuses. Although "Jeff" is only a half-hour sketch, the characters are vividly realized, their relationships economically but richly explored, the themes made to arise out of the dramatic situation. As in "Miss Jenny," though with considerably greater skill, artistry, and control, Peckinpah is showing how women suffer as a consequence of the prejudices of society and the limitations in men's thinking.

Three different attitudes are made explicit: the respectable or idealistic, the cynical or misogynistic, and the sympathetic or realistic. "Just because you're a woman don't mean you got to run perfect," Blassingame tells Jeff; but she knows that many people don't forgive so easily, that what she has become will follow her wherever she goes. "That kind of news everybody likes to talk about . . . you make yourself poison to everyone around you until they want you gone. You don't belong no matter how much you want to." Ironically, it is Denny, her pimp, who embodies both the idealistic and the cynical attitudes, which turn out to be but two sides of a fundamental misogyny. Although he ridicules Blassingame's notions about "the sanctity of womanhood," it is clear enough that his expectations are even more idealistic, albeit twisted, for when a woman fails to live up to them (as who wouldn't?) he degrades her beyond redemption and reclamation. He forces Jeff to wait on drunks he knows will get rough with her so that he can intercede at the last minute, knock them senseless, and thus demonstrate to her how much she needs him for protection. He reinforces the demonstration by slapping her around when she threatens to leave, saying, "This room and that one out there, they're your world. You better get used to it, Jeff, because you're never going to leave it. You won't leave it now, because I won't let you. And when I do, you won't want to go." When Jeff decides to stay, Denny tells Blassingame, "All that noble gallantry gone to waste. Well, I tried to warn you. Knowing what she is you should have—" "I know what you made out of her," Blassingame interrupts. "You left your mark on a lot of people, I guess. My dad used to tell me that women must be God's favorites, because he made them finer than anything else in creation. Well, he must hate your guts for what you done to them."

It is a portrait of innocence corrupted. Jeff's decision to stay is less an expression of genuine desire than an indication of the extent to which she has, by way of threats, beatings, and fear, absorbed Denny's attitudes toward women in general and herself in particular. She has been made to believe she deserves to be punished for what she is, and now she is willing to remain in a relationship that is patently sadomasochistic so that she will get that punishment for the rest of her life.

Peckinpah externalizes one of the social consequences of these attitudes in a framing device. On his way into town Blassingame passes a haggard evangelist (played by Peckinpah's wife at the time, Marie Selland), the only other woman in the story. She is handing out pamphlets describing "the road to everlasting peace." When he asks the price, she says, "There's no charge for salvation," and when he pays her (without taking a copy), she protests it's too much: "Prudence is one of the Lord's blessings, son." When he passes her again on the way out of town, she asks if he has found salvation. "Have you?" "Yes, I have," she answers, as the still night air is broken by the soft laughter of a woman's voice coming from a window in the brothel. The implication is that the woman herself was once a whore, hence her reluctance to accept Blassingame's money. Moreover, her age—she is not old, only old-looking, as if used and worn out—suggests an allusion to Blassingame's warning to Jeff, "Think about yourself five years from now when you're busted up and dying in the gutter." The evangelist and the gently mocking laughter of the prostitute epitomize the polar roles into which men like Denny and respectable people invariably cast women. Whether a woman becomes an emaciated angel or a vital whore, suffering the enervated sanctity of the one or the degradation of the other, it is exploitation and alienation either way.

The underlying meaning of the sketch is its effect on Blassingame himself: a burgeoning awareness of depths and complexities, primarily moral and psychological, that his limited codes and experience do not yet encompass or permit him to comprehend. Jeff and Denny, he discovers, share a relationship that, however sick and perverted, serves a deep need in both of them. At one point, Denny plays ruthlessly and desperately upon Jeff's sympathies, telling her he needs her in a way that indicates he is pleading for her not to go away (it is here that the woman's laughter, coming now from upstairs, is first heard). Later Jeff tells Blassingame that the woman he thinks she is no longer exists and maybe never has existed. For all the "realism" of his attitudes, then, the Westerner too cherishes fictions about people and is thus implicated, however inadvertently, in the suffering of the two women. It is therefore a kind of initiation for him—into a heightened perspective on human experience—and can be seen as an extension of the possibilities Peckinpah saw but was prevented from developing in *The Rifleman*. It is also an appropriate opening for a series about a drifter. Unable now to settle down with the woman he wants to marry, Blassingame no longer has any home to return to, only a road to travel and a lesson that he has just begun to learn: everlasting peace isn't to be found in this life.

The subject matter and, for the time, frank language—it was one of the first times "damn" was heard on nationwide television—almost kept "Jeff" off the air. Over three decades later, it may be difficult fully to appreciate how daring and controversial this and some other episodes of *The Westerner* were in their day. It wasn't just the language that concerned the NBC censor. He was even more alarmed by the presence of a dance hall girl who is obviously a prostitute, and in a memo he insisted, "Dialogue establishing Jeff's profession as a saloon singer will clearly be put across. We should avoid her being mistaken for a prostitute." Of course, Peckinpah wrote no such dialogue, and no one mistakes Jeff for a singer. The censor was equally alarmed by the sheer amount of alcohol that was consumed throughout the series: "To date, four of the episodes have alcohol 'necessary' to development. A fifth mocks temperance."[13] (Judging from the televised episodes, these memos must have joined the others in the round file nearest Peckinpah's desk.) Levy and Powell intervened and somehow managed to assuage the fears of the front-line NBC officials and the affiliates, so *The Westerner* was premiered as scheduled on Friday, 30 September 1960. The next morning *The Hollywood Reporter* called it "a great show, a stand-out series, and its strongest competition in the weeks ahead will be its own standards."[14] Later the same day, NBC received telephone calls from nine affiliates threatening to leave if the show went any further. "We ran a comedy next time," Peckinpah said, "so I guess they stayed."[15]

One can see why. In the comedies he directed—"Brown," "The Painting," and "The Courting of Libby"—Peckinpah didn't have much to say that would offend anyone. They consist of a lot of brawling and drinking and lewd banter between Blassingame and Burgundy Smith, a con man (played by John Dehner) who appears from time to time and is given to bursts of florid, often drunken rhetoric. There are moments and even whole scenes of genuine wit and tangy humor, but mostly Peckinpah seemed to use the comedies to sharpen his filmmaking technique. In "Brown," for example, there is a crane shot that begins on a closeup of Burgundy's boots as he comes out of a saloon, follows them along the walk until he stops and ties a bottle of whiskey to a dangling cord, moves up with the bottle as it is hauled to the roof where a pair of dance hall girls sit, and then keeps moving up and beyond them to become the first long shot of the main street, where a Fourth of July celebration is in progress.

"Brown" is also noteworthy for its form: the plot, which has Burgundy trying to con Blassingame into selling him his dog, is but the merest pretext for a series of loose, improvisatory sketches about a three-day bender that climaxes in an extended brawl that leaves no cliché unstoned. "This is Sam's idea of boys will be boys," someone once remarked, and it wasn't a criticism. The sense of a binge with no other purpose than to get down and dirty and uproariously drunk is raucously, hilariously conveyed.

With "Jeff," the best of *The Westerner* episodes Peckinpah directed is "Hand on the Gun," scripted by Bruce Geller (who wrote frequently for the series) and involving a situation often used in Western stories (probably its classic statement is Stephen Crane's "The Blue Hotel"). It has Blassingame as a trail boss for a pack of mustangers; one of them is a young easterner named Cal Davis, whom Blassingame has hired in return for being taught how to read. The kid knows nothing about being a cowboy except what he has read in books and the fast draw he has apparently taught himself. His melodramatic preconceptions about the West leave him always ready for trouble and thus always provoking it. Living in a fantasy world of dime-novel heroics, the kid is constantly seen drawing his pistol, twirling it, and aiming it at the others, until Blassingame, exasperated, asks,

> Look, you know what this is? That's a .45-calibre, 240-grain hunk of lead that can splatter your brains out like a jumped on squash. You ever seen a bullet hole? I mean up close. Oh, it goes in little enough, but when it comes out, that's if you're lucky and it comes out, it leaves a hole about like that. Now a gun ain't something to play with, it's to kill people with, and you don't reach for it unless you're going to shoot, and you don't shoot unless you're going to kill. You understand?

Still cocky, Davis says, "I think I would have just snapped him in the leg a bit." Blassingame replies, "Oh, you'd have just snapped him in the leg a bit? Well, I've seen men lose a leg that got snapped out a little." His point is given urgency later on when the man he was forced to shoot dies, although Blassingame had tried his best only to wound him; and prior to that he had even walked away from several insults to stop the argument before it came to violence. To clinch the point Blassingame asks Oresquote, a Mexican friend and an experienced

gunman, to show Davis his scars. The older man pulls up his shirt to
reveal a small scar on his stomach, then turns around to reveal a scar
the size of a softball on his back. "I don't want to shoot nobody," he
says, "and I don't want nobody shooting me." But Davis doesn't learn.
At the end of the drive, he goads Oresquote into a gunfight by insulting him. When he refuses to apologize, the older man tells him
to go outside and stand up the street a little.

This scene is beautifully filmed. Blassingame follows Davis out the
door, goes to his horse, and mounts up. Moments later, Oresquote
appears in the doorway, his gun already drawn. Davis fires wildly a
couple of times as the Mexican takes careful aim, plugs him with a
single bullet, and then mounts up. As Blassingame and Oresquote
pass the kid, Peckinpah follows them with a low-angle shot indicating the kid's point of view. Then he cuts to a crane shot looking down
on the kid and gradually pulls up and back as bystanders converge
to investigate more closely. When the camera finally stops in overview,
Brown barks and lopes up the street after his master. The dog's movement through the crowd inscribes one line of motion, the crowd's
movement toward the kid inscribes another line, the kid lies dying
where the two lines intersect. Brown reaches Blassingame as the first
few bystanders reach the kid, the two lines of motion completing
themselves simultaneously and bringing the composition to stasis just
before the rapid fadeout.*

Like "Jeff," this story has a frame, in the form of two parallel scenes,
and, as in a number of the early *Gunsmoke* shows Peckinpah wrote,
violence and innocence clash. Davis first appears at the camp in the
middle of an argument between Blassingame and one of his men,
who is drunk. The man turns on Davis, who picks up the challenge
despite Blassingame's patient explanation that the man's quarrel isn't
with Davis, who is being used, but with Blassingame himself. But the
kid won't go away, and when the man draws on Blassingame, Blassingame shoots him. In the penultimate scene it is shown that what
the kid has learned is not how to avoid violence, but how to use one
man to provoke another into a fight:

---

*Peckinpah flew into a rage when Four Star at first wouldn't approve the expense
of a crane. And he almost had to fight to keep the bit of Oresquote appearing at the
saloon door with his gun already in hand. Peckinpah personally added this touch to
the script where Geller had written a conventional Western duel. When Powell read
the revision, he asked Keith, "Can't you get Sam to tone it down, make it a fair fight?"
Keith suggested Powell approach the director himself, "He's pretty near a grown man,
you know." But Powell decided against it, and the bit was filmed as the director wanted
it (Weddle, unpublished draft, pp. 339–40).

Oresquote: You know, he would rather you come out that door than
  me. Would you like to try him for me?
Blassingame: What if I wanted to, would you let me?
Oresquote: No, amigo . . . what a waste.

Both scenes are distinguished by Peckinpah's command, acquired
early, of material that involves small provocations and retaliations,
testings, among men, which in turn create situations that grow beyond any single person's power to control, eventually flaring into
violence. Of particular note—and one of the things that distinguishes the episodes he directed—is how often he uses pauses, silences,
and silent cuts to draw out the tension, build moments, or suggest
what the characters are thinking and feeling. In both scenes the latent motif is space: serious, sober men, not looking for trouble, back
off, as if to create more space for the tensions to dissipate without
bloodshed, and both times the available space is insufficient.

This theme turns up again in "The Line Camp," the best episode
not directed by Peckinpah, and, with "Jeff" and "Hand on the Gun,"
one of the three best of the series. (There were times when he wasn't
sure it wasn't the best.) Written and directed by Tom Gries, it finds
Blassingame working as a cowhand in a line camp along the perimeter of a large cattle spread.[16] Three cowhands, a cook, and a foreman
occupy the camp's small bunk house where the episode is mostly set.
The story is about the conflicts that develop within this group of men.
Owing to the welter of motivations and submerged tensions that eventually flare into violence, a summary of the plot, such as it is, conveys
little sense of the drama and none of its effect. There are two main
conflicts (and several minor ones). The first, between Blassingame
and the cook—who wrongly suspects him of killing the man whose
job he now holds—is resolved in a fist fight, which the others allow
to go on just long enough for the two men to "get it over with." There
is no winner, but tensions are somewhat relaxed, and the cook soon
eases off Blassingame.

The second, and central, conflict is between Blassingame and
another hand, Prescott, who knows Blassingame from a previous job
and regards him as a friend. Despite company rules forbidding drinking, Prescott trades some cartridges for a jug of whiskey from some
market hunters while the foreman is gone. Soon enough all the cowboys are drunk and gambling, which is also against the rules. Blassingame quits while he's ahead, which provokes Prescott, who is by
now very drunk and a bad loser as well. Before he can pick a fight,
the foreman returns, sees the empty jug of whiskey, and fires both

men. When Prescott complains, Blassingame says, "We broke the rules. You got to take the tail with the hide." Impressed by this attitude and since Blassingame is new, the foreman hires him back, but Blassingame insists it's only fair to hire Prescott back too. When this is done Blassingame announces he's leaving anyway. "Punching cows, you got to know where the other man stands," he tells Prescott. "In case I was to need you, why, I don't think you're enough to call on."

Once Blassingame is outside, Prescott, stewing in his own drunken resentment, tells the cook that maybe he was right, maybe Blassingame did bushwhack the other guy for his job.

> *The cook:* Well, now, I never came right out and said so. But he's your friend, you know him better than I do.
> *Prescott:* Well, we wasn't all that good friends, you know. For all I know he's out there now laying for me.
> *The cook:* Could be, if he had a mind to.
> *Third cowhand:* I don't think so.
> *Prescott:* You figure he is?
> *The foreman:* You're still drunk, Prescott.

The third cowboy goes out to warn Blassingame, but before the latter can saddle up, Prescott appears, wearing his gun. Blassingame, as in "Hand on the Gun," does everything he can to avoid a gunfight. Opening his coat to show he's unarmed, Blassingame says, "Ain't no sense in a shooting, it ain't like I was mad," adding, "If I was laying for you, I sure ain't ready, am I?" "He's sure got you there," chuckles the cook. Confused, teetering on the edge, Prescott relents. But as Blassingame moves simply to pick up his holster so he can be on his way, Prescott fires and hits him in the leg. Blassingame fires back, hitting Prescott, who falls. Again Blassingame tries to prevent matters from going any further. Slumped on the porch, Prescott agrees, picks himself up in great pain, and stumbles back toward the door. But at the last moment, he wheels and fires at Blassingame, who fires back. When the dust clears, Prescott is dead and Blassingame is wounded so badly he can't go anywhere. "You sure as heck brought a pack of trouble with you!" the foreman shouts. "How am I going to explain two dead men and one so shot up he's good for nothing?" Blassingame mumbles back, "Well, if things go bad, you just got to run the string out, I guess." He is held in tight closeup for a beat, then the image fades to black and the story is left to end as abruptly and unsentimentally as a Puccini opera.

Several things are noteworthy. To start with, and characteristic of the series as a whole, "The Line Camp" is determinedly unromantic and realistic in the details, the sets, and especially the clothing, which is worn, wrinkled, and dirty. These men look like cowpunchers and trail hands. In the cabin they are as often as not shown in their long-johns and performing mundane tasks like mending their socks. In the shootout Gries sets up a nice comic counterpoint by dressing Prescott in cowboy hat, gunbelt, and boots but leaving him in his longjohns from the night's binge. The fist fight between Blassingame and the cook, like other fights in the series, is not a carefully choreo-graphed stuntmen's ballet but a serious physical brawl between two men who are too angry to look fancy doing it. As in "Jeff," Blassin-game doesn't fight fair, at one point grabbing a skull from a post and bashing the cook on the head with it. Then there is the convention used against itself, as in "Hand on the Gun": the old-fashioned show-down that goes farther than anyone intended. "I sure didn't mean for it to come out this way," Prescott says, already shot but still too drunk to have sense enough to stop. Another realistic detail is that the third cowhand is black, which is historically accurate: many cow-boys were ex-slaves. Everyone associated with the episode was con-cerned that the character's race be treated as a simple matter of fact, not highlighted or otherwise made an issue. He's just there, one of the cowhands, working the line. Finally, there is the alcoholism, prev-alent throughout *The Westerner.* By this time in his life Peckinpah him-self had long been a serious drinker and a problem one too, so it may be no accident that he chose a script in which booze precipitates the lethal climax.

What mostly makes this episode outstanding is the quality already observed in *The Westerner:* the complexity of the characters and their relationships, however small the canvas. The cook, for example, doesn't really believe Blassingame has killed the cowhand he replac-es, it's just that the man was his friend, he can't make any sense of the senseless death, and the only way he knows how to express his grief is through blame and rage. As for Prescott, sober he's genuine-ly affable; but he drinks too much, can't hold it, gets mean, then paranoid, and, finally, real dangerous. When the foreman refuses the market hunters food, he is not being greedy or merely inflexible about company rules: though the hunters have killed none of herd, they kill game, which riles the Indians ("The only thing between us and the whole hungry Cheyenne nation is a line on the map"), and it's the cowhands who are left to deal with the consequent trouble. As for the rules against drinking and gambling, the episode as a whole becomes its own commentary upon them.

Seen together, "The Line Camp" and "Hand on the Gun" also

point us toward something else in Peckinpah's work. In a penetrating comparison Weddle suggests that in the stark closeup that ends "The Line Camp," Gries eschews context altogether in favor of "an intimate look at one simple but terrible event in a man's life"; whereas in the carefully composed crane shot that ends "Hand on the Gun," Peckinpah reveals the story in a "mythic" aspect.[17] This is an early appearance of what might be called a contextualizing tendency in Peckinpah's imagination. Other early variants can be found in the frame scenes of "Jeff" and "Hand on the Gun." Before long this tendency will become a recurring practice that will take many forms, sometimes simultaneously—mythic, romantic, generic, aesthetic, allegorical, historical, social, to name but a few—throughout all the remainder of his films. Considerably sharpened and intensified, it will also become an informing principle of his filmmaking style. This development will not be complete until *The Wild Bunch*, with its multiple perspectives and rapid, radical shifts in points of view, by which he tries to see a dramatic situation from as many angles of vision as the narrative line will allow without disintegrating. But thereafter it will virtually define his style and inform everything he shoots.

These episodes are exclusively about men, but it would probably surprise a good many of Peckinpah's critics to discover how prominently women figure into the series and indeed into his television work as a whole. It will likely appease these critics little (and surprise them less) that the women are often prostitutes, background characters in several episodes and protagonists in three of them (counting "Jeff"). As noted, this worried the NBC censor no end (as did everything involving sex, including Blassingame's philandering with married women). But more than likely, what really caused the worry was less the number of prostitutes than Peckinpah's essentially sympathetic attitudes and his disinclination to condemn them.

These women are portrayed as strong willed and tough minded. Like the characters in *The Wild Bunch*, they "know how to take care of themselves" and make no apologies for the life they lead. The protagonist of "Going Home" (written by Jack Curtis and directed by Elliot Silverstein), a prostitute named Suzy, virtually flaunts it. "I'm not what folks would call a nice girl," she tells Blassingame. "Wouldn't like it if I was. Being no good beats plowing, it's warm, and you got company." Sal, the saloon-owner madam of "*Dos Piños*" (written by E. Jack Neuman and directed by Donald McDougall), is so hard bitten that when a lover is badly wounded and needs a place to rest until Blassingame can remove the bullet, her response is, "He's just another customer with an unpaid bill." Both women are seen as temptresses, trying to get Blassingame to forsake honor for money or a life with them. Suzy is allowed to be redeemed at the last minute but pays for it with her life. Sal and Blassingame spend a quiet moment talking about their childhoods, and Sal briefly entertains the thought of going off with Blassingame. But when he protects the wounded man against the crazy cowhands who shot him, she can't understand why he would risk their future trying to save someone who isn't worth it. "You didn't have to prove you're a man to me," she tells him. "I wasn't trying," he answers. "I didn't spend all night keeping him alive so they could kill him in the morning." He leaves, and she retreats back into her shell of cynicism and misanthropy.

The woman as temptress returns in "Mrs. Kennedy," written by Peckinpah and John Dunkel and directed by Bernard Kowalski. The story suggests Tennessee Williams flavored with Erskine Caldwell; and though somewhat overwritten and unsubtly directed, in one key respect it finds Peckinpah drawing upon his parents' marriage. Blassingame is working for a couple whose ranch is failing about as fast as their marriage. The title character is a fragile young Southern woman, not "raised to hardship," who loathes the ranch and has lost all feeling for her husband, Marsh. Desperate to leave but lacking the strength and courage to do it alone, she sees Blassingame as a way out and makes plain her interest in him, amorous and otherwise. Sensing how bad things are, her newly rich Uncle Henry offers to take the couple back home with him, but Marsh has too much pride to return to the menial clerking jobs he would face there. When the uncle declines to invest in the ranch, knowing what a losing venture it is, Marsh is consumed with envy. And when his wife tells him their marriage is finished, he realizes he has lost everything and his rage becomes violent. He takes the saddle bags full of the uncle's gold coins and clubs the old man to death; then he rushes to the barn, grabs a pitchfork, and tries to kill the sleeping Blassingame. Blassingame awakes just in time to save himself but is forced to kill the crazed man in the process. The man's dying words enjoin Blassingame to take good care of his wife. In the final scene Blassingame tells Mrs. Kennedy he won't be taking her with him. Her husband may not have been much, he says, but "he cared about you and deserves more than you stepping over his body to get to my horse." He offers to take her into town as he goes to get the sheriff. "No thank you," she says. "I'll stay here where I belong. I'll wait for the sheriff with my people."

In most respects the story is in no literal sense about Peckinpah's father and mother or their marriage. There was never any infidelity on the part of either parent. Far from a failure, his father was a great success, and the son talked often and admiringly of him. But about his mother, Fern Louise, he was far more circumspect, when he talked about her at all. As a nineteen-year-old girl Fern had fallen in love a man who later left town under sudden and mysterious circumstances, never to be heard from again. Two years later she married David Peckinpah, but to the day she died, she never forgot the other man. In this respect the reason Blassingame gives for not taking up with Mrs. Kennedy is most to the point. "You had somebody all built up in your mind before I ever got here," he tells her. "That's something I ain't, I never was, and I can't be." Peckinpah did not write the original screenplay, but he shares a writing credit; and these lines appear for the first time only in the drafts *after* he personally took over the revisions. In view of the unrequited love Fern Louise brought to her marriage and of Peckinpah's own admission that Blassingame is partly based on his father, it is difficult not to see here an association between fictional people and their counterparts in life so intimate that it virtually becomes identification. The father who in life married a woman who also had somebody all built up in her mind before he ever came along returns for a scene as the drifter who in fiction manages to avoid the same trap. As with the addition of the son to *The Rifleman*, so here Peckinpah uses a piece of family history so that he may reimagine it with a more desirable outcome.

Peckinpah's alleged misogyny will doubtless be debated as long as his films are watched, and we are far from finished with it here. But it should be noted that he nowhere blames Mrs. Kennedy for not loving her husband, just as Marsh is not blamed for being too proud to be a clerk and unsuited to be a rancher. These people were not raised to the hard lives they've mistakenly chosen for themselves, the desperation of their circumstances forcing them to acts they would not otherwise commit. This does not exonerate them from responsibility, but neither does Peckinpah judge them, preferring to observe and trying to comprehend. In Mrs. Kennedy's decision to remain on the ranch for the sheriff to arrive, there may be a glimmer of redemption in the suggestion that she is beginning to accept a responsibility that was beyond her at the outset.

It is also worth noting that the scripts for both this episode and "Going Home" were unusually worked over—much more than was typical for the series—and in a way that suggests there is more to Peckinpah's attitudes toward women than the misogynist label can encompass. In both cases the women protagonists became far more sympathetic characters than in the original scripts, which were not by Peckinpah. As originally conceived by Jack Curtis, Suzy was little

more than the greedy "bitch" the outline calls her. But memos indicate that Peckinpah insisted she be shown as a woman whom circumstances made dependent on men and that he exerted a decisive
though uncredited hand in a rewrite toward that end. In John
Dunkel's first script for "Mrs. Kennedy," practically everybody but
Blassingame is a greedy, bloodthirsty maniac, the title character coming on first to Blassingame, then to her husband, unconcerned about
who murdered whom but only who has the gold. It was only when
Peckinpah took a strong hand in the writing that the characters were
scaled down and made flawed in recognizably human terms. It was
then that the gold assumed the place it always does in Peckinpah's
work: not as a primary motive but as a catalyst that releases other,
admirable motives, although in thwarted, twisted forms. Love, pride,
fear, jealousy, loyalty, honor, friendship, devotion, responsibility, loss
of love, family, and land—these are the things that drive Peckinpah's
characters, male and female, young and old, "good" and "bad." If this
is a misogynist, he is plainly a complex and complicated one.

Loss and rage are the principal motivations of the women in an
odd episode called "Ghost of a Chance," written by Milton Gelman
and directed by Bruce Geller, but also extensively changed along the
way to filming. The opening suggests *The Westerner* has wandered into
The Twilight Zone, as Blassingame enters a Mexican village that shows
every sign of life except for people, who are nowhere to be seen. He
leaves, sees some circling vultures, and then returns to find the village now populated, but only by women and children. The rest of the
plot is almost too absurd to summarize. Suffice it to say that an evil
Mexican bandit named Serafin and his gang have kidnapped all the
men and are holding them hostage so that he can steal an ammunition shipment that will pass through. When Carlotta (played by Katy
Jurado) asks Blassingame if he saw the men on his way into town, he
remembers the circling vultures and concludes that Serafin has already had the men killed. With Blassingame's help, Carlotta and the
other women lure Serafin's henchmen away one by one with promises of sexual favors and then kill them until only the leader himself
is left. He pleads to be turned over to the *federales,* but Blassingame
leaves him to the women, who, shrouded in black and full of hatred,
descend on him like avenging furies. The episode contravenes the
common view of Peckinpah's women as only passive and compliant;
and the climactic scene anticipates a sequence in the director's World
War II film *Cross of Iron,* made almost twenty years later, where a Nazi
soldier is turned over to a group of Russian women, one of whose
number he has attempted to rape.

In "School Day," written by Peckinpah and Robert Heverly and directed by Andre de Toth, a schoolteacher is brutally murdered fighting off a rapist. She figures only in the very beginning, but the way she fights to protect herself again depicts the kind of strong, active woman that we're not supposed to find in his work. Blassingame is wrongly accused of the murder and almost lynched. In high school Peckinpah was bowled over by the film version of *The Ox-Bow Incident,* and this part of the plot may be something of an homage to that classic, which is one of the first "revisionist" Westerns. There is some playful revisionism too—and maybe an insolent flip toward Levy and Laven for all the kids' stuff they wanted him to do on *The Rifleman*—in a bit that has Brown leaping like Rin Tin Tin through a window to free his tied-up master, only the dog just licks Blassingame's hands, turning his full attention to leftovers on the table.

The world of Peckinpah's Western films could sometimes be quite small and marked by coincidences that are a little eerie. Two *Westerner* episodes have plots that are like blueprints for his first two features, yet this has to be coincidental, as Peckinpah did not generate the original scripts for either film. In "Going Home," a man with a price on his head is shot while fleeing bounty hunters. He dies in the company of his wife and his mother, who insists they return the body to their home forty miles away where he can be buried next to his siblings. Blassingame, who has joined the hapless trio, rigs a makeshift wheelbarrow to carry the body through the desert. This is, of course, the basic plot of *The Deadly Companions,* which also stars Brian Keith as the hero who does the hauling.

Scarcely less coincidental is "The Old Man," written by Peckinpah and Jack Curtis and directed by Andre de Toth. Here an old cattle baron is dying as his many relatives converge upon him, all hoping for some portion of his wealth. He favors his grandson Billy, a young man who "hasn't been through the fire yet, and when I pass on this ranch, I want to have the feeling he can handle it." When a pair of distant, degenerate cousins and two of their pals threaten to burn the house down with him, his grandson, and Blassingame in it if the deed isn't signed over to them, the cattleman shouts, "You full of fear at meeting the old man head on?" When one of the cousins wants to ambush the old man as he comes out, the other shames him into fighting fairly. The three emerge, the old man out in front, Blassingame and Billy flanking him. Guns are fired, the greedy cousins are killed, and the old man goes out in a blaze of glory, his dying words, "I wouldn't have had it no other way."

If all of this sounds just a little familiar, it is because the old man, the white-trash heavies, the decision to fight head on, and the gunfight in the yard all constitute what in retrospect appears as a dress rehearsal for the climax of *Ride the High Country*. The old's man last words come back as a famous line in *The Wild Bunch*, while the name of his ranch, the Agua Verde, will be given to the Mexican town that is the site of the Bunch's final showdown. But more important than any of this is the old man himself. In the screenplay here is how Peckinpah describes him just before the shooting starts: "The old man stands in the sunlight, his eyes bright, his hands steady, drinking in the feel of the wind on his face, the anticipation of the coming fight, knowing these are his last moments, and glorying in them. Then he turns slowly, looking over his ranch, his holdings, almost drowning in the memories of the good times and the satisfaction of a fine life now at an end."

It would not be accurate to call this mythic, but there is more than a passing nod in that direction. The old man is arguably the only character in the whole series that Peckinpah self-consciously tried to make considerably larger than life. In the directing and filming, de Toth realized little of that, keeping everyone scaled to what Hawthorne liked to call the ordinary and probable in the course of human events. But like so much else in *The Westerner*, this episode marks the beginning of things Peckinpah was later to master. It suggests too that for all his insistence upon realism, there was inside him a romantic, at once hard edged yet full of sentiment, just biding his time.

Despite its high quality, almost unprecedented for a television series at the time, *The Westerner* was canceled not halfway through the season. Asked why, one hardened television journalist cited "Jeff," saying, "You can see it right there. It was good."[18] Perhaps, but there also are less cynical explanations. *The Westerner* was a thirty-minute dramatic series at a time when hourlong series were becoming more and more popular. It debuted opposite *Route 66*, one of the more highly acclaimed of the longer series, which featured a pair of more or less neo-Beat drifters traveling around the country in a Corvette, and *The Flintstones*, the first prime-time animated sitcom. Despite the competition, *The Westerner* attracted a remarkably large and devoted audience, including many critics and columnists, all of whom vociferously protested the cancellation. And NBC received over a thousand letters and telegrams from viewers alone.

This sort of fuss raised over a small, unpretentious if offbeat Western series was more than enough to generate talk in the industry and soon in the press of this new director around whom a cult was forming. Still, other television shows have been as good, even better, without acquiring anything like the reputation this one did. Perhaps the explanation lies in Peckinpah's personal commitment to the series—in a medium not conspicuous for that quality—which lends the best of the episodes a strength of conviction and a depth of feeling that make them difficult to forget.

The high quality of *The Westerner*, its abrupt cancellation, and Peckinpah's later accomplishments in theatrical films have all conspired to give his very early television work a reputation decidedly out of proportion to its actual achievement. Peckinpah too could wax rather lyrical about this period in his career. Caught in less sentimental moods, he told a different story. Recalling his first three years of television directing, he said, "Every time I started a show I would walk on a set, lay out the first three or four shots, then go back to the head and throw up. Then I'd get a milk shake, settle down, and make a picture."[19] Allowing for the hyperbole that suggested this went on for three years and on every show, the programs themselves reveal the strain and Peckinpah's lack of experience. Despite a pale glimmer here and there, all the work he did before late 1959 has a cramped, boxed-in look and feel, with none of the dynamism and expansiveness of his mature style, the sure control of tempo and rhythm, and the almost fanatical care and precision lavished upon editing and detail (there are shots that don't match, for example, one moment a character's bullet strap is full of bullets, the next moment it's empty; the actors mostly stand and deliver their lines; and so forth). The writing is sometimes even worse than the directing (with lines like "That Greek is a pretty mean hombre," "Yeah, but he's smart"). It is difficult to believe that were Peckinpah to have taken a good, hard look at most of these shows he would have wanted them around.

The big improvement, as sudden as it was dramatic, in writing, directing, and filmmaking came with *The Westerner*, on which Powell and Levy gave Peckinpah probably more freedom than he ever enjoyed with any other producers. The series also provides an answer to a minor but puzzling question about his career: how did he become such a skillful filmmaker so quickly? Shows like "Jeff," "Hand on the Gun," and "Brown" tell us how; he simply shot them as if he were making movies, not television. One notes the frequent use of deep-focus lenses; the balance struck among closeups, medium shots, and long shots; the increasing attention paid to preserving point of view by careful selection of camera setup and placement; and an extraordinarily comprehensive grasp of filmic space—how to fill it significantly, exploit it dramatically, and use it expressively. One also sees the beginnings of the textual richness and density familiar from

The Wild Bunch, Junior Bonner, Ride the High Country, and other films (dust choking the customers in a crowded saloon, a drunk piano player taking a hall tree for a dancing partner in the background of one shot, a brass band that marches in and out of one set and eventually starts a brawl, a stuffed raven adorning a bar, an Indian bartender who carries a sickle instead of a knife), the recurring visual motifs (low-angle tracking shots, sudden cuts from closeup to overview and back again), a wonderful feel for the way people look and smell and for naturalistic grotesques, and a recognition of the explosive power of firearms (glasses and mirrors shattering like shrapnel, a beam of wood splintering as bullets from a high-powered rifle thunk-thunk-thunk into it).

Above all, one recognizes the beginnings of his primary interest as dramatist and storyteller, which is with character: Western in its terms, universal in its significance. Many years later Peckinpah told Garner Simmons, then an aspiring screenwriter, "If you can't find the humanity even in your villains, you're not doing your job as a storyteller, you're making things too easy for yourself and your audience."[20] From the very beginning, even when Peckinpah's writing was inexperienced, uninspired, or just plain bad, his conception of character was remarkably complex and sophisticated, and was already taking him in the direction of those twisted ironies and gnarled ambiguities that make his later films so difficult and disturbing. He seemed incapable of conceiving people in only one dimension, of seeing them in only one aspect.

As in his scripts for *Gunsmoke,* this extended even to his heroes. Most of the stories present Blassingame as a man of honor, often testing his honor in the form of temptations, usually monetary, sometimes sexual, occasionally both. He passes the tests, but upholding honor, decency, integrity—indeed all of what Faulkner once called the old time virtues and values—is always shown to involve real and dear sacrifice, prices to pay, losses to bear. In "The Treasure" (written by Cyril Hume and directed by Ted Post), the temptations are almost irresistibly great and the dark side of the hero makes a far more menacing appearance. As Blassingame carries a treasure out of the desert he becomes so infected with gold fever that he refuses to share his water with Brown, who collapses and would die except that someone else discovers and saves him. Before long Blassingame has become an outlaw and is headed for Mexico with gold that is not rightfully his. By the end he comes to his senses and returns the gold, but the point is already clear. "Things are always mixed," Peckinpah once said, by which he meant also that people are always mixed.[21]

One can search *The Westerner* from the first to the last episode and hardly find a thoroughly good or thoroughly evil character—they're all a little, or a lot, of both.

The basic look of Four Star's productions, which, in common with most television shows, favored sound stages over actual locations, could blight many of Peckinpah's best visual effects and his attempts at verisimilitude. But as often as not he would also turn these to advantage by setting the stories indoors or in quite small spaces when out of doors, the visual style usually dark, close, even claustrophobic; and many scenes are set at night. It was as if he were intuitively playing to the strengths of the small screen and the limitations of his budgets and facilities. Nor was he merely making virtue of necessity: the relationship between restricted spaces and the violence people do unto one another is one of his abiding themes, and he started developing it here.

But a television series is still a series: the strain of producing a minidrama on schedule each week eventually made itself felt even on Peckinpah and the talented pool of writers and directors Four Star allowed him to draw upon. Impressive as "Jeff" is, for example, it is undermined by a weak performance in the title role. While none of the episodes is wholly without merit, and most of them help to fill in the picture of Peckinpah's filmmaking apprenticeship, some of them, like "Brown" and "The Painting," are at once padded and thin.

Despite the control Peckinpah had at the time of its production, *The Westerner* eventually suffered the same fate of unauthorized cutting that befell so many of his features later in his career. Four Star syndicated it with three other short-lived series under the generic title *The Westerners*. Presumably to make it seem as if they had been conceived originally as an anthology series instead of an *ad hoc* one, the shows were "unified" by a kind of emcee, a grizzled cowboy, played by Keenan Wynn at his hammiest, who frames each episode with an introduction and a homiletic conclusion that are subliterate and of stupefying banality (e.g., "Like you just seen," he says after "The Line Camp" fades out, "a man's best friend is still this," and holds up his sixgun). What is worse, in order to make room for the framing scenes and still stay within the half-hour time limit, all the episodes were shortened by a couple of minutes, usually by dropping first scenes, but sometimes by trimming or removing internal ones, too (in "Jeff," for example, the dialogue in which the pimp tells Jeff, "This room and that one out there," etc., was removed).

A selection of Peckinpah's television work should nevertheless be made available in a responsible format, perhaps for the home-video market (preferably on laserdisc for its superior resolution and sound reproduction). *The Westerner* in particular deserves a far better fate than the one to which it remains consigned. This work as a whole reveals a young artist, soon to be a master, discovering fairly early his themes and materials and working in conventional forms that he was already beginning to manipulate in fresh and original ways. For all that the hasty production schedules constricted his style, they also forged in him both a strong discipline and an ability to work under extreme pressure that, although he couldn't have known it at the time, would stand him in good stead on his first two feature films.

III

When the three remaining *Westerner* episodes were completed in the fall of 1960 and the series was canceled, Brian Keith signed a contract to star with Maureen O'Hara in a Western film entitled *The Deadly Companions.* Keith, who had immensely enjoyed his association with Peckinpah, talked the producer Charles FitzSimons into hiring the young director. Itching to direct features, Peckinpah accepted quickly, with great enthusiasm and, since Keith was part of the package, it may be assumed with high hopes. As things turned out, the conflict implied in the title was enacted on both sides of the camera, and the picture became a first for Peckinpah in more ways than one, setting a pattern of arguments with producers and moneymen that was to continue throughout his career. But FitzSimons's style of interference was preposterous even in the context of this director's difficult career. He told key crew members, including the cinematographer (who referred to him as "a goddamn idiot"), not to listen to Peckinpah; he actually stood next to the director on the set and tried to tell him how to stage the scenes and direct the actors; and eventually he forbade Peckinpah from even speaking to Maureen O'Hara (who is FitzSimons's sister). "It wasn't the best deal in the world for either of us," Peckinpah said. "He wanted someone he could push about. I wanted to make the best picture I could."[22]

The trouble started with the script, which Peckinpah thought he had been hired to fix. Written by A. S. Fleishman (who later made it into a novel), it tells of an ex–Union soldier named Yellowleg searching for the Confederate renegade who tried to scalp him seven years earlier at Chickamauga, leaving him scarred across his hairline (he never takes his hat off unless alone). Near the beginning, Yellowleg tries to halt a bank robbery and accidentally shoots and kills a boy when his aim is thrown off due to a wartime shoulder wound, the

The people in *The Deadly Companions* were all based on gimmicks—the scarred head, the dead boy being carried across the desert for five days. The thing I will take credit for doing, at least I kept off that long enough so that you weren't too conscious of it.

—Sam Peckinpah

bullet still lodged against his collarbone. The main action of the story sends Yellowleg and the boy's mother, a dance hall girl named Kit Tilden, on a journey across the desert to Serengo to bury her son next to his father.

Peckinpah's strongest objection, apart from the often atrocious dialogue (which FitzSimons thought excellent), was that the characters were "all based on gimmicks—the scarred head, the dead boy being carried across the desert for five days" (the body never putrefying in the heat) just to get the hero and heroine alone together in the wilderness, and other ploys.[23]* Peckinpah offered to rewrite; FitzSimons promptly refused. The producer had spent three years developing the script and considered it in no need of further work, a judgment shared by no one else. "Every time I'd volunteer anything, he'd tell me to go back to my own corner," Peckinpah recalled. "Brian had sense enough to know that we were in trouble with the script, so between us we tried to give the thing some dramatic sense."[24] In all, he and Keith, working nights, between scenes, on breaks, and generally on the sly, managed to rewrite about a fifth of the dialogue, primarily Keith's. (Little was done to O'Hara's lines as Peckinpah couldn't speak with her.) Peckinpah realized early that the script he was handed was the script he was going to have to direct, "so I just kind of went around the edges, trying to bring some life into it."[25]

Amazingly, the film does have life to it. One likely reason is that, even though it is set much earlier, *The Deadly Companions* can in many respects be regarded as a kind of two-hour episode of *The Westerner*, its hero an extension of Dave Blassingame. The casting of Brian Keith virtually guarantees this. But the character too is surely a strong possibility for the kind of man Blassingame would have become as he grew older: far darker and more troubled, still a drifter and misfit but now carrying a past that weighs heavily upon him (which is neatly evoked: the character is named for the stripe on the Union trousers he continues to wear five years after the war).

Also like the series, the script gave Peckinpah ample opportunity to exploit a couple of his more prominent gifts: his sense of irony and his taste for colorful, eccentric characters. The ironies begin with the

---

*As absurd as this gimmick may be measured against the strictures of realism, it has enjoyed a remarkable life in both literature and popular art (to say nothing, doubtless, of folklore). It appears in, among other places, Faulkner's *As I Lay Dying*, Larry McMurtry's *Lonesome Dove*, and William Humphrey's *The Ordways*; and a variant of it crops up later in Peckinpah's own *Bring Me the Head of Alfredo Garcia*, where the hero must deal with problems "tastefully" left out of the earlier film (flies, for example, or how to preserve a severed body-part) (Jerry Holt to P.S., 1994).

title itself, an oxymoron, prophetic of things to come in Peckinpah's work, for here we meet the first of several sets of companions in uneasy alliance that will appear and reappear in his subsequent films. In this one the characters are mostly types, even stereotypes, but they are close enough to those he had created and would create to appeal to what he has since called a "weakness for losers on the grand scale," "a sneaky affection for all the misfits and drifters in the world."[26] While that grand scale would have to await later projects, for the time being he could at least watch, experiment with, and endeavor to see these people as thoroughly as conditions permitted.

Most clearly seen are the three companions to whom the title initially refers: Yellowleg and his two newly acquired sidekicks, Billy (a cocky gunslinger) and Turkey (the renegade from Chickamauga). Billy is pure stereotype, to which Peckinpah could do little more than counterpoint his menace against his sporadically charming "little-boy bravado." Turkey, however, is something of an original and anticipates many of the low-life characters in Peckinpah's later films. Adorned with beads and feathers, dressed in a long buffalo robe, Turkey is a hulking psychotic bear-man who speaks in a whiskey-soaked rasp that occasionally breaks into a clogged laugh (when his psychoses come on strong, the music score, which Peckinpah detested, goes into a tortured rendition of "When Johnny Comes Marching Home Again"). Turkey and Yellowleg are linked dramatically as hunted and hunter; and they also share a psychological association, as Turkey is Yellowleg's foil, the embodiment of his past and past self that haunts and obsesses him. Peckinpah economically symbolizes the relationship with costume and film technique. In the first shot we follow a pair of legs, dressed in Union trousers, walking through a set of swinging doors; then the camera travels to another pair of legs, clad in buckskin, atop a barrel turned on its side, and tilts up to reveal Turkey, a noose around his neck and some cards pinned to his shirt. Turkey's buckskin contrasts with Yellowleg's military blue, yet it forms a kind of match to the hero's own buckskin jacket, while the camerawork unites both in the same cinematic space. Turkey is in this predicament because he cheated at cards; Yellowleg gets him out of it, thus saving the life of the man he plans to kill.

This opening is significant because it introduces one of Peckinpah's basic storytelling techniques: he rarely opens a film or a scene with an establishing shot. Instead, his camera will light upon a naturalistic detail that leads to another detail and still another, until gradually the setting is built up from and revealed through a careful process of selection and accumulation of significant details. His aesthetic is thus novelistic inasmuch as setting becomes a function of discrete details; and his intention is more psychological than pictorial (the pictures, images, and compositions are means, not ends). It is as if he were forcing us to discover for ourselves the world the film inhabits, as if it is being "created" out of our own sense impressions. Peckinpah refined this technique and continued to explore its uses and implications throughout his career, but here in his very first film he gives it one of its earliest applications.

That Kit, the mother, is seen less clearly than the other main characters is probably more a result of the constraints under which the director was working than of any deficiency in his eye or technique. In the absence of the freedom to make changes, he could do little more than treat her according to the standard Western euphemism allowed for prostitutes—a barroom or dance hall girl—leaving unexplored both her shame (briefly alluded to in the script) for what has become of her life after her husband died and the contradictions in her attitudes: on the one hand, her contempt for the self-righteous citizens of Gila City who judge her, and on the other, her desperate need to reach Serengo and prove (partly to Gila City, partly to Yellowleg) that she was legally married and that her son was legitimate. Bits and pieces of this glimmer through, but mostly Kit remains a collection of possibilities.

Yet Kit—who she is, what drives her, the nature of her obsession with conventional morality—is doubtless one of the things that attracted Peckinpah to the script in the first place, the other being the paradox inherent in the hero's mission of vengeance. On the trail Yellowleg tells Kit he once knew a man who carried on a vendetta for five years. One day the man caught up with the fellow he wanted to kill, killed him, and then discovered that he had killed the only thing he lived for. Yellowleg is of course talking about himself as well (it is five years since the war), and the anecdote predicts a self-defeating future. By the end of the film, he has caught up with Turkey, and, ignoring Kit's exhortations to stop, goes to scalp him. At the last moment he desists in a neat wrap-up: he has discovered that his love for her is a more valid reason for living than his hatred for the renegade. Together the man and woman ride off into the sunset.*

*FitzSimons, who declares himself "a great believer in the auteur theory as it applies to a producer," actually said that he didn't think Peckinpah understood "the problem of revenge for a man of moral fiber. . . . It was a morality play in Western clothing which we had constructed around the quotation 'Revenge is mine saith the Lord'"(Quoted in Simmons, p. 37). This is a literally astounding thing to say about a director who made an authentic revenge-tragedy in *Bring Me the Head of Alfredo Garcia*

The problem here is less the gimmicks than the love story. The ease and speed with which Kit manages to warm to, then fall in love with, and finally forgive the man who killed her son, however accidentally, are almost absurd. It's not that such a development is beyond belief, merely that the script fails almost completely to chart the emotional stages by which it happens. Equally damaging is the absence of even a single scene that depicts her grief over her son's death. Indeed, despite the presence of the coffin containing his corpse, the boy figures amazingly little in any of the dialogue between Kit and Yellowleg throughout the whole five-day journey.

Omissions like these are pretty uncharacteristic of Peckinpah's work. When he finished shooting, he made the first cut of the film himself. FitzSimons didn't like it, recut it, and got into such a mess that he had to return to the original cut the director made. As the film now stands, it consists mostly of Peckinpah's editing, except for a crucial moment in the climax where, as a result of a cutaway that FitzSimons put in the wrong place, it appears as though Turkey shoots Billy when in fact it is and should be Yellowleg who shoots Billy. When Peckinpah complained that the sunset was not his touch, what he seems to have meant is not that he would have removed it but that he wanted it to function ironically. In his version, he said, when it was absolutely clear that Yellowleg "did the killing, the ride off into the sunset was a bit of a finger to 'The West.' Very few people picked it up."[27] Perhaps so, but it is doubtful many more people would have picked it up from his cut, especially as Yellowleg refrains from scalping Turkey, thus redeeming himself for Kit.

Years later FitzSimons denied ever returning to Peckinpah's cut. Fleishman's original script, the producer pointed out, called for "an old-fashioned gunfight between Yellowleg and Billy in which you didn't know who was going to win, and if anything, the hero was at a disadvantage because of his old shoulder wound."[28] The ending Peckinpah staged has Billy attempting to force a showdown as Yellowleg, marching to find Turkey, orders Billy out of his way. When Billy instead prepares to draw, Yellowleg shoots him dead without so much as breaking stride. "How can you have a man shoot another against whom he bears no grudge and then turn around and be unable to kill the man he's hated for years?" the producer asked, not without some reason.

---

and three other films—*Major Dundee, The Ballad of Cable Hogue,* and *The Killer Elite*—with vengeance as one of their central themes; who was obsessed with the theme the whole of his artistic and personal life; and who never once anywhere in his art showed or otherwise suggested that for perpetrator and victim alike the wages of revenge are anything other than quite literally death.

But the director had his reasons too. For one thing, in both structural and dramatic terms he knew it was surely wrong to postpone the final confrontation between Yellowleg and Turkey any longer. For another, Yellowleg's shoulder wound has been shown to be so debilitating that empty-handed he cannot lift his arm to shoulder level or, holding a gun, even halfway up, so how could he outshoot Billy in an old-fashioned Western gunfight? And last, something in Peckinpah must simply have rebelled against staging a conventional gunfight, not because it was a cliché but because it was so completely unjustified by the story and unmotivated by the characters. It seems clear that the real finger Peckinpah flipped at both the West and the conventional Western here was not that sunset but what he called "the brutal, realistic act" of Yellowleg, obsessed with revenge, shooting Billy dead while Billy is quite literally playing kids' games with his sixshooters.

In any case, the true theme Peckinpah discovered in this film has little to do with any ironic treatment of the Western as genre. The true theme is so central to much of his own work, to a good many Westerns (*Stagecoach* is a classic expression of it), and to a sizable chunk of American literature (*Adventures of Huckleberry Finn* and "The Bear" are two outstanding examples) that he couldn't help feeling the shock of recognition. That theme is a trek into the wilderness where, away from society, a person may be reborn or in some sense redeemed, often through an ordeal of physical crisis or a trial of violence. Much of this journey finds Yellowleg and Kit tearing at each other with a savagery that is partly mirrored, partly exacerbated by the savagery of the landscape. "You don't know me well enough to hate me!" Yellowleg shouts. Yet Kit knows him clearly enough. He teamed up with Billy and Turkey to rob the bank, so he finds himself in a doubly compromised position. He accidentally shoots the child while attempting to halt a crime he himself was planning to commit. The polarities in his psychological makeup are thus externalized in those with whom he associates and in what he does—the "accidental" killing revealing more truth about him than any of his good intentions does. The journey through the wilderness is necessary so that he can reveal to Kit those aspects of his character that she doesn't know (and that he himself doesn't know either). His moral awakening at the climax is thus as much a revelation to himself as it is to Kit.

However sketchy much of this appears in the completed film, the landscape is nevertheless extraordinarily well realized. Gila City, where the film opens, hardly qualifies as a backwater, let alone a city. It rests securely in the tradition of the sparse, dusty, windswept towns from such revisionist Western films as *The Ox-Bow Incident* and *The Gunfighter* that attempt to supplant dime-novel, B-movie romance with much sterner stuff. Peckinpah obviously means to evoke that tradition, but in terms that are wholly his own and that derive as much from his experience as from previous films. Most of the early action is set in the saloon, which serves the triple function of house of ill repute six days a week, house of worship the seventh, and house of justice whenever legal services are called for. (Near the beginning there is a church service presided over by an armed preacher, behind whom a bartender discreetly covers the nude painting above the bar.) Surely the surrounding wilderness by contrast can offer only refuge and succor.

If anything, however, it is even worse. *The Deadly Companions* opens onto an almost obsessively unpretty Western landscape: scarred, burned out, sparse, desolate, dry, cracked, peeling—and violent. Once on their own, the couple find themselves stalked by an Indian. Some critics have suggested that the Indian symbolizes the dark, savage side of Yellowleg. This is plausible enough, but Peckinpah does little to encourage the interpretation (with Turkey around to assume that function, who needs an Indian?). Instead, he seems to use the Indian primarily to heighten the sense of the bizarre, to underscore the precariousness of the couple's situation, and to extend and amplify the ironies. Yellowleg steals the Indian's horse, and the Indian dogs him to reclaim it because of a point of honor among his tribe. Peckinpah thus provides a compact inversion of the primary plot, as Yellowleg the hunter becomes for a while the hunted. At the same time, Peckinpah shows us that this wilderness is not "lawless," that even in a so-called savage culture there are abstractions—forms, codes, and rules—that govern human behavior. The inversion culminates in a chilling confrontation in a cave where Kit, from the outset adamantly opposed to killing, must kill to protect her own life. Women are not exempt from the imperatives of this world.

The Deadly Companions is neglected in most assessments of Peckinpah's work. But given the obstacles of a poor script, a hostile producer, a severely attenuated shooting schedule, and a near-total breakdown of communication between director and leading lady, the film emerges, tabulating effects against defects, as more successful than not. "I think I failed," was Peckinpah's own assessment, adding that the one thing he was willing to take credit for was that he stayed off the gimmicks sufficiently so that audiences weren't too conscious of them.[29] Actually, he can take credit for more than that. *The Deadly*

Companions—not only his first film but also shot in CinemaScope—contains no evidence that Peckinpah had any trouble making the transition from small screen to large. As he himself suggested, one of the reasons may be that, prohibited from rewriting the script, he concentrated instead almost exclusively on the filmmaking. In the process he learned how to stay close to the action, the characters, and the situations (leave the messages, he would later say, "to Army Special Services")—in short, how to tell a story cinematically.

Regarding this last point, *The Deadly Companions* has one quality in common with Peckinpah's later films that alone makes it worth seeing. Several critics have commented on his ability suddenly to expand the scale and enrich the texture of his films, often introducing dizzyingly discordant elements, without breaking the continuity or violating the tone. Cited in particular are the mining camp and brothel sequences from *Ride the High Country* in which the texture of the film, up to these points affectionately naturalistic and rather nostalgic, suddenly becomes by turns grittily realistic and subtly surrealistic. When asked about this, Peckinpah replied that he just tried to play the sequences from the girl Elsa's point of view. What he meant is that he tried to show how the sights and sounds of these places, thoroughly alien to her experience, impressed themselves upon her. In *The Deadly Companions*, once Yellowleg has driven off Billy (who has tried to rape Kit) and Turkey has run away, it is as if the last vestiges of even so measly a "civilization" as Gila City are gone and the couple are now isolated in an utterly strange and forbidding land. Soon they see a stagecoach far in the distance being chased by a band of Indians. On closer inspection it turns out that the Indians, drunk and wearing top hats and bloomers, are only staging a parody of their attack, which has already occurred. (It is while the Indians sleep off their stupor that Yellowleg steals the horse.) Peckinpah sets up and shoots the incident with great care, selecting his lenses and camera positions to preserve the integrity of the main characters' point of view, so that we experience what is happening even as they themselves do.

The slight alteration in scale, the injection of the bizarre and the gothic (culminating in the cave sequence), the sudden fluctuation from initial terror to comedy (which, because grotesque and unexpected, only reinforces the sense of threat), the countervailing intensification of focus and concentration—all of this, as in the later films, is generated by implications already organic to the material, is firmly located in dramatic necessity, and is made to serve an overriding expressive purpose. This sort of thing is what is indicated when early critics spoke of Peckinpah's fresh eye and dazzling technique; it is also what probably provoked the more obtuse among them to say that he couldn't tell a story; it is certainly what makes his sudden ascent to the high country of the next film altogether more explicable but no less impressive.

In simple terms *Ride the High Country* was about salvation and loneliness.
—Sam Peckinpah

2
The High Country

The hero is the man of self-achieved submission.
—Joseph Campbell

Not long after *The Deadly Companions* was released, the company that financed it, Pathé-America, went out of business. Peckinpah meanwhile had been invited by the producer Richard E. Lyons to direct a Western at Metro-Goldwyn-Mayer. Lyons had already assembled the package, including the casting of Joel McCrea and Randolph Scott as the aging heroes Steve Judd and Gil Westrum. All he needed was a director. An agent at William Morris, where both Lyons and Peckinpah were clients, told the producer about the young director. Lyons watched four episodes of *The Westerner* and was so impressed he arranged for Sol Siegel, MGM's head of production, to see them. Siegel's reaction was the same: "Hire him." A script went out to Peckinpah and the next morning Lyons received a call: "I've been reading and rereading this script all night. It is the finest script I have ever read in my life. What do I have to do to direct it?"[1]

"Fix the script," might well have been Lyons's first answer. *Guns in the Afternoon* was an original screenplay by a writer named N. B. Stone Jr. Stone had a drinking problem, and when he finally turned in a first draft it was an unwieldy 145 pages long and just "awful," said Lyons, "I couldn't believe anything could be that bad."[2] Stone had been recommended by a writer friend of Lyons, William Roberts, who was so dismayed by how things turned out that working nights and weekends Roberts "virtually rewrote the whole damn thing. But he wouldn't put his name on it because he wanted to do something for Stone, who really needed a break." Roberts effected a substantial improvement, but both Lyons and McCrea felt it still needed work.

Once hired, Peckinpah spent about month doing a new draft. He rewrote over 80 percent of the dialogue; reconceived the story of the two old westerners and their friendship with far greater emotional depth and thematic complexity; and made a decisive change by having the McCrea character, rather than the one played by Scott, die at the end. (In all versions prior to Peckinpah's, it is Westrum who dies.) Peckinpah also changed the title to *Ride the High Country*. In view of all this, one wonders what he must have in mind when he told Lyons it was the finest script he had ever read. Apparently he was referring less to what he had been handed than to the potential he saw in it. McCrea would later say that without Peckinpah's revisions and direction, the film would have been "just another Western, and I know, I've been in a lot of them."[3]* Peckinpah was once asked if for precisely that reason there was any temptation to leave McCrea and Scott (also a veteran of many Westerns) to their own devices. The director replied: "That's not the case at all. We rehearsed—we had only four days—and I worked very closely with them on the set. They want to work, they are looking, I won't say for help but they give a lot on the set, and they expect a lot, which is exactly the way I like to work."[4] Sixteen years after making the film Scott could still remember Peckinpah's "rare ability" to help actors get back into the mood of a scene that is shot over a few days or that relates to surrounding scenes shot days, sometimes weeks, earlier.[5]

One reason for this ability, apart from his much remarked upon meticulousness, is that Peckinpah, unlike most film directors, had quite a lot of experience directing theater, which taught him the importance of building and modulating a performance over a long span. Another is that he had some fairly unconventional ideas about how to get performances, and by this time the personal authority to implement them. For example, the Hammond brothers are a clannish brood of white-trash, backwoods miners, socially graceless and insular. Lyons remembered that once Peckinpah "wardrobed them he said to them: 'Now you guys are a unit. I want you to stay away from the rest of the cast. You are the Hammond brothers. You eat by yourselves, you live in the motel by yourselves. You hate everybody here!' And he kept them all as a unit and it worked."[6] According to L. Q. Jones, a Peckinpah regular who plays one of the Hammonds, "Peckinpah goes for the little bits in a scene. He has far-out ideas, but he makes an actor feel one can trust his instincts. . . . remember when those brothers came riding in to that marriage ceremony in the broth-

---

*Lyons tried to get Peckinpah a shared screenwriting credit, but the Writers Guild, of which Peckinpah was a member, refused. Guild rules require a director contribute more than 50 percent of "construction" for a shared credit. Despite Lyons's arguments, the arbitration did not consider the director's—from every reliable source, truly sweeping—changes sufficient.

el? Peckinpah told me to sing during the ride. 'You're crazy, man,' I said. 'I'm not going to sing—it doesn't seem right!' But he insisted. So finally we sang. And it was a fantastic scene on the screen. That's what I mean by trusting his instincts."[7]

With a budget of only $813,000, the shooting schedule a tight twenty-four days (which became twenty-six owing to bad weather), it was a "small picture, by MGM standards," Peckinpah said, but "there was a great excitement about it."[8] He was especially fond of the contributions of the art director, Leroy Coleman, who stole sails from MGM's remake of *Mutiny on the Bounty* for the tents in the mining-camp sequence; and of Lucien Ballard—one of the great cinematographers, he had shot "Jeff" and would shoot four more features for Peckinpah, including *The Wild Bunch*—who came up with the idea of using soapsuds to simulate snow when the temperature rose to 115 degrees. The crew spent only four days on location in the California high country of the title—Inyo National Park and Mammoth—when they were snowed out and had to return to Los Angeles, where the remainder of the film was shot, including the Knudsen farm and mining-camp sequences. Nor was *Mutiny on the Bounty* the only MGM superproduction the *High Country* crew availed themselves of: one night they sneaked onto the set of *How the West Was Won* to film the confrontation between Judd and Westrum over the gold.

Nor did the enthusiasm stop with cast and crew; it spread even to Sol Siegel, who, without telling Peckinpah, bucked the New York offices when they wanted to shut down production. Soon after that Siegel phoned Peckinpah and said, "Stop shooting like John Ford. Learn to behave." As Peckinpah remembered, "Not knowing what the hell he meant, I kept shooting the way I had from the start. Later, on putting together a first assembly, he called me up again and said, 'You gambled on that funny style of yours—and you've won. Go ahead and make the final cut.' All of which cheered me enormously."[9] One reason he won is that he had an advantage missing from his first film. "It's very difficult," he once said, "to write about things you don't know. Those mining camp sequences and the brothel sequences, for instance, took a great deal of research—but it paid off." He received "letters from all over the Western United States, from people who wrote in and said 'That's how it was!' And they're right."[10] He knew they were right because a lot of his research was already packed into a memory that stretched far back into the California where he was born and raised. "All that's left now are the names to remind you," he said some years later, "and what names: towns like Coarsegold and Fine Gold, Shuteye Peak, Dead Man Mountain, Wild Horse Ridge,

Slick Rock."[11] Coarsegold became the name for the mining camp in the film, "an actual place" down Finegold Creek (just below his grandfather's ranch), which he visited when he was five years old.

As a consequence these scenes are among the most vividly realized in the film. Shot from Elsa's point of view, they nevertheless record feelings that are equally Peckinpah's own: the terror and bewilderment he felt as a child when, like Elsa, he saw this place for the first time, and the reverie and regret he felt on its passing. "It was kind of like going home. Today the ranch is gone. There are motels. It's all gone."[12] In actuality, yes. But it is part of his special achievement that it is alive in this film, thick and pulsating with all the vitality that impressed itself upon him many years ago when his father took him, even as Steve Judd takes Elsa, far up into the high country.*

Felt with equal strength is the beautiful conclusion. The old hero, fatally wounded in the climactic shootout, bids farewell to his best friend and then turns to face the mountains one last time before sinking down out of the frame to die as the high country and the big sky, now in full view, bear witness to the life that has just heroically ended. The power of this scene has several sources: Steve Judd and Gil Westrum are the first of Peckinpah's aging westerners to have survived the days that formed them and gave them their values. The presence of McCrea and Scott, by this time Western-film stars in the autumn of their careers, could not help but confer an extra measure of pathos on the roles they played. Most important, however, were Peckinpah's memories of his father, David, who died on 30 November 1960, almost a year to the day before the completion of principal photography on *Ride the High Country*. The director's sister, Fern Lea Peter, suspects that far more than memory, an actual photograph, taken on their father's last hunting trip only weeks before his death, inspired the composition of the famous closing image of the film: "Sam took the picture. It's a long shot. And since it was taken from his back, you wouldn't know it was our father standing there unless you knew him, and then it's unmistakable. He's looking out at the mountains for what turned out to be the last time. He was wearing his leather jacket that was lined with lamb's wool and he had his ten-gallon cowboy hat on. It was in color, and I think it was taken around sunset."[13]†

---

*Elsa is played by Mariette Hartley in a lovely performance that launched her career. Though she never worked with Peckinpah again, she retained a closeness to him and at the memorial service at the Directors Guild of America in 1984 hers was one of the most moving remembrances.

†If Fern Lea is correct in her suspicions, then this photograph (which was lost years ago by a frame shop) inspired a lot more than just the last shot of *Ride the High Coun-*

It is difficult to say how much of the father the son put into Steve Judd, but from all reports it was considerable. Both were old lawmen, Steve an ex-marshal, David a lawyer and a judge. In conversations with McCrea, David Weddle writes, the director "kept bringing up his father obliquely—casually relating anecdotes, things his dad had said, what he had stood for, what he'd meant to Sam."[14] The most famous single instance is Steve's declaration, "All I want is to enter my house justified." Peckinpah came up with that line, which has become one of the most widely quoted in all cinema, by paraphrasing a biblical verse his father had taught him. The judge and the director talked about it not long before the judge died. "He was a great student of the Bible," Peckinpah said, "and this is one of the things I remember from my childhood."[15] The allusion is to the parable of the Pharisee and the tax collector (Luke 18:9–14), in which the Pharisee thanks God that he is not a sinner like other men while the tax collector, so humble he cannot lift his eyes toward Heaven, simply begs for God's mercy. "I tell you," Jesus says to his disciples, "this man went down to his house justified, rather than the other; for every one who exalts himself will be humbled, but he who humbles himself will be exalted." This is exactly parallel to what happens to Gil (who is humbled) and Steve (who is justified) in the course of the story; and in reference to Steve's death, Peckinpah means for us to recall Paul's remark in the letter to the Romans, "whom he justified, them he also glorified" (Romans 8:30).[16]

Perhaps the most compelling evidence of all is a letter the director wrote to his oldest daughter, Sharon, in the months between his father's death and the filming of *Ride the High Country:* "I would like to tell you about him. . . . What is important is how you leave the world and how you live when you are here, what you left behind. . . . He gave me the knowledge of what honor means. . . . He told me and showed me by his example the glory and wisdom a just and good man can bring to this world."[17] But if Peckinpah's admiration for his father found expression in Steve Judd, then his ambivalence may have found expression in the character of Joshua Knudsen, Elsa's father, a widower who quotes the Bible constantly, is obsessed with his daughter's purity, and bears certain resemblances to Steve. "The law and the Bible and Robert Ingersoll were our big dinner-table topics,"

---

try. In his later films whenever Peckinpah wanted to pay some tribute to his isolated, beleaguered characters, he often filmed them from the back, usually directing them to move away from the camera even as it follows them. The most famous instance is Pike Bishop riding over the sand dune in *The Wild Bunch.* But there are also Garrett disappearing into the desert at the end of *Pat Garrett and Billy the Kid;* and Ellie, the mother in *Junior Bonner,* gathering herself as she crosses the street after seeing her estranged husband in the parade.

Peckinpah once said of his childhood; and in one scene Steve and Knudsen carry on a verbal duel over dinner, tossing back and forth scriptural quotations that become gnomic statements of theme, revelations of character, or ironic foreshadowings.[18] When Knudsen discovers that Steve, Gil, and Gil's young partner, Heck Longtree, are on their way to the mining camp Coarsegold to pick up a shipment of gold they will deliver back to the bank in the town at the base of the mountains, he charges them with trafficking in gold, "which if to possess is to live in fear, to desire is to live in sorrow." Steve replies that they are only transporting the gold, not trafficking in it, adding, "A good name is rather to be chosen than great riches, a loving favor rather than silver and gold." But Knudsen has unwittingly forecast the truth, as Steve doesn't know that Gil and Heck are planning to steal the gold; and he replies with the key reference to Isaiah 30:6: "into the land of trouble and anguish from whence come the young and old lion, the viper and fiery flying serpent, they will carry their riches upon the shoulders of young asses, and the treasures upon the bunches of camels, to a people that shall not profit them."*

Steve is of course the old lion and, at least on the way up the mountain, Gil is the viper and Heck, first seen racing a camel against horses in a contest he cannot possibly lose, the fiery young serpent ("skinny as a snake and about as mean," Steve says, comparing his own younger self to Heck). When Heck first meets Elsa, he whispers to Gil, "Think of all that going to waste up here," to which Gil answers, "Gold is where you find it," and Steve adds, "If it's not yours, don't covet it." Appositely, Elsa, who leaves her father to go with them to Coarsegold to marry Billy Hammond, becomes the treasure, and the mining camp the land of trouble and anguish (where the Hammonds do not profit from her). Except for Steve's, these roles and relationships by turns reverse and otherwise shift as the story progresses; but here we should note that the identification between Peckinpah as child—and even as young man—and Elsa tends to be cemented:

---

*In the best early essay on Peckinpah's career, Colin McArthur has noted other instances in which biblical verse functions either as prophecy or commentary. In particular, the inscription on the marker of Elsa's mother's grave—"Wherefore, O Harlot, hear the word of the Lord. I will judge thee as women that break the wedlock and shed blood are judged. I will give thee blood in fury and in jealousy"—is worked out "though in a typically paradoxical way" (McArthur, p. 182). The inscription functions as both ironic commentary and ironic prophecy, revealing Knudsen's assessment—obsessive, puritanical—of his wife in particular and of women in general, while by the end of the film everyone associated with Elsa is either dead or wounded, in part because she refuses to become a harlot. Peckinpah's films continually surprise and delight by "little" things like this, but very little that is in them is there by accident or without design.

Elsa: My father says there's only right and wrong, good and evil,
   nothing in between. It isn't that simple, is it?
Steve: No, it isn't. It should be, but it isn't.

Growing up with all those judges and lawyers, Peckinpah soon "realized that there was no such thing as simple truth" and developed in
response a more complex, open, and questioning moral sensibility
than could ever be contained by his family's law books.[19]
   A moral awakening forged by experience in a larger world was
important to Peckinpah. He had chipped away at it in his television
shows with their recurring stories of innocence confronting violence,
and here he gives it his first full artistic treatment. Heck, who has been
tagging along with Gil for three years, is "a good deal less than green,"
but his education thus far consists in knowing how to fight, shoot, and
cheat people. "Kid, you've got an awful lot to learn," Gil tells him;
appropriately enough, it is Steve, after Heck tries to force himself
upon the unsuspecting Elsa, who identifies the gaps Gil has left in
Heck's education. "When I questioned you about that boy," Steve says,
"I should have gone a little deeper into the subject of character."
Heck acquires character in the process of replacing Gil with Steve as
the more desirable model of behavior, and the agent for the change
is Elsa. "Mr. Longtree was a perfect gentleman," she ironically remarks
when Heck delivers her to Billy Hammond, who replies, "Why? Something wrong with him?" In Billy and his crude, gross brothers with
their dirty jokes, Heck is put face to face with another side of himself, and he doesn't like what he sees. His identification with Steve
reaches its culmination on the night of Elsa's wedding, when the two
of them rescue her from the threat of gang-rape by the Hammonds.
   Elsa's education, which consists less in a moral awakening than in
a loss of naiveté about some of the ways of the world, directly parallels Heck's, and it culminates in the same scene. The wedding, like
so much else in this beautiful film, has become a classic sequence—
full of violent contrasts and a double sense of mounting hilarity and
accumulating dread. It begins with a processional up the main street,
a mud path lined with tents, at the end of which is Kate's Place, saloon and brothel; Elsa, dressed in her mother's gown, rides in front,
followed by the Hammonds, who sing, "When the roll is called up
yonder we'll be there."* At the ceremony, Elsa's maid of honor turns

---

*As McArthur points out, this is more prophecy, as is a new lyric, "Judge Tolliv-
er's awaiting with a prayer book in his hand / For to tie the knot that binds them 'til
they die" (McArthur, p. 182). According to Randolph Scott, the new words for this
old tune were not in the original script but were written and added by Peckinpah on
the set (Randolph Scott to P.S., 1977).

out to be Kate herself, immensely fat, dressed in shiny, gaudy purple, and the flower girls four of Kate's ladies. Everyone gathers together, poised for song, and no sooner do we expect "Here Comes the Bride" than the whole assembly bursts forth with a raucous chorus of "For she's a jolly good fellow." When the ceremony proper begins, Judge Tolliver, seen in closeup against a lurid red wall on which hangs a pastel-blue painting of a partially clad woman, delivers a little sermon that is by turns funny, stupid, and curiously touching—a good marriage "is like a rare animal, hard to find, almost impossible to keep"— and then has to be reminded of Elsa's name before he can pronounce the couple man and wife. After the formalities, everyone gets drunk (or, as the case may be, drunker), the liquor finally having the softening effect on Billy that his four brothers count on to make him receptive to sharing the wealth. When the couple retire to one of the back rooms (Kate shouting, "Have fun, honey!"), Elsa pleads, "Not here, Billy, please," and he strikes her almost unconscious and then is himself knocked unconscious when he falls from a chair he has climbed to close the window against any of his Peeping Tom brothers. At that moment, Sylvus and Henry Hammond appear in the doorway, the expressions on their faces spelling out their intentions clearly enough and recalling what was really meant when they sang, "Billy's got that love-look in his eye." Elsa manages to escape their clutches and be rescued only because the brothers are too busy fighting with each other to catch her.

This sequence ends with one of Peckinpah's subtlest groupings: sober, honorable, imposing in his rectitude, his gun drawn in absolute command of the situation, Steve holds the Hammonds at bay, while Elsa, her wedding gown torn at the shoulder, stands at his side, clutching his arm. The imagery is a richly suggestive iconography— of Steve as father-protector-husband—that demonstrates how thoroughly Peckinpah had assimilated the lessons of John Ford yet made them uniquely his own: the picture of the stalwart marshal, dressed in his black suit, light-colored shirt, and neat string tie, and the young bride in virginal white on his arm, suggests an epiphany of the wedding day he might have had, the different life he might have lived and roles he might have played, if decades earlier he had married the woman he loved, Sarah Truesdale, of whom Elsa so reminds Gil.

Peckinpah uses Elsa to provide, among other things, an additional perspective on the theme of education. With characteristic irony he has Elsa's father speak the truth about Coarsegold (that place "is a sinkhole of depravity") and has Gil, reading a wall plaque—"When pride cometh, then cometh shame. For with the lowly is wisdom"—

observe, "There's a lot of truth in those words, Heck." It is a truth the film demonstrates, but only by way of demonstrating first that preachment in and of itself is an insufficient way of learning it. If values are not tested by experience and if behavior is not learned at least in part by way of several models, what happens is that one becomes like the puritanical Knudsen, who festers in his cloistered self-righteousness. The reason Elsa gets into this ill-advised marriage in the first place and is in general prey to the depravity in Coarsegold is that her father has permitted her exposure to nothing and nobody except himself, his instruction, and his little farm. When she runs away, it is an act of rebellion born of loneliness, weariness of being constantly lectured to and beaten, and hunger for a more exciting and vital life. "Sometimes I get to thinking that my father and I are the only two people left in the world," she tells Heck. There was once a third, Elsa's mother, but she too fled with another man when she could no longer stand her husband's incessant preaching and choking protectiveness (this is, at least, the strong implication, as her name is Hester, a possible allusion to *The Scarlet Letter*).* Elsa is thus revealed to be the second woman Knudsen has driven away, and also the second he has made, for all the lopsided truth contained in his sermonizing, ill equipped to cope with the complex, many-faceted world that lies beyond the farm.

Peckinpah once declared, "I have never made a 'Western.' I have made a lot of films about men on horseback."[20] Coming as it did after *The Wild Bunch,* this remark is not so much pretentious as testy:

---

*Peckinpah said that "Hester came a little more from the Bible than from Hawthorne," adding, "I must reread both." He also said that whatever the source of her name, the impression he wanted to convey is that she was driven from home by her husband's cruelty and religious fanaticism (Sam Peckinpah to P.S., 1977). In view of this there is an episode of *The Rifleman* that can be seen as a kind of back story to the relationship between Knudsen and Elsa. Called "The Baby Sitter" and both written and directed by Peckinpah, it has a rather independent woman, a singer named Leona Bartell, fleeing with her baby daughter from her husband, Wood Bartell, a Bible-thumping fanatic who carries a bullwhip and uses it. When he finds her in a saloon and she protests she was only singing a song, he asks, "Why ain't you singing a hymn?" Later Lucas asks Leona, who is his cousin, why she married Bartell. She replies, "He was quiet and clean, and talked real soft to me, talked about loneliness and about love and family, work and devotion. He talked of everything, I guess, except what was on his mind . . . to confer salvation upon what he considered the worst kind of woman he could dig up. And then when the baby came along, he decided she was the one needed to be saved. Well, I decided the only salvation we needed was from him." In a happy ending, Leona escapes with her daughter as Bartell is driven off for good. But Elsa's story tells the grim alternative: what might have become of the daughter if a convenient hero hadn't been on hand to keep her father from taking her.

he was reacting against a certain kind of thinking that tries to dismiss a work of art by giving it a label, preferably a condescending one. He had been pouring his deepest feelings into the Western since the beginning of his career. *Ride the High Country* heralds his emancipation from the genre even as it demonstrates how thoroughly he had absorbed and for the most part mastered it. There are still too many times when Peckinpah merely relies on, as opposed to uses, convention, notably in how often a sock on the jaw is enough to incapacitate someone, especially when a scene needs to be moved on. And one might also wish away the brawl in the restaurant, however much it can be justified as demonstrating that Heck knows how to fight. The complaint is not that these things in and of themselves are poorly executed; rather, they feel like vestiges that the director himself hasn't quite realized he has moved beyond.

But these lapses are exceptions. Far more typical is how the film marks for the first time his full command over the polarized structural motifs that inform this and all his subsequent films. These motifs are most evident in the pair of old westerners whose divergent paths late in their careers constitute the primary story. The love story, which as convention is as common to the Western as to comic opera, is secondary, but Peckinpah makes its incorporation organic by using the education of the victimized Elsa and the ambivalent Heck as a way of focusing and thus giving dramatic urgency to the issues at stake in the main conflict between Steve and Gil. The basic issue of that conflict is, appropriately enough in view of a lot of the talk in the script, a biblical question. What does it profit a man to gain the world if he lose his soul? Peckinpah doesn't ask the question abstractly. He gives it a flesh-and-blood reality by telling the story of a man who has grown old and been nearly forgotten and by shaping it as a journey that goes from the low country (the town) through a pastoral wilderness (the farm and the trail) to a primitive frontier mining town far up in the mountains. The journey describes a kind of passage—moral, ecological, mythical—that cuts through time or, rather, that conceives time as spatial rather than temporal. The story is so securely grounded in its geography that the thematic argument can be followed simply by observing how the values change as the landscape the characters pass through changes and by observing how they look and act in one setting as against how they look and act in another.

In the town, with its horseless carriages, traveling carnival (complete with merry-go-round and ferris wheel), and policemen, Steve and Gil are already anachronisms, the clothes they wear telling us as much as anything else does about the changes time and circumstance have wrought upon their lives. Steve continues to wear the austere black suit he probably wore in the old days when he was marshaling, the cuffs of his shirt now frayed rather like the reputation he still carries with him, even though most people have forgotten about it. Gil, by contrast, is attired in the latest fashion, a tailor-made glen-plaid suit, and has outfitted himself with a new reputation, equally well tailored. Cheating customers out of nickels, dimes, and dollars in a rigged shooting contest, he is a sideshow attraction at the carnival, appearing as the Oregon Kid ("the last of the Western town tamers"), with a fake beard and long red locks, who subdued the infamous Omaha Gang. "Tell me, Gil, who *was* the Omaha Gang?" Steve asks, "I don't seem to recollect them fellows." "It's easier than punching cows," Gil answers, "and it pays off with free drinks every time I walk into a saloon."

The theme is diminishment, disillusion, and compromise. Gil's tacky new identity serves as its own commentary, while Steve, for all his quiet dignity, appears just a little comical and quaint. When he first enters town, he doffs his hat to cheering citizens who line the main street. Suddenly a policeman shouts, "Watch it, old man, can't you see you're in the way?" Both a little hard of hearing and, we soon discover, too vain to wear spectacles, he does not at first realize that the cheering is in fact jeering, as he moves aside just in time to avoid being run over by Heck's camel and the horses that race down the street. One humiliation follows another, as Steve is almost run down by an automobile before he enters the bank, where the bank president, a portly, balding, beady-eyed little man ironically named Samson, tells him, "Frankly, Mr. Judd, we expected a much younger man." "Well, I used to be," Steve replies, "we all used to be." Far from the quarter-million the letter mentioned, the shipment of gold is worth only twenty thousand dollars (which will be reduced nearly to half in Coarsegold). "The days of the forty-niners are past," Samson says, nodding to his son (who, in a nice touch, seems to be about as old as he is), "and the days of the steady businessman have arrived." Steve signs the contract anyhow, for before shame comes pride, and with the lowly is wisdom. It's a steep drop from famous marshal to bank guard, but it's a step above the only work he has been able to find these last years: bartender, stickman, bouncer in places like Kate's. To his way of thinking it is more honest than Gil's opportunistic sell-out, which a line near the beginning suggests weighs more heavily upon Gil than he lets on: "It takes all the free drinks I can get just to put me to sleep at night," Gil tells Steve in jest. But his joke acquires a poignance much later when, his wrists bound after the attempt on the gold, he asks Steve to cut him loose because "I don't sleep so good anymore." The prospect of an easy score aside, it is little wonder that Gil jumped so eagerly at Steve's offer of some "old-time activity."

When they arrive in Coarsegold, Peckinpah throws the positions they represent into a different perspective. We begin to appreciate how brilliant the conception is when we realize that Peckinpah gets his contrast by taking a modern city, splitting it horizontally, and situating the business community (with its pretty shops and middle-class homes) at the base of the mountains and the working community (with its slums and tenements) in the high country. The two communities have a symbiotic relationship, as the camp feeds the town gold (coarse gold), which is banked and then presumably invested or otherwise refined into supplies some of which are in turn are sold back to the camp. There is a corresponding transformation of sensibility from the coarse and vulgar to the refined and respectable. In one witty bit of business that Peckinpah, with characteristic nonchalance, almost throws away, a mother threads her way through the carnival crowd up to a pair of boys watching a belly dancer, takes them by the ears, and leads them away. Instinct is carefully segregated and set off in the town, and desire is given expression in voyeurism. By contrast, in Coarsegold the instincts are given full and carnal release, especially during the saturnalian wedding celebration in which the vulgar will attempt to rape the respectable with the sanction of official authority, at least inasmuch as Billy has been legally married to Elsa by a judge licensed to do so by "the whole state of California."

There follows a turn of events that seems subtly to undermine Steve's integrity while strengthening Gil's relativism. Steve's dedication to the law leaves him awaiting the decision of the miners' court about whether Elsa will go or stay while Gil's expediency insures the outcome: he takes Judge Tolliver's license at gunpoint and threatens to kill him if he doesn't testify that he was never licensed to marry. This ironic reversal juxtaposes the limitations of the law against the occasional necessity to take it into one's own hands. But it should not be read, as it sometimes has, as an endorsement of Gil's methods over Steve's, for the film is far from conclusive on the question of what Steve would have done had the miners reached a different decision. It is evident that Steve's agreement to abide by the court is provisional, predicated less upon any inflexible devotion to legality at the expense of justice than upon a willingness to exhaust every possible alternative to violence. This is perfectly consistent with his former profession as lawman and with his character (as exemplar, Steve represents nothing if not the principle of a person's accepting responsibility for his word and his actions). When he tells Elsa, "The problem is you were legally married to Billy of your own free will," what is suggested is his awareness of the full complications of the situation, which involves not only legal and ethical but also practical considerations: "There are a lot more of them than there are of us." Although Gil says it, Steve knows it's the truth. And when Steve frets, "Let's hope the court lets her go with us, otherwise we'll be a little short handed," his worries are revealed both in the expression on his face and in the veiled reference to the fight they're going to have on their hands in case justice and legality don't coincide. His real assessment of the situation is shown accurately enough the night before, when he wrests Elsa from the Hammonds at gunpoint and informs them that she will be returned to her father. It is reinforced when, the afternoon following the trial, Steve makes no move to take her back to Coarsegold even though Gil has just torn up the license before his eyes. Still later the next day, Steve refuses to hand Elsa over to the Hammonds, even though he now knows they have a legal claim to her. One can almost never go wrong remaining responsive to Peckinpah's ironies, but the real ironies consist not in a shift of tonal allegiance from Steve to Gil, but in the reprisal—the Hammonds beat the helpless judge to a pulp when they discover how they've been fooled—and in Gil's motivations. He takes the law into his own hands not to spare Elsa but to protect his interest in the gold, and thus he prevents the law from ever being pushed to the ultimate test.

The real change lies not in the film's tone toward the two men and the positions they represent but in the revelation of the attitudes that underlie their positions. As the story progresses and the settings change, Steve—the so-called absolutist—is actually revealed to be the more flexible man, while Gil—the so-called relativist—becomes almost brutally inflexible. It is Steve, the lawman, who defies a point of legality in favor of a greater point of justice by refusing to give Elsa over to the Hammonds; and later Steve realizes that in the scheme to steal the gold, Heck is less culpable than Gil, and thus he will speak for Heck at the trial. Gil, on the other hand, is so bitter about society's ingratitude for all his years of service as a lawman helping to "make the West safe for decent folks" that he has become a total cynic: his one single and absolute standard for evaluating everything, including his friendship with Steve and his own past and past self, has become money. Peckinpah intensifies our sense of just how slavish Gil's devotion to his new standard is by having his resolve to steal the gold become more desperate and single minded as the actual sum involved decreases from a quarter-million to twenty thousand and finally to a

little over eleven thousand. In other words, what Gil is tacitly demonstrating is that even by the puny standard of money his friendship
with Steve is worth less and less. There is a wry counterpoint to Gil's
obsession with money in the scene where Steve calculates "what it's
worth to get shot at." Figuring all the ambushes, bushwhackings,
fights, months out of work recuperating from wounds, and so forth,
Steve concludes, "I'd say I was owed all the gold we could carry out
of these mountains." (This remark is alluded to at the end when,
dying, Steve says, "Those boys sure made me a lot of money.") "My
sentiments exactly," Gil replies. But he misses the irony of Steve's
calculations, of how inadequate money is to measure a person's
worth, which is why Steve insists that all any man has a right to expect is the sum his contract calls for. A job can have a money value,
but not a life, let alone a whole way of life and love and friendship.

Inasmuch as Steve is pious, crusty, and rather parsimonious, it is
tempting to develop a romantic attachment to the wittier, more glam-
orous and colorful Gil, a temptation that Peckinpah doubtless invites.* At the same time, however, he is careful to keep before us how
thorough and ruthless Gil's opportunism is. On the trail Steve and
Gil reminisce about the old days, becoming friends all over again. But
their solidarity is continually undermined by the role Gil's scheme
forces him to play, which is suggested early by a witty touch so obvious it's subtle: as they bed down in the Knudsen barn, Steve wears
white longjohns, Gil red ones. "The Lord's bounty may not be for
sale," Gil whispers to Heck, "but the devil's is, if you're willing to pay
the price." But the price is high and includes total denial of self and
betrayal of trust. Gil's opportunism reaches probably its most overt
and despicable expression when he reminds Heck, who by now is
wavering, to "remember . . . that we made a deal." The language gives
him away: a corrupt bargain is not the same as an honest pledge,
however tacit, and making a deal is not the same thing as keeping
your word. Gil's readiness to exploit the whole honorable concept of
the word by twisting it and then using it to coerce the confused Heck
into helping him betray Steve is only the last incident in a long development that nails Gil into his role as tempter-devil-whore. Peckinpah emphasizes just how heartless the betrayal will be by placing
the robbery attempt immediately after Steve, in the most moving

*If Steve suggests Peckinpah's father, then it goes almost without saying that the
director saw something of himself in the crafty, worldly Gil, who has left the law and
set himself up in a form of show business that is even, from a certain point of view, a
progenitor of the Western: a carnival gunslinger parodying the very myths of the West
he himself helped to create.

exchange in the film except for the farewell, has made himself most vulnerable to deceit by saying how good it feels to be back to work again, how much his self-respect means to him, and how he intends to keep it "with the help of you and that boy." By this time, however, Gil—so caught up in his scheme and so convinced by his own cynical arguments, which he initially advanced to persuade Steve, that the gold is only their just payment for the years of unrewarded service—can only ask what self-respect is "worth on the open market" and go for the gold.

All the issues of the story converge in the moment of confrontation, which takes place on the trail:

> *Steve:* It all pointed this way, all that talk about old Doc Franklin, ungrateful citizens, what we had coming but never got paid. I knew in my bones what you were aiming for but I wouldn't believe it. I kept telling myself you were a good man, you were my friend.
>
> *Gil:* This is bank money, not yours.
>
> *Steve:* And what they don't know won't hurt them. Not them, only me!

Steve slaps Gil hard across the face twice, then holsters his pistol, saying, "You always fancied yourself faster than me. Go ahead, draw. Draw, you damn tinhorn!" Steve's insult is the unkindest cut, but it tells the truth about what Gil has become. Gil quietly unbuckles his gunbelt and tosses it to the ground.

Steve's treatment of Gil thereafter—tying him up and planning to put him behind bars—has received much comment but little understanding.[21] However much Steve may represent an ethical touchstone, he is, like all of Peckinpah's heroes, not without weakness, fault, or infirmity. When he tells Elsa he will plead on Heck's behalf but not on Gil's because Gil was his friend, his harshness has to do less with judgment as such than with the depth of his pain owing to the profundity of the betrayal. And when he tells Elsa that matters of good and evil should be simple but rarely are, one of the things he is alluding to is his internal conflict between his principles and his feelings. Despite all, Steve clearly does not want to believe the friendship is utterly destroyed or beyond redemption. It is precisely this capacity for feeling that renders invalid the comparisons frequently made between him and Knudsen. Both are figures of righteousness, but they are different in kind: Steve's "code satisfies easily enough," whereas Knudsen's never satisfies at all. Steve is capable of being touched by sentiment, Knudsen is not.

Ride the High Country has often been treated as an allegory about moral inflexibility versus moral relativism, but no close viewing will support so narrow an interpretation. When Gil returns, Steve is the first to welcome him back. And when Gil promises to deliver the gold "just like you would have," Steve says, "Hell, I know that, I always did. You just forgot it for a while, that's all." What is revealed is not only Steve's great generosity and capacity for forgiveness, but the strength of his belief in his friend. Peckinpah once said that the basic theme of *Ride the High Country* was "salvation and loneliness," which in the terms of the film became redemption through friendship.[22] Steve's purity consists not in the rigidity of how he enforces the law but in the steadfastness of his faith in Gil.

Peckinpah's location of the farewell and the final gunfight on the Knudsen farm indicates how richly he can exploit setting to embody meaning. He uses his polarized structural motifs not as ends in themselves but to inscribe boundaries—dramatic, thematic, spatial—which he then fills with elements that confound any simplistic dialectics. The farm is the only one of the three main settings that is used twice, once on the way to Coarsegold and once on the way back. Situated roughly between the town and the mining camp, the farm is distinguished by a disjunction between appearance and actuality. The middle-class respectability and puny citizens of the town look like what they are, while Coarsegold's vulgarity and vitality exist right there on the surface in Kate's raucous laughter and the Hammonds' lechery and drunkenness. On the farm, however, all is deceptive (a motif Peckinpah puts to dramatic use at the end, when Steve, as a result of his failing eyesight, falls for the Hammonds' ruse of placing the dead Knudsen at Hester's grave). The farm is first seen from inside the barn, where father and daughter carry out their afternoon chores in silent drudgery. Elsa wheels a cart full of hay from the main door past a window to a side door, the camera following her as the sunlight seems to be fighting its way through the openings to cast some light on the dark interior. The effect is as if, even out here in a resplendent forest, the people are unaware of the natural beauty, as if nature is seen mostly from shelter, the barn enclosing Elsa and her father even as Knudsen's oppressive moralism limits her freedom and range of experience. It is not until, spying the party approaching, Elsa drops what she is doing, turns, and runs back through the barn and to the house that Peckinpah cuts to the first long shot, establishing the house, the barn, and the corral as nestled amid a rich, lovely, and peaceable clearing. The openness and serenity of this image has, however, already been qualified by the initial claustrophobic darkness inside the barn.

Metaphorically too the farm differs from the town and the mining camp. The town has a police force, and the mining camp, which is an earlier version of the town, has the beginnings of a legal system, with the miners' jury and the judge (even if he is usually "too drunk to hit the ground with his hat"). But the only authority on the farm is the patriarchal Knudsen with his Bible and his fierce retribution (once, he slaps Elsa across the face when she talks back to him), which has the effect of making the farm a genuinely primitive society and thus displacing it further back in time. When Knudsen's authority is wiped out by a single Hammond bullet, the farm is pushed even further back to become an authentic, lawless wilderness (the chickens clucking around the dead Knudsen subtly heighten the feeling of disorder). At this point, the scene is set for the final, radical inversion of irony that stands the motif of illusion versus reality on its head and reveals everyone in his truest colors. In the absence of external authority of any kind, the farm becomes the one and only place in the film where that old-time activity the two westerners are always talking about can justifiably move from nostalgic reverie to vital necessity. Pinned down and wounded by the Hammond gunfire, Steve and Heck are trapped and Elsa would be lost but for Gil, who, spurred by their plight, gallops to the rescue in a stirring one-man charge. Reunited as comrades in arms, the two old friends go off to face the Hammonds head-on, "just like always."

The journey into the past is thus triumphantly completed, and with it Gil's redemption, which, with almost classic inevitability, has taken the form of a rebirth in the wilderness and has left him fortified against temptation and fit at last to deliver the gold when Steve is no longer able. Even the Hammonds are revealed in a better light, as the education theme reappears to clear them of any taint of cardboard villainy. When Elder moves to ambush Steve and Gil as they rise up, Billy asks in disgust, "Ain't you got no sense of family pride?" Even these limited, gross people are seen to be capable of modeling themselves for one brief moment after the superior example set by the two men, becoming in the process worthy foes.

The filmmaking, excellent throughout, is masterly here, especially as regards the use of space for expressive and dramatic purposes. Before the shooting begins, the two sets of antagonists are seen in a long shot, Steve and Gil on one side of the screen, the Hammonds on the other, the barnyard an expanse of empty space that seems to stretch infinitely between them. The composition is absolutely static. As the men advance upon each other, Peckinpah shifts to an interior view of the action, recording it mostly with tracking shots that move increasingly closer to the actors, reducing the air around them as the available space diminishes and the bullets inevitably become more accurate. Immediately after the last bullet is fired, Peckinpah jumps back to the long shot, equally static, the figures now clustered together toward the center of the wide yard, with only Gil left standing. After he and Steve exchange their final words in alternating two-shots, Peckinpah returns once more to the long shot, this time with Heck and Elsa appearing at the bottom of the frame as Gil leaves Steve to join them and the three walk off toward the horses. Then Peckinpah is ready to give us the famous closing image, a low-angle setup similar to the one already used when Steve and Gil said farewell, the effect of loss made visually poignant by the absence of Gil in the frame as Steve is left alone to look for one last time at the Western horizon before turning slowly and lowering himself to the ground and to death. With no movement from the camera, no cutting, no alteration of focus or setup, the shot is transformed from a closeup to a long shot, the man no longer blocking out the sky and the mountains far in the distance.

While there is much in *Ride the High Country* that Peckinpah would return to, elaborate, and otherwise develop, this film represents in at least one respect a decisive culmination in his career. Laurence Olivier has said, "When you are young, you are too bashful to play a hero; you debunk it. It isn't until you're older that you can understand the pictorial beauty of heroism." He was speaking of the work that he had done when he reached his first maturity. If he was right, then *Ride the High Country* is one of those remarkable coincidences, as *The Wild Bunch* would later be, of artist and subject, made when the director was exactly the right age, thirty-six—almost the same age Olivier was in 1944 when he did his own magnificent treatment of the subject in *Henry V,* one of Peckinpah's favorite films. Peckinpah would return to heroism again and again, would even send one bunch off in a triumphant blaze of redemptive glory, and would be preoccupied with it right up to end of his life. This film, however, marks the last time he would visualize it so straightforwardly, so pristinely, and so appealingly. From here on out, all his doubts and ambivalences, his ironies and ambiguities would dominate and prevail. But to this little patch of wilderness, halfway down the mountain, where the kind of heroism Steve Judd embodies is not only possible and necessary but susceptible of unequivocating assent—this way the director did not pass again.

Major Dundee ran beautifully at two hours and forty-one
minutes by my cut. When I saw the final release print,
which is to say Columbia's final release print, not mine,
I was sick to my stomach.

—Sam Peckinpah

3

The *Dundee* Story

The essential American soul is hard, isolate, stoic, and
a killer. It has never yet melted.
—D. H. Lawrence

I

While Peckinpah was preparing the final cut of *Ride the High Country*, the president of Metro-Goldwyn-Mayer, Joseph Vogel, decided to
take a more active part in the company's filmmaking. Early one afternoon, after just finishing a big lunch, he screened *Ride the High
Country* and fell asleep during the first reel, snoring loudly a few rows
in front of a disbelieving Richard Lyons and his apoplectic director.[1]
Vogel awoke in time to see the Coarsegold sequences and managed
fitfully to stay awake until the lights came up, whereupon he pronounced it the worst film ever made, saying that if it were not for
contractual commitments, "I would sell it for the cost of the negatives."[2] Peckinpah rose and shot back, "You give me three days with
that picture in first-run houses, and you'll have your cost back with a
percentage of the profit!"[3] It was the wedding in the brothel, Peckinpah figured, that offended Vogel the most. According to Lyons, Vogel had been led by his aides to expect "a nice, warm family picture
on the order of Disney." That, coupled with his having watched the
film the same day as two other MGM features that were irremedia-
bly bad, was probably what led him to treat it, in director's words, "as
a low-budget quickie they could throw away in the second halves of
summer double-features, and if I'd tried to talk to them about the
basic theme . . . which was salvation and loneliness, they'd have fired
me on the spot."[4]

Peckinpah was fired anyhow. He had spent thirteen weeks on the
editing, and although this is a remarkably short time to spend putting a feature film into fine cut, some lower-echelon management
feared that if he took as long dubbing and scoring, the release dates
would not be met. He was barred from the lot. Sol Siegel, so helpful
throughout production, had by then left owing to differences with

Vogel on several matters. Lyons had to finish dubbing and scoring himself. At one point he was playing portions of the music over the telephone to Peckinpah.* MGM released *Ride the High Country* in May 1962 on the lower half of a double-bill that featured a cheap costume "epic," *The Tartars*. Despite enthusiastic notices in publications like the *New York Times,* the *New York Herald-Tribune, Life, Saturday Review, Time,* and *Newsweek,* the studio did not alter its marketing strategy (though once the reviews came out there were numerous reports of theater owners around the country reversing the billing on their marquees). William Goldman, the novelist and screenwriter, once asked an MGM executive why the film had been just dumped on the market that way. The executive told him that it had been previewed and that the "cards were sensational." But, he added, "We didn't believe those preview cards. *The movie didn't cost enough money to be that good.*"5 However, it found an audience overseas and within months became one of MGM's highest grossing films on the European market. By year's end it had appeared on many ten-best lists, was voted best picture at the Belgium International Film Festival (over Fellini's *8½*, among others), and won awards for best film or best foreign film in Mexico (the Silver Goddess), in Sweden (the Silver Leaf), and in Paris (from *Le Conseil des dix*). In sum, Peckinpah said, "it was a de-layed victory for all of us."6

No new film offers came forth, so Peckinpah returned to Powell and Four Star to direct a pair of hourlong shows. The first of these, telecast on 4 December 1962 on *The Dick Powell Show,* came from a story by Harry Mark Petrakis that Peckinpah and Petrakis fashioned into a script entitled *Pericles on 31st Street.* Although this show is a problem drama with a contemporary setting, the basic plot has been used in hundreds of Westerns: a stranger comes to a town that is lord-ed over by a bad man (gambler, saloon owner, whatever) who forces the merchants to pay him protection money so that his thugs won't wreck their businesses. Here the stranger becomes the Pericles of the title—Nick Simonakis (played by Theodore Bikel), an old Greek peanut and hot dog vendor—who one day sets up on 31st Street, a row of tenements badly in need of repair, owned by the neighbor-hood's alderman (played by Carroll O'Connor), who promises bet-ter times but squeezes the people more and more and doesn't have

*Despite a haunting main theme, used affectingly during the farewell scene, Peck-inpah detested the finished score. It is for the most part poorly orchestrated, far too pervasive, and just plain too loud throughout; and it is constantly italicizing effects and whole scenes that need no additional emphasis and are harmed by it. (The tympani during the closing gunfight are particularly distracting, often provoking laughter.)

to pay for any goods or services he receives from them. Nick, on the other hand, believes "a man should be prepared to pay for what he receives," runs his wagon strictly on a cash-and-carry basis, and eventually through sheer stubborn fearlessness convinces the others to rise up against the alderman, refuse to pay the rent increase, and threaten to deduct expenses for necessary repairs from rent payments.

The group action that provides the inspirational surge in the last scene is practically a requirement of the genre, so there isn't much that Peckinpah could do with it (it's not even well staged, one of the surest indices to the strength of his convictions). That aside, however, he turns the story into a character sketch, and he has a wonderful character to draw. Periodically, Nick, who calls the merchants sheep (and the alderman the goat leading them to slaughter), goes into a traditional Greek folk dance, snapping his fingers and slapping his heel with a silk handkerchief, which releases Peckinpah's gift for extending the revelation of character into moments of the best kind of theatrical artifice. When the children of the neighborhood begin to imitate Nick's dances, he becomes something of a Pied Piper, and in one nicely played scene he teaches two of them how to sell hot dogs. In the most touching scene, he returns from breakfast to find his wagon has been destroyed by a pair of thugs the alderman hired to teach him a lesson. When the adults—who, including the policeman on the beat, had witnessed the crime from the coffee shop without lifting a finger to prevent it—come out to help him, he shouts, "Get away from here, all of you! Go and hide your heads in shame," but lets the children approach. As they pick up the pieces of the wagon, one of the children asks what he will do if the next time someone tries to hurt him. Nick answers, "A man's life does not really belong to himself. It belongs to his sons and his daughters, to the rain and the stars, to the voices of the past that live in a man's heart, to God."

Now that's a risky speech, but Peckinpah is always at his best working out on some edge or other, balancing himself between excess and restraint, between genuine sentiment and sentimentality. Here he walks the tightrope right straight to the other side, not least because his conviction is absolute. In a sense this speech is what the death of Steve Judd is all about in *Ride the High Country,* and its sentiments will reverberate throughout the rest of Peckinpah's films.

The other Four Star production is altogether slimmer stuff. First televised on 15 January 1963 on *The Dick Powell Theatre* and titled *The Losers,* with a script by Bruce Geller from a story by Geller and Peckinpah, the show resurrects David Blassingame, Burgundy Smith, and

Brown from *The Westerner*, but the resemblance ends with the names. Here played by Lee Marvin and Keenan Wynn (Brown is played by the same dog), the characters have been updated to the contemporary West (Blassingame now a con man like Smith), where we find them on the run from a quartet of cowboy-style gangsters (looking forward to the Stetsoned hitmen in *The Getaway*) they've hoodwinked in a card game. The two fall in with a blind itinerant gospel singer and his assistant, an orphaned child, and eventually serve as matchmakers between the singer and a spinster with a scarred face, who lives with her cranky father on a farm (a comic version of Elsa and Joshua Knudsen). The match is brought to an appropriately sentimental conclusion that leaves Blassingame and Smith still on the run. "Keenan and Lee had a ball," Peckinpah said, "and the whole thing was a joy to do."[7] It looks it. He treated it as an occasion for a real workout, trying everything he had ever learned and a lot of what he hadn't, including fast motion (for a Keystone Cops-style chase) and, for the first time, slow motion (to record a pratfall). *The Losers* is strictly a cartoon, a "criticism" Peckinpah anticipates by twice turning it into a near-literal cartoon with montage sequences of still images cut to the beat of the music. All in all, it's a light, entertaining, and in parts frighteningly self-confident piece of filmmaking. Just as television prepared him for films, so his first two films wrought an improvement in his television directing.

With good reviews and consistently high ratings for each of its five replays during the remainder of the season and the summer, there was some talk of making *The Losers* a series with Peckinpah as its producer. However, Dick Powell had by then been stricken with the cancer that would soon claim his life, and his replacement at Four Star, Tom MacDermott (under whose management the company eventually lost all but one of its prime-time series), wavered so long despite the show's continuing popularity in reruns that everyone involved in the production lost interest or got angry. When MacDermott finally called Marvin with a million-dollar, multiyear contract, Peckinpah recalled, "Lee told him to go stick it up his ass! I've always liked Lee for that—it cost me a lot of money at the time but I would've done the same thing in Lee's place."[8]

In fact, he had already done a similar thing. After NBC canceled *The Westerner* in the fall of 1960, CBS offered to pick it up, providing it was expanded to an hour. But when Peckinpah and Brian Keith were told it was to air an hour and a half earlier, they declined, figuring, the actor said, "we'd have to cut the realism and make it for kids—in other words, cut everything out of it that made it good."[9]

Without doubting the sincerity of this, one cannot help but wonder if Peckinpah were not secretly happy for the excuse to turn down the offer. The same is true of *The Losers:* how long would he have been content producing a whimsical series about a pair of droll drifters cavorting around the "new" West? In passing on both, he gave up a great deal of money (literally millions if either series had had even an average run). But the truth is, if *The Westerner* hadn't been canceled, he would have had to cancel it. This director was born to make films.

In the way that the entertainment industry has of making strange bedfellows, Peckinpah wound up writing for Walt Disney "a *Shane*-type picture called *Little Britches,*" from a novel of the same title. He eventually scrapped the novel and "came up with the best script I've ever written. Walt read it and said, 'Too much violence and not enough dogs.' Well, the violence I plead guilty to, but as for not enough dogs. . . . End of project, though like most things I work on it'll probably turn up some day."[10]* It never did, but even if it had panned out—Sam Peckinpah on the *Disney* lot? And then, would he ever have made *The Wild Bunch,* a film that crowned the decade and redeemed his career? The questions are unanswerable; but given the advantage of hindsight, it is difficult to see how he could have been much worse off by the time 1967 rolled around. If passing on the series cost him a lot of money and the Disney misadventure his best script, then the next two projects would take a much higher toll: five years out of his career.

II

It is a convention of that journalistic genre called the film review to refer to the director as the "author" of a film. But every film critic

---

*How much stock may be placed in Peckinpah's various pronouncements of this script or that film as the best thing he ever did is anybody's guess. He had a habit of making hopped-up statements like this with little consistency and apparently no regard for whether they contradicted things he said on other occasions. He judged *Major Dundee* "possibly my best film," likewise at other times *Pat Garrett and Billy the Kid, The Wild Bunch,* and *The Ballad of Cable Hogue.* When someone told him the editing in *The Wild Bunch* is as good as that in Kurosawa's Samurai films, he said he thought it was better; yet elsewhere he also once said *The Wild Bunch* was terribly cut. One explanation is that, as with most directors, his favorite was for a time his latest. Then too a special place in the heart is always reserved for the maimed children, the what-could-have-beens. Peckinpah also loved being provocative, often gratuitously so, especially when he showed up for press conferences, interviews, and talk shows drunk, which was often (*more* often than not the last ten years of his life).

knows that films, by the very nature of the medium, are collaborative efforts and, given the immense sums of money required to make them, also business enterprises. While directors may make most of the important decisions, they don't necessarily make them alone, of their own volition, or even happily; nor do they usually get the right to final cut, that being the trump card producers and executives reserve for themselves. *Major Dundee* affords an almost classic case history of how, owing to the circumstances under which motion pictures are made and financed, compromises, cross-purposes, conflicting aims, misplaced priorities, and plain bad judgment can ruin a film and, for a time, an artist's reputation.

Columbia first approached Peckinpah not out of any interest in him or the project, but simply because the studio had a commitment to Charlton Heston to make a film for around three million dollars. "They had a script of sorts," Peckinpah said, "something Chuck and I both saw potential in, providing I could do some rewriting."[11] The story, by Harry Julian Fink, is about an obsessed cavalry officer (the title character) who leads a punitive expedition into Mexico against a band of Apaches led by a renegade chief named Sierra Charriba. Peckinpah and Heston discussed their ideas with the producer, Jerry Bresler, who liked what they had to say and gave his approval. The original deal called for a three-hour picture that was to be given a road-show release (first-run theaters, selective as opposed to saturation booking, critics' screenings, advance previews for audiences). On that basis Peckinpah started Fink writing the first draft and went off to scout locations in Mexico.

When Peckinpah returned he read Fink's first draft and was aghast. "To put it bluntly," he wrote Fink, "I am appalled not only by what I have read but the fact that our discussions of these last six months have proven completely fruitless."[12] Fink's draft stopped after 163 pages and covered only about a third of the story. "Projected," Peckinpah pointed out, "this means a shooting script of 450 pages, which is ridiculous; . . . your representation regarding your first draft completion date has set this project back for months and cost thousands and thousands of dollars." Fink also failed to elevate the character of Tyreen to full costar status. And the director was disgusted by the violence: "the consistent brutal and unbelievable blood bath that accompanies each scene of violence is beyond sickness—the horse urinating on the boy and the use of such words as shit, fucking, etc., is beyond bad taste." There is less contradiction to Peckinpah's objections about the violence than may meet some eyes. His method was never to dwell on the gore, and violence for him always had to be motivated by story, situation, and character. Still, as offensive as the draft was to him, one wonders if it didn't give him any ideas as to how many envelopes he might push, and how far.

This dispute was in mid-September; the start date was the first of December. Bresler managed to get the schedule pushed back to the first week in February, the latest possible date that would not conflict with Heston's previous commitments to another film. A new writer, Oscar Saul, was brought in, and together he and Peckinpah went to work on a script they intended to be about how men in war soon forget their ideals and become lost in the lust for blood and glory. As February approached, the first half of the screenplay was in good shape, but the last fifty pages still needed much attention—too much, in Saul's opinion, for shooting to proceed. Peckinpah assured him it would all work out.

Then two days before shooting was to begin, the company set, the cast and crew lined up, and the locations at last agreed upon, Peckinpah received a call from Bresler informing him that fifteen days and about a million dollars had been ordered cut from the budget. It was essentially an accounting and marketing decision. In common with other major studios during this period of declining attendance, Columbia decided that three million dollars was too much money to spend on a Western, even one starring Charlton Heston. If the decision came down inconveniently late, well, since half the script was unfinished anyway, how hard could it be to lose a third of the whole—in two days? This thinking didn't emanate from some studio functionary who might not be expected to know any better, but from the producer himself. When Peckinpah said they were asking for the impossible, Bresler, pleading pressure from New York, assured him, "Leave it to me, I'll take care of it."[13] Whereupon he promptly called the front office and said, "No problem, look, I'll get Sam to cut the script we're shooting. It needs to be tightened up anyway. We'll cut, we'll simplify, and we'll eliminate shooting days that way."[14]

It is difficult to say just what a director should do in a situation like this, because no matter what he does someone is sure to attack him for it. It was unwise of Peckinpah to start shooting a script as unfinished as this one. But perhaps only those who work in the film industry can fully appreciate the precariousness of what is involved in setting up a project at all. Ask most directors what the hardest part of making a picture is and they'll answer that it's getting the financing. Once the money is locked in place, the last thing a director wants to do is risk losing it by raising concerns about the script to the studio, even if there is good reason to be concerned. What is more, *Major*

Dundee was not just a go picture, it was a go picture *right away*. A further postponement would lose Peckinpah his star, which, in view of the eleventh-hour cut in the budget and schedule, might have been all the studio needed to cancel the project entirely.

Looking back several years later Peckinpah wondered if the wisest course wouldn't have been "to tell them all in no uncertain terms . . . what sort of film I was after rather than taking it for granted they would let me have my way."[15] At the time, however, he felt that the only alternative to staying was delaying or leaving. Either course would require sacrificing the thing he wanted most: a chance to do a big picture on a big scale. Leaving would mean disappointing his colleagues (paramountly Heston, whom he liked and admired), who shared his high hopes for the project. His contract still guaranteed him the right to edit the film for advance screenings by critics and preview audiences, so up through then at least he was certain he would exert a fair degree of control. He also figured that once down in Mexico, far from the main offices, he and his crew would be left alone to make their film. After all, Bresler had assured him things would be taken care of with New York. Peckinpah believed that once the film was shot, Bresler, whom he still trusted and considered a reasonable man of good taste and sound judgment, would recognize its quality and respect its integrity. He was dead wrong on every count.

On location the situation worsened. His relationship with the producer and the studio became increasingly antagonistic, the strain on himself, cast, and crew almost intolerable. One day tensions reached such a pitch that, over a minor disagreement as to whether Peckinpah had instructed him to lead the troop at a trot or a canter, the usually calm and patient Heston turned his horse and charged the director in an attempt to run him through with a sabre:

> I think it had become necessary for Sam to see whether he could get me mad, and he did. Unfortunately, he got a lot of other people mad, too. He fired, in the course of production, some fifteen people on the crew, some of them more than once, and became, in the clinically paranoid sense, convinced that he was surrounded by conspiracy and plotting. To a certain extent this is a self-generative condition because he promptly did become surrounded by conspiracy and plotting, most of it from Gower Street where Columbia Studios is headquartered. Finally we began to get those delegations of men in Italian silk suits and black attaché cases picking their way across the Mexican landscape out to where our sweaty troop of horse soldiers milled in the sun. That becomes a particularly difficult way of life, because the fellows in the shiny suits come

down and say, "Hi," and have lunch with you and talk about whatever the problem is they've come down about. Then they go back
into the motel and have a nice nap in an air-conditioned bedroom
waiting for you to come drooping at 7:30, having driven forty miles
across the desert from location. You go into the bar and there they
are waiting and they say, "Now, what about this scene?" You go to
see the dailies and there they still are; you come back at one o'clock
in the morning, you've had a drink, indeed several drinks and, if
lucky, a sandwich. You are still in wardrobe; in Sam's case the same
pair of blue jeans through the entire production. The talk goes on
and on and finally you say: "Look, fellas, we've got to get up at six."
This can go on for days at a time.[16]

Peckinpah's version tells the same story: "Making a picture is . . . I
don't know . . . you become in love with it. It's part of your life. And
when you see it being mutilated and cut to pieces it's like losing a
child or something. When I saw it happening I went a little crazy."[17]

Apparently everybody went a little crazy. Heston recalls several
conversations in which he and Peckinpah were heard "telling each
other how terrible They are; that's 'They' with a capital 'T.'" And
Peckinpah's way of making a film, which essentially involved driving
the cast and crew until they felt it as strongly as he did (or firing them
if they didn't), kept the screws turned pretty tight. It also got one of
the results he wanted, a quality of realism that led Heston to observe:
"The people seemed like horse soldiers . . . not actors. This was part
of Sam's contribution to the film. I think much of that contribution
was unconscious, achieved through the way he apprehends film and
what you do with it. These Mexican villages have not yet changed in
a hundred years. The reality is more total. Sam made it work for all
of us. We were living a lot of the experience."

It was perhaps because of this or in anticipation of it that Peckinpah, maybe not altogether consciously, at some point made a decision to stick to the original shooting schedule and budget, the studio be damned. Not until he had run several days and $600,000 over
the revised schedule and budget did the studio executives fully realize what was going on—at which time they threatened to close the
production down, take the footage already shot, and do what they
could to get it into a form that could be released. Heston, who wielded more power than did the relatively unknown director, intervened
with an offer to return his entire salary if Columbia would grant Peckinpah the extra time needed to shoot the remainder of the script
(primarily a Halloween party at the Rostes ranch and a surprise attack by the Apaches, both of which occur at the beginning of the

film). The studio at first declined, then thought about it a few days, took Heston's salary back, and still put a stop to production. It is not known exactly who made the decision, but the reasoning behind it was that with the additional material at the beginning of the picture, the introduction of the stars would be delayed some twenty minutes, which was considered commercially risky. The consequences were that Heston wound up making the film for nothing and that in dramatic terms some of the urgency to capture or destroy the Apache is missing (and along with it some nice ironies, like the Rostes children, soon to be captives, dressed as Indians at the party).

However, the worst was yet to come. Though prevented from shooting the opening massacre, Peckinpah had shot the aftermath of the massacre, its discovery by C Troop the next morning, and he knew the film could begin there (as it does) with no damage to the continuity. So he returned from Mexico to prepare the film, as his contract stipulated, for advance screenings for critics and preview audiences, happy that they at least would see a close approximation of what he might have made under more congenial circumstances. His first cut ran two hours and forty-one minutes—"beautifully," in his judgment, though he decided another ten minutes should go back in.[18] Before he could do that, Columbia decided to bypass all advance screenings of any kind, which then freed the studio from the contractual obligation to honor any version prepared by the director. For the remainder of his involvement with the picture, Peckinpah had to watch a hatchet job: "What I worked so hard to achieve—all of Dundee's motivation (what it was that made him the man he was)—was gone. This was material I'd both written and shot and cared very much about, but which Bresler or Columbia had thought unnecessary to the total effect of the film."

In all, fifty-five minutes of material that Peckinpah considered essential were removed or never included in the first place. In addition to what has already been noted, the deletions consist of the following: the early escape and subsequent apprehension of Tyreen and some of his men (including the clubbing of the guard, whose death provides Dundee with the leverage by which, threatening capital punishment, he coerces Tyreen into giving his word to serve and volunteering twenty of his best men); the information that Sergeant Gomez, of Mexican birth, was captured by Apaches as a child and later fought with them against his own people, thus reinforcing the theme of families fighting families; a playful knife fight between Potts and Gomez that Dundee, who misunderstands its meaning, breaks up; Dundee and Tyreen reminiscing about their West Point days (which the film sorely needs); a scene in which Dundee gives whiskey to the whole command, Sergeant Chillum proposing a toast to the South, the preacher Dahlstrom proposing a toast to the North, whereupon everyone dumps his drink except for the mulepacker Wiley; Dundee, his horse shot out from under him during the first skirmish with the Indians, trying to get the mule he must ride to move while the men try to suppress their laughter; and a short prelude to the comic rescue in Durango showing that Tyreen and Gomez, initially hostile comrades at arms, have become genuine friends.[19]

As if this were not enough, much of what remains, Peckinpah claimed, was "wrongly cut"; and the studio further crippled it by adding a music score built around a banal march tune orchestrated with piercing trumpets and twice sung by Mitch Miller's Sing Along Gang to lyrics like, "Fall in behind the Major / Fall in and I will wager / Fall in and keep your guard up," and so on. When Peckinpah saw the release print, he was sick to his stomach and tried to have his name taken off the film. It was too late for that, and the picture, which he called "one of the most painful things that has ever happened in my life," died a fittingly ignominious death when Columbia, with no previews or advance screenings, simply dumped it onto the market.[20]

There are two basic problems when a film fails as *Major Dundee* does, one for the artists and one for the critics. Both were touched upon by Peckinpah in an interview: "Writing has one very big advantage over directing: you only have to deal with yourself; you can escape into your fantasies and be a king. The outside world, as far as a writer's work goes, is limited to dealing with an agent and maybe a couple of editors, some of whom can be pretty good people. . . . The worst that can happen to a novelist is that his book goes out of print, but it survives, somewhere, in libraries, at least, in its original form."[21] But when a film fails, whose failure is it? If it is in part the filmmaker's, how do we criticize it without at the same time sounding as if we are tacitly endorsing the studios' despicable practice of mutilating films? All of these problems come to the fore with *Major Dundee* because the studio did mutilate it, because what is left is not in the form the director intended, and finally because it must be admitted that the picture has substantial problems quite apart from anything the studio did to it.

Asked once if "they" had cut out a lot of *Major Dundee,* Peckinpah answered, "Yes, they cut a lot of it. They left out what it's about."[22] Trying to figure what it's about is not the easiest job in the world. With all due allowances made for the pressures under which Peckinpah worked and the interferences with which he had to contend, the film remains in conception and execution among the most confused of all his films. Much of the confusion stems from weaknesses in the basic structure (still apparent despite the missing fifty-five minutes) and from certain intractable elements in the raw materials, the potential that Peckinpah and Heston saw in that script of sorts being not at all the same. "We still haven't isolated exactly what this picture's about, maybe because we can't agree, or just don't know," Heston worried in a journal he kept, "but we have to decide."[23] The actor himself wanted to do "a film really about the Civil War, which I think is one of the great watershed American experiences, in that it was the proving ground for the viability of the United States as a federation of states. There has never been a film made that began to explore the significance of the war in those terms and what I had in mind was a film which in some way did this. What Sam had in mind was, I think, *The Wild Bunch,* and what the studio had in mind was just a film that made a lot of money and was about cowboys and Indians." Peckinpah indicated something of the same when, talking once about violence as an artistic subject, he remarked, "They cut it in *Dundee.* I did it in *The Wild Bunch.*"[24]

The similarities between the two films are striking. Both pictures feature pairs of protagonists, once friends, now forced by circumstance against each other, and one of each pair is bound by his word of honor to an agreement he detests; both center on groups of men divided against themselves; and the groups in both films cross the Texas border into Mexico and become embroiled in conflicts that have international implications. There are also whole scenes, and even specific shots and compositions, in the earlier film that adumbrate the later one. When the Confederate trooper Benteen taunts the black trooper Aesop, touching off a dispute that almost ignites the entire command to violence, it is practically a rough draft of the scene from *The Wild Bunch* in which the Gorch brothers demand a larger share of the loot than they have coming. The fiesta in the Mexican village looks forward to the Bunch's visit to Angel's village and to Agua Verde, and the scene even comes complete with a guitar-strumming Mexican band, drinking and carousing, and a farewell that has the whole village turn out to serenade the departing soldiers who, like the Bunch, are regarded as liberators. Peckinpah even films the leave-takings similarly: Dundee saluting Teresa as he rides by, just as Pike Bishop salutes Don José, both passings caught with a gently rocking tracking-shot that suggests the gait of their horses. The villages are also introduced the same way, by opening out from shots of a starving dog. In addition, there are cutaways to children watching acts of violence, the children arranged and photographed as they are in similar cutaways in the later film. The rising crane-shot of Dundee's command riding into Texas at the end is almost identical to the crane-shot that records Thornton and Old Sykes riding off with the Mexicans. Finally, there are two exchanges that, considerably deepened and amplified, would become informing themes of *The Wild Bunch*. In a report to the Major, the scout Sam Potts says that Charriba "figures on leaving stories about you that'll be told around the campfires of his people for a thousand years." Sometime later when Teresa asks Dundee why all this fighting is so important, he replies: "Men can understand fighting. I guess maybe they need it sometimes. Truth is, it's easy. Forget about your problems, responsibilities . . . let someone feed you, tell you what to do."*

According to Heston, the only thing these three films—his, Peckinpah's, and the studio's—shared is the title character. And something else. The longer one thinks about *Major Dundee*, the clearer it becomes that the story in the film and the story of the film are one and the same, a company divided against itself. With so many mutually exclusive allegiances, responsibilities, and priorities, it is probable that most of the normal distinctions between fact and fiction blurred to some extent for everyone involved, especially the director. With the script incomplete when shooting began, it was inevitable that Peckinpah, caught off guard in the first place by a radical change of the corporate mind and kept off balance thereafter by the ever-shifting demands placed upon him, would let much of what was happening to his film make its way *into* his film. What got him into trouble is that too many elements and aspects of the materials resisted being developed in the way he wanted to develop them; and the one element that was needed to unify them all, the character of Dundee, both caused many of the problems and suffered most from them.

---

*Major Dundee also recalls Howard Hawks's *Red River*. Given Peckinpah's admiration for that film, it can hardly be coincidence that a line from Hawks's film turns up in *Major Dundee*. During the execution of O. W. Hadley, Dundee orders the deserter off his horse because "I don't want to have to look up at him," exactly what Tom Dunson, the cattle-baron protagonist of *Red River*, says when some deserters are returned to him. It may even be that Dunson served as a rough model for Dundee (notice the identical first syllables of their last names, their fanaticism, and their obsession with their own authority). If so, Hawks's protagonist may not have been the only model, as Dundee also echoes the embittered, ambitious colonel from John Ford's *Fort Apache*. The plight of Ford's character is not unlike Dundee's: assigned, he believes unjustly, to command an outlying fort in the Southwest, he deliberately provokes the Indians into a war so that he may in turn win it and sufficiently impress the top brass back in Washington to promote and transfer him.

Three of Peckinpah's other Western films are wholly fictitious, telling stories that could have happened but did not; one of the others (*Pat Garrett and Billy the Kid*) tells a version of a story that did happen in history. But *Major Dundee,* like *The Wild Bunch,* is a work of fiction set against a backdrop of historical events, some of which are moved to the foreground. During the Civil War there was Indian action in the West; and it was not uncommon to find forts manned with what were called "galvanized Yankees," Confederate prisoners of war who agreed to join the Union army and fight Indians instead of sitting out the war in freezing prisons trying to survive on bad rations. Black troops were also used in the Indian wars, but not until a few years after the Civil War. Peckinpah invokes artistic license here because he wants to increase the number of factions under Dundee's command and keep before us a reminder of an issue of the war. This is also why the French are in the film. Maximilian I occupied Mexico and fought the Juaristas in a conflict that is important to Peckinpah. By sending Dundee's troop from one country torn by civil war into another, the director is able to universalize the theme of internal conflict and insecure identity. He can also play an old civilization against a new one by way of a primitive one. The French lancers, all dashing show and preening display but soft inside, are pitted against Dundee's ragtag bunch of deserters, thieves, cutthroats, and renegades who are nevertheless tough and hardened (here license became liberty, as the French troops were most emphatically not soft). The various national, social, and cultural groups—Indians, the French, the Union, the Confederacy, blacks, whites, soldiers, civilians, and peasants—express Peckinpah's theme that savagery remains barely latent, whatever a society's development. An irony he often works is that the more civilized a society, the more capable it is of barbarity, hence the exchange following the French atrocities in the village:

> *Potts:* Them boys in the pretty hats make the Apaches look like missionaries.
> *Tyreen:* Never underestimate the value of a European education.

This much Peckinpah manages to incorporate effectively and well.[25] The big problems set in with the Southern background of the two principals, Major Dundee and Captain Tyreen, the latter's British origins (he comes from Ireland), and the Civil War itself. Some critics have taken Heston at his word and are willing to view the film as a metaphoric treatment of the Civil War, seeing Dundee's divided command as a microcosm of a nation desperately in search of a unifying identity. But this is a tenuous viewing at best. More than likely, for Peckinpah, the Civil War is a symbolic backdrop only, the large-scale national conflict reflecting the smaller, more concentrated conflict in the command. The country was not unified after the Civil War by closing ranks against a common enemy, either an enemy within (the Indians) or an enemy without (the French). Some historians maintain that no real unification, at least in the military, occurred until the Spanish-American War, the first conflict in which former Confederate officers served since the Civil War. It can be argued that Peckinpah, invoking artistic license again, is using the battle with the French to suggest the only way the country could have been unified—militaristically, which in history happened to come some thirty years later. This defense has some validity, and the director has one large historical fact on his side: almost immediately after Appomattox the United States marshaled troops along the Texas border with the explicit intent of invading Mexico if the French did not pull out (they did, but no Confederate officers were there).

What really makes the film at best an aborted metaphor for the Civil War, however, is the character of Dundee himself, whose private obsession is wholly inadequate to the task of representing and thus focusing the national problems of identity that could be said to have led up to the Civil War: the social issue of slavery, the political issue of a quasi-feudal collection of states occupying the same boundaries as a more democratic collection of states, and the economic issue of an agrarian society versus a mercantile-industrial society. Indeed, Dundee's problems as soldier, as leader of men, and as man are almost completely unrelated to the country's problems as a confederation of states.

Peckinpah initially must have been drawn to these materials by the polarized relationship between Major Dundee and Captain Tyreen and the moral issues that the contradictions in their postures implies. Tyreen says Dundee betrayed friends and family by remaining in the Union; Dundee calls Tyreen a traitor to his country. Tyreen serves the wrong cause—the South—but for an admirable reason: loyalty to friends and family. Dundee serves the right cause—the North—but for the wrong or at least for questionable reasons. A year before the war broke out, Tyreen, serving under Dundee, killed a fellow officer, a Yankee, in a duel of honor, for which he was cashiered out of the regiment, with Dundee casting the deciding vote at the court martial. "You voted to please the generals in Washington, you voted a promotion for Amos Charles Dundee," is Tyreen's accusation, which is echoed by Captain Waller, who asks, "Are you pursuing the Apache,

Major, or a promotion?" Dundee evades the question both times, which is not an unfair description of how gingerly Peckinpah handles it for most of the film's length.

Because theirs is a polarized relationship, Dundee and Tyreen have often been discussed in terms of the male pairs in *Ride the High Country* and *The Wild Bunch*. Specifically, Dundee has been linked with Steve Judd and Pike Bishop as heroes devoted to their own best image of themselves. However, Steve is devoted to maintaining a past self that actually did exist; and Pike, for all his personal failings, has nevertheless acquired an imposing reputation that he is proud of. Both men measure themselves against past achievements. Their devotion to ideal selves is a defense against the encroachments of old age and changing times that together prevent them from being the men they once were and that thus erode the basis of what self-respect they have left and what dignity they can claim. But Dundee's ideal image of himself never existed, which is why his superiors have made him a "prison keeper" instead of a "professional soldier."

Still unable to learn from his mistake at Gettysburg, which cost him his position, Dundee sets out to prove his worth only to make the same mistakes, systematically reducing the strength of his command, alienating his men and his fellow officers, and getting a great many people needlessly killed. When the French commander invokes international law and Potts says, "The Major ain't no lawyer," we laugh. But Peckinpah throws the joke back in our faces when the peasants become the victims of a vicious reprisal by the French troops for Dundee's attack on their garrison, as do the members of his command who are killed in the climactic battle with the lancers. Throughout Peckinpah is careful to keep Dundee located in an ethical position far more equivocal than that of Steve Judd and Pike Bishop, for whom the twin concepts of friendship and the word given and kept are entirely personal. When Gil Westrum returns to help Steve, it is by choice, the persuasion engendered by the superior example the other man sets and the feelings of friendship; when Pike orders his men to follow him to reclaim Angel, their ready assent is a clue that he has only expressed their secret wishes. Dundee, however, uses the sanction of his position of authority to enlist others by force in the service of his ambitions, while matters of personal honor and dignity are subordinate to his desire to be welcomed back into the fold of the army and be justified according to an official set of standards. His repeated attempts to impress the generals in Washington and his insistent laying of the charge of traitor upon Tyreen make him quite distinct from Pike Bishop, who says, "We share very few sentiments with our government," and from Steve Judd, who, in answer to Gil's argument that nobody will be the wiser, says, "Only *me!*"

Dundee has also been linked with Gil Westrum and Deke Thornton as a moral relativist. But this isn't quite the case either. The precise contours of Dundee's moral position are clarified in the execution of O. W. Hadley, which also draws together and resolves the seemingly contradictory facets of the Major's character. He orders Gomez to get the deserter off his horse because "I don't want to look up at him." Wounded in the leg, Hadley crawls along the ground, picking his way through the rocks and cactus as the Major calls for a firing squad, taking a thinly disguised pleasure in the life-and-death power he now holds. It is a brilliant, scathing, and uncompromising portrait of a fascist mentality. Peckinpah makes us realize that the near gloating satisfaction Dundee takes in the spectacle of Hadley begging for his life is only an explicit and concentrated instance of the satisfaction he has taken all along in giving orders and watching others carry them out, often against their will. The root cause of the Major's obsession, what lies behind the fanatical pursuit of the Apache—carried on long after the children have been rescued—is power; and his drive for official recognition and promotion is directed toward the acquisition of still more power. When he extracts from Tyreen the pledge to serve "until the Apache is taken or destroyed," it is only so that he may watch Tyreen squirm, even as O. W. squirms, so that he may goad him to break his word and then remind him of it, prodding and teasing and needling him, relishing the power he holds over his friend (a power that, ironically, derives from Tyreen's devotion to a principle of honor). When Tyreen finally shouts, "Forget about the book," it is clear that Dundee is not and never was a book soldier (if he were, he wouldn't be where he is). Rather, he uses the book when it suits him—just as he uses his friendship with Tyreen and the concept of the word—to be invoked when it is advantageous to him.

From its strategic place in the structure, it is clear that the execution scene is supposed to be the film's watershed, where all of Dundee's belligerence, his deluded sense of his own importance, his wrongheadedness, and his sick thirst for power are brought to a head in a fatal decision that should, as a logical consequence, set the seal of doom upon the whole expedition. Tyreen makes this explicit when he warns Dundee, "If you kill that boy, that's the beginning of it, Major, not the end." What happens instead is this: Hadley is no sooner shot than Corporal Ryan remarks—in his journal that is read in voiceover as a way to twist together the disparate strands of the narrative—that the Major "bears the burden of command and I do not feel fit to judge him"; Teresa, sympathizing with Dundee and wanting to feel something besides hatred, takes him outside the picket lines and gives herself to him. Afterward they are ambushed by Indians and Dundee is shot in the leg; he is sent to nearby Durango, where a doctor removes the arrow. Dundee spends some days recuperating, all the while drinking himself into a state of self-pity and self-loathing and seeking solace in the arms of prostitutes (with one of whom Teresa is shocked to find him, after which she leaves him for good); and eventually Tyreen and some of the men rescue him (an ironic reversal of Dundee's earlier prediction that Tyreen is corrupt "but I will save him") in a comic interlude of drinking and brawling that seems to have come from some other film.* All of this so humiliates the Major, forcing him to realize the depths to which he has sunk, that the next morning, his stupor slept off, it is as if he has awakened from a bad dream, and thereafter he comports himself with great dispatch and unfaltering good judgment. In one of the oldest tricks in the book (stuffing their sleeping bags and lying elsewhere in ambush), he and his men outfox and destroy the heretofore shrewd and elusive Apache, engage and defeat the French lancers, and finally regroup in Texas, the tattered remains of the command at last unified under the colors. And the Major wears a smug look of approval that for all appearances the filmmaker does not intend to be read ironically.

What has happened? Early on there is an exchange that is the first of two instances of Peckinpah's unalloyed sympathy for the Major:

> *Captain Waller:* Your transfer to this post was a disciplinary action pure and simple, and if you try to fight your own war again, as you did at Gettysburg, they'll break you.
> *Major Dundee:* They won't break me, not if I get Charriba and those kids.

It is difficult to believe that Peckinpah did not at some level here identify with Dundee, seeing in the Major's fight with Washington a distorted reflection of his own fight with the studio, and in Dundee himself a man unfairly maligned by his superiors, desperately needing to prove to them that he is a better man than they think. (This is one of the few scenes in which Peckinpah directs Heston to let Dundee drop his mask of grim, tight-lipped guardedness, giving us a

---

*Specifically *Lawrence of Arabia:* minus the drinking and the humor, Dundee's breakdown in Durango is curiously reminiscent of Lawrence's humiliation in Deraa; and in both films the protagonists' degradation is associated with sordid sex.

glimpse of what is behind the armor.) At the same time Peckinpah must have realized that his interpretation was an imposition upon the character as broadly drawn. The director's attempt to juggle his diametrically opposing views of Dundee as wronged hero and as power-hungry maniac is manifested in the tonal insecurity that makes the film wobble throughout and finally crumble in the seduction scene that comes immediately after O. W.'s execution. It is surely no accident that these two scenes—one the film's best scene, the other the film's worst and one of the silliest scenes in all of Peckinpah's work—occur back to back. He must have noticed that in striking to the very bedrock of Dundee's motivations, he had forfeited any claims to sympathy for the character. However, since this is the character with whom he was in part identifying, he did an about-face and tried to recover the lost sympathy. After all, what is so bad about the love scene is not that it is cynical and disingenuous, but that it is desperately, almost nakedly sincere, as if the director were trying to remind us of everything "They" were doing to him. By the time he got into post-production, his identification with Dundee was so strong that he had long since lost whatever artistic distance he might have maintained through the shooting. Here, for example, is one of his last memos about the editing, dated 3 September 1964:

> Dundee is a strong-minded man whose inability to admit personal failure—to recognize his own weakness—almost breaks him. He is a man unable to bend who finally learns not to judge himself or others too harshly. A man who finally learns to listen and to understand. A man who reaching the bottom of personal degradation recognizes his weaknesses and through his own strength of character and Tyreen's anger, becomes the Commander he thought he was at the beginning of the picture.
>
> I think we should all remember *Major Dundee* is the story of the making of a great officer.[26]*

*If this description applies only partially to Dundee, it is surely dead on for Pike Bishop, the hero of *The Wild Bunch,* whose story is precisely that of someone triumphing over failure to become the man he imagines himself to be. (Heston's argument that the later film is what the earlier one was meant to be is again confirmed.) It is also a pretty accurate description of Peckinpah himself; but the *redemptive* side of it applies less to the director of *Major Dundee* than of *The Wild Bunch,* which is where he truly became the "commander" he always thought he was. In laying bare Dundee's thirst for power, Peckinpah was perhaps offering a truer portrait of some part of himself than he was willing or able to countenance at this time in his career. Come *The Wild Bunch* and after he would be ruthless in depicting his own worst selves, but not here, not yet.

The other explanation for the structural disintegration during the last third of the film is that this is where the studio cut the most material. According to Peckinpah,

> where it fails, where it refuses to make sense, lies in the fact that all of Dundee's motivation, the why behind it all, is all gone. I shot a series of progressive incidents in which Dundee kept failing in what he was doing—punching up the difference between what he set out to achieve and what he achieved. I looked at him very closely, zeroing right in on his locked-in approach to his own ego. All of which was cut and junked. I figure I must have shot about forty-five minutes of Dundee under the microscope.[27]

There is no reason to doubt Peckinpah, nor is there any reason to infer that the studio was in any way justified in removing these scenes, for they are clearly not extraneous to the unfolding of the character. At the same time, however, it must be said that a detailed examination of the disparity between Dundee's aspirations and failures is not necessarily synonymous with a continued probing of his motivation and ambitions. At best the former would contribute to and support the latter. The biggest problem is that if we take Peckinpah at his word, it means that somewhere along the line he shifted his attention from what basically drives Dundee and from the moral implications of his decisions to the mistakes that are merely consequent upon those decisions.

Peckinpah thus found himself pushing an odd interpretation, for he seemed to be saying that if Dundee hadn't made so many mistakes, he would have been a better man and his moral (and professional) position would have been far less questionable. This makes no sense at all. It is like saying that Ahab's obsession would have been justified if only he had managed to kill the white whale and survive. In the first place, the point, after all, is that even if Dundee had conducted himself with greater professional competence, he would still have been in the wrong for pursuing the expedition long after the children had been reclaimed, in the process getting most of his men (and more than a few innocent bystanders) killed and his country nearly embroiled in wars with two countries. In the second place, Peckinpah's interpretation fails to account for Dundee's independent action at Gettysburg and for his vote against Tyreen at the court martial, both events that predate the punitive expedition. And third, it is just a little hard to believe that a man this messed up could straighten himself out so quickly and so easily simply because he is twice humiliated, by a woman (the story unconvincingly tells us) he loves and is loved by and by a friend who tells him he isn't "worth killing." Yet these are the two turning points that lead to his amazing and speedy self-improvement, and they have the effect of removing his mania, which is the film's main subject, far to the background.

Whatever the explanation, when Peckinpah allows his grip on Dundee's obsessiveness to slacken, the obsession itself evaporates, taking with it or else diluting to the point of dissipation much of what he wanted to say and do in this film. The clearest indication of this, because it is structural and thus concrete, is that none of the implications of the execution scene is realized. Neither Tyreen's warning that if Hadley is shot the command will be split even further nor Ryan's fear, after the execution, that "nothing will ever heal this breach, even some of our own people are bitter against the Major," comes to pass in the plot. Rather, the opposite happens, for the men seem to become a more cohesive group after the execution. This has the additional effect, reinforced by Dundee's fast recovery following the Durango episode and solidified beyond all questioning with his successful destruction of the Apache and his survival of the battle with the French, of setting a seal not of doom but of tacit approval upon many of the things he has done. Perhaps most egregious of all, it suggests that in wanting to spare Hadley—that is, in tempering justice with mercy—Tyreen really is, as Dundee charges, "crumbling like old chalk" instead of remaining the "rock" he used to be.

The reference to Ahab has more than incidental relevance. Peckinpah was not unaware of the parallels between *Major Dundee* and *Moby-Dick;* indeed, they were among the main reasons he wanted to make the film. Several years later he replied to a letter inquiring about the influence of the novel on *The Wild Bunch:* "Actually, it was *Major Dundee* where I tried to take on Melville, and then I guess a little hung over on *The Wild Bunch.*"[28] And when R. G. Armstrong first read the *Dundee* script, he excitedly phoned the director, saying, "Sam, this is *Moby-Dick* on horseback!" Sam replied, "Goddamn it, R. G., you and Oscar Saul are the only ones who realize that!"[29] In view of the manifest influence, Peckinpah would have been better off to follow the parallels out to their logical conclusion and have Dundee, like Ahab, be consumed by his obsession. There is a rumor that one direction in which Peckinpah considered developing the script was to have the Apache wipe out or nearly wipe out Dundee's men one by one as they retreat toward the border. No script pages or notes exist to substantiate the rumor; but if that course had been taken, a lot of what is now distended and disjointed in the film would have been made coherent and unified. For example, if there were at least one scene analogous to "The Quarter Deck" and related chapters in which we were shown how Dundee manages to "shed his characteristic" on his command, how the men get caught up in Dundee's obsession, soon forgetting about their animosities toward one another and their problems, then what Peckinpah wanted to express about the attraction of a life of violence for certain kinds of men would have had force and clarity.

What he obviously had in mind was not the banality of the men rallying around Old Glory, let alone any freezing of the United States "in a barbaric posture."[30] What he had in mind was the men being forged into a powerful fighting outfit because they are swept up by the mania of a terrifying force of personality much stronger than their · own individual or collective personalities, a personality that knows how to play upon their most malignant instincts for blood lust and vengeance or upon their best qualities of courage and valor. As it stands now, what is left to carry the brunt of this development is one pathetic entry in Ryan's journal to the effect that the men were angry and wanted to continue the pursuit and Dundee's few words to Teresa about why men like to fight—which is no development at all.

If Peckinpah had portrayed Dundee as being consumed by his obsession, then the theme of personal identity would also have found a logical place in the film. The Civil War materials would then have served a real function, as we would see how readily the men allow their complex problems of identity (which point toward social and political issues) to be brushed aside and replaced by the simpler passion of the Major (who promises the essentials of food, drink, and clean air in return for blind obedience). In this way the story might have taken real shape as an oblique metaphor of the Civil War and its immediate aftermath. The surviving members of the command would have been left leaderless to face the appalling discovery that their inability to resolve their conflicts by any means other than violence had divided them in the first place, unified them in the second, and left their number decimated and still disparate at the last. This would have left the structure open-ended, but that is both truer to its themes (and to history) and preferable to the false and falsely contrived resolution that now disfigures it.

When Peckinpah turns his attention from the title character to the other characters, the film suddenly improves.* Partly this is because

*This does not include, however, the various scenes that dwell on Graham's inexperience as an officer or on Ryan's with women, or the bits of stock "masculine" comedy involving drinking, brawling, and "whimsical" morning-after hangovers—all of

the secondary characters are played by actors who were part of the
Peckinpah road company (Dub Taylor, R. G. Armstrong, L. Q. Jones,
Ben Johnson, Slim Pickens, John Davis Chandler, and, best of all,
Warren Oates as O. W. Hadley), and partly it is because Peckinpah
has them securely in his grasp, his involvement being not personal
as such but artistic.

The most vividly seen and interesting of the secondary characters
is James Coburn's Sam Potts, with whom the director is involved in a
way that is both personal and legitimately artistic, the one serving the
other. Potts and Peckinpah share the same first name and initials.
Considering the trouble he was having with the studio, Peckinpah
may have viewed with envy the scout's role as a detached participant
in the expedition. In contrast to Dundee with his career, Tyreen and
the other Confederates with their freedom, Aesop and his "six col-
oreds" with their equal worth as soldiers, Ryan and Dahlstrom with
their vengeance, Graham with proving himself an able officer, and
even Wiley, who comes along mostly because of the free whiskey, Potts
has no personal stake or self-interest in the pursuit. He just does his
job the best he can and keeps largely to himself, emerging thereby
as something of a progenitor to the men in later Peckinpah films who
become whores by selling their services but not their sensibilities. A
detached participant, Potts functions as observer and commentator
on the events. It would probably be too much to call him the group
conscience (he's more like the resident cynic), but Peckinpah does
use him from time to time as a mouthpiece to qualify, clarify, or otherwise place into deeper or enlarged perspective the various moral
pretensions of the others. Potts makes the key comparison between
the French and Apache atrocities; he makes explicit the Major's hollow legal posture; and he repeatedly undercuts the Major's other self-
righteous postures, in particular in his reply to Dundee's question as
to whether Riago would turn against his own people—"Why not?
Everyone else seems to be doing it." Potts may also be intended as
the most mature member of the command, which is neatly suggested by the number of times Dundee and Tyreen refer to him as "Mr.
Potts" and which is further reinforced near the end when he inter-

---

which are by turns stiff and arch or limp and flat. Like John Ford and Howard Hawks
before him, Peckinpah had a lamentable weakness for this kind of hokum at this point
in his career but little of their conviction in realizing it. Perhaps he was so distraught
he wasn't aware how banal these scenes really were. But couldn't he have resisted the
bit about Ryan getting his first shave the day after he gets his first lay, itself applaud-
ed by catcalls and hoots from the other men as the obliging young lady kisses him
goodbye?

rupts their personal duel to remind them of the French lancers across the river, saying, "If you boys want a fight, I've got one for you." Finally, Potts is the only member of the command from whom the Major asks and even eagerly seeks advice and from whom the Major backs down. Ordered to find Hadley, Potts refuses, "Ain't my job, Major, I didn't sign on to go chasing after no homesick soldier boys." (But why did he sign on, since he advises against the whole expedition in the first place? As it is Peckinpah who raises the question, we're not stepping beyond his subject when we ask for an answer.)

Tyreen too is rendered quite vividly (with Richard Harris giving exactly the right histrionic performance to counterbalance the rather unrelieved impassiveness that Heston by necessity must bring to Dundee; when both stars are on screen, we are equally drawn, as called for, to the charismatic presence of each). Tyreen has been called a moral relativist, but where it counts—in the twin imperatives of friendship and of keeping one's word—he is an absolutist. "I've got what I need," says Dundee, "I've got his word." Tyreen originally pledges to serve in order to buy freedom for himself and his men; but once having given his pledge he is bound to honor it and thus by extension bound to play a role that gets him further and further into self-contradictory gestures and postures. He personally executes O. W. Hadley not only because, as he has already said, the Rebels can take care of their own or because, as is commonly assumed, he wants to deprive Dundee of the satisfaction, but also to discourage as urgently as possible any of the rest of his men who may be contemplating escape. The Major has not only the authority to shoot them "out of hand" as Hadley has been shot, but also the power to back it up, the Confederates by now no longer outnumbering the Union soldiers and the civilians as much as they did at the beginning. Tyreen's determination to honor his word becomes, thus, an obsession of his own that parallels the Major's, yet the point is contrast. Tyreen's concern is for his men, and this enables him to stand apart from his role and, even as it claims him, to learn from it and grow in resistance to it. His is the only real development in the story (the other characters are mostly unfolded), as we watch him move from the adolescent bravado that he displays early in the story to an increasingly mature realization of the tragic consequences of his pact with the Major. Facing the French he says, "At last, Major, you have found yourself a real war." But so has Tyreen. The Apache destroyed and the pledge fulfilled, he must now willingly ally himself with Dundee because the French lancers make no distinction between the command at large and his own men or for that matter the Union soldiers he has come to know and admire as a consequence of his association with them and of his moral growth.

The ironies that complicate Tyreen's role and finally entrap him in it are pursued to the very end in an outcome that is both tragic and peculiarly triumphant for him (making this aspect of the film even more of a test run for *The Wild Bunch*). Tyreen has been three men in his lifetime: Irish potato farmer, cashiered Union officer, and Confederate renegade. "I don't like any of them," Dundee says, to which Tyreen answers, "Now isn't that a coincidence?" What he wants to be is suggested early on when Dundee labels him "a would-be cavalier." Tyreen certainly looks and talks the part, and in the closing battle he at last gets to act it. Mortally wounded while retrieving the Union colors, he wheels his horse and, swinging his sabre high in the air, heroically charges the approaching French cavalry, occupying them just long enough to give his comrades the chance to escape into Texas. In the process he becomes both figure of gallantry from another era and sacrificial victim to the Major's obsession and to his own romantic idealism. The rest of the men look on wide-eyed and envious, almost like the children who are fascinated by acts of violence in this and other Peckinpah films. Tyreen has shown them for one brief moment how glorious warfare at its best can be, exposing at the same time the senseless brutality of the war Dundee, they, and their country are fighting. That he is able to do this only after he has been fatally shot suggests simply another twist of the ironic screw that Peckinpah never stops turning for very long.

What keeps Tyreen from being one of Peckinpah's fully realized protagonists is that certain things the character says and apparently believes do not jibe with other things he says and believes, but are not dealt with either. Peckinpah will typically pit the ethos of the word and friendship against a repressive and commercial society that reduces all values to monetary values. But the scene in which Benteen taunts Aesop, ordering the black man to remove his boots, reminds us that Tyreen, for all his justifications, is fighting to preserve a severely stratified society that is scarcely less greedy than it is oppressive. And some of his justifications are not very noble. When Dundee accuses him of "fighting for a white-columned plantation house you never had and never will," Tyreen doesn't answer the accusation immediately, but sometime later he condemns himself all the same: "After the war the Tyreens of County Clare will become the landed gentry of Virginia." Peckinpah doesn't know where to apply these colors because there is clearly nowhere he can apply them and still paint the portrait he obviously wants. It is after all one thing to show a man keeping his word and honoring his friendships because his very soul and selfhood are at stake and quite another to show a man doing these things because they will enable him to be elevated to higher social status in a society founded upon slavery. Even that assessment is confounded by Tyreen's remark, "I'm fighting for the only country I have left and I kill men in a hopeless war for it," which is both more in keeping with some aspects of the character and less in keeping with others.* All of this has the effect of deflecting the moral complexities Peckinpah saw in these materials away from meaningful elaboration and perilously close to thematic chaos.

There is obviously no way of knowing for sure how many of the non sequiturs, the dangling motifs, the unraveling themes, to say nothing of the conflicting attitudes toward the title character, would have been written out, tied up, or otherwise resolved had Peckinpah been working from the outset with a cooperative producer and a supportive studio. Doubtless it would have emerged a better film than it is, but despite his claims to the contrary, it was never even "possibly" his best picture. He was unprepared both conceptually and experientially to tackle a project of this size and scope when he did; and from several reports he was terrified from the moment he left for Mexico to begin principal photography, if not before. Granting all that, however, the film remains an impressive demonstration of his ability to handle, relatively early in his career, the logistical side of a really big production. His accomplishment in this aspect is most dramatically on display in the battle scenes, which have been widely and justly praised: they are expertly staged, beautifully set up and shot, and stunningly composed with a sure eye for the juxtaposition of detail and panorama.

The battles unfortunately bring us right back up against the problem of studio interference. To begin with, Peckinpah shot quite a lot of slow-motion footage that mystified and sometimes offended Bresler. But it was the director who finally wound up removing it. According to Howard Kunin, one of the editors, while Peckinpah "used slow-motion extremely well in his later films," "on *Dundee* he just shot it wild, there was no concept at all of how it would be used.

---

*Some of the inconsistencies in the character of Tyreen were caused by an unforeseen problem in the casting. Tyreen was originally to be a Southerner by and from birth and remained so until the rehearsals, where it became obvious that Richard Harris would never be able to master a convincing Southern accent. After holding out as long as possible, Peckinpah told Harris to scrap the accent and changed the character into an "honest Irishman" seeking his fortune in the antebellum South (Heston, p. 191).

Sam tried many, many things to make it work. We even once did a whole slow-motion version of the French battle, of the hand-to-hand fighting. Sam hated it. It just didn't work."[31] Whether the footage was as unwieldy as all that or was just so unusual there was no time really to work with it is something that will probably never be known. There are, however, several places in the battles, in particular the closing one, where, from the hindsight of *The Wild Bunch,* slow-motion shots could be inserted with an effect that, stylistically speaking, would be recognizable as vintage Peckinpah.

It is a pity the music, damaging throughout, was not also thrown away. It is ruinous in the closing battle (the prevailing tune sounds like a martial "Three Blind Mice"), as Peckinpah almost never sets his violence to music but uses the sounds of fighting percussively. And as magnificent as the battles look, they too are sometimes, as Peckinpah complained, wrongly cut, yet all the requisite setups seem to be there.* According to Peckinpah, the studio deleted about eighty percent of the "really bloody, awful things that happen to men in war," leaving the fighting merely "very attractive and colorful."[32] The sort of thing the he had in mind and once had in the film was a moment following the river ambush by the Apaches. Corporal Ryan dips a ladle into the water for a drink and lifts it to his lips only to find the bowl filled mostly with blood. Grimacing, he empties it back into the river and dips again. It is not beside the point here to note that one reviewer began his column with the observation that as specific wars recede in time we begin to forget about their horrors and to exploit their possibilities for entertainment.[33] The reviewer is not an insensitive or unintelligent man; he was simply responding to the evidence before his senses, the film he saw on the screen, much the same as others similarly sensitive and intelligent will respond. Meanwhile, the director was left to vent his impotent rage and protest to interviewers, reporters, and anyone else willing or unwilling to listen.

*Another entry from Heston's journal, this one dated 6 March 1964, is very much to the point here: "Sam's cold nerve astounds me. With the production brass breathing down his neck, he continues to shoot every shot he feels he needs" (p. 193).

A writer has his pencil and paper and goes hungry only for time to use them.
A director must start with this driving need to make his picture.
—Sam Peckinpah

4

The Farmer and
the Farmer's Wife

The terrible thing is, everyone has his reasons.
—Jean Renoir

I

In the fall of 1964 Peckinpah left *Major Dundee* and returned to MGM
where he started work on *The Cincinnati Kid,* starring Steve McQueen.
There is evidence that Peckinpah was here willing to become the
good whore he later took to calling himself and do a solid professional job on a routine picture. According to David Weddle, he signed
on with "no illusions about the material," but "the money was great,"
which he needed "after forfeiting most of his salary on *Dundee*."[1]
(Another big enticement was that one of his favorite actors, Spencer
Tracy, was to play a part.) But it was to be not so much out of the
frying pan into the fire as out of the kitchen altogether.

When Peckinpah came aboard there was not even a script, only a
long treatment by Paddy Chayevsky with little or no dialogue. A subsequent parade of prestigious writers that included Frank Gilroy, Ring
Lardner Jr., Charles Eastman, and Terry Southern never managed to
come up with a satisfactory script. No one could agree on what kind
of picture it was supposed to be; and the producer, Martin Ransohoff,
always flying off to make other deals, was never in town long enough
to approve changes with any decisiveness. (The only two real decisions that seem to have been made were the studio's refusal to meet
Tracy's fee and his replacement by Edward G. Robinson.) Peckinpah
was just off a film that had started under uncomfortably similar circumstances—an incomplete script, the same lack of conceptual una-
nimity—and that had never recovered from them. He was not about
to begin a new one the same way. Though not paid for a rewrite and
reluctant to do one, he nevertheless began to spatchcock a script from
the various drafts. Once he started working with the material, he be-

came—inevitably, helplessly—involved, seeing an opportunity to do a period piece, to give, as he put it,

> a fairly honest look at life in the thirties, in a Depression area, and what happens to a man who plays stud for a living, how it affects his life and those around him. I thought the picture came out just like a story in an old *Cosmopolitan* or something. . . . I had a feeling I would never do the picture, but I really didn't expect to be fired after I got started. . . . I found out later that no matter what I'd shot—and I thought it was some astonishingly good footage— I was going to be fired, or shall we say sandbagged.[2]

It happened after just four days of shooting.

"I did a damn good riot scene," Peckinpah recalled, "then another long scene between Rip Torn and a Negro prostitute in bed, and that was it. Oh, I was also shooting in black-and-white. They had wanted color, but I didn't."[3] It hardly mattered. Ransohoff by his own admission wanted a "popsicle" that could be sold on the basis of sex and a fleeting resemblance to *The Hustler*, the Paul Newman–Robert Rosen hit of two years earlier. When his subordinates began telling him of the hard-edged period downer the dailies suggested, he started looking for a reason, any reason, to dump his director. The one he decided on was some nudity in the prostitute scene, and afterward he released a statement that Peckinpah had been let go for making a dirty movie. Both the trade papers and some gossip columnists, notably Sheila Graham, printed it without so much as a phone call to the director.

This was a particularly scurrilous charge coming from Ransohoff. In a seven-page letter to MGM detailing his version of the events leading to the dismissal, Peckinpah wrote: "I had been told again and again by Ransohoff that the commercial value of the picture would be based on only its sexuality but I have tried to make this sexuality come from the characters and not from any rank exploitation factor. When I brought up my doubts, which I did many times, I was told by Ransohoff 'Fuck the code, if Wilder can get away with what he's doing [in *Kiss Me, Stupid*], we'll go twice as far.'"[4]

In view of Peckinpah's reputation for being difficult and uncooperative with producers, this letter is a revealing document. Among other things he grants that he and the producer wanted to make different films, "but Ransohoff had known my intentions . . . from the beginning and the only change I made was *to go along with* his demand to highlight every aspect of sensuality and sexuality" (emphasis added). In other words, Peckinpah was trying to be cooperative. To be

sure, he insisted that the "highlighting" be justified by character and
arise out of situation, and he changed the script accordingly. Take
the scene at issue: as written by Terry Southern on quite specific instructions from Ransohoff, it was truly puerile, calling for a cheerleader's costume, a vibrator, and nudity. Peckinpah eliminated the vibrator and replaced the cheerleader's costume with a drab raincoat. As
to the alleged nudity, Peckinpah wanted an actress who would not be
uncomfortable baring her breasts on the set: "*Not that they would be
seen on film* but it was necessary for her to open her coat and since I
intended the audience to think she wore nothing under it I felt it
would be easier to shoot if she could open the coat without worrying about brassiere, tape, and the constant problem in having her
stop a movement that would be continued in another cut on her
back. I told the casting man to be sure the girl cast understood this.
He assured me she did" (emphasis added). According to every reliable account, the nudity was only a very small aspect of a much longer
scene, was in no way gratuitous, and as edited was suggested rather
than shown. The scene depicted a cruel, callous man using, then
discarding, some pathetic hooker for his own amusement. "I find it
provocative but not distasteful," Peckinpah wrote, "except the point
I wanted to get across to the audience that [he] was basically a distasteful man."

    Ransohoff knew his accusation was bogus, but he hoped to estab-
lish a violation of the so-called "moral turpitude" clause in Peckinpah's contract and avoid paying the remainder of his fee. The director's attorneys held fast and got him the money, but it was the last
money he would see from directing for the better part of two years.
Sam Peckinpah was effectively blacklisted by every studio in town.

    Given Peckinpah's history of fights with the moneymen, there are
a number of people, including some of his friends, who have constructed a pet theory to the effect that his problems were largely of
his own making and stemmed from a mean, nasty, argumentative
streak in his personality. Well, Peckinpah's personality was certainly
all of that: he was fiercely combative, nothing if not angry, and seriously paranoid about studio executives. But what is wrong with this
theory is that it doesn't fit anything like all the facts up to *this* point
in his career. He was certainly tough, exacting, and uncompromising in his artistic demands, and he could be cruel, mean, and unreasonable toward cast, crew, and studio personnel alike. However, apart
from *Major Dundee* and *The Deadly Companions,* where the circumstances were surely extenuating enough to grant the benefit of some
doubt, he was rarely gratuitously quarrelsome and almost never irre-

sponsible, at least not measured by the latitudes customarily granted exceptionally talented, temperamental artists working under the
high-pressure conditions of feature filmmaking.[5]

The theory also ignores the strong connection between Peckinpah's attitudes and his working methods. Rightly or wrongly he felt
that confrontation and conflict—stirring things up and getting his
cast and crew riled or scared or just plain excited—sharpened people's wits, kept them on their toes, forged them into a cohesive unit,
and most important intensified their *feelings* about the material. All
of this, he believed, both released and focused their creative energies toward the common goal of making the best film. Already this
early in his career he had some impressive achievements to back him
up, while *The Wild Bunch* and the string of films that came in its wake
would be a triumphant vindication. Even *Major Dundee,* for all its
many problems, can boast an unprecedentedly realistic picture of
horse soldiers in a punishing, brutal desert, which most people in the
cast and crew attribute to Peckinpah's basically having run the set the
way Dundee runs his command.

This is not the only way to make films, but it was Peckinpah's way.
What he mostly needed in producers were people shrewd enough to
know how to handle his combativeness so as to get maximum pro-
ductivity out of him while wasting minimum energy on infighting and
bickering. This is a balance that was not easy to achieve, especially
during the early stages of a shoot when Peckinpah was laying the
groundwork and discovering, as it were, the film *as* a film. But it could
be done, and once he was off and running, the smartest thing to do
was to get the hell out of his way, which is exactly what Sol Siegel, Dick
Powell, and later Ken Hyman at Warner Brothers did. When he
worked with supportive producers like David Levy and Richard Lyons and, later, Daniel Melnick, Phil Feldman (most of the time),
Martin Baum, and Joe Wizan, there were rarely any problems that
were not professionally resolved. But practically everybody on their
respective crews wished Charles B. FitzSimons and Jerry Bresler away
(only Heston has ever had a kind word about the latter). And Ransohoff has a history that would force him to hide his head in shame
anywhere but in Hollywood. He produced *The Americanization of Emily,*
dismissing the director, William Wyler, two weeks into shooting; he
also produced both *The Loved One* and *The Fearless Vampire Killers,*
mutilating them so badly that their respective directors, Tony Richardson and Roman Polanski, wanted their names removed.

Yet each of these directors continued to work. Why did Peckinpah
suffer? Richardson was British and worked mostly out of England,

where he was free from the slander of Hollywood; Polanski is Polish and had not yet entered the American phase of his career. And Wyler was one of the industry's oldest, most well established, and widely respected directors, so he had powerful friends. Peckinpah was still relatively unknown, and with Bresler and Columbia on *Major Dundee* scarcely months behind him, he was an easy target, ripe for "disciplining" (which is Hollywoodese for punishment). Ransohoff wasted no time. "Hollywood is a small, ingrown community," Pauline Kael once observed, "where people live in terror that 'word will get back.'"[6] Peckinpah never showed much fear in his career, but the word got back all the same. "I couldn't get a job anywhere," he said of these years, "couldn't even get into a studio."[7] By his own reckoning he was broke, his second marriage was in ruins, and he was writing under five different pseudonyms, sometimes new material, other times peddling old scripts. "I went through Hell," he said, "because if you're a director and you don't get a chance to direct you start to die a little."[8]

The story Weddle tells of this dark hiatus is of great professional frustration and personal anguish, accompanied by much self-destructive behavior and abuse toward those closest to him. But Peckinpah's recollections in interviews give little or no idea of how active he was. He did an almost bewildering amount of writing, much of it with his good friend Jim Silke. He wrote or cowrote at least five full-length screenplays (including adaptations of James Michener's *Caravans* and James Gould Cozzens's *The Castaway*) and several television scripts (usually pilots for proposed series—he even returned briefly to *The Losers*). Very little of this material ever found its way into production, and what did was not directed or produced by him, which left him in the end all the more frustrated. Most of this material he wrote neither for love nor for money but for leverage to bargain his way into a directing job. Ironically, the only script of his that ever went into production during this period was written back in 1956. Originally titled *The Dice of God*, it was Peckinpah's second feature-length screenplay, a fictionalized account of Custer's Last Stand and an early attempt to treat several themes that later informed *Major Dundee*. It had been commissioned by the *Rifleman* team of Levy-Gardner-Laven, who liked it but were unable to put a package together. It languished for the better part of six years until they managed to line up financing, coincidentally around the time that *Major Dundee* was already in production. It is an indication of the reputation Peckinpah had already made for himself and the distinctiveness of his style that when the finished film came out in 1965—under a new title, *The Glory Guys*—what attention it got from serious critics tended to concentrate on the script, which was considerably changed from the original. Discerning what he could of Peckinpah's touch as obscured by the changes and by Arnold Laven's uninspired direction, Kenneth Tynan observed, "Peckinpah's shadow is better than most other Westerns' substance."[9]

II

One day in the summer of 1966 after what must have felt like an eternity, Peckinpah received a phone call from a producer, Daniel Melnick. Melnick, then a partner with David Susskind in a production company called Talent Associates, wanted to do an adaptation of Katherine Anne Porter's short novel, *Noon Wine*, for a new anthology series, *ABC Stage 67*, scheduled for the approaching fall season. Was Peckinpah interested in directing it? A former associate of Melnick had told him she thought Peckinpah had been unfairly fired from *The Cincinnati Kid*. Melnick knew and admired *Ride the High Country* and *The Westerner*; and after one meeting, he believed he had found the right man not just to direct it, but to write the screenplay as well. Although Peckinpah hadn't been on a set for nearly two years, the gossip mill was still grinding on. FitzSimons, Bresler, and Ransohoff all telephoned Melnick immediately, telling him Peckinpah was nothing but trouble. "Melnick got calls," the director said, "from people who not only had never worked with me but who didn't even know me. They all tried to warn him off me."[10] Peckinpah himself had been forthcoming about the blacklisting, but Melnick thought he was referring to the McCarthy period. When the callers made clear that it had nothing to do with politics, but with everything else from artistic intransigence to personal drunkenness and violence, Melnick vacillated, then became intrigued, and finally dug his heels in deeper each time he hung up the phone. The reward was a collaboration that both men valued as highly as any they had ever enjoyed.

As a team Peckinpah and Melnick were a study in complementary contrasts. The director worked intuitively and disliked talking about why he made his creative decisions. The producer was more intellectual, however, and would often force Peckinpah to "articulate what for him was visceral. I made him think intellectually just so that *I* would understand what he wanted to do. When he got mad he would storm out of our meetings shouting, 'You fucking New York intellectual Jew!' Five minutes later he would come back in and give me a big bear hug."[11] After *Noon Wine* aired, on 23 November 1966, Peckinpah told an interviewer, "I would say that *we* made the picture, not me."[12]

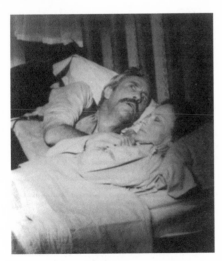

I had no way of figuring out how I could do [the long flashback] in the way that she wrote it, exactly. . . . So I did it very simply, I let it, you know, progress in time, and it worked.
—Sam Peckinpah

Porter's story afforded Peckinpah a near ideal combination of the new and the familiar. On a small farm in south Texas in 1895, Royal Earle Thompson, a poor middle-aged farmer, lives with his sickly wife, Ellie, and their two young sons. One day a tall, lanky Swede named Olaf Helton appears looking for work. There is something unsettling about his haunted gaze and refusal to look directly at anybody, but Thompson needs the help and hires him anyway. A tireless worker, Helton eventually transforms the rundown farm into one of the most well kept and productive in the county. Nine years pass. One lazy hot August afternoon another stranger appears. A shifty, unpleasant man with an irritating laugh, he introduces himself as Homer T. Hatch, a bounty hunter, and identifies Helton as an escaped lunatic who had been incarcerated for murdering his—Helton's—brother many years ago in North Dakota. Reluctant to give Helton up, Thompson angrily orders Hatch off his property. Things rapidly escalate into a moment of confused violence that leaves Helton on the run and Hatch struck dead with an ax wielded by Thompson. Thompson insists that Hatch drew a knife and stabbed Helton, and that he killed the bounty hunter in defense of the Swede's life. He asks his wife to say she saw the whole thing—a lie, as she did not, but she reluctantly agrees to support her husband.

When a posse later apprehends Helton, the men find no knife wounds. Despite a trial that ends in acquittal, nobody believes Thompson; and he becomes obsessed with telling the world his version of the killing. With his wife beside him, he visits each of their neighbors, telling his story over and over, turning to Mrs. Thompson for support ("My wife will tell you, ask my wife, she won't lie!") and each time meeting the same disbelieving faces that belie their words of assent and sympathy. Exhausted from the lying, Mrs. Thompson refuses to visit any more neighbors. When it is clear to Thompson that not even his wife and sons believe him, he walks out to the farthest edge of his property one dark night and writes a note explaining, "It was my belief at the time that Mr. Hatch would of taken the life of Mr. Helton if I did not intervene." He then places the barrel of his shotgun under his chin.

Melnick had long loved *Noon Wine*, and an adaptation had been a dream of his for some time.* Once Peckinpah was signed they soon

---

Noon Wine was originally published with two other short novels, *Old Mortality* and *Pale Horse, Pale Rider* (the latter also the title of the collection). In the introduction Porter admonished her readers to call her short novels "short novels" rather than "novelettes" or, particularly odious to her, "novellas" (*The Collected Stories of Katharine Anne Porter* [New York: Harcourt Brace Jovanovich, 1972], p. vi. This collection also includes *Noon Wine*).

lined up a dream cast: Per Oscarsson as Helton, Theodore Bikel as Hatch, and, best of all, Jason Robards and Olivia de Havilland as Mr. and Mrs. Thompson. (This marked the beginning of Peckinpah's working relationship with Robards, who also became a close friend.) The only sticking point was Porter herself, so dismayed by the Stanley Kramer–Anthony Mann adaptation of her novel *Ship of Fools* that she insisted on script approval before she would grant any further permission. Melnick agreed, which was a chancy thing to do, as he knew that she could abort the project, even with cast and crew already hired.[13] Peckinpah visited her in Maryland; they became fast friends (getting "drunk," according to Robards, "on bourbon and swamp water"),[14] and he returned with her confidence to get down to the business of writing, always the most difficult task for him.

For a man who claimed to suffer the tortures of the damned while writing, Peckinpah's approach to the job seems to have been remarkably methodical. He would analyze the structure and outline the plot, carefully breaking it down into scenes and sequences. Years later when adapting an inferior novel, *The Siege of Trencher's Farm*, into the screenplay that became *Straw Dogs*, Peckinpah would write elaborate back-stories for the characters. None of this material ever made it to the screen as such; but writing it, he felt, gave him and his actors a better understanding of the people and the story. This practice no doubt accounts for the unusual depth, weight, and substance of even the minor characters in his films. Porter's novel, which he had read and loved years before, already provided a fair amount of back-story. He soon came up with an adaptation that was exceptionally faithful without being literal. He condensed the action, reduced the time span from nine to a little under four years (presumably to avoid having to cast two sets of actors to play the Thompson children), and used montages to depict the passing years and the improving fortunes of the farm.*

The most difficult problem Peckinpah faced is the last part of the novel. Almost all of the events between the murder and the night of the suicide—including Thompson's asking his wife to lie for him; Helton's flight, capture, and subsequent death in jail; the sheriff's

---

*The third of the montages contains just about the only out-and-out mistake in the whole show: a pair of cuts with Thompson and Helton smiling at one another, presumably to suggest the beginning of a real friendship. But Helton is obviously a schizophrenic, incapable of this or any other normal social relationship. He spends his time in the isolation of his compulsions, which consist in working the farm and playing one of the several harmonicas he collects. (It is always the same tune over and over, from a Scandinavian folk song that provides the novel with its title, about a worker who awakens feeling so good he drinks all the wine he's saving for the noon layoff.)

relating these events to Mrs. Thompson and advising Thompson to get an attorney; and the scenes of Thompson with the attorney, the trial, its aftermath, and the Thompsons visiting the neighbors—are presented as an extended, almost impressionistic flashback through Mr. and Mrs. Thompson's thoughts and feelings, not as a straightforward sequential narrative that is in any way dramatized. "I had no way of figuring out how I could do it in the way that she wrote it," Peckinpah said. He rejected anything fancy, "which would have been so much fun to do and yet so kind of campy, in bad taste. So I did it very simply, I let it progress in time, and it worked."[15] Although he had not specifically talked about the flashback with Porter, his approach to the material it covered turned out to be her alternative structure when she first conceived the story. If she had decided to write it differently, she told Melnick, Peckinpah's way would have been it, "exactly," which made watching it "absolutely witchy."[16] In the end his adaptation demonstrated so acute an ear for idiom and so comprehensive a grasp of theme, character, and structure that Porter wrote Melnick "a wonderful letter saying she wished she could have been as imaginative as Mr. Peckinpah was in the new scenes he created. It was the best communication I could have hoped for."[17]

Peckinpah had an unusually sensitive feel for one of the trickiest procedures in adapting literary works to stage or screen: transposing passages of prose into spoken dialogue. In the novel, here are Mrs. Thompson's thoughts as she walks toward the house at the end of the last day she and her husband will visit any of the neighbors:

> Life was all one dread, the faces of her neighbors, of her boys, of her husband, the face of the whole world, the shape of her own house in the darkness, the very smell of the grass and the trees were horrible to her. There was no place to go, only one thing to do, bear it somehow—but how? She asked herself that question often. How was she going to keep on living now? Why had she lived at all? She wished she had died one of those times when she had been so sick, instead of living on for this.

A passage like this obviously cannot be performed, so Peckinpah created a scene for earlier the same afternoon as the couple are on their way home. Thompson's lines are entirely by the director; Mrs. Thompson's are prose reworked from the novel.

> *Mr. Thompson:* I keep hoping, Ellie, I keep hoping you might say, "I remember now, Mr. Thompson, I really came around the corner in time to see everything." I keep hoping you'll quit saying it's a lie, for I truly trust to God it is not.

> *Mrs. Thompson:* There was a time when my husband hadn't killed
> a man and made me lie for him and I could tell the truth to
> anybody about anything. But now, life has become all one dread,
> and there's no place for me to go. Oh sweet Jesus, I just don't
> know how to go on living anymore.

Beyond even the superb writing and acting, what really transforms
this scene from literature to drama and finally to cinema is the way
it is visualized: a series of traveling shots, some of them singles, some
subtly moving from one face to the other, alternately isolating and
uniting them, culminating in a medium closeup of Mrs. Thompson.
Now Ellie Thompson is hardly the kind of woman Peckinpah was by
temperament disposed to like, but as an artist he always empathized
beyond his private sympathies. He knew in his bones how much it
costs this woman to lie, whatever the reasons, and his film arguably
conveys it even more strongly than the novel. The sense of her being trapped is perfectly caught in that understated but pitiless
straight-on medium closeup, almost claustrophobic despite the exterior setting, Mrs. Thompson tense with anxiety as she gives voice
to her deepest feelings, the tiny lenses of her dark glasses her only
protection against the glare of humiliation and judgment from a
world at once familiar yet now almost unrecognizable.

Her nearly frozen rigidity here is in contrast with her attitude in
an earlier scene when the sheriff tells her there will have to be a trial, which inspired one of the most impressive pieces of staging in all
of Peckinpah's work. In a loose full-shot we look past the sheriff, who
stands in front of Mrs. Thompson to her right; on her left, his back
to camera, is Mr. Thompson, tight with tension, his head turned
slightly, watchfully, in her direction and the sheriff's. When she realizes she will have to lie under oath, which is to say before God, Mrs.
Thompson quickly grows agitated, moving one direction, blocked,
turning, then another, blocked again, turning once more, almost me-
chanically, like a whirligig, literally unable to find any place she can
come to rest or anyone she can turn to.

Long after publishing the story, Porter wrote a famous essay called
"*Noon Wine:* The Sources," which Peckinpah read while preparing the
screenplay and marked up almost as much as he did his copy of the
novel.[18]* The discovery by an ordinary man of his capacity for violence is obviously one thing that struck him forcibly. Another is the

---

*He was in need of inspiration and moral support at this time in his career and he
found both in Porter's essay. In the margin at the bottom of the second page, he wrote,
"She has—as all the great ones do—this instinctive sense of her own destiny—."

way the violence suddenly erupts, shattering the lives of all it touches. Still another is the wholly unsympathetic, judgmental attitude of society toward anyone who steps outside its narrow boundaries of right and wrong. Porter described this "society of my childhood" as "in the main a civilized society, and yet, with the underlying perpetual ominous presence of violence; violence potential that broke the smooth surface almost without warning."

Peckinpah underlined that passage. It points toward ways *Noon Wine* relates to his other work. The main characters—a family of farmers, the hired hand, the neighbors—are people who generally occupy the backgrounds and fringes or play supporting roles in most Western stories. Here they are brought to the foreground and the domestic setting is moved center stage. When the violence breaks out, it is not cushioned by the presence of outlaws and gunfighters, from whom we expect it. Set entirely in the ordinary world of this small farm and the surrounding community, *Noon Wine* is the most stubbornly realistic of all Peckinpah's work. Nor did he ever go further in the direction of naturalism than here (not even in *Pat Garrett and Billy the Kid*), apropos of which he underlined another sentence in the essay: "there is nothing in any of these beings tough enough to work the miracle of redemption in them." He had dealt with such characters before, as early as his scripts for *Gunsmoke* and in several *Westerner* episodes (paramountly "Jeff"); and by every rule of storytelling logic and psychology, Major Dundee is or should be incapable of such a miracle, even if the director's eventual identification made him pull back from the character's darkest implications. But *Noon Wine* marks the first time they've been the *only* such people in one of his films. Redemption through loyalty, salvation through friendship, regeneration through violence—these are his abiding themes, even when his structures are those of tragedy. But he fully honored the integrity of Porter's vision and aligned his own with it.

The bridge that connects them is a theme that is even more basic to Peckinpah's work than that of redemption. "Everyone in this story contributes, one way or another directly, or indirectly, to murder, or death by violence," Porter writes; it is "a story of the most painful moral and emotional confusions, in which every one concerned, yes, in his crooked way, even Mr. Hatch, is trying to do right." When Peckinpah read that, he not only underlined it (the last part twice), he added an exclamation point. A few years later, after he had finished *The Wild Bunch,* he expressed much the same idea: "Things are always mixed. We're all guilty to some extent."[19]

Porter thus throws a net of guilt and complicity over the central

act of violence, which starts in what she calls that "apparently aimless talk between Mr. Hatch and Mr. Thompson which barely masks
hatred and is leading towards a murder." Hatch, writes Porter, is "evil
by nature, a lover and doer of evil," who "works safely within the law,
and has reasoned himself into believing that his motives, if not good,
are at least no worse that anyone else's." Peckinpah knew these self-
righteous types; his Western films especially are populated with them.
Hatch is a particularly odious example. With an annoying laugh and
a sneaky manner, he never approaches any subject directly. He lets
the two crucial pieces of information about Helton—his insanity and
his crime—slip out as if by accident, though in fact he is carefully
manipulating Thompson, keeping him off guard. In the novel it is
principally Hatch's nastiness and his devious manner that strike us,
which Porter can italicize without fear of descending into a melodramatic villainy because she depicts him mostly through Thompson's
unsympathetic eyes.

Working without this advantage on film, Peckinpah nevertheless
manages to suggest the character's full repulsiveness—the laugh especially well realized, a nasal snarl so irritating that it alone invites
thoughts of murder—without ever letting us lose contact with him
as a human being. Yet by the time the ax has fallen, we are also made
to feel how Thompson's repugnance for this fat vile man with his
insults about the farmer's heritage, his wife, even his tobacco could
get all mixed up with the heat of the day and the bounty hunter's
disgusting brown "rabbit teeth" and irritating laugh and threats about
the law and what the neighbors will think if he doesn't cooperate and
the handcuffs he pulls out until suddenly disgust has become rage
and he is lying on the ground, blood seeping from his caved-in head.

How to film the murder and yet fully convey the confusion and
ambiguity presented Peckinpah his biggest problem. In the novel
Porter uses a third-person–limited point of view to introduce Hatch,
play out the dialogue, and suggest the barely suppressed hostility that
precedes the violence. Although the point of view is mostly Thompson's, there is a sufficient sense of objectivity about the narrative to
let us feel that the data we are being given is reliable. But for the
murder and the events immediately surrounding it Porter sharply
narrows the perspective to the wholly subjective so that we experience
them only by way of Thompson's enraged, now almost feverish mind.
"Get out of here before I knock you down!" he shouts; and then he

took a step towards the fat man, who backed off, shrinking, "Try
it, try it, go ahead!" and then something happened that Mr. Thomp-

son tried hard afterwards to piece together in his mind and in fact it never did come straight. He saw the fat man with his long bowie knife in his hand, he saw Mr. Helton come around the corner on the run, his long jaw dropped, his arms swinging, his eyes wild. Mr. Helton came in between them, fists doubled up, then stopped short, glaring at the fat man, his big frame seemed to collapse, he trembled like a shied horse; and then the fat man drove at him, knife in one hand, handcuffs in the other. Mr. Thompson saw it coming, he saw the blade going into Mr. Helton's stomach, he knew he had the ax out of the log in his own hands, felt his arms go up over his head and bring the ax down on Mr. Hatch's head as if he were stunning a beef.

The commotion draws Mrs. Thompson from inside the house, but by the time she comes out all she sees is Helton fleeing in the distance "and Mr. Thompson, supporting himself on the ax handle," "leaning over shaking by the shoulder a man Mrs. Thompson had never seen, who lay doubled up with the top of his head smashed and the blood running away in a greasy-looking puddle. Mr. Thompson without taking his hand from the man's shoulder, said in a thick voice, 'He killed Mr. Helton, he killed him, I saw him do it. I had to knock him out,' he called loudly, 'but he won't come to.'"

Porter's manipulation of point of view throughout this section is so subtle that, like Thompson himself, we can never be sure of exactly what has happened, let alone how. Did Helton actually come between Thompson and Hatch, as Thompson believes? Did Hatch really have his bowie knife drawn? The last time he had it out was to cut a chew from his tobacco. After that there is no reference to the knife until Thompson sees it; but by then the narrative is totally inside Thompson's excited mind, which is such a bundle of anger, fear, and panic it's almost incoherent. Also, since Hatch last took a cut from his plug, he indulges his nervous tic of clasping both hands together as if the one were shaking the other, so we know he cannot have had his knife out then. A little later he takes the handcuffs out and puts them in his jacket pocket and pulls his hat down tight over his eyes, but there is still no mention of his drawing the knife again. As for Helton, the only thing we know from a point of view other than Thompson's is that Mrs. Thompson saw the Swede running away; later the only wounds found on his body are those made by the posse subduing him.

In order, then, to preserve the ambiguity of what happened in these few seconds, all Porter has to do is further focus the subjectivity of a narrative that is already subjective, and the effect is achieved with ease and seeming naturalness. But in a dramatic medium like film this sort of ambiguity is virtually impossible to realize. If Peckinpah had wanted to be literal about it, he could have cut away at precisely the point that Porter goes completely inside Thompson's mind. This would preclude our seeing *anything* of what happened immediately before the murder, but the effect would feel clumsy and contrived, even rather like a cheat. It would also be false to the meaning of Porter's story: it is not that Thompson remembers nothing of what happened, only that he is confused about it and cannot get it straight. Taking his cue from that, Peckinpah sacrifices some of the novel's ambiguity: in the film we clearly see Hatch pull the knife; we see Helton come between Thompson and Hatch and then flee as Hatch advances. Almost without thinking Thompson swings the ax, and we cut immediately to a closeup of Mrs. Thompson in the house reacting to the sound of the blade crushing the bounty hunter's skull. Peckinpah intuitively realized that the ambiguity of events at this point is less important than Thompson's simple uncertainty about what happened and his part in it. In a film that has for most of its length been seen at medium distance and in fairly long takes, there is a sudden proliferation of quick cutting, close camera-placement, and deliberately fragmented action to make these few crucial moments—that will ultimately leave three men dead, a family destroyed, and a community divided—tumble in upon one another with a bewildering speed that intensifies our sense of Thompson's confusion.

In a typically subtle touch, Peckinpah reinforces the sense of confusion even more by never actually showing Thompson wielding the ax. It is seen in a closeup sticking out of a stump; there is a cut to a hesitant Thompson as Hatch moves toward Helton; next the ax is coming out of the stump in a closeup so tight we can't see any hands removing it; then Thompson is swinging it, but again framed so close we cannot see the ax itself; and the completion of the swing occurs offscreen. The effect is almost as if Thompson—driven by something deep within, far stronger than his ability to control it—has *willed* the killing of Hatch rather than actually done the deed, which is crucial to a full understanding of his claim to innocence. Peckinpah has realized here a cinematic equivalent to the literary technique of third-person–limited point of view: just as in the novel, except in terms unique to film, the narrative, through the selection, framing, and editing of the shots, does not merely illustrate the character's fragmented perceptions but in some sense actually embodies them. Peckinpah was a quick study in this technique, and *The Wild Bunch* would soon demonstrate how thoroughly he had mastered it.

Once Peckinpah figured out how to do the central murder, he turned to another of Porter's narrative ellipses. The posse's capture of Helton is only reported in the novel, the violence necessary to subdue him left unspecified except that it was unavoidable, that the sheriff sincerely regrets it ("They *had* to be rough, Miz Thompson, he fought like a wildcat"), and that it was of sufficient violence to cause the Swede injuries that will result in his death a short time later in jail. In Peckinpah's telling Helton is, like Hatch, clubbed to death with a fierce blow to the head that kills him immediately (in a nice touch, the man who delivers the death blow is the white-trash farmer McClellan whose self-righteous wife later preaches, "Now we don't hold with killin'"). The sheriff tells Mrs. Thompson, "He acted like a mad dog. We didn't mean to kill him, but he was crazy as a loon. He picked up a club and tried to brain every man that come near him. Then he almost killed a man. We had to get tough, Miz Thompson. Nobody likes killing a loony, but we had to protect ourselves." These lines, once more fashioned by Peckinpah from Porter's prose into a new scene, together with his visualization of the capture, make the two killings resonate ironically off each other in a way that strengthens the structure, while the sheriff's justifications come out sounding uncomfortably close to Thompson's.

To keep the costs down *Noon Wine* was shot mostly on video tape. In those days the standard practice was to use three cameras, again for economy. But Peckinpah wanted a dark, shadowy look that would have been impossible from the saturation-lighting required for running three cameras simultaneously. Though the style of the show cries out for film, it is amazing how many of the limitations of video tape Peckinpah managed to transcend.* The capture of Helton, for example, is set at night in a small corral off a barn. The men swarm over him as he grabs a piece of wood and swings it about crazily. The master shot is a high-angle setup that delimits the corral more or less

---

*Owing to the condition of the surviving prints, even a practiced eye might find it difficult to recognize the achievement. In order to make room in the vaults some twenty years ago, ABC destroyed the negatives for several of its series, including all the *Stage 67* shows. There remain only two color copies of *Noon Wine* that were made from the original: one is in the Museum of Broadcasting (New York, New York), the other belongs to Jason Robards. (Peckinpah had a black-and-white kinescope in his archives, but it is almost unwatchable, especially in a tape transfer.) It is Robards's print that is usually shown at retrospectives of the director's work. The color is faded, and even with a meticulous transfer to tape one has to imagine what the original must have looked like. Current digital technology now makes it possible to correct this sort of degradation to an amazing degree, though at some expense. But in this instance it would be worth it.

with the borders of the screen, thus sounding another of the director's familiar themes: a small space filled with too many scared and angry men and too much antagonistic energy for violence to be avoided. When Helton is dealt the death blow, he lets out a short, high-pitched screech, as if some terrified animal had been struck down.

The same high-angle setup is paralleled in the penultimate scene, in the Thompson's bedroom. The room is so claustrophobic it feels airless, conveying an almost unbearable impression of a couple trapped in a dynamic that is destroying them. In the small bed Thompson tosses and turns, wracked by second-guessing and self-doubt, while his wife sleeps beside him, her arms crossed over her breast and holding herself so rigid she suggests a cadaver laid out in a coffin. In voiceover we hear Thompson's thoughts fighting to get clear on what he could have been thinking and why he didn't do things differently, questioning his every move and motive as the walls of denial are torn down only to be built back up again just as tenaciously. Phantom images from the fatal afternoon return to haunt him—the knife brandished, the handcuffs out, Helton backing away in fear, Hatch laughing as he moves forward, the swing of the ax, his own uncomprehending visage—and before he is aware of what he is doing, Thompson is rising from the bed, his mounting anger toward his dead victim become now a torrent of raging words hurled into the empty darkness of the small room, his fists clenched around an imaginary ax that he swings again and again and again in a grotesque reenactment of the murder that gives the lie to all his protestations of innocence. Mrs. Thompson awakens with a prolonged howl that recalls Helton's dying screech, and then in a guttural voice cries, "No, no, no, no!," her hands clutching her hair, twisting her head back and forth. In one blinding epiphany all four principals and both killings are thus drawn together and bound around a core of rage, fear, and denial.

Peckinpah often talked in interviews about men who could not recognize deep within themselves the violence of which they are capable and which as a consequence leaves them open to greater violence than they could ever suspect or fear. These are men who sit on their anger until it becomes rage and then sit on their rage until it explodes. Yet for all the ferocity the flare-ups are over so fast they are hardly experienced, let alone remembered, for what they are. Thompson is one of these men. "He was a murderer," Porter writes. "That was the truth about himself that Mr. Thompson couldn't grasp, even when he said the word to himself. Why, he had not even once *thought* of killing Mr. Hatch," and he could never remember actually "hitting Mr. Hatch." In this sense Thompson's compulsion to clear his name can be seen as a dark, ironic version of the quest to enter one's house justified. As Porter writes in another passage the director underlined: "afterward [Mr. Thompson] could not live without justifying himself."

There has always been something of an enigma at the center of this story. Thompson's hatred of Hatch, or, to be more precise, the intensity of his hatred, doesn't make full sense on the face of it. Where it comes from is elusive and obscure, and is nowhere even hinted at in Porter's essay. The manifest reasons seem obvious enough: there is Hatch himself, evil, obnoxious, and personally disgusting (Thompson "kept thinking he couldn't remember when he had taken such a dislike to a man on first sight"). There is the economic motive: rather lazy, with no real interest in dairy farming, Thompson has failed to work the farm, letting it go undeveloped and fall into such disrepair that it barely provides a living for his family. He is also a man of considerable, albeit foolish pride, his first two names—Royal Earle—obviously ironic, invoking a dominion he will never rule and a social position he will never enjoy. But in the tireless Helton he finds a hand to do all the work and for remarkably little pay, leaving him free to manage the place and market its products, very much acting the earl to the Swede's serf. Never prosperous, the farm, thanks to Helton's efforts, becomes productive enough to enable the Thompsons to start accumulating some savings; Thompson hates to pay wages, but he increases Helton's twice, without being asked, for "he knew a good thing when he had it."

Less important but not beside the point is Thompson's drinking, which, owing to his wife's stern disapproval, he does on the sly. On that hot August afternoon as Hatch keeps talking and Thompson's irritation for him grows, he becomes aware of the dust and the heat and remembers four bottles of beer he had stored "deep in the pool at the springhouse, and his dry tongue squirmed in his mouth. He wasn't going to offer this man anything, though, not even a drop of water." This is another effect that can't be filmed, but Peckinpah managed to allude to Thompson's drinking in a wonderfully subtle bit of staging: Hatch removes an empty bottle of beer from the stump on which, uninvited, he seats himself.

Still, none of these explanations seems sufficient in itself or even in the aggregate to account for a rage that explodes into the murder of a complete stranger. But what if the rage itself is misdirected? The dialogue that leads up to the murder has been widely celebrated, in part because Porter herself justly called attention to all "that apparently aimless talk between Mr. Hatch and Mr. Thompson which barely masks hatred and is leading towards a murder." But it may be other dialogue that is more to the point. Just after Hatch drops the first hint of Helton's insanity, Thompson, raising his voice, declares, "He never acted crazy to me. He always acted like a sensible man, to me. He never got married for one thing, and he works like a horse, and I bet he's got the first cent I paid him when he landed here."

Hatch laughs with excessive joviality, "Yeah, that's right! Let's all go crazy and get rid of our wives and save our money, hey?" This isn't what he meant at all, Thompson thinks, and motions them to the side of the house, away from the open window, pointing out that his wife is not very strong, "kind of invalid now goin' on fourteen years"; after four operations that "didn't do any good," "I just turned every nickel I made over to the doctors. Upshot is, she's a mighty delicate woman." Hatch replies, "I never had much use for a woman always complainin'. I'd get rid of her mighty quick, yes, sir, mighty quick. It's just as you say: a dead loss keeping one of 'em up." This, too, is not at all what Thompson felt he had said: "he had been trying to explain that a wife as expensive as his was a credit to a man."

Far from aimless, the sarcastic twists and turns that Hatch keeps giving Thompson's sideways complaints about the burden his wife has become begin to seem closer to the truth of his feelings than all his silent protestations to the contrary. The resentments the bounty hunter unwittingly taps here have been sounded right from the beginning of the story. Explaining the job to Helton, Thompson says, "This is more of a dairy farm. My wife, she was set on a dairy farm, she seemed to like working with cows and calves, so I humored her. It was a mistake. I got nearly everything to do, anyhow. My wife ain't very strong. She's sick today, that's a fact. She's been porely for the last few days." A few pages later we discover how thoroughly Thompson detests dairy farming, not least because he feels it is "woman's work." "Killing hogs was a job for the boss," he believes, but slopping them "was hired hand's work": "All his carefully limited fields of activity were related somehow to Mr. Thompson's feeling for the appearance of things. . . . 'It don't *look* right,' was his final reason for not doing anything he did not wish to do."

A portrait soon enough emerges of Thompson as a rather ineffectual man of some arrogance, considerable pretensions, and no small ego, whose view of himself is quite at variance with his actual place in the world and his situation in life. He is similarly unaware, or at least keeps it well off in a distant corner of his mind, how much he blames his wife for the failure the farm has become and for his own fading hopes and disappointed dreams. Caring mainly about "his dignity and his reputation," he

> saw after a while, how short-sighted it had been of him to expect much from Mrs. Thompson; he had fallen in love with her delicate waist and lace-trimmed petticoats and big blue eyes, and, though all those charms had disappeared, she had in the meantime become Ellie to him, not at all the same person as Miss Ellen Bridges, popular Sunday school teacher in the Mountain City First Baptist Church, but his dear wife, Ellie, who was not strong. Deprived as he was, however, of the main support in life which a man might expect in marriage, he had almost without knowing it resigned himself to failure. Head erect, a prompt payer of taxes, yearly subscriber to the preacher's salary, land owner and father of a family, employer, a hearty good fellow among men, Mr. Thompson knew, without putting it into words, that he had been going steadily down hill.

Long before Helton shows up, Thompson has slid so far that much of his time is spent sitting for hours chewing tobacco and worrying about things. "God amighty," he notices, "it did look like somebody might take a rake in hand now and then and clear up the clutter around the barn and the kitchen steps." But nobody does, and after pondering it long enough Mr. Thompson finds himself looking "forward to the boys growing up soon; he was going to put them through the mill just as his own father had done with him": "those two boys were going to earn their salt, or he'd know why." Then he grows "quite enraged" imagining them as lazy "big lubbers whittling or thinking about fishing trips." Plainly this is a man who is no stranger to rage, and as often as not it is taken out on the two boys, never on their mother. We see that rage in action when he returns home from town drunk and is ready to take a calf rope to the boys for playing with Helton's harmonicas. "Maybe you'd better leave the whipping to me," says Mrs. Thompson. "You haven't got a light enough hand for children." When the farm starts to do well and things are going better, however, Thompson begins to believe "that he had never spoken a harsh word to [his sons] a day in their lives, much less thrashed them." This is also a man who is no stranger to self-delusion and denial.

The two most ambiguous lines in both the novel and the film occur in the last two scenes. When Mrs. Thompson awakens screaming, the two boys, teenagers now, rush to her side. The older, mistakenly thinking his father has hit her, savagely turns on him, raises his fist, and shouts, "You touch her again and I'll blow your heart out!" In the face of this Thompson loses any fight he has left and just gives up: "I never did your mother any harm, on purpose." On purpose. In the filming Peckinpah gets even more mileage out of the ambiguity of these two words. The camera setup is a full-shot past Thompson to his sons and wife grouped together on the other side of the bed, the composition itself suggesting his estrangement from the family. Peckinpah directs Robards to deliver only the first part of the line to the family; then Thompson pauses, turns from away them toward camera, and as if in soliloquy quietly speaks the last two words to himself.

In the springhouse he begins his suicide note: "I do solemnly swear that I did not take the life of Mr. Homer T. Hatch on purpose." When a writer who uses language as carefully and as self-consciously as Porter, wasting hardly a word, repeats a phrase as loaded as this one— at all, let alone so close together—it cannot be through carelessness or without design. The repetition points to a pattern that runs beneath and counter to Thompson's pleas of innocence: in both cases he admits to the harm or violence he has done while disavowing any malicious intent. Thus by way of two seemingly innocuous words Porter virtually identifies Mrs. Thompson with Hatch, the first victim of an unexpressed rage that burns so deep and uncontrollably inside Thompson himself that when it erupts he can only claim, with all the conviction of a man who cannot bear to turn his gaze inward, that he had no purpose in it. Despairing of his good intentions ever being believed, Thompson continues: "This is the only way I can prove I am not a cold blooded murderer like everybody seems to think. . . . I still think I done the only thing there was to do. My wife—." Here he pauses for a moment, but neither the novelist nor the filmmaker makes us privy to his thoughts. Then he wets the tip of his pencil and blackens out "my wife" so thoroughly that all that remains is "a neat oblong patch." The note concludes: "It was Mr. Homer T. Hatch who came to do wrong to a harmless man. He caused all this trouble and he deserved to die but I am sorry it was me who had to kill him."

It is impossible to know what would have followed the reference to his wife—a final confession of the truth that he forced her to lie for him; an admission of at least his own uncertainly as to motive and responsibility; some expression of disappointment in Ellie as wife and companion; or another insistence upon the lie that she witnessed it all? However one decides, it cannot be an accident that Porter for one last time chooses to link Mrs. Thompson and the violence against Hatch; and then has Mr. Thompson, in a final desperate act of denial, push away all further thoughts of his wife as he prepares in his last testament on earth to blame everything once again on the bounty hunter.

Peckinpah took the themes of denial and complicity one step further in a closing image of shattering power. In the book Thompson walks out to the farthest perimeter of his property to kill himself. In the film he walks only across the yard to the small springhouse. As he places the barrel against his chin, there is a cut to a high, wide exterior of the house at night. The shotgun sounds, its report carrying over the next cut to an extreme closeup of Mrs. Thompson against a dark background, a look of confused, frightened incomprehension on her face, an ominous note sounding in the music, then a quick fade to silence.

This closeup, it is said, left the audience at the cast and crew screening absolutely devastated. Yet Porter strenuously objected to it in a letter she later wrote to Peckinpah, protesting that Mrs. Thompson "was not alone, her sons were with her trying to soothe her terror and grief."* But the setup is obviously close enough that it doesn't preclude the presence of her sons offscreen; just as obviously, Peckinpah, taking a cue from Porter herself, wanted to allude to the murder for one last time, which he also played offscreen except for the sound of the death instrument over a somewhat looser closeup of an equally uncomprehending Mrs. Thompson. The final closeup is Peckinpah's way of suggesting that she has failed her husband as much as he has failed her. But it achieves something more: so tightly framed her face seems to have no reference points beyond a background as black as the night in which her husband has just blown his head off, the composition at once freezes Mrs. Thompson in a bleak present and posits an equally forlorn future, leaving her as isolated as her hapless husband, as confused, and as deluded about her own complicity in the dark chain of events that has brought them both to this place of desolation and despair.

---

*Porter also had other problems with the film. "So far as I could trace your hand in the play, and remember the script, all went well," she wrote. But she felt that at an hour (which means about fifty minutes for the film itself) the show was too short; she was also irritated by the commercials and complained that the folk song was not the right tune. But Jerry Fielding, who wrote the score, said that when she sang the song to him, "just as she'd remembered it," what she sang was not some Scandinavian folk song, but "Look for the Silver Lining," which "couldn't have been that song because that hadn't even been written when she was a child" (quoted in Simmons, p. 77). As Melnick remembers, the commercials bothered her the most; and her response left him particularly disappointed, not just because of her early enthusiasm for the screenplay but because he had offered to set up a special screening precisely so that she could watch the film without commercial interruption (Daniel Melnick to P.S., 1995).

III

Peckinpah often said that in one way or another all his work is auto-biographical. This will raise some eyebrows considering that much of his work is in the Western, a genre that is period by definition and remote and rather romantic even when rendered realistically. It is also remarkable inasmuch as he did not invent most of his primary story material. But to doubt his word too much is to reckon without his peerless ability to make almost anything he touched authentically his own, and to forget that he had an extraordinary gift for finding stories and scripts that he could bend to his needs.

Not that *Noon Wine* needed much bending. It is a reasonable guess that Peckinpah spent so much time reading and marking up Porter's essay on the sources because he might very well have written a companion one himself. Royal and Ellie Thompson reminded him so strongly of his parents, David and Fern Peckinpah, that he often, though quietly, referred to scenes from his parents' marriage by way of guiding Robards and de Havilland toward the emotions and feelings he wanted from them. He had already drawn on his parents in several scenes and sequences in his earlier television work—"Miss Jenny," parts of *The Rifleman* and *The Westerner* (paramountly "Mrs. Kennedy")—but *Noon Wine* is by far the fullest treatment. It is also regarded by the family as the fullest portrait he ever did of Fern Peckinpah—along with one other, the small film he made as part of his master's thesis at the University of Southern California. But before looking at that, a short account of his parents' marriage and his relationship to them may shed some light on just how much the family shaped and conditioned the emotional and thematic content of his art.

The Peckinpahs and the Churches were the among the oldest, most distinguished families in Fresno, California, and the surrounding area. Fern Louise was born the second child of Denver and Louise Church in 1893. Although Louise was a strong woman, the birth was exceptionally difficult and almost killed her. During her long recovery Denver cared for the infant, and between the father and daughter there developed a deep bond from which she learned that her strength lay in her dependency. Her father's favorite, she was troubled her whole life by fears of abandonment. As a teenager she fell in love with Bob Nichols, a pharmacist from Long Beach, of whom her father disapproved because he felt he wasn't enough of a man. Denver expressed his misgivings in a letter to his daughter, but he promised he would not interfere, whereupon he went behind her back and did exactly that: with a combination of threats and a bribe, he sent the young man packing. Fern never saw him again.

In a way, Denver's deception subverted his own purposes. For long before Nichols was sent away Fern had met David Peckinpah, one of the hands who worked Denver's ranch and of whom the old man heartily approved: "well nigh a perfect specimen of young manhood," he described the young cowboy to Louise.[20] Though two years younger than Fern, David fell in love with her, and pursued her respectfully but ardently. The two spent a lot of time together when the pharmacist was away (which was most of the time), and Fern obviously enjoyed and welcomed David's attentions. Entries in her diary from this period indicate that if left alone her romance with Nichols might have run its course. Instead, by interfering Church merely ensured the pharmacist of a preeminent place in his daughter's fantasy life, where she kept his memory alive until she died in 1983 at the age of ninety. She never forgave her father his deception and betrayal.

Less than two years after Nichols disappeared Fern accepted David's proposal and they were married. In the early years of the marriage they were very much in love and quite the active couple. Denver, a lawyer and congressman, helped his new son-in-law to go to law school. A few years later David established a highly successful practice in Fresno, where he was widely respected and immensely well liked. His father-in-law was a pillar of the community, and in time he would be also. As his professional obligations and community work began to occupy more and more of his time, David and Fern fell into the pattern typical of both their families: the men went out into the world, the women stayed at home with the kids and the house. (Sam would eventually replicate this pattern in his own first marriage.) This only served to exacerbate Fern's fears of abandonment. Unwilling to share David and resentful of the time he spent away from home, she soon reverted to the dependency that she came to believe was her only source of power. Following the birth of their first child, who was named Denver Charles (after each of the grandfathers), she started taking to her room with exhaustion, headaches, spells, and assorted other aches and pains, real and imagined. Before long, between David's activities, Fern's retreating to her room more and more, and the couple's social obligations, Denny, as the boy was called, was abandoned to Denver and Louise, who raised him through much of his infancy and early childhood. Fern, who always wanted a daughter, never warmed to her first son. (An unspoken enmity existed between them until her death; Denny did not attend the funeral and to the end of his life—he died in March 1996 at the age of seventy-nine—seldom mentioned her.)

The director's parents, David and Fern Peckinpah, on their ranch (circa 1938).

My parents had a strange relationship. They were very much in love, very much, but boy did they eat on each other psychologically.
—Sam Peckinpah

Sam (age sixteen or seventeen) and his father (circa 1941).

Sam (between ages eighteen and twenty-one) and his mother (circa 1943–46).

My mother [believed] absolutely in two things: teetotalism and Christian Science. My father believed in the Bible as literature, and in the law.
—Sam Peckinpah

Fern was still pining for a daughter by the time Sam came along (it was the reason she got pregnant a second time). Her initial disappointment turned to elation when she looked into what she described in her diary as "the most beautiful eyes a child ever had"; "God gave me a treasure to have and to hold."[21] She lavished upon her new boy all the love and devotion she had withheld from his brother. Christened David Samuel, he soon came to be known around the house as "D. Sammy," since he and his father shared the same first name. Despite her devotion to Sam, Fern still wanted daughters. Years later she and David adopted a baby girl and named her Fern Lea; and sometime after that, they adopted another, whom they named Susan. (The girls would call their father "DeDa.") Repeating the pattern with the girls that she had established with the boys, Fern favored the younger over the older; but neither of them ever came close to displacing Sam as the center of her world. It was not long before several observers noticed that the parents had rather effectively divided the boys between them: Denny for David, Sam for Fern. The mother and son shared an unusual intimacy throughout his childhood and adolescence. They bathed together until he was four; when the practice ceased he did not respond happily. It was a little custom between them that he would get to sleep with her each year on his birthday night, a custom that, to judge from Fern's diaries, was observed at least until he was fourteen. (After reading her mother's diaries and letters many years later, Fern Lea remarked, "If you didn't know Sam was her son, you'd think she was writing about a lover.")[22]

Fern was a painter of middling ability but a gardener of truly awesome gifts. "She could touch a stick of wood and tomorrow you would find it blooming," Peckinpah said. "There are trees she planted that are a hundred-and-fifty feet tall now in front of houses all over Fresno."[23] Her garden at home was an enchanted place. In addition to myriad species of flowers and foliage, it featured an artificial brook and miniature waterfalls, bridges, and castles. The family all believe Sam inherited her meticulous attention to detail and her eye for composition and design. "Mother, fortunately and unfortunately, was the most powerful figure in his life," Fern Lea says.

He got his creativity from her, though I'm certain he would have denied it. Sam was basically a woman emotionally, and I think he was embarrassed by it because in our family, "By God, the men are men! We don't cry and we don't allow our emotions to show. We're the guys!" I think of a man as being systematic in his reasoning, to come to a certain point. Sam would get to the answer emotional-

ly—the way he felt about it, the way he visualized it. He would see
the flowers and the beauty in the flowers, whereas another fellow
might say, "Yeah, that's a pretty flower, that's a nice shade of red."
But Sam would smell it, the reaction would be more feminine. I
don't think he ever worried about being homosexual, that was
never it, but I think he might have been aware that his emotions
weren't "masculine." Sam didn't want that side of him to show.[24]

Hearing that cannot help but bring to mind how often in his films
the characters, male and female, will turn away in their moments of
greatest vulnerability, and how much pathos he could wring simply
from observing the receding backs of his lonely individuals.

Sam learned a lot from his mother, but by no means was all of it
absorbed in ways that would have pleased her. "My mother believes
absolutely in two things," he once said, "teetotalism and Christian Science."[25] She sternly disapproved of all drinking and swearing, and Sam
was a frequent target of her puritanical moralizing. (She made him
promise he wouldn't drink and use profanity. He made the promises
over and over, and just as repeatedly broke them.) As for his father,
he "believed in the Bible as literature, and in the law," Sam said. "I grew
up with those people sitting around a dining room table talking about
law and order, truth and justice, on a Bible which was very big in our
family."[26] David was not religious as such—he became a Christian Sci-
entist at the same time his wife did because he thought it would help
her overcome her illnesses better—but he was a student of the Bible.
He was also easily Fern's match in the rigidity of what he considered
right thinking and proper behavior. If the girls wore shorts outside the
house—"And we're talking shorts that came down almost to my *knees*,"
says Fern Lea—he considered it tantamount to leaving home naked.[27]
His conversations were liberally peppered with "shoulds," "oughts," and
"musn'ts" and with expressions like "It isn't done," "It's not right," "How
will it look?," and "What will people think?" The kids regarded him "as
an *authority*," Peckinpah recalled, "and we all grew up thinking he could
never, ever be wrong about anything."[28] David certainly found it hard
to admit he was ever wrong. And he had a quick, violent temper that
unleashed a terrifying rage. He absolutely forbade backtalk or disre-
spect of any kind from them, especially toward their mother; and signs
of it were dealt with severely: they were often sent to find a switch, and
they'd better return with a stout one. These whippings were infrequent,
but they were never forgotten.* And there were occasions when his
temper was scary enough that Fern stepped between him and the chil-

---

*It is perhaps easy to get the wrong idea here. The whippings were intended as
punishment; once they were administered, David carried no grudges. Nor was he a

dren. But matters rarely got that far. A tongue-lashing from David was much more the rule, and often inspired a lot more fear than the switch. When the kids stepped out of line, he would dress them down with a combination of stern judgment and piercing shame. Fern Lea remembers that David could be especially hard on Sam.

In view of this it is reasonable to ask why the kids didn't hate their father as much as they did their mother. For one thing, according to every available witness from inside or outside the family, Fern was so unyielding in her demands, so monstrous in her selfishness, and so disagreeable in her day-to-day crankiness that the sympathies of the kids, who spent much more time at home, naturally went to the forbearing father rather than to the overbearing mother. "My father went along with a lot of things my mother did that I didn't like," Fern Lea says, apparently speaking for them all, "but I never blamed him for it."[29] Then too, David's fearsome temper notwithstanding, there was his almost fabled likableness. They all have many pleasant memories of him (Sunday mornings when he cooked them all huge breakfasts were especially cherished). What is more, they were never in any doubt that he deeply loved them. About Fern they were much less sure (except for Denny, who was absolutely sure—that she didn't love him at all). But David was always there for them. It is doubtless true, as Betty Peckinpah (Denny's wife) claims, that David never understood Sam's theatrical ambitions; but despite his reservations (many and not to be minimized), when he was called upon for assistance, he supported and encouraged his son. After Sam married Marie Selland, an actress he met in college, and they moved to Los Angeles where he started directing community theater, David regularly sent the couple money to help make ends meet. So far as is known, he attached no conditions or in any way made them feel his generosity as a form of largess. The same could not be said for Fern, who once threatened to have the money stopped when she discovered alcohol in their house. For David, however, it was enough that Sam believed in what he was doing and was working very hard at it.

---

bully. He seems to have been afraid of nobody. One day a young man was trespassing on the family property, shooting at some of the animals. When David told him to leave, the young man, who was armed with a shotgun, uttered some wisecrack or other. David, who was unarmed, swelled his voice to a hair-raising volume and with the full force of his rage ordered him to get the hell off the property. The smart-aleck turned white and ran. "It scared me too," said Denny, who was at his father's side the whole time (David Weddle to P.S., 1994). There is no record of what Sam thought of the incident, but one wonders if some clue isn't to be found in the shocking scene from *Straw Dogs* where a similarly unarmed magistrate tries to wrest a shotgun from a drunken rowdy and is blasted nearly in two when the gun accidentally goes off.

"My parents could have had a wonderful marriage," Fern Lea says, "but my father treated my mother like a child, and she never grew up."[30] Outside the house David was strong, forthright, and assertive, but at home he deferred constantly to Fern, never challenging her on any subject. "He was always afraid to face her on issues," Fern Lea recalls.[31]* The reasons were several. For one thing, every time he or anyone else in the family confronted Fern with something she found unpleasant or didn't want to talk about, she got a headache and went to bed. For another, however neurotically based, Fern's illnesses were real in the sense that she suffered great pain and discomfort (the headaches especially debilitating). And though she stretched everyone's patience beyond endurance, she was also obviously deeply troubled and desperately unhappy. "I don't see why you're unhappy. You have a big house, you can go horseback riding, you have everything you need," Fern Lea remembers her father telling her mother. "Of course, Dad never really understood Mother, how lonely and lost she was, waiting for him to come home everyday. . . . He had no idea how to deal with her, couldn't see that she didn't have what she needed. And she didn't know how to help herself, except by trying to control him."[32]

But David too was controlling, and his obsession with appearances extended, not surprisingly, even to his home life. Just as he could not admit to being wrong, he could not admit that his marriage was anything less than ideal. He had in his mind a picture of what a happy home should be, which certainly did not include scenes of domestic strife or emotional and psychological problems. Mostly it seems to have consisted in a vision of order and tranquility, everyone contentedly playing his or her preordained role to great satisfaction. Fern Lea remembers one afternoon when she "was mending something and mother was occupied with something else, and DeDa looked up from his reading and said this was exactly the way he liked his life. This was the way it should be."[33] The way he tried to realize this ideal was by the simple expedient of pretending there were no problems at all.

Yet problems there surely were, and the suppression of them hurt everyone. Who of the children was damaged most it is impossible to say—each suffered in his or her own way—but the harm done to Sam was almost certainly the most visible in later life. If the family trace

*When the husband tells the wife in the "Mrs. Kennedy" episode from *The Westerner*, "I am sick of your whining, I am sick of your feeling sorry for yourself," he is expressing sentiments the children felt about their mother at one time or another and in language they all wished their father would have used directly to her.

his creativity to Fern, then no less do they feel he inherited her ma-
nipulativeness. For all her neurasthenia, she was an extraordinarily
strong woman, but in a passive mode. "Lord, what a power of will!"
Peckinpah once exclaimed. "If she did not want the sun to rise tomorrow, it would not rise."[34] Her strength in this regard was colos-
sal, as her son's would later be. Reaping all the guilt she could from
her fragility and dependency, she usually got her way around the
house and her demands rarely went unmet. If she decided to take
her rest in the living room, the shades were drawn and everyone was
required to tiptoe around her. When the Republican party wanted
David to run for a seat in the 1952 congressional race, which most
observers were certain he would easily have won, Fern absolutely
forbade it, threatening to leave him. Despite a personal phone call
from Dwight Eisenhower, David bent to his wife's wishes. Not long
afterward he suffered his first heart attack.

Seven years later he was offered a judgeship on the Superior Court
of Madera County. Again Fern threatened to leave and again David
told her he would decline. But this time he accepted the position and
never told her. The day the appointment was announced, he didn't
bring the newspaper home. But she heard the news from a friend and
was crushed, going right back in her mind to that time decades earlier when she discovered her father had lied to her.* Months later
when the appointment ran out, David had to decide whether to campaign for the judgeship. He told his wife he wouldn't; but he did, and
once more she found out from others.

Fern threatened divorce, but she never followed through. For the
first time, however, David's rage burst through his self-control and was
turned directly upon his wife. In language and a tone he would have
thrashed the children for using, he accused her of being selfish,
morbid, mean-spirited, and ungrateful. In response, her ailments got
worse and she went nearly to pieces: "after the bitter talk," she wrote
in her diary, "I went down on the creek alone and had hysteria worse
than ever in my life. I could not stop screaming and crying for oh
so, so long."[35] In truth they were both pretty close to the end of their

---

*According to Fern Lea, her mother detested lies, and little wonder, she had to
endure so much of it from some of the most important men in her life (Fern Lea
Peter to P.S., 1994). But in view of how difficult she was to please as a wife and mother and how continuously she demanded it, if she was not a cause of many of the lies
in her later life, then she was at least a full partner in the dynamic that produced them.
Here was a double-bind that must have particularly galled the teenaged Sam: in order to placate his mother, he made promises to her—about drinking and swearing—
that both of them surely must have known he would inevitably, invariably break.

tethers. With the anger now in the open, the house was charged with such hostility and bitterness that they could hardly stand to be in each other's presence. When home David spent much of his time alone in a small cabin he had built in the back of the property as a sort of study and retreat, complete with a fireplace. But he didn't spend much time at home those days. As a requirement for the judgeship was residency in Madera County, he had already rented a small apartment there, and he commuted to and from Fresno. He easily won the campaign and threw himself into his work with renewed vigor, continuing that way until his heart gave out once more. Within a week of the second attack he was dead.

Sam took an especially hard attitude toward his father's death and lost opportunities, and he focused it all on his mother. He often said she killed his father by way of the constant stresses to which she subjected him and the way she made him subvert his own dreams for her; for that matter, David himself accused her of virtually causing his first heart attack. Sam's behavior had an immediate explanation. To start with, still unable to accept that her husband actually had a life outside the house, Fern wanted information about the funeral withheld. Though her wishes were overridden—the community closed the courts while three thousand persons turned out to pay their respects—Sam remained bitter his whole life about what she tried to do. As if that weren't enough, in an act of denial breathtaking even by the standards of what prevailed between this couple, Fern wanted an autopsy performed because she believed that David's heart attack years earlier "had done something to his brain and that's why he took the judgeship and had done all these things that she didn't want."[36]

But more important, perhaps, than either of these is that in the year or so before David's death, Sam felt closer to his father than ever before. Deep in preparation on *The Westerner,* he had turned to David for story ideas. They talked and corresponded extensively about people David had known from the old days and local history that showed promise for scripts, which Sam was already writing up as treatments for the second half of the season.[37] Although he still called him "the Boss" and began letters "Dear Judge," Sam believed he was finally getting the relationship he had wanted his whole life with his father. One of his last letters to his father closes, "Let's hold tight to our agreement to meet much, much more often. All my love."[38] This was written a little over two months before the judge died. David saw only one of his son's films, an episode of *The Westerner* at a screening for the NBC censors. "After it was all over," Peckinpah remembered, "the

Boss came up to me and said, 'A little rough, but—.' And he gave me a nod and a smile, and I knew that I had made it."[39]

Sam's anger toward his mother had in fact been building for quite a long time. Years earlier when Denver Church died, his ranch, the old Dunlap spread and the boys' summer home, was left to Fern, who sold it in a hurry, though she knew that her sons wanted it and were trying to raise the money to buy it. According to Weddle, she said the place carried too many painful memories for her to keep it. But the children suspected some kind of vengeance toward her father for betraying her years earlier and toward Denny, "whom she viewed, with increasing distrust and animosity, as an ally with David against her and as a rival who had usurped her position as her father's favorite."[40] If this was so—and the evidence supports it—then an original wrong became in the repetition a baneful pattern as once again a child for whose supposed good a parent committed a wrong in the first place became the child most harmed by it in the last: Sam took the transgression personally and, like his mother, never forgave the offending parent.

But this only fueled resentments that had begun to burn much, much earlier. Fern was fiercely possessive of Sam from his infancy. He was not only her favorite, he was also her companion and perhaps even a kind of shield against her husband and an intimacy she both desired and held at bay. As the boy grew older and wanted to spend more time with his friends and with the men of the family, she became more and more depressed and her possessiveness grew fiercer. It was doubtless this that formed the basis of the animosity he began to develop toward her. Becoming a man in the hypermasculine world of David Peckinpah and Denver Church was hard enough, but being a mama's boy made it a whole lot harder than it had to be. Sam loved his brother, who was nine years his senior. But he idolized his father and worshipped his grandfather, and was forever trying to win their approval. This could be purchased only on their terms, which, as his sister has already indicated, often required that Sam suppress or otherwise split off much of what came naturally to him. Expressions of feelings, displays of emotion, signs of sensitivity—these were all weaknesses to Old Denver, who met them with shame and sarcasm. Yet "sensitivity" is the single most recurring adjective in recollections by friends and family of Sam as a boy and a young man: *unusually* sensitive, to be more precise, and introspective, with a tendency toward solitude, and projecting an almost worrisome vulnerability. "There's something about the little fellow," his father once fretted, "that makes you want to protect him from the world."[41] (Peckinpah never lost this quality, which was one of the things that kept people so loyal to and protective of him throughout his life, however cruel he was to them.) He loved to read and spend time alone in his room thinking, drawing, experimenting with his chemistry set, or just getting lost in his imagination reliving his favorite stories. Old Denver had little patience for any of this, and he criticized his grandson mercilessly for the time he spent indoors.

The great outdoors was absolutely serious business for the Peckinpahs and the Churches. The boys were expected to master the skills of roping and riding on the ranch and of hunting, fishing, and tracking. They also had to know the lore necessary to keep them from getting lost in the wilderness or to find their way back out if they did. In all of this Denver put them to the test with a passion that was almost tribal. Sam grew up with a healthy respect for firearms and a reverence for all things wild, what his grandfather called "God's bounty." Not long after he first started fishing, Sam returned home with about a dozen trout he had caught and proudly displayed them before his grandfather. "Well, I hope you like to eat them," Old Denver said; he cooked them up and made the boy eat every one of them.[42] Sam never forgot the lesson: you hunt and fish for food, not sport, and you don't kill more than you and your family can eat. Peckinpah always prided himself on shooting game chastely and responsibly, honoring all the ancient rules and rituals of the hunt. When he told Garner Simmons about his third deer, the words could almost have come from the pages of Faulkner's "The Bear":

It was snowing. I was walking. I snuck around a tamarack and shot him in the neck. When I circled round to where he was, he was hanging half over the edge but still alive. As I approached him he watched me with this mixture of fear and resignation, and I wanted to say "I'm sorry" because I really didn't mean to kill him. I got caught up in the chase. But there was nothing I could do except pull his hindquarters away from the edge and put a bullet through his head to end his suffering. When that was done, I knelt beside the carcass in the snow to gut it and found myself unable to control my tears. I had such incredible communication with that animal. I would have done anything to see him run again. But when you're really hunting there is a relationship between a man and what he kills to eat that is absolutely locked. It's hard to explain to people who think that meat comes from their local grocery store or to these cats who come out and shoot anything that moves for trophies. But I cried for that deer with more anguish than at any other time in my life.

For all of his mother's influence, experiences like this suggest that the men in the family also made substantial contributions of their own to Sam's creativity. When the boy first started going out alone, his grandfather would constantly question him about where he had been and what he had seen. "He made me tell him all these things," Peckinpah said, "because when you were hunting all by yourself in the high country that was the difference between making it back to camp and starving in the woods." But it also sharpened his powers of observation and developed in him an unblinking concentration, and both are everywhere visible in his films. In view of the constantly shifting and colliding perspectives that make up an important aspect of his editing style, there is one thing his grandfather showed him that he must have learned until it became second nature: "Do you realize that with every step you take your perspective changes?" Peckinpah told his brother-in-law, Walter Peter: "You take one step, you look, you take another step and your point of view changes."[43]

Yet valuable as all this obviously was, there was a curious side to the kind of masculinity embodied in the grandfather and to a lesser extent the father that seemed to forswear pleasure and to resent any enjoyment the boys might take or, worse, *express* in these activities. One reason is easily found: Denver and even David too were both old enough to remember the days when hunting and fishing, and farming and ranching, really did determine what and whether you ate. But they surely pushed it all too far. "DeDa never wanted anything bad to happen to us," Fern Lea says.[44] But his concerns were sometimes manifested in ways scarcely less unfeeling than his father-in-law's. When Sam entered high school and his keen interest in girls really began to show, David made him sit through the trial of a seventeen-year-old boy charged with statutory rape. When Peckinpah recalled this experience in interviews—which he did often—he liked to make it sound as if it did him a lot of good (doubtless echoing his father). But friends from the time tell a different story. "That hit him really bad. He had nightmares," one of them remembers. "He was a very sensitive boy."[45] Evidently even David's friends thought it was a pretty questionable thing to put a teenager through.

These were also the years when Sam joined the high school drama club and tried his hand at acting. There is no record of the effect upon Old Denver of seeing his grandson come home from rehearsals with makeup still on his face, but it confused David (who thought the debating team more appropriate for a son he imagined becoming another lawyer). But by this time Sam had long since proved himself a good enough cowhand and an excellent tracker and hunter, so there could be no concern about his "manliness"; and though he was neither tall nor brawny—instead, of medium height, lean, wiry, and scrappy—he had got himself into enough fistfights that physical cowardice was never an issue. His grandfather learned this *very* early: a notorious teaser, he was one day hassling the three-year-old Sam so mercilessly that the boy "grabbed up a pitchfork—which he could hardly handle because he was so small—and took off after Denver and ran him around the pile of pine needles and eventually treed him."[46]

Stories like this are in and of themselves amusing enough; but when we consider their effect upon the development of a personality as sensitive as Peckinpah's, they become sobering and disturbing. "For me, the tragedy of Sam was that he spent his life trying to find acceptance from that family," says Betty Peckinpah. "The macho posturing" "wasn't Sam. It was, but it wasn't. That was him trying to win approval from his family. He spent his life trying to do that and it tore him apart inside. He never did get acceptance. It made him one of the saddest people I ever knew."[47] It also made him one of the most complex, conflicted, and volatile personalities that ever directed film. For he was as drawn to the outdoors as he was to reading and writing. He loved to hunt and fish, ride and work the ranch. A different family might have celebrated the range of his enthusiasms. But in his family there was no one from whom he could find a wholehearted support and encouragement for the full spectrum of the things he liked to do. If his mother's love was suffocating and his father's was sometimes tough to the point of vengeance, neither's was even remotely close to unconditional. No matter what he did, some figure of love and authority in the family was sure to ridicule or otherwise find fault with it. He became divided not just down the middle but every which way, within and against himself—divisions the boy and later the man never managed to integrate into a single whole personality that could ever find peace with itself. Before long what Emerson said of Thoreau could also be applied to Peckinpah: he did not feel himself except in opposition. This is not completely true, but it is true enough that we don't have to look much further to account for all those polarities, antitheses, ironies, and ambivalences that tear his films apart.

It also helps to explain a lot of the outrageous behavior by which he made himself notorious once he became a celebrity. The drinking, the sexual profligacy (including prostitutes), the personal gaucheries in interviews and other public appearances, the temper tantrums, worse drinking, the fights, the knife throwing, the drugs—all this and more obviously answered many needs. But one of the most pressing was surely a deep-seated rebelliousness that such behavior could at once nourish and direct toward both parents. And what was all the reckless waving around and shooting off of handguns on the sets, in his trailer, in his hacienda, wherever, about if not in one respect a flip of the finger to his father and his grandfather and everything they had taught him about firearm safety? Even the drinking seems as much a rebellion against them as against his mother, for David rarely drank and never to excess, and Old Denver never drank at all. With all his anger, it is impossible to imagine that Peckinpah did not at some level resent his father, and perhaps his grandfather too, for abandoning him all his early years to his mother.

As Peckinpah grew older he vilified his mother more and more in private at the same time as he idealized his father more and more in public. Some would argue that he had already begun the process of sanctification in *Ride the High Country*, but they would be wrong: Steve Judd's heroism is solidly realized in a genuine human being of recognizable faults, infirmities, and even some comic aspects as well as great strength of character and virtue. But in life Sam eventually washed the memory of his father clean of every flaw, defect, and shortcoming until he emerged a figure of towering strength, high moral rectitude, and absolute though benevolent authority, boundless in his encouragement, generosity, and love. It was a make-believe father, seen with a child's desperate need for an unblemished hero and a lack of complexity that Peckinpah would never have countenanced in his films (and to which of course his films continually give the lie: "We represent the *law*!" shouts the domineering railroad boss in the *The Wild Bunch*; "How does it feel to be so goddamn right?" shouts the reluctant leader of his posse right back). Sometimes Peckinpah himself couldn't even sustain the fiction. He was in his forties—well over a decade had passed since his father's death—when a close friend, Camille Fielding (the wife of the composer Jerry Fielding), became lyrical about how wonderful his childhood must have been growing up in the high country. "No it wasn't," Peckinpah retorted, almost savagely. "He was so sad, talking about being a little boy, learning to ride," Mrs. Fielding recalls. "You couldn't fall down and be hurt, you had to get up and go on. Not like any childhood I knew. You fell down and wanted to cry and your dad wouldn't let you. Hit you if you cried. It's a nightmare thing, and I heard this coming out of him. It hurts when you fall off a horse and nobody gets up to help you. 'Get back on!' A little kid. Not to be able to cry, to show pain. I think a lot of his rage stems from that."[48]

James Hamilton, who did a revision of the *Cross of Iron* screenplay and got to know the family quite well, arrived at much the same conclusion after writing a biographical sketch of Denver Peckinpah.[49] In the course of his research Hamilton quickly found himself up against "lines you didn't cross; and the father seemed even then a sacrosanct figure."[50] He came away from the experience seriously questioning whether the kind of authority David Peckinpah represented was "truly benevolent, morally constructive, or loving in the best sense." Referring to the famous line near the beginning of *The Wild Bunch*—"It's not what you meant to do, it's what you did I don't like"—Hamilton said he'd wager "a thousand bucks those words come straight from the father, and that the sons had heard them more than once. There's a lacerating quality about that sort of cruelty, and . . . the ensuing wounds from such unforgiveness played a huge part in Sam's life as an artist and man."

Peckinpah was never able to heal those wounds. He never found the resources to mediate the conflicting demands of his father and his mother, which is to say his own masculine and feminine selves (except in his films, where the resolutions are always unstable and fleeting). But as much as David and Fern stood in opposition to one another, the lines separating them were far from clear cut and often blurred entirely. His father was strong except for always giving in to his wife; his mother was sickly but in her passivity absolutely unmovable; his grandfather taught him much that was valuable, but with a mean and biting sarcasm. His father studied the Bible as literature and his mother treated it as scripture; both strains were passed on to him. The father was all about law and duty; so was Fern, only it came out as piety and moralism; both were driven into him. The grandfather, the father, and the older brother were all real men's men, cowboys and hunters (and lawyers and judges). But what is less well known is that Louise Church was an excellent shot and an expert rider, and her daughter was at least an accomplished shot and a good rider. (In a rare light-hearted recollection of his mother, Sam said, "On her wedding day she and my dad received a leg of lamb and seven dollars, but what she really wanted was a saddle.")[51] Their resulting legacies were thus all mixed up, complicated, and confused, and they would do the same to a boy as sensitive as this one was.

"My parents had a strange relationship," Peckinpah once said. "They were very much in love, very much, but boy did they eat on each other psychologically."[52] Theirs was, he concluded, "a sad story," which is exactly how many friends and relatives describe Sam's own story. It is difficult to escape the feeling that long after his par-

Left to right: Denver Church; Billy Walker (a family friend, part Indian); and David Peckinpah with his sons, Denny (age thirteen or fourteen) and Sam (age four or five), holding the rifle (circa 1929).

My father, David E. Peckinpah, my grandfather, Denver Church, and my brother, Denver C. Peckinpah, [were] all Superior Court judges. When I was a kid I grew up with all those people sitting . . . around a dining room table talking about law and order, truth and justice, on a Bible which was very big in our family. I suppose I felt like an outsider, and I started to question them. I guess I'm still questioning them.

—Sam Peckinpah

ents died they continued to eat on each other as introjects in the heart and mind of their talented son. Just about the only constructive resources Peckinpah ever found to deal with his inner struggles consisted in his films and filmmaking, which, lord knows, brought him little release and less respite. But art cannot resolve the conflicts it pulls together and concentrates, much less untangle the problems to which it alludes; it simply reveals them with a clarity otherwise unavailable. It was with his mother's rifle, a .32 Winchester carbine, that Sam, age sixteen, killed his first deer. In the context of how large a role guns, shooting, and violence—especially toward figures of authority—play in his films, this is a symbol fairly rich, indeed almost comic, with irony. It will be recalled that Peckinpah provided Dave Blassingame, the first westerner wholly of his own creation, with a specially modified Winchester rifle and that among the people he modeled the character on were his father and himself. (Dick Powell even wanted *The Westerner* to be called *Winchester,* but the title was already owned by another company.) Guns continued to proliferate in the household long after the men were gone. Garner Simmons is the last writer on Peckinpah to have interviewed Fern. He visited her in 1973, ten years before she died. Denny's wife, Betty, drove him to the house, where Fern greeted them at the gate, toting the same .32 Winchester, which she also carried, neighbors reported, walking the perimeter of her property at two o'clock in the morning.

IV

When Melnick asked if Peckinpah had experience in three-camera video production, the director replied that he did but was vague about it. What he had in mind was the film he made for his master's thesis, which was a production of Tennessee Williams's one-act *Portrait of a Madonna.* The play was rehearsed, staged, then filmed at a local television station. As the station was donating its facilities after hours, time was of the essence and the play had to be shot in a single, uninterrupted performance. The result is a rather crude-looking 16mm kinescope (that looks cruder still on tape) of a good, perceptive production. Once allowances are made for the schedule and what appears to be a faulty switcher that often flashed when going from one angle to another, the camerawork is about as accomplished as what was to be found in all but the best of live television circa 1953, when this production was mounted. In other words, Peckinpah wasn't just gilding an unusually modest lily when he told Melnick he knew how to work with three cameras. Where his inexperience showed most was in his failure to scale back the theatricality of the performances. Gestures, expressions, and readings that would be perfectly acceptable, even nuanced, on stage were often just too big for the proximity of the cameras. It is a mistake he would not make again.

But the main interest in this early effort is not the technique or the style but the story and the title character and what they meant to him. Peckinpah once made a statement to the effect that he guessed he had learned more from Tennessee Williams than from anyone else: "I think I learned more about writing from having to cut *Menagerie* than anything I've done since."[53] He was referring to his senior project, which required that he trim the play to an hour's length. His feeling for Williams's work goes much deeper than that, however. Peckinpah eventually directed *The Glass Menagerie* at least three more times on stage, and those who knew him well were aware of how closely he identified with Tom Wingfield, whose domineering mother, Amanda, drives him from home, abandoning his sister to the mother's care. (Susan, the younger sister and never as close to Sam as Fern Lea was, remained at home with Fern long after the others had left.) But though Tom has escaped bodily, he will never be free psychologically; and he will always carry the burden of his guilt, his helplessness, and his love with him the rest of his life. It is reported that in these productions Peckinpah made Amanda Wingfield an usually hard, strong, and powerful woman.

If *The Glass Menagerie* allowed Peckinpah to depict his mother at her most baleful and overbearing, then *Portrait of a Madonna* became for him a way of understanding how she got that way, and why. In the analytical portion of his thesis, he describes the heroine, Lucretia Collins, as a Southern spinster who

> has been creating a disturbance in the apartment hotel of a Northern city. A virtual recluse, she has lately been imagining that a man has entered her room and raped her. This imaginary visitor is an old beau who twenty years ago turned to a prettier and evidently more physical type of woman. Although Lucretia protests these visits and calls for the police, she attempts to protect her illusion when it is threatened. Her deeply religious and extremely inhibited upbringing force her to subordinate and repress all physical desires. She looks upon these natural desires as unclean.
>
> The effect of this repression shows in the form which her illusionary love affair takes. It is wrong, and therefore she must not: but as a victim of assault she is helpless, and blameless. Therefore, she can take part in this subconsciously desired love affair.
>
> It is within Lucretia Collins's illusion that the crisis of the play

comes. She dreams of having a baby by her phantom lover, and for this imaginary child she makes the most important decision of her life. Her child will not grow up in the domineering shadow of a church whose moral dictum smothers the individual, and then lets the individual be exposed to the pitiless glare of society. The climax of the play is the arrival of the representatives of the state asylum.[54]

Fern Peckinpah had also spent far too many solitary hours languishing in her room. And she had her own version both of a long lost lover and of an oppressive society in the most important men of her life, Denver, David, and Denny. (Sam, of course, was still special.) Peckinpah knew all of this when he made *Portrait*. What he could not know—and what gives this early film an eerie prescience that raises goose flesh—is that his mother's mind would eventually slide into dementia and, like Lucretia, she would spend her remaining years (seven were left) in an institution, hardly aware of her surroundings. "The enforced confinement in an institution," her son concluded almost thirty years earlier in his analysis of the play, "will complete the destruction . . . begun so long before by her parents and her church."[55]

The Bible that was so big in the Peckinpah household says that the sins of the fathers will be visited upon the sons. Modern therapy puts it a little differently: if you do not work it out, you will act it out. However it is stated, few families can have illustrated the underlying principle more thoroughly, even tragically, than the Peckinpahs and the Churches. Almost nothing that was going on emotionally or psychologically was ever mentioned, let alone talked about. Feelings were carefully placed in compartments and the lids were tightly fastened. The bad stuff got out anyway, of course, and things became messy all the same—messier, really. "Everything I do comes out in anger," Peckinpah liked to say. But it is a supreme irony that in a family where there was so much unvoiced antagonism, almost no one really knew how to be angry, let alone how to express it constructively or beneficially, least of all, it would seem, Sam himself. Like his father before him, Peckinpah never confronted his mother. He would frequently vent his hatred, bragging that he would piss on her grave, but only to others and far away from home. However infrequent the visits became as time passed, one thing never changed: the pattern set in childhood, stronger than any stone. No matter who accompanied him (usually his latest wife or girlfriend) or how much he inveighed against his mother on the way, when he arrived at the house he would give her a big hug and they would disappear into her room where they would talk their private talks. A little while later he would emerge quiet and subdued. It was not until he and his companion were well on the road back to Los Angeles that he would begin to rail against his mother all over again. Weddle has drawn a chilling picture of the last visit shortly before Fern died.

> They found her lashed in a chair so she could sit upright, her once-thick curls of brown hair shorn to a white stubble, her skin pale and slack, eyes glassy as she babbled incoherently. Fern Lea couldn't handle it; she turned and fled the room in tears. But Sam sat there calmly beside his mother, nodding his head as if he understood her every word, murmuring in response. "Yes, Mother, of course. I know you do . . ." Like their heart-to-heart talks of the old days. To the very end, in her presence, he played the dutiful and attentive son and kept his anger locked out of sight.[56]

Thus does Peckinpah's television work, which climaxes with *Noon Wine*, end in its beginning: with a short film about his mother.*

In the way of a generalization that is intended to be suggestive rather than definitive, it can be said that in his television films Peckinpah dealt much more centrally with women than he did in his features beginning with *Ride the High Country*. In some of them women are important, even main characters; but, excepting only *Straw Dogs* and perhaps *The Getaway*, they are always players in the men's stories. From this perspective *Noon Wine* is a watershed, and it marks the end of something. Given the intensity of his antipathy toward his mother, it is to his credit that Ellie Thompson emerges as a complex and sympathetic character, and that her last closeup is at once ambiguous and devastating. But at the strictly private level, *Noon Wine* is about his turning away from his mother in favor of his father, and that closeup is perhaps the single most judgmental shot in all his work. It represents his way of putting on film his belief that his mother "killed"

---

*In fact there is one more item, a show he directed almost immediately after *Noon Wine* for *Bob Hope's Chrysler Theater,* another hour-long anthology series. Televised in the spring of 1967 and titled *That Lady Is My Wife,* it is about a gambler who puts up his wife as the stake in a contest with a cowboy who wants to marry her. The contest is a pool game played on horseback in the main hall of the cowboy's baronial mansion. When the cowboy wins, the gambler refuses to give up his wife, and together they leave town on the next stage. Although a minor effort, it is marked by themes characteristic of much of the rest of Peckinpah's television work: women in the West and the limitations of masculine codes. The show is beautifully directed, the setting and the pool game in particular revealing the gothic element that creeps into his work from time to time. He also included a slow-motion shot, from a subjective point of view, of the gambler jumping a horse over an obstacle.

his father through her constant demands, her pressures, her threats and ultimatums, and the sheer drain on his energy and stamina. Peckinpah's was doubtless a simplistic assessment (though a surprising number of people who knew the couple concur in it, including just about the whole rest of the family). He even admitted as much in his portrait of Thompson, who can by no means be held blameless for his misfortunes and in whom are depicted many of David Peckinpah's unattractive characteristics, such as his rage, his denial, his buried violence, and his obsession with appearances. But all the same, as a man Peckinpah never forgave his mother, though it tormented him the rest of his life because he loved her and he hated her.

Fern did not miss the point. Though she liked virtually everything her son did that she saw—even *Straw Dogs*, which annoyed him no end—she never liked *Noon Wine*, ever.[57] Of course, like Tom Wingfield, Peckinpah was never free from his mother's influence, and not even remotely was he ever completely happy in the world of men, as his films grimly testify. But by affording him the opportunity to resolve, however temporarily, a lot of conflicted feelings that he had been struggling with for a long time, *Noon Wine* freed him for what would be, after a couple of false starts on other projects, his next film: a spectacular celebration of male mythology and one of the richest, most complex, disturbing, and passionate epics about men and violence ever put on film. And this time he would not be unprepared.

I wasn't trying to make an epic, I was trying to tell a simple story about bad men in changing times. *The Wild Bunch* is simply what happens when killers go to Mexico. The strange thing is that you feel a great sense of loss when these killers reach the end of the line.

—Sam Peckinpah

5

Men without Women: *The Wild Bunch* as Epic

There is nothing more futile under the sun than a mere adventurer. He might have loved at one time—which would have been a saving grace. I mean loved adventure for itself. But if so, he was bound to lose this grace very soon. Adventure by itself is but a phantom, a dubious shape without a heart.

—Joseph Conrad

I

"I read the screenplay of *The Wild Bunch*," Robert Culp wrote in 1970, "on a gray, empty morning two years ago in Peckinpah's home on the beach above Malibu. I groaned with each foolish page, to think he had to go and do this nonsense for all those bleak months in Mexico."[1] When he saw the completed film, Culp radically reversed his judgment in one of the most intelligent and perceptive essays ever written on *The Wild Bunch*. But the actor was not alone in failing to see the possibilities in the script that Peckinpah did. The original story was by Roy Sickner, a stuntman, who conceived it as a star vehicle for Lee Marvin. Sickner commissioned a screenplay from Walon Green, a documentary filmmaker eager to break into features. Marvin tested Peckinpah by giving him the Green-Sickner "outline of some thirty-two pages."[2] His interest piqued, the director read the screenplay and found it an excellent start. Retaining Green's overall structure and the broad outlines of Sickner's story, he did a substantial dialogue rewrite; changed, deleted, and added scenes; and, most important, invented a crucial back story in the form of what would become several contentious flashbacks. In the meantime Marvin lost interest, while still more of the director's friends wondered why he was making another Western, and one so apparently hackneyed.

In fact *The Wild Bunch* was not the first project Peckinpah turned to when he was called by Warner Brothers. Hyman had a property of his own—*The Diamond Story,* to which a producer, Phil Feldman, was already attached—and the director himself had at least two other projects. Sometime in 1967 Warren Oates had shown him an original script by John Crawford and Edmund Penney titled *The Ballad of Cable Hogue,* which Peckinpah liked so much he purchased it, started revising, and thought about casting. He was also talking about directing James Gould Cozzens's *The Castaway,* a script for which he had already prepared. When casting problems forced *The Diamond Story* to be postponed indefinitely (and eventually abandoned altogether), Feldman sent the script of *The Wild Bunch* to Hyman, who liked what he read and gave it a green light.

Once Warners committed to the project, Peckinpah's involvement was total. In addition to the extensive work he had already done on the script, he personally supervised every aspect of production from casting to cinematography to special effects to art direction and wardrobe. By the conservative estimate of several crew members, he worked fifteen to eighteen hours a day and cared about only one thing: what was "going to be finally realized on the screen."[3] One of the reasons he worked this hard is that he wanted to be as absolutely free from studio interference as possible while shooting the picture. To this end he had his editor, Lou Lombardo, polish a few self-contained sequences, figuring the studio would want to see some cut footage. According to his assistant, Joel Reisner, Peckinpah "outguessed the studio. They did ask to see film and the ten reels they saw were the ten reels Peckinpah wanted them to see." The director was as a consequence left unbothered during production and editing. It wasn't until after the picture opened that the betrayal came. The upshot was that within the first month of its release there were three different "official" versions of *The Wild Bunch*—one European, two domestic—and any of several individual prints that were different from any other mostly because of haste and carelessness.

The first filmgoers to see *The Wild Bunch* were an audience in Kansas City where the film was sneak-previewed on 1 May 1969 at a length of about 151 minutes.* It was this version that started the controversy about the violence: over thirty persons walked out, one or two ac-

---

*The figure has often been reported erroneously (in, among other places, the first publication of this book) as 190 minutes. That was, in fact, the length of the *first* cut of the film—finished shortly after completion of principal photography, before any fine cutting had begun—obviously much too long and, like all first cuts, in a form that nobody, the director most of all, would ever release. (In one of the bigger ironies of the history of this troubled film, several commentators have called for the release of this 190–minute version, on the mistaken assumption that it represents the director's final thoughts. Nothing could be further from the truth.)

tually became physically ill in the alley outside the theater, and there was almost a riot. Peckinpah returned to Hollywood to resume work on the editing. He deleted several repetitive scenes and in general tightened the narrative line. "I had to make the film play better," he said.[4] He also excised several moments of violence, despite the studio's wish for more rather than less bloodshed. As Feldman has pointed out, "Some people have accused Sam of wanting to make it more bloody. Actually he toned down the violence that I wanted, especially in the first fight."[5]

Peckinpah's reasons were several. He felt that some of the violence was "excessive to the points I wanted to make," and he didn't "want the violence, per se, to dominate what is happening to the people," adding, "I have a story to tell, too."[6] He also wanted the violence to enter and accumulate more gradually, to which end he heightened the contrast between the opening and closing gunfights. The point of view in the opening gunfight, an ambush of the Bunch by a posse of bounty hunters and railroad men, is generally that of innocent bystanders caught in a crossfire that suddenly erupts through the fabric of everyday life in a quiet Texas border town. The violence is more elliptical and oblique. The point of view in the closing gunfight is generally that of the Bunch themselves, who in returning for a friend are making a last-ditch grab for glory. The carnage is far more explicit, escalating past horror into a kind of feral exultation.

But there can be little doubt that the response of that preview audience influenced Peckinpah's thinking seriously, and that he came away having learned something about the dynamics of film violence. "If I'm so bloody that I drive people out of the theater," he remarked after he had made *Straw Dogs,* "then I've failed."[7] It is after all easy enough to disgust people (as Godard demonstrated in *Weekend* by having a pig's throat slit on screen). But the real artistic achievement consists in treading that thin line between meaningful excess and mere exploitation, and the first problem in winning an audience's assent to a vision in which violence is part of the very essence is to get people to watch the film. We don't look away, and therein consists equally Peckinpah's argument and his achievement.

Peckinpah's final cut ran 145 minutes. Around this time there arose a disagreement as to how to market the film. According to the director, "The European distributor saw it and said, 'Roadshow.' The domestic distributor saw it and said 'Double-bill,'"—meaning second-run theaters and the drive-in circuit, paired with another film, preferably a Western—and also wanted it shorter.[8] As a conciliatory gesture Peckinpah agreed to remove one flashback from the domestic version only; in return the studio supported him and made *The Wild Bunch* its feature summer attraction. In Europe meanwhile the film received the full prestige treatment with limited bookings, hard-ticket sales, intermission (complete with *entr'acte* music), and prints in 70mm CinemaScope with six-track stereophonic sound. In America it was shown in 35mm Panavision (both versions are widescreen).[9] In either case *The Wild Bunch* was previewed to critics and shown to audiences in a form that Peckinpah was happy to pronounce himself 94 to 96 percent satisfied with.[10]

From here on the tale becomes rather byzantine. If filmgoers had gone to see *The Wild Bunch* in America in early July 1969, they would have seen a 143-minute film; in mid-July, they would have seen a 135-minute film, as Vincent Canby of the *New York Times* discovered when he went to see the film a second time. The missing footage, which will be described in detail later on, consists principally of flashbacks that fill in the past of the Bunch's leader, Pike Bishop, and an attack by Villa's rebels on the army of Mapache. Canby immediately telephoned Feldman, who said that the studio had been contemplating the cuts for a good while and would have made them before the premiere, had there been time.* If this had been done, Feldman argued with curious reasoning, Canby would not have been bothered by the missing scenes because he would never have seen them in the first place. This was hardly the issue, which concerned the director's wishes and the artistic integrity of the film. Feldman was misleading as regards the one and simply wrong as regards the other. Many filmgoers and critics who saw only the short version *were* bothered even if they could not articulate precisely what was wrong, citing instead superficial characters with unclear or insufficient motivation. Assuring Canby that the cuts had been made with the good of the film in mind, Feldman said that filmmaking is a cooperative enterprise and strongly implied that the cuts were carried out with Peckinpah's full awareness and approval.

Here are Peckinpah's comments on the subject: "I do not agree with that in any way, shape, or form"; "all I can say is that these cuts are a

---

*Since Feldman is one of the two chief protagonists at this point in the history of *The Wild Bunch,* it should be noted that he either never answered or summarily refused repeated requests for an interview. When at last he agreed to talk, it was only to say that he deemed "Mr. Peckinpah and that whole period in my life as being too unimportant to comment upon" and that he stood behind every decision he made as producer of the film (Phil Feldman to P.S., 1977). Shortly before his death in 1991 Feldman told David Weddle that he considered *The Wild Bunch* unquestionably the best film of his career (David Weddle to P.S., 1992).

disaster."[11] Canby wasn't aware of Peckinpah's feelings at the time, for when he tried to verify Feldman's statements he discovered that the director, exhausted from having made two films back-to-back, was in Hawaii for a short period of rest and recuperation and could not be reached by telephone. Feldman was, however, in constant touch with Peckinpah by phone or memo and had told him that he wanted to remove two of the flashbacks as an experiment in a couple of theaters. "I okayed it," Peckinpah later said, "on an experimental basis in two theaters *only*." What happened instead, and the next thing he knew, was that two whole scenes and parts of four other scenes had been removed from prints in some three hundred theaters.

Feldman has been made to shoulder much of the blame for the post-release cuts in *The Wild Bunch*, but any of several memos indicate that he was in fact working very hard to protect the film and to persuade the studio to let it find its audience. From the beginning he and Peckinpah wanted the same marketing strategy Warners had used on *Bonnie and Clyde* the year before: few theaters, select cities, letting the word of mouth build, then widening the release after several weeks. Instead, having decided to make the film its feature attraction for the summer, the studio proceeded to launch it out the back door.

An expensive summer Western with big Hollywood stars, *The Wild Bunch* was marketed according to the standard strategy used for John Wayne pictures: it was first opened in about twenty theaters in Texas during June. Given the richness, depth, and complexity of Peckinpah's vision, the returns in this market were terrible, to no one's surprise but that of the studio executives, who immediately panicked and demanded a shorter picture with a wider release. By July the film was playing in over three hundred theaters across the country, a small figure by 1990s standards, but very large in 1969, much too large in those days for the initial release of a prestige film. What happened next was almost predictable. With the film in so many theaters, yet without benefit of adequate word of mouth, ticket sales per theater were relatively low. This did lead some exhibitors, as Feldman told Canby, to ask that the film be shortened, not to "accelerate the pace" or "improve the aesthetics" but simply to generate more box office and concession-stand sales by squeezing in another showing each day.

It seems clear in retrospect that the director and the producer understood how their picture should be marketed much better than the studio did. *The Wild Bunch* became the most talked about, commented upon, and argued over film of the summer (in fact, of the year). Although predictably controversial, well over half of the first reviews were favorable, many of them quite enthusiastic and from publications that mattered, like the *New Republic,* the *New Yorker,* the *New York Times,* the *Los Angeles Times, Life,* and *Time.* Word of mouth is exactly what *The Wild Bunch* needed and exactly what it was starting to get. Though it doesn't work quickly, it *was* working, as the excellent returns in New York, Los Angeles, San Francisco, and a few other big cities were already demonstrating. Unfortunately, it wasn't working fast enough for an impatient studio desperate to take some action, any action, to bolster ticket sales.

To make matters worse, Ken Hyman, the Seven Arts half of Warner Brothers–Seven Arts, had pulled out of the partnership, leaving the film without its staunchest advocate and protector at the studio and leaving Feldman to fight on alone.* Once the new management was in place, Feldman was issued an ultimatum through channels from the office of the new studio head, Ted Ashley, ordering fifteen to twenty minutes cut from *The Wild Bunch.* It is curious that at a juncture like this the producer did not alert the director, who was still in Hawaii, as to exactly what was going on, choosing instead to withhold some things and simply lie about others. Had Peckinpah been told of the studio's plans, he could have returned, and together he and Feldman would have had a good chance of prevailing. One explanation is that in addition to feeling beleaguered, Feldman also found himself in an increasingly compromised position. It was no secret that throughout the months of editing he had argued continually for the removal of the flashbacks and a couple of other scenes. Peckinpah argued just as strongly for keeping them. Their disagreement on this matter, while professional, grew at times quite acrimonious, which may help to explain some of Feldman's actions. Suddenly he was being presented with an opportunity to do something "creative" that he sincerely believed was for the good of the film and with the justification that the studio was ordering him to do it anyway. But not, evidently, without consulting Peckinpah: Gill Dennis, at the time an American Film Institute intern working with Peckinpah, was in Feld-

---

*Hyman is the unsung hero behind the making of *The Wild Bunch.* He took a chance on Peckinpah when no one else in features would. Once shooting commenced and costs and delays began to rise, he just kept encouraging Peckinpah to move forward, even overriding Feldman's pleas to help keep the unruly director under control. Hyman, who watched the dailies religiously, saw footage of a calibre unprecedented in his experience. The last thing he wanted to do was rein this director in. Shortly before the premiere Hyman wrote Peckinpah, "Just for the record *The Wild Bunch* will wind up in history as one of the great pictures of all time. Thank you. Thank you and thank you again" (Ken Hyman to Sam Peckinpah, note, 12 June 1969).

man's office when John Calley, the head of production at Warners under Ashley, phoned and expressly told the producer *not* to cut anything without first talking to Peckinpah. Instead, the moment Feldman hung up he called Lombardo and told him the flashbacks were ordered removed.[12] Nor was Feldman alone in thinking the scenes in question problematic. The first national magazine to review *The Wild Bunch* was *Time,* which in its 20 June 1969 issue published an extraordinarily laudatory review that had just one criticism: "Peckinpah is sometimes guilty of overkill himself," wrote the reviewer (later identified as Jay Cocks). "Action sequences—like an attack by the Villa forces on Mapache—occasionally destroy the continuity of the elaborate story, and flashbacks are introduced with surprising clumsiness."*

What clinched Feldman's decision was probably a bit of professional jealousy. Once the film was released he was, perhaps understandably, resentful that all the talk was about the director, little or none about himself as producer. He went so far as to write Peckinpah a long letter complaining of how little attention the press was paying him. What he couldn't have known is that earlier in the spring, before postproduction was even completed, Peckinpah had already enthusiastically praised both Feldman and Hyman in interviews that would not see the light of publication until later that summer or fall. All the same, the director responded to the producer's letter first personally and then with a full-page ad in *Variety* thanking him and indicating in no uncertain terms his great contribution to the film.

Nor was Peckinpah merely massaging a producer's bruised ego. By any standards Feldman was here a superior producer, and he attended to postproduction with exemplary conscientiousness. During much of the editing Peckinpah was in Nevada filming *The Ballad of Cable Hogue,* while his editors were headquartered back in Los Ange-

---

*For the record, Peckinpah wrote Feldman a short letter, dated 17 July 1969, saying that Villa's attack should stay in but "I am all in favor of keeping all of the flashbacks out." It is difficult to know what to make of this, since the letter begins, "I am disturbed with the lifts from *The Wild Bunch*," and half the lifted material consists in the flashbacks. He concludes by asking, "What are your thoughts?," which suggests he was still thinking experimentally rather than definitively, and was unaware the cuts had already been implemented. (The date certainly places the letter before he could have known that most of the prints were changed or that it was even an option.) Then too he might have been trying to make the best of a situation that he felt was already slipping beyond his control. Whatever the explanation, this is the only time he ever expressed any such feeling about the flashbacks. And once he became aware of the extent of the cuts, he insisted they *all* be restored, a position from which he never wavered to the day he died.

les with Feldman. Most weekends they would take the film to Nevada, run it for the director, then return and make his changes. Memos that went back and forth between him and Feldman during this period document how much he relied on his producer and how deeply Feldman was involved in the process, how sensitive he was to the responsibilities delegated him. For example, as an experiment Peckinpah once tried ending the film simply on Thornton sitting against the wall as the desert wind kicks up the dust, eliminating the deaths of the bounty hunters and the return of Sykes. Peckinpah would never have left it that way, but all the same Feldman wrote an eloquent, impassioned plea for putting it all back. "I know when I put this in words it sounds a little maudlin and a little sentimental, etc. But this picture is a saga. It is not an incident or a plain story. It is a big and fine picture. [If we do not reunite Sykes and Thornton], which shows that people do side together, that they do stick with each other . . . then perhaps we have destroyed everything we have been talking about in this picture."[13] Feldman also lobbied hard for deleting the onscreen deaths of the bounty hunters, for which Peckinpah always gave him full credit: the producer realized, and the director soon came to agree, that no more deaths could or should follow those of Pike and Dutch. As Peckinpah always regarded Feldman as his full partner in the making of *The Wild Bunch*, the *Variety* ad also became a way of making his feelings public before the entire industry. Ironically, the ad appeared in the 14 July 1969 issue, just about the time that, unknown to Peckinpah, the last of the cuts in the last of the prints was being implemented.*

As things turned out, the decision to make the cuts was questionable in economic, logistical, and aesthetic terms. The studio had to lift six scenes in whole or in part from over three hundred prints that by then were scattered all over the country. As recalling them was impossible, the job had to be done at the various distribution centers, either with counts—i.e., beginning and ending footages of the scenes to be removed in their respective reels—or with a template

---

*It is not easy to appreciate how fragile the egos of powerful people can be. Feldman's great contribution to the film notwithstanding, one's sympathies remain a little strained, not just because of his opportunism. *The Wild Bunch* was made before the days when possessive credit above the title became a standard clause in the contracts of directors of Peckinpah's stature, which means that the first name one sees on the screen is not Peckinpah's, as in "A Sam Peckinpah Film," but Feldman's: "A Phil Feldman Production." Clearly nobody regards *The Wild Bunch* as anybody's vision but Peckinpah's; still, one wonders how much more credit a producer could possibly need than to have his and only his name above the title of one of the greatest works of film art ever made.

provided by the postproduction facility back in Los Angeles. In either case those who physically made the cuts did not even look at their work when they were finished. (Had they even been motivated, there were too many prints, not enough time.) This explains why during its initial run several "versions" of *The Wild Bunch* could be seen, including prints in which some of the scenes were removed but not others, and prints in which pieces of some scenes were removed while the rest of the scene was left untouched. And several prints, mostly those playing in small towns, were left untouched entirely. The procedure was also a sloppy way to execute the lifts, especially damaging to a film of the supreme stylistic unity and technical finish of *The Wild Bunch*. When a cut is made in a composite print (i.e., a print with an optical soundstripe), it leaves a visible tape splice on the film and an audible "pop" sometimes preceded by a dropout. As most of the transitions between scenes consist in dissolves, the effect of the cuts on the soundtrack is brutal. Still, barbaric as the whole business was, it had one unexpected benefit: the master negative was left untouched, so that when new prints were struck in subsequent years, they were of the version Peckinpah approved for domestic release.

In the end the cuts had no material effect on the film's box office. Nor did most of the exhibitors bother to rearrange their schedules to get in another showing. Many of them just added the extra time between showings to sell more refreshments, and one theater is known to have filled up the spare time with a "Tom and Jerry" cartoon.

What is so sad about this story, quite apart from any damage done to the film, is the effect upon Peckinpah himself. When he embarked upon *The Wild Bunch*, he was so happy to be making films once more that he couldn't praise Feldman and Hyman highly enough. By the time he was into postproduction, his generosity was lavish. He spoke of "the courage and wisdom of one man—Kenny Hyman" as having made it possible for him to be directing again, and he referred to Feldman as "a miracle man."[14] In the spring of 1969, he said of both of them: "They're enormously creative people, and I feel we work together very well. I respect them, and they respect me. They let me do my thing, so to speak, and whenever they can, they highlight it, and give me all the help that I could possibly need. They're damn good, they're tough, they've got good ideas. And I either have to get a better one, or I use theirs. You don't mind working with people like that; it's a delight."[15]

He couldn't have known then that the "highlighting" would take the form of surgery, and when he did know it, he tried his best to suppress his disappointment, frustration, and anger, as he remained grateful that he could get *The Wild Bunch* made at all. But he was deeply hurt that after all they had been through together, Feldman had still deceived him. What particularly galled him was a letter the producer wrote him shortly after the prints had been cut saying that if he had known Peckinpah cared so much about this material he wouldn't have let it be removed.[16] This was precisely the material they had been fighting over throughout the whole of postproduction. Finally, even Feldman himself seemed to have lacked full conviction in the cuts he had so stridently insisted upon, at least to judge from his subsequent actions: the rest of the summer and well into the fall he tried to get Warners to release the European prints in selected theaters in New York, Los Angeles, and other large domestic markets. He was not successful, but he must be credited with efforts that were substantial and sincere.

But for Peckinpah it was a case of too little, too late. As time wore on and the full extent of the damage sank in, the hurt he felt over what he believed was betrayal became anger, and the anger became a rage less and less susceptible of suppression. Once, in Feldman's presence, a reporter asked Peckinpah to detail exactly what was cut from the film. The director deferred to the producer, who "began ticking off the shots and sequences one by one. Suddenly a crash came, the dishes on the table rattled. Peckinpah had slammed his fist against the table, and he looked livid with anger. 'You mean that's out,' he squeezed out through his apoplexy. 'Yes, Sam,' Feldman said pacifyingly, 'I thought I told you!'"[17] By the spring of 1970, after Warner Brothers had withdrawn all support for *The Wild Bunch* at the Academy Awards and was planning to dump *The Ballad of Cable Hogue* on the market with no advance publicity, Peckinpah was already looking for new associates. Two years after his association with Feldman had dissolved, Peckinpah told a reporter, "I've had my share of headaches with producers. Phil Feldman was another one. I had great difficulties bringing in *The Wild Bunch*—it took eighty-one days of shooting—and then Feldman let those rotten sons of bitches at Warners chop out twenty minutes so they could hustle more popcorn."[18] Those who wish to know why Sam Peckinpah became an angry, hard-bitten, occasionally vindictive man have only to meditate upon how it happened that this film, which Robert Culp has called "more quintessentially and bitterly American than any film since World War II,"[19] could not readily be seen in America in the form in which its maker conceived it.

Over a quarter century would pass, several regimes would come and go at Warners, and Peckinpah would be dead before *The Wild*

Bunch would be shown theatrically in this country in the only version he ever fully authorized for release. This took place on 3 March 1995 when newly struck 70mm prints in stereophonic sound opened in New York, Los Angeles, and San Francisco, with other cities following a few weeks later. The response was sensational both critically and at the box office. The film was almost universally recognized as one of the great masterpieces of world cinema. But the violence continued to generate the controversy it always did and almost caused the restoration to die aborning.

How this came about is a mini-epic in itself. Warners originally planned the event for the spring of 1994 to coincide with the twenty-fifth anniversary of the film's premiere. Mistakenly believing that *new* footage had been added, the studio submitted the restoration to the Motion Picture Association of America's rating board, expecting the R—no one under seventeen admitted unless accompanied by a parent or guardian—it received in 1969. The MPAA slapped it instead with an NC-17—no one under seventeen admitted, period. In commercial terms this is tantamount to an X, which would not be problematic in itself except that Warners will not release films with ratings stronger than an R because many newspapers will not carry the advertising and the powerful Blockbuster Video chain will not rent or sell them.

The new rating stunned the industry. Many filmmakers—among them, Martin Scorsese, Ron Shelton, Oliver Stone, and Robert Harris—fired off angry protests to the MPAA chairman, Jack Valenti. Others, like Richard Donner, asked if there was anything they could do. Everybody wondered how the parents, teachers, social workers, psychologists, and others who constitute the MPAA's ratings groups could routinely give films like *Total Recall, Basic Instinct,* and the seemingly endless supply of stupid *Friday the 13th*–type slasher films R's, but give an absolutely serious film like *The Wild Bunch* an NC-17. An obvious explanation gives little consolation: like the suppression of Joyce's *Ulysses* or the bowdlerizing of D. H. Lawrence, the new rating pays a lopsided tribute to the film's enduring power.

Valenti deplored the rating, declaring himself a great admirer of the film (true) but essentially helpless to change the rating. He didn't want to set a precedent. (For what, someone wanted to know, good sense and sound judgment?) In the meantime, for the better part of a year Warners repaired the dub, adapting it to present-day formats (Dolby SR, SRD, THX, and DTS), and in general got along with the work of preparing the film for theatrical rerelease (and a widescreen-laserdisc for the home-video market). The studio also submitted it twice more to the MPAA—the bylaws of which allow a film to be submitted as many times as the studio wishes—on the chance that another group of viewers would return a more lenient rating. The second viewing brought an even stronger vote for the NC-17 than the first, the third a stronger one still. Things were at an impasse.

At this point the tale became less mini-epic than farce, and, as in farce, what everybody was mostly in need of was enlightenment and clarification. To begin with, for all their genuinely good intentions, the people at Warners who spearheaded the restoration—Barry Reardon, the president of worldwide distribution, and Peter Gardner, the vice-president of home video—did not realize that in restoring the European version of *The Wild Bunch,* no new material was being put back that had not already been seen by the MPAA and rated R in 1969. One of the bigger jokes of the whole imbroglio is thus that the film never had to be resubmitted in the first place.

Warners was eventually persuaded, but the next problem was how to convince the MPAA, which demanded hard evidence. Neither the files at Warners nor those at the MPAA were of much help. David Weddle, Peckinpah's biographer, told the studio that the best place to look might be in the director's correspondence and memos, now in the library of the Academy of Motion Picture Arts and Sciences. Leith Adams, the studio archivist, did the legwork and found it: the original certificate for R-rating, dated 15 April 1969. The implications of the date are no doubt tickling Peckinpah's vast sense of irony wherever his spirit now roams, for it means that not only was the European version rated R, but in fact the Kansas City–*preview* version—which was six minutes longer and much more violent—also had that rating.

The studio scheduled a meeting, the MPAA was convinced, and on 13 October 1994 the original R-rating was reinstated. It is reported that the overwhelming emotion was relief, from no one more so than the representatives of the MPAA itself, embarrassed by the NC-17 in the first place and desperate for any loophole to make it go away in the second.

What if the evidence had not been available or the MPAA had remained unconvinced? Let us not ask, rejoicing rather in the occasional happy ending when it comes along. This film has had enough trouble in its turbulent history. "The important thing is that we never let it drop," Reardon said, with understated though justifiable pride. "We could have, but we didn't." Or as Peckinpah himself said—he was talking about *Ride the High Country,* but his words are even more applicable to *The Wild Bunch*—"It was a delayed victory for all of us."

Thornton's capture

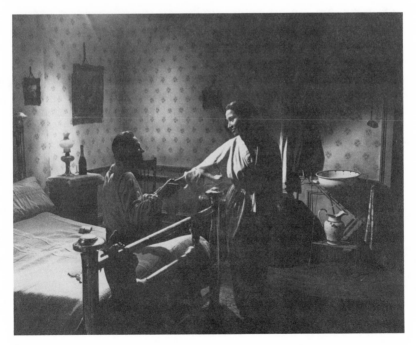

Aurora

Villa's raid

Thornton in prison

II

Arnold Schönberg once warned opera-house managers and conductors about the dangers of trying to reduce, however judiciously, the length of Wagner's music dramas: when you attempt to shorten a long work by removing sections, he told them, you do not make it into a shorter work, merely into a long work that happens to be short in places. What exactly was removed from *The Wild Bunch,* and how does its elimination affect the film? Better to place things in perspective first: even in its truncated version the film remained a great achievement, the mutilation in no way approaching what was done to *Major Dundee* (or what later would be done to *Pat Garrett and Billy the Kid*). The three great action sequences—the opening and closing gunfights and the Bunch's assault on the train—are untouched, and the continuity in general does not suffer. If the film were nothing more than what *Variety* is fond of calling an "action-oater," the cuts might even be said to constitute an improvement. But as there was nothing wrong with the narrative flow before they were made and as the film adds up to much more than just the sum of its action sequences, the net effect of the cuts is to diminish the epic scope slightly, reduce some of the ironies moderately, and lessen the complexity of characters and character motivations considerably. Of this last Peckinpah was especially worried, writing Feldman that "if we the audience see the [characters] only act and do not see their motivation, it hurts the overall effect of the film."[20]

In all, three flashbacks with related dialogue, two whole scenes, and part of another scene were removed, totaling nine and a half minutes. The first flashback reveals how Pike's best friend, Deke Thornton, was captured; the second is of Crazy Lee in the opening robbery; and the third shows how Pike was wounded in the leg. The two lifted scenes consist in a raid by Villa on Mapache and the aftermath of the raid. Finally, part of the festivities at Angel's village was excised.

As there have been at least four different "official" versions of *The Wild Bunch* in release during the past twenty-seven years, some sorting out may be in order before proceeding. The complete films—and the only version to which Peckinpah ever lent his wholehearted imprimatur—is the European version of 1969, which is 145 minutes long and contains all the material just described. The first domestic version—Domestic I, let's call it—is essentially identical except for the removal of the third flashback, which Peckinpah agreed to, albeit with great reluctance; this version runs 143 minutes. The second domestic version—Domestic II (sometimes called the American version)—

is missing all the material just outlined. The 1995 restoration returns
to the European version but drops the intermission, which was originally inserted just before the train robbery, the first half of the film
ending with Pike and Dutch on the trail and Pike's line, "This is our
last go-round, Dutch, this time we do it right." As the intermission
was created in the first place only in response to the European distributor's demand for a roadshow engagement, it has been left out
of the restoration, which is almost certainly closer to what Peckinpah
intended. That he conceived *The Wild Bunch* to play straight through
is suggested by a dissolve—from the Bunch on the trail to the train
sequence—that was made for the domestic release when the third
flashback was still in it. This dissolve is now in the restoration. (In the
European version these two scenes are faded out and in, respectively, to make room for the intermission, and constitute the only scene-
to-scene transition that is not a dissolve.) In any case, at a little under two-and-a-half hours the film not only doesn't need the break, it
is arguably the more effectively experienced as one unbroken arc of
cinematic energy.

Warner Home Video released a widescreen laserdisc of the restoration in the fall of 1995. Ironically, some reviewers charged that the studio still had not fully restored Peckinpah's final cut, and some others
apparently believed that the 190-minute length represents the director's cut.[21] Meanwhile, the more die-hard fans are complaining that
there are scenes in the theatrical trailer missing from the film. Probably none of these people will ever be satisfied, and fans and collectors
seem always to want more regardless of whether it is better. In fact, the
theatrical trailer *does* show one scene not in the film: Sykes telling Dutch
they have to go after Angel, Dutch asking, "How?," as Mapache's men
unload the wagon. Peckinpah obviously cut it because its point is sub-
sumed in the argument the Bunch have after Sykes gets ambushed.
Moreover, the presence of a scene in a trailer means nothing in itself:
trailers often include scenes not in final cuts because they are prepared
months in advance, usually reaching theaters before directors are
finished editing their films. As for the so-called "190-minute version,"
it is hardly a *version* at all, merely the editors' first cut; and if it were
even possible to release this cut, it would constitute a greater travesty
to Peckinpah, his artistry, and his vision than anything the studio did.
Among other things, it contained scenes such as the one in which the
Bunch point out that to avoid suspicion Angel had better come along
when they turn over the guns to Mapache. As the film fell into narrative shape, Peckinpah knew it would be disastrous to leave this scene
in, as it would telegraph a key development in the plot and throw an

alert audience right out of the film. Multiply such instances—redundancies and digressions that vitiate the story's intensity and destroy its narrative drive—and the point is clear enough: more is sometimes not just less but worse. To reiterate the facts in the strongest possible terms: the 1995 restoration is absolutely true to the version that Sam Peckinpah himself prepared and authorized for release in 1969 and it represents *his* final cut of *The Wild Bunch*.

To return to cuts themselves: the trim in the scene in Angel's village, involving little dialogue and only about a minute's worth of screen time, is hardly damaging at all. However, the story is richer for its inclusion, as it shows the Bunch relaxing in Angel's village and establishes more clearly their status as guests of honor among his people. It thereby serves as preparation for the big scene the following morning when the entire village turns out to bid the Bunch farewell, and it helps to account for why these people come to view the Bunch as liberators, which is crucial to the reprise of this farewell at the end of the film. This elision contains, moreover, one bit of business—a Mexican woman dancing with Dutch, and Old Sykes cutting in—that if back in would mercifully eliminate a supposed ambiguity some viewers have claimed to find. Dutch does not join Pike and the Gorch brothers in the brothel, which led one interviewer to ask Peckinpah if Dutch is homosexual. The director laughed and replied: "In the first place, I didn't know where to put him. In the second place, he had the closest ties with Angel, so he was more preoccupied with things, right? It was on his mind—all he wanted to do was get him out. . . . Angel saved his life on the train, and, you see, in many ways Dutch . . . was the conscience of *The Wild Bunch*."[22] A favored reading of the interrelationships within the Bunch pegs Angel as the group's conscience. But Angel is a victim both to the Bunch's readiness to renege upon their code of honor and to his own revolutionary ideals, while it is Dutch who at two key moments draws some vital distinctions. When Pike compares the Bunch to Mapache, Dutch says, "We ain't nothing like him. We don't *hang* nobody." And sometime later, it is Dutch who reminds Pike that Angel, by keeping his mouth shut about the Bunch's complicity in the theft of the rifles, "played his string right out to the end."

The longest lift has Mapache awaiting a telegram that will inform him whether the Bunch have successfully looted the U.S. munitions train, for which he is paying them ten thousand dollars in gold. As there is apparently no telegraph in Agua Verde, the town in which his army is headquartered, Mapache and some of his army have taken a train to a nearby station where, awaiting the message, they are attacked by Villa's rebels. While most of his men scurry for cover, Mapache refuses to budge and, soldiers dropping around him, holds his ground until he receives the telegram. For all his loathsomeness, we are made to see that he is a genuinely fearless man, which Peckinpah reinforces by having a small boy, dressed in a *federale* uniform, deliver the telegram and watch, wide-eyed with admiration and even envy, as Mapache reads it despite flying bullets and exploding shells. Although it has been shown that Mapache is little more than a bandit and a killer, a dupe Huerta has put in charge of a regiment, clearly for this boy the general is not just a hero but someone to emulate.* The boy puffs out his chest, salutes, and together he and the general walk calmly under fire back to the train.

In addition to its importance for character, this scene is necessary because it contains the sole appearance by Villa's army. Without it the only revolutionaries actually seen are the Indians of Angel's village, for whom Pike allows Angel to "steal" one case of rifles and ammunition in exchange for his share of the gold. Yet in the absence of a dramatic demonstration of Villa's military power, there is no longer any urgency behind the advice of Mapache's German advisers to steal arms from a neutral country by employing men who are fugitives from that country. A whole dimension of the international implications of the story is thus lost, and with it an important character revelation and several shades of irony. These points are reinforced and deepened by the brief scene of the bloody aftermath of Villa's raid, which Peckinpah argued for because he felt that it demonstrated Mapache's "concern for his people and his need for guns and ammunition."[23]

In *Major Dundee* Peckinpah said he was trying to tell the story of a man who repeatedly fails in what he sets out to do. The director himself failed in that telling, but he told it in *The Wild Bunch,* and the remainder of the missing scenes deal directly with that aspect of the story. Pike Bishop is an aging outlaw and killer, notorious for robbing trains in the Southwest. By 1913 the pickings have become pretty lean, the available territory more and more crowded. Most of the companions of his youth and middle age (Deke Thornton, for example) are dead or in prison; other companions of those days (such as Old

---

*This point is given great urgency in the final battle when the first of the fatal bullets that cut down Pike Bishop is fired by an almost identical boy-soldier. Peckinpah had always intended that he be played by the *same* child actor; but the production manager had by mistake already returned the boy to Mexico City, and it was impossible to get him back in time for the Agua Verde sequence (Jesse Graham to P.S., 1995).

Sykes) are by now so old as to be infirm and a nuisance; and the younger members of the Bunch (the Gorch brothers, Angel) all have other interests and are fast becoming impatient with him. Pike and the Bunch, dressed in regulation army uniforms and riding army horses, enter Starbuck to rob the train office only to discover they've walked into a trap laid by Pat Harrigan—a railroad boss who is Pike's old nemesis—with the help of Deke Thornton, Pike's close friend and former partner.[24] The Bunch have to fight their way back out of town, through bounty hunters who fire from the surrounding rooftops with manic abandon and through dozens of citizens, including several children and a group of temperance marchers, mostly women. In a moment of confusion, Pike wheels his horse and accidentally tramples a woman fleeing from the gunfire. (On the outskirts of town, he untangles her shawl from his stirrup.) When the remaining members of the Bunch go to divide the take, they find washers, not coins, in the payroll sacks. "Silver rings!" exclaims a disbelieving Tector Gorch, while his brother Lyle shouts at Pike, "All your fancy planning and talking damn near got us shot to pieces over a few lousy bags of washers!" Pike ignores the charge, and mutters, half to himself, "We've got to start thinking beyond our guns. Those days are closing fast."

The theme of entrapment is thus quickly established, and it comes from all directions: advancing age, diminishing space, changing times, and for Pike himself a loss of self-respect owing to a series of blunders, mistakes, and failures of which the botched train office robbery, where the Bunch's number was reduced by half, is only the first to be shown. The second is revealed in the first flashback. Thornton and his bounty hunters sit around a campfire as one of them asks what kind of man Pike is. "The best," Thornton answers, "he never got caught." In Domestic II, this cuts to Pike's camp, where he and Dutch talk about the next job, which might involve looting an army payroll train. "They'll be waiting for us," Dutch warns; and Pike answers, "I wouldn't have it any other way." In the cut version this sounds like mere bravado, and Dutch's repetition, "Pike, I wouldn't have it any other way either," which closes the scene, sounds maudlin. In the original and now the restored versions, Pike's line is followed by a flashback that has Pike and Thornton hiding out in a bordello in a town where they've just pulled a job. Thornton, visibly apprehensive, urges they leave, while Pike orders him to relax, assuring him this is the last place the law will think to look. "How can you be so damn sure?" Thornton asks. With excruciating pomposity Pike replies, "Being sure is my business!" At that moment the door bursts open to reveal a Pinkerton agent drawing a bead on Thornton. He fires and hits him, while Pike uses the diversion to escape out the back way. The flashback is not presented continuously, but is repeatedly interrupted by dissolves back to the present, to closeups first of Pike, then of Thornton, the editing itself establishing a structural arc that binds the two men—formerly partners, now on opposite sides of the law— by way of a common memory.

Unfortunately, when the flashback was removed, it took with it several lines of dialogue:

> *Dutch:* Damn, you sure must have hurt that railroad. They spent a lot of money setting up that ambush.
> *Pike:* I caught up with them. Two or three times. There was a man named Harrigan, used to have a way of doing things. I made him change his ways. There's a hell of a lot of people, Dutch, that just can't stand to be wrong.
> *Dutch:* Pride.
> *Pike:* And they can't forget it, that pride, being wrong, or learn by it!

Pike is alluding to his longstanding duel with Harrigan. When Dutch asks if the Bunch learned anything from being wrong that morning, Pike answers, "I sure hope to God we did." The exchange is both revealing and curiously touching. It suggests the pride Pike himself feels in the reputation he's acquired as an outlaw over the years, and it identifies his principal flaw, that very pride that finds it hard to admit to mistakes or weakness. At the same time the quickness with which he informs Dutch that he got even with the railroad finds an immediate explanation in his recollection of Thornton's capture, and the whole scene establishes the twin components in his motivation: his past failures and his desire for success, for another good score. When we see that it was essentially his fault that Thornton was captured, we realize why Pike talks so much about the old days, and why he is so insistent that the next job the Bunch pull not be easy: he has a terrible need right then both to prove himself and to be reassured that he is worth anything at all. We also realize why throughout the film he is so obstinately disinclined to judge Thornton for teaming up with the railroad: it is because of Pike's carelessness that Thornton wound up facing the alternative of remaining in prison to be whipped day after day or joining the posse. (In an early argument between Thornton and Harrigan, Peckinpah rapidly fades in and out a flashback of one of those whippings, the strong implication being that Harrigan used his wealth and influence to have Thornton beat-

en as a way of forcing him to join up.)* With all of this dialogue restored, when Dutch echoes Pike's "I wouldn't have it any other way
either," the effect, far from maudlin, is to provide an undercurrent
of pathos, Dutch's refrain becoming a response to the need he senses in his friend for reassurance.†

The next flashback reinforces the motif of desertion. During the
opening robbery Pike orders Crazy Lee, the youngest member of the
Bunch, to hold some customers hostage "as long as you can until after
the shooting starts." CL replies, "I'll hold them here until hell freezes over or you say different." The order is initially puzzling, as it has
no strategic value for the Bunch's escape (the customers are unarmed). It is not until the kid is shown to be a near psychopath that
we realize CL is obviously too reckless (and too stupid) to be reliable,
too dangerous even for a "wild" Bunch, and Pike was using this opportunity to get rid of him. The following day Pike learns that CL is
Old Sykes's grandson. Sykes hadn't told him because he figured Pike
had enough to worry about, and anyhow he didn't want the kid getting any special treatment. All the same he wants to know how the
boy handled himself when things got hot, wants to be sure the kid
didn't run out on anybody. Before Pike can answer, Peckinpah rapidly dissolves in a flashback of CL in which we hear Pike's "Hold 'em
here" reverberate a few times, much as his earlier "Being sure is my
business" echoed and reechoed throughout the whole flashback of
Thornton's capture. Pike simply mutters that the kid did "fine, just
fine."

In addition to some ironies of its own—Pike's readiness to lie about
the kid's actual performance to preserve his friend's illusions—the
scene is placed so that together with the flashback of Thornton's
capture, it frames the big scene in which Pike declares his code. Earlier that same day, Tector wanted to get rid of Sykes, but Pike inter-

*Peckinpah shot but did not use still another flashback, showing Thornton at hard
labor in prison uniform.

†Peckinpah felt an especially intimate connection to this scene, in particular the
lines about pride and admitting being wrong. In rehearsal he instructed Borgnine
to turn toward camera after saying, "I wouldn't have it any other way either." In the
first take Borgnine turned instead away, putting his back to camera. "And then there
was this prolonged silence," the actor recalls, "and the camera kept rolling and rolling and I thought: What the hell happened? Did Sam fall asleep? And then finally
from Sam I hear, 'Cut!' but there is a distinct quaver in his voice. So I waited a moment to be certain the camera wasn't still rolling, and then I turned over and looked
at Sam, and there tears rolling down from behind those dark glasses" (quoted in
Simmons, p. 95).

vened: "You're not getting rid of anybody. We're going to stick together, just like it used to be. When you side with a man you stay with him, and if you can't do that you're like some animal. You're finished. *We're* finished! All of us." However much Pike may fail to honor these sentiments, they express the deepest article of his faith and articulate the only code of honor he knows. The disparity between the lip-service he pays this code and his actions that betray it is already eating at him when the film begins and will demand a tragic reckoning before his story has ended.

The third and last flashback shows how Pike was wounded. He was courting a woman named Aurora whom he wanted to marry. Late one night her husband returned, caught them in the bedroom, and fired several shots into the dark room, killing her but only wounding Pike in the leg. The staging, the lighting, and the set are telling and will reverberate later in the film. The room is dim, illumined only by the soft glow from an oil lamp that, in a lovely moment, Aurora extinguishes. Behind her there is an armoire with a mirrored door. When her husband bursts in, we see him first as a back-lit, shadowy reflection in the mirror behind her. As Pike tells it, the husband was supposedly gone for good—"He's never coming back," Aurora had said—and Pike had gotten careless and dropped his guard. As with the other flashbacks, this one occupies a crucial place in the structure, coming immediately before the assault on the train. When Dutch asks if he ever caught up with the husband, Pike says, "No, but there's not a day or an hour goes by that I don't think about it." Then he adds, "This is our last go round, Dutch, this time we do it right." As before, it is the triggering of a memory of failure and loss that makes us aware of how desperately Pike needs to have something in his life go right, and it is with this particular memory that the line "Being sure is my business" finds its saddest resonance. Being sure is his business, but he got careless, and the woman he loved was killed.

This flashback also resonates in that moment in the final battle when Pike backs into a room for cover. On one side there is a woman who is reflected in a mirrored door on the other. Noticing a slight movement, Pike fires, shattering the reflection and killing an officer hiding behind the door. Pike does not shoot the woman; but when he turns from her, she raises a pistol and shoots him in the back. Almost reflexively he wheels, shouts "Bitch!," and blasts her with his shotgun. The moment is deliberately, intentionally shocking, but it is not gratuitous. The small room, the mirrored door, the triangle of one woman, two men, Pike now the intruder, the double killing, the single wounding—this time near the heart—all these are clearly meant to invoke the earlier scene and to play off it themes of buried rage, revenge, and retribution.

The Wild Bunch is thick with subplots of revenge, and they extend to the women and children as much as to the men. For example, just as Peckinpah meant for us to understand that the boy soldier shoots Pike out of a desire to avenge the killing of his hero Mapache (not just because he has learned to imitate his violent elders), so too he tried to establish revenge as the reason the woman shoots Pike in the back. In a memo to Feldman, Peckinpah wrote:

> I have seen [Villa's raid] with Mapache's reaction cut out as *per* your request, two times. I think it is obvious to us both, as previously cut, that Yolanda looks at the general and his reaction to her was overdone but not having *any* reaction is now even worse. I find that it is possible . . . to add a brief reaction to her, which, as I'm sure you know, will tie the two together. I have tried to do this throughout the picture, as the position she has is inevitably close to the general. She is "his woman," even while being in second place to Sonia. It is because of this that she shoots [Pike] in the back.[25]

The footage evidently could never be manipulated to everyone's satisfaction, and Peckinpah failed completely to make it indicate the Mapache-Yolanda relationship in a way that would be apparent to an audience. It should be obvious, however, that the women characters are no more driven solely by treachery than the men are. This is certainly clear enough when the mother of Teresa, the girl Angel kills, betrays him to Mapache. The point is not that all women are treacherous, or even that this particular woman is treacherous. She is angry and grief-stricken, and informing on him becomes the only way she has of getting some justice for the killing of her daughter. It is also clear that there is much more to the relationship between Teresa and Angel than any simple matter of desertion and betrayal—that Mapache had become for her a way of getting out of the village and of surviving. But when she flaunts it, insulting him and his village, Angel moves to hit her, but Pike stops him. Her closeup, as Pike pulls Angel back to the table where the rest of the Bunch are sitting, is a marvel of ambiguity: close to tears, she breaks slowly into a smile, then starts to laugh. At the risk of stretching a point: is it ridicule only or is she using mockery as a way to make it as easy as possible for Angel to forget her?

Scenes like this or the third flashback should be sufficient to contravene the general objection that all the women are wholly unsympathetic. Even when the Aurora scene was out, it was a specious criticism. For one thing, Peckinpah is being true to his story, and part of that truth requires that he populate the film with the kind of women the Bunch would probably be associated with—whores, mostly, or camp followers, like Teresa. For another, unsympathetic compared to whom—the men? Which one of *them,* including the main characters, is not shown to be untrustworthy, greedy, and bloodthirsty? That the men are much more fully characterized is freely granted. But this is the given of the picture, what Henry James calls the subject we must grant the artist. Part of that subject is precisely the "place" of women in a world as dominated by masculine attitudes as this one. For example, one of the most important subjects of *The Wild Bunch* is masculine forms of honor, which Peckinpah dramatizes in many aspects, including the sexual. In this context, his understanding of how large and deadly a role saving of face can play in the lives of men like these is so astute that Angel's killing of Teresa is clearly shown to be motivated by more than just jealousy. The killing is instigated at least as much—in the strictly immediate sense, perhaps more so—by the ridicule of the Gorch brothers, who, insensitive to his mounting rage and frustration, make wisecracks like, "She sure ain't your woman no more" and "Look at her licking inside that general's ear." The killing happens with shocking suddenness, but what may be even more disturbing is its resolution in laughter. Mapache's soldiers, guns drawn, surround the Bunch as Dutch shouts, *"Calma! Calma!"* When some semblance of order returns he explains to Mapache that Angel "went a little crazy when he saw her with you. *Era su novia,"* meaning she was his sweetheart. Mapache finds this hilarious, those around him joining in the laughter; and soon, at the urging of his German advisers, he has invited the Bunch to have a drink with him.

Peckinpah has been criticized for treating the girl's death equally lightly instead of dwelling upon it. But this is to stay on the surface only of a scene that, like practically everything else in this richly layered film, operates on several levels at once. What else would these men do in this situation? When Mapache laughs off Teresa's death, it is isn't as if the Bunch, who've been disarmed, have any option but to go along with him and defuse a situation that, if they resisted, would get them all killed. If we look a little closer we discover that, like the Gorch brothers' wisecracks, the laughter of Mapache and his cronies reveals something about how men in this culture relate to women and through women to other men. Women are obviously just chattel to Mapache, Teresa merely his latest acquisition. But when he is told that she was Angel's *novia,* it makes the prize only that much tastier. For while *novia* may mean "sweetheart," it distinctly connotes a romantic relationship that is not yet sexually consummated and that is even rather adolescent in its idealization. "Angel dreams of love and Mapache eats the mango," Pike had observed back in the village. Mapache's laughter is thus pure machismo and indicates his dominance over another man, the girl and her death merely incidental "amusements" to the specifically sexual joke and power he now enjoys at Angel's expense.

The resolution of the sheer fact of the girl's death comes two scenes later, when Peckinpah has her body, dressed for burial and borne aloft by a cortege of old women shrouded in black, return to disrupt the negotiations between the Bunch and the Germans over stealing the arms shipment. Pike and Dutch try to show some respect, but Mapache just brutishly shouts for the women to hurry up and get her out of there. Yet he makes no move to force them along, and they do not quicken their pace so much as a beat. Here is one area in this society where the power these women wield is nearly absolute (because much of it derives from the church, which is suggested by the prominent crucifix carried by the leader of the procession). Moments like this are surely a more accurate indication of the director's attitudes, as is the way the themes of sexual jealousy, masculine pride, and revenge are mirrored in the later flashback of Aurora. But she is killed for no betrayal—for all practical purposes, her husband had abandoned her—let alone any honor worth the name, merely a man's sick thirst to salve his pride. In both cases, however, women wind up dead.

The film also contains several instances of women as victims of violence—the woman Pike accidentally tramples, the women that Dutch and the other members of the Bunch kill or use as shields in the final battle, the women killed, mangled, and also used as shields in the opening gunfight—which are not offered for our delectation or presented in such a way as to invite approbation. And when any shooting starts, consider how often the women think first of protecting not themselves but their children and their husbands. It is this sort of thing and the ubiquitousness of children, usually accompanied by women, throughout the backgrounds that led Ron Shelton to observe that Peckinpah has made it possible for us to view all the events of the story from the perspective of women and children, if we care to.[26] But Peckinpah dwells on little of this, because he is able to show it so well.

Peckinpah once said that *Major Dundee* had "a very tight script, intricately intertwined," so that "if you removed a part of it, something else would fall out fifteen pages later."[27] The same is obviously true of *The Wild Bunch,* and it is nowhere better illustrated than in the now-missing flashbacks. We have already noted how in *Ride the High Country* Peckinpah used the convention of the young lovers to reflect the issues at stake in the conflict between the two heroes. In an analogous way the flashbacks here give a private urgency to Pike's dilemmas, for it is in them that Peckinpah crosses and thus fuses the personal and professional aspects of Pike's life. Each of the flashbacks is marked by a personal loss that is the direct result of a professional mistake, miscalculation, or equivocation. Collectively, the flashbacks thus serve to ironize Thornton's description of Pike as "the best": he's often the best, it seems, because he never got caught, being sly, deceitful, or heedless enough to let others get caught or killed in his stead.

That the flashbacks are therefore to the point is beyond dispute; what has been disputed is the manner of their introduction, which is by way of dissolves, a device that has been criticized as old-fashioned and clumsy.* But Peckinpah has rarely been interested in style for its own sake; he wants style to serve meaning, technique to convey the right feeling. The image does not so much dissolve as appear to quiver momentarily before deliquescing, and the effect is as if the present tense of the film were struggling to suppress the past tense, which nevertheless fights its way to the surface. Inasmuch as the flashbacks are from Pike's point of view, what is this but an exact objective correlative to the way these painful memories intrude themselves upon his consciousness? He would like to forget them, as they remind him of failure, and he tries to repress them, because the recollection of them humiliates him. He can do neither. The very look of the flashbacks was meticulously worked out by Peckinpah and Lucien Ballard

---

*According to Lou Lombardo, the flashbacks were originally edited as straight cuts, but the studio "got cold feet because it had never been done that way before and they insisted on using oil dissolves" (quoted in Simmons, p.103). Actually, an oil dissolve—the image becomes wavy, as if seen under water—is used for the first flashback only in the campfire scene; all the rest, including the back-and-forths in the first one, are introduced with standard dissolves (sometimes called overlapping dissolves or lap dissolves). The point about confusion aside, it is doubtful that Peckinpah would have implemented a change he didn't like just because he was told to. For one thing, with Ken Hyman still at Warners, that was not the kind of relationship the director had with the studio at this time. For another, it is arguable that he would eventually have abandoned the straight cuts anyway given the overall narrative style of the film, which, as noted, uses dissolves for nearly every scene-to-scene transition. And the pause that he *directed into* the campfire scene just before the flashback is introduced—Pike stops talking, turns away, and rubs the back of his head, his face clearly troubled—practically demands the more easeful, less abrupt transition that it finally got.

to give the images the characteristic of something hidden and haunted: the settings dark, flat, claustrophobic, the decor and furnishings
carefully chosen for their dated, antique character, the lighting an
alternately harsh and muted chiaroscuro that contrasts with the dust
and desert sand and the blue sunlit sky elsewhere in the film. The
cumulative effect of both their style and the manner of their presentation—including the artificially reverberant acoustic in which Peckinpah records the sounds of the past, and the way each flashback is
never run continuously but is faded in and out of the present—is to
suggest the existence of a past reality, living still in memory, that runs
parallel to and never far beneath the surface of the present reality
and that bursts through at key moments to remind Pike how, when,
and with whom he has failed to live up to his reputation as "the best."

It is perhaps the oppressiveness of this sense of the past that has
led several critics mistakenly to align Pike too closely with Steve Judd.
"I'd like to make one good score and back off," Pike says, and Dutch
asks, "Back off to what?" This much-quoted exchange is usually tak-
en to indicate that Pike's problem, like Steve's, is that he is so far into
his life that he is incapable of doing anything else. Yet whatever these
two may have in common, resistance to changing times isn't part of
it. To be sure, they share some characteristics: both are well past their
prime, with established reputations they care very much about and
are proud of, while William Holden, as Pike, bears an unsuspected
resemblance to Joel McCrea (unsuspected perhaps by everyone except Peckinpah, who took care to attire them similarly in austere
black and white and to set up and photograph identically the closeups in which they declare their codes—tight, slightly low-angle, with
just enough blue sky to outline the faces). Both men are also aware
of the distance they've traveled and the self-respect they've lost along
the way. And both of them make a lot of mistakes in their work, mistakes that have less to do with getting old (which would explain physical infirmity but not the lapses in judgment) than with how much
they have on their minds: Steve, the betrayal by Gil and the dilem-
ma of what to do with him; Pike, his memories and his guilt (in this
context the manner of the flashbacks' introduction—in particular the
way they overwhelm and obliterate the present for Pike—is telling).
But Steve has no plans to retire; indeed, his whole concern is to find
means of employment that will restore his dignity and allow him to
remain the man he was. Pike, no less in love with the life he used to
enjoy, is nevertheless a lot more tired than Steve, and when we meet
him, he is not only ready for a change, he wants one. In this respect,
he is quite unlike the rest of the Bunch, the sense of his alienation

subtly heightened by groupings and compositions that leave him isolated from the others at precisely those moments when he must insist most strenuously on their solidarity, lest their petty gripes, mean
hostilities, and personal animosities flare into violence.

After the one particularly nasty dispute in which he narrowly prevents Tector from killing Sykes, Pike lifts himself partway to the saddle only to come crashing back down on his weak leg when the stirrup breaks. As he lies there in pain, the Gorches trade abusive
wisecracks: "It appears Brother Pike needs help, Brother Lyle" and
"Riding with Brother Pike and old man Sykes makes a man wonder
if it ain't time to pick up his chips and find another game." Pike
mounts up without saying a word, quietly turns his horse, and rides
slowly away. The camera follows with a very slow zoom, the telephoto lens conferring upon the solitary figure a stature that magnifies
as he recedes in the distance. When the horse and rider fill the screen
from top to bottom—in what is surely the film's most beautiful single image—Peckinpah fades in the next shot underneath, a long view
of the Bunch strung out across an expanse of desert, and leaves the
two shots overlapped just long enough for Pike's immense figure to
dwarf the others and tower above the sandy terrain. The composition
is simplicity itself, built out of primary forms and materials reduced
to an absolute minimum: man and animal, earth and sky. Yet it is
made to open onto depths of feeling, areas of experience, and extremes of loss we have only begun to suspect exist in this lonely man.
The steady gait of the horse climbing the dune, the slight hunch of
Pike's shoulder as he winces in pain striving to straighten himself
against the ridicule, and the seemingly infinite space stretching back
and beyond horse and rider suggest the weight of responsibilities sto-
ically assumed, the burden of a reputation recklessly made and now
courageously sustained, and the weariness of trying to live up to it
even as he longs to be rid of it. Above all the image foreshadows Pike's
destiny—which is to fulfill his reputation in spite of himself—in the
very reluctance with which the shot yields to its successor, the gradual disappearance of the wounded heroic figure so subtly photographed that it seems to have become indelibly impressed upon the
environing wilderness, lingering ghostlike in the mind's eye long after
the horse and rider have faded from view.

Even though it is placed later in the film, the flashback showing
Aurora's death is most to the point here, for it is there that Peckinpah
makes manifest the full extent to which Pike keeps his deepest feelings to himself. This is the only flashback accompanied by voiceover—
Pike affecting a toughness of attitude, telling Dutch all he thinks

about is getting even with Aurora's husband. The images, however, focus chiefly on Pike's own sometimes careless treatment of Aurora (he arrives two days late for a rendezvous, offering neither explanation nor apology) and on their last few moments of tenderness together before she is killed. The contrast is once more between what Pike says and how he says it, and what is actually on his mind and how he is feeling, the latter always revealed by the images. It is clear that what he thinks most about is not getting even; rather, it is about having lost her. This flashback confers a retroactive poignance on Pike's earlier order to Angel about Teresa—"Either you learn to live with it or we'll leave you here"—as that is exactly what he has had to do about Aurora, and not at all easily.

It is this unflinching assumption of responsibility for the life Pike has made for himself and his resoluteness despite (perhaps because of) his failings and his losses that Peckinpah may want to acknowledge. These find a more or less explicit expression when Thornton's exasperation with the inept bounty hunters reaches the point of outburst: "You think Pike and Old Sykes haven't been watching us all the way down here? They know what this is all about, and what have I got? Nothing but you egg sucking, chicken stealing gutter trash, with not even sixty rounds between you. We're after men, and I wish to God I was with them. If you make one more mistake, I'm going to ride off and leave you to die." No banal machismo is being trotted out here. Thornton is expressing an outlook neither childish nor cynical but simply realistic and therefore serious, indicating the necessities of such attitudes and modes of thought in a world as dangerous as the world the film contains. It is perhaps difficult to appreciate the full measure of Peckinpah's achievement in this respect until the film is placed against the many shopworn films and novels in which these subjects—the skills, knowledge, and discipline of men of action—have been poorly handled because of inadequate observation or insufficient characterization. But Peckinpah knows this milieu, feels it keenly, and obviously believes in it deeply. Thanks to his attention to detail, he has managed to revitalize these subjects and restore them to the realm of serious art simply by tying them securely to character and in turn locating character in an appropriate filmic world fully visualized. As a consequence *The Wild Bunch* became the best film since *The Seven Samurai* about men whose lives and work involve violence and killing.

Not the least of Peckinpah's achievements consists in getting from his actors performances of unselfconscious ease and naturalness, utterly free from the kind of pomp and display that in more overtly "stylized" action films signals the actor's awareness of the onlooking camera.* The men we see here are the men we would see if there were no camera present; there is no empty gesturing or hollow striking of poses, because their validity is made to inhere not in their generic roles but in their very physical being, and it finds expression in the way each of them sits or stands or rides in this hostile setting. Or in the way Pike enters a new place. In an exceptionally sophisticated piece of film editing, Peckinpah makes the very cinematic tissue of the narrative convey what it is like to be on guard every waking hour. Pike passes through an enclosed walkway that leads to the main square of Agua Verde. He pauses at the threshold, while Peckinpah cuts back and forth between Pike's closeup and three successive pans that sweep the area, taking note of the places that provide cover, the high aqueduct with sentries positioned on it, the supporting arches that permit egress or entry.

It is things like this—or the way that Pike, without raising his head, surveys the surrounding rooftops when he dismounts at the beginning, or the piece of hide wrapped around his binoculars to prevent telltale reflections from the sun—that give force to Thornton's description of Pike as the best. ("Think you can handle this?" Lyle asks when they discover the machine gun. "What I don't know about," Pike answers, "I sure as hell am going to learn.") But the others know their business too, as in a tense moment that has the Gorch brothers, without any word from Pike, put down their glasses and turn from the whores they've been eagerly awaiting to prepare themselves for trouble when an unexpected dispute arises, or in an earlier scene that has Sykes soundlessly cock his rifle when the Gorch brothers demand a larger share of the take than is rightfully theirs. Even the few self-conscious displays of bravado originate in necessity, as when Pike, tipping his hat, offers himself as a target, buying just enough time for the spark to touch the dynamite.

Each of the Bunch achieves a kind of personal style, which Peckinpah exploits to magnificent effect in those great images of Pike,

---

*It is a bit late in the day to be praising the performers, but this group of Hollywood regulars—William Holden, Ernest Borgnine, Robert Ryan, and Edmond O'Brien—is something special and leads one of the best casts ever assembled. Peckinpah's magic with actors is legendary, and these men imbued their performances with an unusually strong sense of lived experience. Of the four, only Borgnine is still alive; while among the supporting cast Albert Dekker, Warren Oates, Strother Martin, Emilio Fernandez, and Ben Johnson have all passed away. Add to them Peckinpah, Feldman, Fielding, Ballard, and the editors, Lombardo and Wolfe, and the elegiac aspect of *The Wild Bunch*, pronounced from the beginning, becomes stronger with each passing year.

Dutch, and the Gorch brothers going off to rescue Angel. As they stride past the camera, Peckinpah cuts to a reverse angle. When they reach middle distance he has the telephoto lens once again initiate a gradual push-in that creates the illusion of figures growing in size while receding in space until it stops just as, their backs still toward us, they fill the screen shoulder to shoulder, marching and marching and marching like some knights of old resurrected out of myth and legend. These are men whose every movement tells us they've lived lives close to the edge, largely on the run, and have thereby acquired lethal skills that have long since become second nature to them. "The clothes seem to smell of the people who wear them," Stanley Kauffmann observed.[28] The scent is the scent of danger, a quality to which Peckinpah is continually alluding in the recurring scenes where the slightest provocation is enough to call their skills into play. It is an irony he inflects throughout that the Bunch seem able to forget their internal differences and bring their skills under full control only when they are forced to close ranks against enemies or are involved in daring and violent exploits. This is a group of men for whom fighting really is the easiest solution to all problems, a position Pike himself is forced to assume when, during one dispute, he says, "I don't know a damn thing except that I either lead this Bunch or end it right now." It is significant that the first time we see the Bunch function as a group is during their assault on the munitions train, which becomes in this context not only a superbly crafted action sequence (the virtuosity of the filmmaking mirroring the expert operation of the caper), but also an ironic vision of brotherhood, each man performing his appointed task to perfection as Pike's perseverance is at last rewarded with that good score.

If it is in moments like this, or when the Bunch celebrate their success by breaking out the whiskey, that Pike finds a provisional justification, there are nevertheless many other moments where his craftiness, his equivocations, and his opportunism suggest stronger parallels with Gil Westrum than with Steve Judd. Pike telling Angel, "Ten thousand cuts an awful lot of family ties," is not unlike Gil telling Heck, "The Lord's bounty may not be for sale, but the devil's is, if you're willing to pay the price"; and Pike's desire for one good score so he can retire is not unlike Gil's scheme to steal the gold so he can enjoy champagne and beautiful women in ease and comfort for the rest of his life. Late in the film, after Pike's good score is tainted by the capture of Angel and the ambush of Sykes, there is this exchange:

Dutch: Damn that Deke Thornton to hell!
Pike: What would you do? He gave his word.

Dutch: Gave his word to a railroad.
Pike: It's his *word!*
Dutch: That's not what counts, it's who you give it to!

This too has been widely misinterpreted, perhaps because Peckinpah, with typical irony, allows Dutch the last word. But Pike knows that for himself it is both simpler and more complex than that; and when Dutch suggests making a run for the border now that the bounty hunters are closing in, Pike answers, "They'd follow us every step of the way. I know Thornton. I'm tired of being hunted." Dutch may still be the conscience for the Bunch as a whole, but for Pike himself Thornton comes to occupy the same position as Steve does for Gil, and Thornton's persistent reluctance to dishonor his word (if only to a railroad) recalls Steve's refusal to violate his contract (if only with a bank). Thornton becomes thus both Pike's nemesis and the touchstone by which Pike's own failings and compromises are thrown into fuller relief ("It's his *word!*"). And inasmuch as Thornton's dogged pursuit symbolizes Pike's past, it is obvious that far from searching for that past, Pike has been trying all along to escape it.

Escape is impossible, of course, which is a realization that begins to close in on Pike like a vise. The Bunch return to Agua Verde and find Mapache and his soldiers celebrating their new weapons, part of the festivities the spectacle of Angel tied behind the general's new motorcar and dragged through the dirt. Pike offers to return half his share of the gold for Angel, but the general, having too much fun, refuses to sell, instead offering the Bunch the pleasures of free women and whiskey. "Why not?" Pike says disgustedly, as the four of them ride off to a bordello. Some time later, after he has finished dressing, Pike sits on the bed watching the young prostitute wash herself at the table across the room, while, behind him, her baby lies on the dirt floor crying. He drinks the rest of his whiskey, looks once more at the young woman, then away, the quietness broken by the voices of the Gorch brothers in an adjoining room, haggling over prices with a whore they've just shared. Pike throws the empty bottle aside, crosses to the doorway, and, parting the shabby curtain, stands there a moment, fixing each of the brothers in a cold, fierce glare. "Let's go," he says at last. The Gorches trade looks of uncertainty, then in one awful moment grasp his meaning. "Why not?" Lyle answers, the assent paradoxically stated in the negative.

This scene, the most delicately inflected in the film, is the pivot point, and not the least of its subtleties is how little it says explicitly, how much it draws together and concentrates. Peckinpah had

learned something in the years since *Major Dundee,* where he had
planned to splice in a montage of Dundee's memories during the
breakdown in Durango. What he learned was how to omit the most
important things from a scene and make them conspicuous by their
absence. For such a method to work, however, what is missing in one
place must be present in another, and this is why the flashbacks are
so necessary in their appointed places elsewhere in the film. Peckinpah knew there was no need to reprise them here, for the past that
Pike has been running from has finally caught up with and surrounded him, has become present by association and analogy. The prostitute and her baby are an ironic reminder of the family he might have
enjoyed had he been, once in the past, just a little more careful. As
he watches her and listens to the baby crying, he thinks as well of a
member of the only family he has left, who lies broken and bleeding
a short distance away. At this point Angel is no longer just Angel; he
is Thornton asking, "How can you be so damn sure?"; he is Crazy Lee
saying, "I'll hold them here until hell freezes over or you say different"; he is Old Sykes wounded and left to die; and he is Angel after
all, near death yet playing his string right out to the end.

Pike's decision has in the final analysis nothing to do with an inability or unwillingness to change. He has options left and a stake to
pursue them with. It's just that they're no good in the face of a personal revelation born of self-disgust and self-contempt that shows him
that no matter where he goes, what he does, or how far he backs off,
he will never be free from these humiliating memories. He knows that
if he were to leave now, he would only add another increment of
shame to a load of guilt that has already become nearly intolerable
and that all the gold, whiskey, and whores in the world will be insufficient to salve, lighten, or obliterate. The next woman will only
remind him of the one killed beside him long ago; at the bottom of
the next bottle he will find only the same desolation; and solitude will
not bring him even the cold comfort of isolation, for he will always
be haunted by the voices of the past that live in his heart, whisper-
ing of debts unpaid, words broken, and friends abandoned because
all he cared about was saving his own skin and making another good
score. It isn't enough, it cannot sustain, and so it places him in a situation as authentically tragic as any a man can know: walk away, his
life's a fraud; stay and fight, his life is over. It defines not one string
but two, each demanding to be played right out to the end. And either way—slow, mean, ignominious, or quick, violent, apocalyptic—
it is the same end: death.

Drawing the noose even tighter is an issue far more profound than the style of a man's passing or the manner of his dying. Pike himself identified it early on: when you side with a man you stay with him, and if you can't do that you're like some animal, you're finished. Pike is finished anyway, but his decision to reclaim Angel represents his decision to become a human being, and it is the full weight of what this choice means that confers upon the carnage to follow its terrifying dimension of tragic irony. For in that squalid room where a strange woman and her baby mock by their very existence every excuse and deceit by which he has tried to evade or justify his past, Pike makes a discovery that he is quite unprepared for and that comes too late for payment by any price less dear than his life: no matter how, a man alone ain't got no bloody fucking chance.

III

It is doubtful that Peckinpah ever made a film that spoke more eloquently to his deepest needs, that struck more piercingly to the dark heart of his most private fears and demons than *The Wild Bunch*. If the flashbacks are made to carry the brunt of Pike's personal story, it is the character of Pike himself that embodies Peckinpah's. The first visible connection was small, almost trivial. For most of his adult life Peckinpah sported a pencil-thin moustache. He asked William Holden if the actor would consider growing one for the picture. Initially hostile to the suggestion—he had never worn a moustache on screen before—Holden was gradually persuaded and, according to Weddle, as the shooting progressed, "began, more and more, to resemble Peckinpah."[29] Lou Lombardo got the point soon enough: "I told Holden one day after dailies, 'I got you figured, you're doing Sam.' He was running that Wild Bunch just like Sam was running the movie. His gestures, his tone of voice, it was Sam. He picked up on that."

By then, however, Peckinpah had long strengthened and multiplied the connections. "Of all the projects I have ever worked on," he wrote to Ken Hyman, "this is the closest to me."[30] In the ten years preceding *The Wild Bunch* Peckinpah had gone from obscurity to early recognition to disgrace to banishment. He had gone through two marriages, and whatever his public pronouncements, he was wracked with anger, with guilt, with pain, confusion, and fear. The breakup of a marriage is rarely one or the other partner's "fault" alone, but at some level he blamed himself for the failures of both, and not without reason. He had abused both wives emotionally, psychologically, and physically. He had manipulated them, often cruelly, manufacturing quarrels so that he could project his own failings, real and imagined, onto them. He had philandered much, yet maintained the classic male chauvinist double-standard that left him free to wander while holding them to their vows. It is little wonder that he fought for over nine long months to keep the Aurora flashback in the film. An extramarital reverie disrupted by a jealous, abusive husband determined that if he cannot be happy with his wife, no one will—this was almost a reenactment of a scene from the end of Peckinpah's first marriage. In life no one was literally killed, as the intruder was a photographer who did his shooting with a camera. But the shame Peckinpah felt for what he had orchestrated was almost unendurable and was certainly, as *The Wild Bunch* reveals, unforgettable.

Despite his love for his children—at that time, three daughters, one son—he had fairly few internal resources to express that love; and there were more times than he could bear to admit when his work really was more important to him than anyone or anything else in the world. These are feelings to which no artist is a stranger, but Peckinpah seems to have had more trouble than most owning them. Had he been able to bring them out in the open he might have weakened their power over him and perhaps even found some relief from the guilt with which one part of himself constantly, almost ritualistically, tortured another. Instead, he projected his fears and frustrations onto the kids—especially if their needs as children collided with his as an artist—and he was often petty, mean, and, worst of all, shaming to them, especially the boy.

These years also bore witness to his worsening alcoholism, which both exacerbated and was exacerbated by his increasing difficulties reconciling responsibilities to his family and to his filmmaking. If he could control the drinking only sporadically at home, at least it didn't seem in these years to impair his performance on the job. By all reports he worked soberly, seriously, and obviously well. This discipline doubtless resulted in what is perhaps his most impressive single achievement as a personal filmmaker: that he managed to pour so much deep personal feeling into *The Wild Bunch* without ever violating the structure of the story. This is a balance that he struck much less successfully in some other films and that he never found in the last part of *Major Dundee*. Yet not only is it maintained in *The Wild Bunch*, but paradoxically the objective story is nourished, charged, and vitalized by the private subtext. What are the flashbacks, after all, but memories of desertion and failure refracted through drama? Peckinpah knew all the guilt, the shame, and the despair Pike Bishop feels in that bordello as he stares at the empty bottle and the young woman he has just bought. Trust and betrayal, violation and ven-

geance, loyalty and greed, love betrayed and love reclaimed, friendship abandoned and friendship redeemed, the word given and played
right out to the end—these are not themes that Peckinpah "decided" upon. It would almost be more accurate to say they decided upon
him. By the end of the decade they were haunting every corridor of
his heart and mind: they had become his interior life.

As for his professional life, the disputes with producers on *The
Deadly Companions, Major Dundee,* and *The Cincinnati Kid* and with studio executives on *Ride the High Country* and *Major Dundee* had made
him so cynical about anyone who controls the money and tries to
control the creativity that he eventually took refuge in a paranoia that
made most of his film deals deadly companionships too. This process
was not complete by the time of *The Wild Bunch,* but it was far enough
along so that Harrigan, the unreasonable, penny-pinching railroad-
boss who won't give Thornton the men and materials he needs to do
the job properly, could represent every greedy producer Peckinpah
ever had as a partner. And Mohr, the German commander, could
become a surrogate for studio executives like those at MGM or Columbia, all the men in suits who think they can give orders that destroy artists and their dreams but remain clean themselves by staying
uninvolved, standing back and up high. If Peckinpah understood
Pike's sadness from the inside out, then in his very bones he also knew
his killer-hero's rage. In the standoff just before the final battle starts,
Pike spies Mohr almost hidden inside the portico, takes careful aim,
and shoots him dead.

This was no actor's improvisation but a specific instruction from
the director himself, whose identification with his protagonist had
become complete: the cold hatred acted out in that moment is lethal, is apocalyptic. Like Pike, if ever there was a man desperate for
redemption, it was Peckinpah by the time he had come to make this
film. He had felt so personally devastated by the trashing of *Major
Dundee* that he actually wrote letters to just about every critic who
panned the film, explaining that, yes, he agreed with them, the film
was a disaster, but at one time it made sense, if only you could see *my*
version before "they" ruined it. There is something at once touching
and disturbing about this, suggesting a personality almost patholog-
ically sensitive. And yet, somehow, through all the booze and self-pity
and desperation, Peckinpah found the resources to protect, save, and
gather himself, if not personally, then at least as an artist. He often
said that the film he really wanted to make when he came off the
blacklist was *The Ballad of Cable Hogue.* But it is difficult to take him
at his word. He knew better than anybody that if his claims for *Major*

Dundee as an epic ruined by forces beyond the artist's control were to be regarded as anything other than a song and dance, he could not come back with a small, lyrical film, however beautiful. He needed a big, bold, powerful film, an all-out assault that would show everybody just what he could do given half a chance and left alone. This is why the violence in the final battle has always been, will always be ambiguous—horrifying yet exalting, sickening yet exciting, damned yet redemptive. But perhaps more than anything else what gives it an urgency that remains undiminished with the passage of time and despite the hundreds of films that have tried to imitate it, is that it is so authentically, terrifyingly personal and yet so inextricably linked to some of the deepest forces of his creativity. It was fueled by a hatred of those who had trashed his work and by a ferocious desire to prove himself. But in the filmmaking these emotions were transformed into a furious, savage joy in the sheer exhilaration of being able to work again and on a film he cared so deeply about. The train heist may be Pike's good score; but *The Wild Bunch* is Peckinpah's, and it was no prelude to backing off.

IV

The Wild Bunch has been criticized for its lack of ideas, but that tells us less about the intellectual shortcomings of the film or the filmmaker than about the inability of most reviewers to comprehend how ideas really enter and operate in works of art. One reviewer claimed that for all the beauty of craft and image, never has so much virtuosity been made to serve so few ideas: "The moral idiocy of *The Wild Bunch* (it's all right to kill if you stay loyal to your buddies) was fairly obvious."[31] Fairly obvious to whom—people who go to the theater or open novels as a substitute for reading philosophy? One of the things that distinguishes Peckinpah's treatment of the themes of friendship and loyalty is that they are not mere obeisances to genre but unmistakably *felt* realities in his films, and he accomplishes this by staying close to the specific story he is telling. Cordell Strug, in a superb essay, put it this way:

[In] *The Wild Bunch,* many themes are stated explicitly . . . but these are simply part of the fabric of the film, whose characters and incidents are so particularized that it is folly to make of them instances of universal truths. The return for Angel and Pike's shot at the German officer bring to a head the discussions of loyalty and the American identity of the gang, but in a dramatic, not an allegorical, sense. The final battle is a dramatic solution that makes sense in the lives of the characters themselves—not a conceptual solution that makes sense as an answer to an abstract problem. This is art, not philosophy, and such art that it cries out against being used as philosophy. If we are ever to contemplate such things, we can contemplate them in this film.[32]

If we must systematize Peckinpah's filmic visions into philosophical statements—which is, in a word, impossible—it would be more accurate to say that what he is doing is showing us that one of the consequences of extreme loyalty is bloodshed. What interests him is the particular dramatic situation in which these men—these limited, somewhat brutal, apparently "bad" men—make, once in their lives, a decision that is, as Robert Culp put it, "neither Good nor Bad . . . simply a Right decision, balanced on a hair" and backed "with their lives."[33] All the rest is tragic consequence: and although the fighting that follows "accomplishes" nothing (inasmuch as Angel is already dead) and although its moral implications can be argued into perpetuity, the last thing that it can be said to express is "Peckinpah's personal vision of the meaninglessness of life" or his "conviction that humanity is worthless."[34] Even many of the film's most enthusiastic critics subscribe more or less to these notions, laying great stress upon Lyle's "Why not?" as evidence of Peckinpah's nihilism. But Peckinpah doesn't provide an explicit answer to Lyle's question because the answer is implicit throughout the film: in Pike's humiliating memories, in the torture of Angel, in the degradation of Thornton by the corrupt Harrigan, in the sadistic, murderous Mapache and his opportunistic, manipulative German advisers, in the crass and degenerate bounty hunters. And also because Peckinpah realizes that in this particular situation, the Bunch's "no" contains an implicit "yes," like the "no" of Camus's rebel, who by saying "no" means "that this has been going on too long, up to this point yes, beyond it no, you are going too far, or, again, there is a limit beyond which you shall not go. In other words his no affirms the existence of a borderline." Presumably most of these reviewers would have been happier had Peckinpah altered the story to have Mapeche accept Pike's offer, and there would be a neat end to it. But this would be truly egregious as regards the things closest to Peckinpah's heart: his film would then be about how ten thousand in gold surely can cut an awful lot of family ties and—to him even more questionable—just as surely bind them back up. It seems clear enough that for Peckinpah camaraderie is a counterbalance against the temptations of materialism, which is why in *The*

Wild Bunch and *Ride the High Country* he pits gold and greed against friendship and family.

Even to say that much, however, takes us in the direction of biographical criticism, in which there is no real need to go except to discover the sources of Peckinpah's art in his personal life. Pike's big speech about sticking together is thoroughly contained by the situation that gives rise to it. Sykes, Pike's oldest friend in the present membership of the Bunch, has botched the job of packing the horses, sending riders and mounts tumbling down a steep dune. When Tector picks himself up, he is so angry he's ready to kill the old man. But Tector's anger has been simmering since the previous day when he and his brother had to back down in the dispute over equal shares and Sykes had ridiculed them all for walking into Harrigan's trap. Pike knows that Sykes's accident has only scraped a lot of still freshly bruised egos (including his own), and he has to get everyone calmed down. He comes up with this speech about siding with a man to cover for his friend's mistake and to smooth things over in general. Since the first flashback has shown us that abandoning Thornton is tormenting him, it is only right, natural, and logical that sticking together should be on his mind. The implications of the speech will eventually entrap him, but that only strengthens its function in the structure of the story.

By the same token, there is no need to look for evidence of Peckinpah's cynicism or his alleged misanthropy in his extraordinary gift for black comic-relief, as some have done with the aftermath to the opening robbery, where the bounty hunters descend upon the bodies and squabble over who killed which and thus gets the loot. After the final battle TC and Coffer are so overcome with joy at the sight of all the bodies and the bounty they'll be collecting that they're speechless. This is one of the most audacious single moments in all of film. It is difficult to say what we might need after the terrible bloodshed of that climactic battle, but the last thing we surely want is this grotesque little spectacle of human avarice and opportunism at its most carnal. Yet that is exactly what the events of the story dictate. The posse, which has been chasing the Bunch for the reward, finally catches up when the fighting is raging in Agua Verde. Rather than enter right away, the bounty hunters wait, like the vultures they are, until the shooting stops and then converge upon their human prey, delighted the job will now be so easy. As before, this is the work of a storyteller being true to the integrity of his story, and here that truth involves the bounty hunters' responses to an appalling carnage in which they can see only material gain for themselves.

Another critic, who once called Peckinpah's ideas "puerile as such," actually wrote: "The pronouncements about future Mexican democracy are so blatantly impasted that they don't even taint the film."[35] Of course they don't, they're *part* of the texture of the film. Pike's remark—"If [these people] ever get armed, with good leaders, this whole country'll go up in smoke"—functions primarily as a revelation of character. To use this and other overt pronouncements as indications of Peckinpah's thinking not only reduces it to the limited level of his characters' thinking, but it misses the point that he is using these limitations dramatically, that is, *as* limitations, thereby deepening our sense of these particular lives.

One regrets belaboring this point so, but some of the objections that have been and continue to be raised against Peckinpah and his films suggest a widespread misconception about the kind of artist he is and the kind of films he made, and seem to be based on a critical fallacy. That fallacy consists in drawing a one-to-one relationship between the ideas that characters express and the artist's personal beliefs—as if an artwork were nothing more than a veiled sermon or confession. There is obviously some relationship between the overt ideas in an artwork and the artist himself. But if the artist is any good, the relationship is far from direct, and surely it can be established only—and then just tenuously, with the most scrupulous qualification—by giving full weight to the totality of the artwork. Peckinpah's is, as we have seen, an intensely personal art, informed by his deepest feelings, his most emotional memories, and no doubt his most cherished beliefs. But by the time this essentially private material has reached the screen, it has been transformed and objectified into narrative and drama, at least in his best work. This is precisely why it is folly to try to yoke him to what this or that character says as a way of getting at his so-called ideas. "I'm not going to get between my audience and the story," he once said in what is perhaps the best single summation of his philosophy toward directing.[36] "When I work, I become all the characters in the script. I'll be playing Jason Robards one second and the next second I'll be doing a McQueen number, and I act out. It's very dangerous. I act out for myself in real life for the illusion of what I'm going to shoot."[37]

What he is really saying here is that he literally has no ideas but in things, which is not the same as saying that he has no ideas at all or that his ideas are puerile. It is rather to say that his imagination is such that it cannot coalesce except upon substance, whether that substance be character, event, story, convention, structure, even props, items of clothing, and details of settings. Peckinpah has frequently been called a visual poet; and if this has any meaning at all, it is that his imagination conceives in the terms of metaphor, simile, image, and symbol. Northrop Frye, in *A Natural Perspective*, his great critical study of Shakespeare's romances, describes this kind of imagination and alludes to the aesthetic issues it raises:

> It is curious that we can think of impartiality only as detachment, of devotion to craftsmanship only as purism, an attitude which, as in Flaubert, turns all simple life into an enormously intricate still life, like the golden touch of Midas. We can hardly conceive of an imagination so concrete that for it the structure is prior to the attitude, and prescribes the attitude. Shakespeare's impartiality is a totally involved and committed impartiality; it expresses itself in bringing everything equally to life.[38]

Now Shakespeare is, as Frye suggests, the supreme example of this kind of artist, an artist who is virtually without ego because his ego is so thoroughly absorbed into his imagination. In American literature Faulkner, Twain, and James at their best are examples of this kind of artist; and in films Ford, Renoir, Kurosawa, Huston, Satyajit Ray, and Peckinpah are similar examples. This is why Peckinpah has so frequently been drawn to the Western—much as Shakespeare was drawn to his "moldy tales," Faulkner to his mythical county, or Hawthorne to his Puritan ancestry—because everything was there waiting for him: a repository of plots, characters, icons, conventions, settings, and themes. He found, in sum, a whole language of myth, symbol, and metaphor waiting to be exploited and capable of freeing his imagination to give form to its dictates, to express his feelings, thoughts, and ideas in character, narrative, and drama and in some of the most emotionally charged, sensually beautiful, and mythically resonant images any one has ever put on film.

In the case of Peckinpah's imagination, the paramount dictate originates in his discomfiture with all certainties and absolutes and finds expression in those polarized structural motifs we have already noted and in the antitheses, ironies, and ambivalences that rend his films and make them studies in ambiguity not unworthy of comparison to James or Conrad. (Peckinpah's discomfiture no doubt derived in part from all those dinner-table discussions of law and the Bible he participated in as a child, and it may help to account as well for his attraction to the Western, which of all popular genres has the most dialectical, that is to say, the most conflicted language.) When he first apprenticed with Peckinpah, Gill Dennis said: "Sam is the one person in American films who has truly caught the idea of ambivalence. Sam respects his characters. He doesn't judge them, and that annoys people. They keep asking, 'Where does he stand?' Even in *Bonnie and Clyde,* you've got your villain in 'society.' Sam won't make it that easy, not ever."[39] Peckinpah himself was more laconic: "Things are always mixed." It is precisely his "mixtures" that reviewers distort when they try to harden this line of dialogue or that declaration of code into a dogmatic statement that is meant to define what he supposedly believes.*

Since Frye published his essay on Shakespeare's romances, our critical vocabulary has changed a bit, so that impartiality is now called cynicism and purism is now called nihilism. But neither gets the picture quite in focus. An artist's affirmation of life can find expression only in the vitality of his art, his commitment only in his devotion to craftsmanship. At roughly the same time as *The Wild Bunch* was first released, two other films, *Z* and *Midnight Cowboy,* were greeted with great enthusiasm by the same reviewers who jumped on *The Wild Bunch.* However, what is morally ugly about both of these films is that the filmmakers diminish and even obliterate the humanity of several characters in order to score easy polemical points or buy cheap sympathy for the main characters. By contrast, what is so morally beautiful about *The Wild Bunch* is inseparable from what is so aesthetically beautiful about it; both are a function of the same imaginative impartiality that is so involved with and committed to its artistic materials that it cannot help granting even the vilest characters a full measure of the rich, pulsating vitality that animates every frame of the film and that leaves us with the unmistakable sense that each character, no matter how minor, exists in the fullness of his particular being. The extent to which this applies to all of Peckinpah's best films forces us to reevaluate the whole question of his so-called mindlessness and anti-intellectualism. When Dwight MacDonald defended Fellini's *8½* against similar criticisms, he wondered, "Why 'ignorance' is a fault in an artist I don't see, nor why he has to solve any problems except those of constructing a work of art, which are difficult enough. . . . And don't the critics remind one of those all-too-serious students who try to discover 'Shakespeare's philosophy' and always fail because Shakespeare hadn't any; his 'ideas' were all *ad hoc;* their function was to solve dramatic rather than philosophical problems."[40]

*"I'm not even sure anymore what I believe in," Peckinpah said after he had made *Straw Dogs* and *Junior Bonner* back to back (the one his most violent, the other his gentlest film). "I once directed a Saroyan play in which one of the characters asked another if he would die for what he believed in. The guy answered, 'No, I might be wrong.' That's where I am." (*Playboy* interview, p. 72.)

Sam Peckinpah is a great storyteller and filmmaker. Is it necessary that our appreciation of his artistry have as corollaries these attempts to make him into a second-rate thinker and a third-rate philosopher, especially when it is so plainly obvious that he was intellectual enough about what mattered to him, which is manifestly and by his own admission making storytelling films?

With its story of men as deadly companions, unified through fighting and eventually through an ideal of personal loyalty, *The Wild Bunch* takes up where aspects of *Ride the High Country* and *Major Dundee* left off, and it has additional roots in other films, in history, and in the epic tradition. Of the films by others, the most manifest influence comes from John Huston's *The Treasure of the Sierra Madre,* which Peckinpah on more than one occasion declared a favorite film. Old Sykes is obviously patterned after Howard (right down to his gale of laughter and his joining up with the mountain Indians at the end of the film) and Mapache suggests a more corrupt, sadistic version of the savage bandit leader, Gold Hat. The two films also share the same setting and one thematic strain: gold and greed coming between friends. Kurosawa's *The Seven Samurai* is widely thought to be an influence on *The Wild Bunch*. It is, but this may owe more to Walon Green, for whom it is a favorite film, than to Peckinpah.[41] And there are several thematic similarities—professional fighting men who have been forced to become "whores" just to survive, uniting for one last honorable cause, achieving both camaraderie and nobility through fighting, dying, and self-sacrifice—and of course the use of slow motion in the action sequences. But Peckinpah's favorite Kurosawa film was *Rashomon,* which he once pronounced "the finest picture ever made."[42] One can see why he might think so with its links to myth and legend and with its theme of perspectivism, shifting views of the same material, a method that was to become—though in a radically different, more elaborate way—the informing principle of *The Wild Bunch*. And in the setting of the last scene, evocative of old ruins with a distinctly religious ambience, Peckinpah subtly fused allusions to *Rashomon* and his beloved *Treasure*.

Peckinpah said that Emilio Fernandez, the famous Mexican director who plays Mapache, gave him the idea for the game the children play with ants and scorpions at the beginning of the film. But Peckinpah greatly admired the French director Henri-Georges Clouzot's 1953 action film, *The Wages of Fear,* which opens on a child teasing several insects; and there is a later scene in which a truck backs onto a rickety turn-platform over a gorge only to have one of its wheels break through the rotted wood—not unlike the wagon wheel breaking through the bridge in *The Wild Bunch*. Peckinpah also specifically cited the influence of Clouzot's use of slow motion in this film.[43]

Two other filmic influences on *The Wild Bunch* are Elia Kazan's *A Streetcar Named Desire* and David Lean's *The Bridge on the River Kwai*. That of the Kazan—whom Peckinpah frequently named as one of his favorite directors, just as Tennessee Williams was his favorite American playwright—is quite specific and owes to the way the voices from Blanche's past are introduced as memory, echoing and reechoing in an artificially reverberant acoustic, exactly as the voices return to haunt Pike in the flashbacks. As to *The Bridge*, like *The Wild Bunch*, it stars William Holden, is concerned with camaraderie among uneasy companions, and has a major set-piece in the explosion of a bridge.* The films also share a couple of remarkably similar lines of dialogue. When the British officer played by Alec Guinness, at one point recollecting past hardships, remarks, "I wouldn't have had it any other way," the context is analogous to the moment when Pike tells Dutch, "I wouldn't have it any other way." And elsewhere the Holden character tells his wounded commander, "If we go on, we do it together," in a scene that suggests Pike telling Old Sykes, "We started it together, we'll end it together."

The strongest link between the two films is, however, William Holden himself. Peckinpah was once asked why he always felt the need to revise and rewrite scripts, even scripts he liked or scripts he wrote himself. He replied, "No matter how good a script is, you have to adapt it to the needs of the actors."[44] In the early drafts of *The Wild Bunch*, before the cast was lined up, the characters ranged from slightly to considerably different from the way they are in the finished film. Dutch, for example, was a young man; and both he and Pike resembled the Gorch brothers to a far greater degree. Much of this would no doubt have been changed with subsequent drafts anyway, but there is equally little doubt that the casting influenced Peckinpah's later revisions and reconceptions, particularly in the case of Pike, who in the finished film is a far more complex and troubled character than he is in the earlier versions of the script. This is because, as we have seen, Peckinpah put a lot of himself into Pike. But it is also because he put something of William Holden as both actor and star into the character. There is a type Holden had been playing, developing, and

---

*In his original script Walon Green wrote a cable crossing with rafts. When Peckinpah changed it to a bridge, Green exclaimed, "Christ, you're not going to blow up another bridge? But Sam had a good retort: 'It's not just blowing up a bridge; it's the way you blow up a bridge.' And he was right. It was terrific" (quoted in Simmons, p. 99).

refining throughout his career, beginning with a 1941 film called *Texas* in which he and Glenn Ford play boyhood friends who wind up on opposite sides of the law, with Holden the hell-raiser and eventually the outlaw. Throughout the fifties—in films like *The Horse Soldiers*, *The Bridge on the River Kwai*, *Picnic*, *Sunset Boulevard*, and *Stalag 17* (the last two directed by Billy Wilder, another director Peckinpah admired)—Holden played characters who are loners, outsiders, cynics, skeptics, misfits, compromised and compromising men who turn out at the very end of their lives to be reluctant, sometimes accidental idealists, men who often wind up dying for that residue of integrity they are surprised to discover they still possess. Pike Bishop, as Peckinpah conceives him and as Holden plays him, can be thought of as an older, even a definitive version of this same composite character, which is what the director meant when he once described the film as being "about what Bill Holden is today—fifty, middle-aged, wrinkled, no longer the glamor boy."[45]

The last group of sources for *The Wild Bunch* come from the history of the West both as fact and legend. "The outlaws of the West have always fascinated me," Peckinpah said.

> They had a certain notoriety; they were supposed to have a Robin Hood quality about them, which was not really the truth, but they were strong individuals; in a land for all intents and purposes without law, they made their own. . . . I've always wondered what happened to the outlaw leaders of the Old West when it changed. . . . It's a very uncompromising film—the language, the action, the details, the lives of these people are as I imagine they were. We tried to re-create an environment, an era, and I think we were reasonably successful with it. . . . The strange thing is that you feel a great sense of loss when these killers reach the end of the line. . . . I'm exhausted when I see it, I'm literally exhausted for hours, and all it is really is a simple adventure story.[46]

But none of Peckinpah's films is elaborately plotted. What he seems to need is a basic dramatic structure, the simpler the better, for the complexity comes from the richness and variety of texture, the elaboration from the way he dramatizes character and visualizes incident and event. The story he told here is a beauty, and it brought together the requisite ingredients—outlaw men living beyond their time, bargaining for freedom, compromising for gold, engaged in exploits that seem already the stuff of romance and legend, all set within a historical framework of violent social and political upheaval—for him to make the story support the fullest, richest, most comprehensive vision of life he ever gave us. Although he said he wasn't deliberately trying to make an epic, *The Wild Bunch* became, and remains, his epic all the same.

In *Pericles on 31st Street*, which Peckinpah helped write, he demonstrated some knowledge of Greek history; in *The Wild Bunch* he demonstrates an awareness of the epic forms and conventions from which much of the film is derived. Pike Bishop, the Bunch's leader, is different from other men in degree but not in kind, a killer-hero but not a god or demigod; the immediate setting is large in scale (the United States and Mexico of 1913, a decade of cataclysmic social change and conflict) and even larger by extension and implication (the imminent world war, the presence of German advisers on Mapache's staff). The story begins *in medias res;* and Peckinpah's purpose is a retelling of history not as documentary but as metaphor angled toward recovering a mythology. About this last, he was more or less explicit: "I don't make documentaries. The facts about the siege of Troy, of the duel between Hector and Achilles and all the rest of it, are a hell of a lot less interesting to me than what Homer makes of it all. And the mere facts tend to obscure the truth anyway. As I keep saying, I'm basically a storyteller."[47] Peckinpah's materials here are drawn from history, some of which he researched and some of which, given his Western background and his frequent trips to Mexico, he must have absorbed as a matter of course. A good bit of the research, however, was quite fresh: after he had finished *Noon Wine*, he spent the first part of 1967 at Paramount writing a screenplay about an American pilot who crosses paths with Pancho Villa. Peckinpah was very excited about his script; but when the star, Yul Brynner, read it, he hated it, declaring Peckinpah knew nothing about Mexico, and brought in another writer.[48] The result became the film *Villa Rides*, which Peckinpah detested; but he didn't squander the opportunity. Paramount had given him full use of its research department, and soon his office was filled with books, photographs, films, and other materials of the Mexican Revolution. Within the year he was putting all of this knowledge toward the preparation of *The Wild Bunch*.

Among other things, Peckinpah discovered there was much gun-running by Americans for both sides. Pike Bishop was based on several such historical characters, and he also has a progenitor in Butch Cassidy, who was notorious for robbing trains and whose Hole-in-the-Wall Gang was often referred to as the "Wild Bunch." The model for Harrigan is E: H. Harriman, a tycoon whose railroad lines were often looted by Cassidy's bunch and who hired a posse of detectives and gunmen to track the outlaws. When Cassidy realized that the posse was not about to give up, he and the Sundance Kid left for South America, where they perished under unknown circumstances. Even the dialogue about keeping one's word has precedent in history and legend (not to mention the ancient epics). The story is told—whether it's apocryphal hardly matters in view of its survival in folklore—of how Cassidy on the night before he was to leave for prison asked if he could be let out to say goodbye to a girlfriend. He promised the sheriff he would return by morning. The sheriff let him go, and, sure enough, come daybreak Cassidy was back at the jailhouse.

It is by now commonplace to call any long or sufficiently "big" story an epic, but the term connects to this film in enough illuminating ways to make its application far from factitious. The flashbacks, for example, reinforce the epic structure, because they are introduced as told or recollected material. And there are other formal devices that seem taken from the epic or at least are equivalents, like the fixed epithet, formulaic repetition, and the catalogue. The analog to this last is to be found in the numerous slow-motion shots of action and violence, which are also examples of formulaic repetition inasmuch as Peckinpah uses them both for rhythmic variation and accentuation and for comparison and contrast (as when he crosscuts between one outlaw falling from his horse to the street in normal speed and another outlaw falling from his horse in slow motion through a storefront window filled with mannequins, or the way the posse floating down to the water from the exploded bridge recalls the Bunch tumbling down the dune). Characters are also given taglines that identify some important characteristic, sometimes straightforwardly (as "Old" Sykes or "Crazy" Lee), and sometimes ironically (as when Pike tells Dutch, "C'mon, you lazy bastard," or in the appellation of "general" to Mapache, who is also called a "killer").

In addition, there are countless musical, visual, and verbal motifs whose function is not unlike that of fixed epithets or formulaic repetitions: the clothing the various characters wear or the kind of weapons they carry; the deployment of groups of children or of musicians at key moments in the drama; the use of similar musical phrases at similar dramatic junctures (as preludes, for example, to those lethally charged silences); the charged silences themselves, impacted with energy that sometimes dissipates, sometimes bursts into violence; the flame racing along the fuse; the rallying cry of "Let's go!" or "*Vamonos*"; editing together parallel actions or using the same setup to photograph different groups of characters (especially well employed during the chase following the train robbery, where the Bunch, the posse, and the cavalry are each seen in identical compositions yet the point is contrast); and the frequent use of laughter as a refrain to tie off major sections of the story, thus giving the film a balladlike quality that links it more closely to an oral tradition of storytelling. Three instances are noteworthy: when the Bunch laugh off their mistake after the opening ambush, celebrate their success after the middle train robbery, and consecrate the (figurative) reintegration of Thornton among their number at the end of the film. Juxtaposed against these, in which laughter indicates solidarity, are several other moments in which it is sinister and disturbing: the giggling children surrounding the thatched cage full of ants and scorpions, or their amusement when they contribute to Angel's suffering at the end; the laughter that siphons off the tension after Angel shoots Teresa; the laughter that ridicules Angel when he is captured; and the almost psychotic giggle of Dutch and Tector that breaks the silence just before the closing gunfight. Peckinpah also uses these recurring visual, verbal, and musical themes and motifs (and countless others like them), with their constant variation and development, to provide a kind of ballast that helps support and unify the sprawling narrative.

There also appear to be—especially in view of Peckinpah's singling out, of all works, *The Iliad* as an example of a historically based story that isn't a documentary—two deliberate allusions to Homer. The spectacle of Angel being dragged behind Mapache's automobile is not unlike the spectacle of Hector being dragged behind the chariot. And Angel himself, as regards the function he serves in the plot, suggests Patroclus, Achilles' friend whose death in battle inspires the warrior to take up arms once again on behalf of his countrymen. In both cases—Achilles' and Pike's—the immediate impulse is for revenge, the long-term motivation an expiation for accumulated guilt born of pride.

While *The Wild Bunch* lacks an analog to the opening invocation of and response to a muse, it does contain the equivalent to the machinery (gods and supernatural intervention) of the classical epic—the actual machinery like the automobile, the train, and all the advanced weaponry (rifles, grenades, and the machine gun). Peckinpah once said, "I detest machines," and while there is no reason to doubt his word, at the same time he has also said, "You're not going to tell me the camera is a machine; it is the most marvelous piece of divinity ever created."[49] The language here—the camera as divine, not invented but created—may indicate nothing more than an understandable chauvinism on the part of a filmmaker toward his medium, which, though an artistic one, relies more heavily than most upon technology. But it also suggests that Peckinpah's feelings toward technology are considerably more complex, even contradictory, than any simple expression of antipathy is able to contain. If, as Lévi-Strauss has shown us, every age has its mythology, its religion as it were, then Peckinpah is especially attuned to the mythology of technological progress, which he often views cynically. Yet he also has an extraordinary sense—perhaps unparalleled in cinema since Buster Keaton—of the absurdist possibilities for drama in the confrontation of living organisms with mechanical contraptions, and it is this sense more than anything else that prevents any pat moralizing or easy editorializing against the evils of progress in his depiction of technology. And the surrealistic element that creeps into his work from time to time is nowhere more apparent than in what he does with machines in his Western settings.

A good illustration is afforded by the first appearance of Mapache's automobile, for which a lesser director might have tried to prepare us. Peckinpah, by contrast, emphasizes its suddenness. With no warning at all, the score sounds a brass fanfare, gates swing open, and the automobile is chugging straight at us.* The note struck is one of comic surprise. The automobile is not only a new element in this world, it is a completely different kind of element, which by its very distinctness looks by turns comic and grotesque, while the suddenness of its appearance, heralded with the fanfare, gives it a comically miraculous air, making it seem like something created or deposited rather than merely invented. Its bright gleaming metallic red contrasts baroquely with the prevailing earth tones and the light-blue sky, constituting an intrusion not only upon the world in the film but also upon the visual texture of the film itself. To emphasize the car's comic-grotesque aspect Peckinpah records its passage from far to near distance not in a single, unbroken shot but in a series of jump cuts, interspersed with reaction shots of the spectators, though at one point cut directly together with no cutaway. The effect is manifold. It confers upon the car a jerky, mechanical movement that emphasizes its

*This is only one of many effects that depend upon the extraordinary music score by Jerry Fielding (who worked on seven of Peckinpah's films). Notice, for example, how at the very beginning the ominous growl from the low strings sets the tone, literally and figuratively, for the entire film, signaling that all is not as it appears to be. Or take the moment near the end when Thornton pauses over Pike's body, then reaches down and takes his friend's revolver as a remembrance. The gesture is a symbolic farewell, but the way in which the music softly, almost imperceptibly, reprises the lyrical main theme reminds us that it is also a moment of reunion. Both Peckinpah and Fielding were in especially close accord on this effect: in one of their early conferences they discovered that each had independently come to feel that the entire film built to this moment.

comic, toylike quality and that contrasts with the smooth movement of horses and people, thus introducing a new motif—organic versus mechanical motion. The filmmaking itself is, moreover, made to convey what it must have felt like to see this strange thing for the first time. No one prepared the people in this village for the automobile— suddenly it was there, and suddenly life was different. The effect of the separate shots cut together is to force us to see the car as the spectators see it, still so amazed they can't follow its movements continuously, as if they were blinking their eyes, which is exactly what the editing is doing. Every time we open our eyes (that is, with each successive cut), the car has moved on, only—owing to the jump cuts— we haven't seen it cover the intermediate space. Finally, in a typically subtle touch, Peckinpah has saddle holsters strapped to the sides of the automobile. It may be something new, but its owners are in no doubt as to the use to which it will be put. The holsters foreshadow the car's later application as an instrument of torture—Mapache using it to drag Angel through the streets of Agua Verde.

Most of the machines are eventually used for death and destruction, yet they are given comic introductions. Our first sight of the train, for example, recalls our first sight of the automobile: chugging along jerkily in a succession of cuts that jump it progressively closer. The first time we see a demonstration of the power of the machine gun is in a wild, slapstick episode in which Mapache tries to operate it without the tripod, sending the entire village scurrying for cover from the spraying bullets. Yet these comic introductions only heighten the menacing quality of the machines, which Peckinpah develops by making them appear as a different order of living thing in the landscape of the film. And they are always getting out of control. When Pike puts the engine in reverse and sends the train back to the cavalry, it seems to acquire a life of its own, which is subtly reinforced by some camera setups that endow the train with its own point of view.

Owing to the transitional setting—from a primitive, agricultural society to a mechanized, industrial one—and to the civil and international warfare with which the action is involved or to which it alludes, all of the advanced weaponry acquires an almost supernatural aura, which, as regards convention, makes the weaponry an equivalent to magic swords or sacred shields. Much of the conflict among the various forces involves their trying to gain the advantage of this superior form of knowledge because it will give them a superior form of power. Peckinpah introduces this motif quite early with the shot of TC, tight with anticipation, kissing his rifle barrel, and in three parallel scenes he establishes the central preoccupation with the rifles. Don Jose, the village elder, tells Pike, "If we had rifles like these," the villagers could defend themselves against raids; Angel tells Pike, "My people have no guns; but with guns, my people could fight"; and Zamorra tells Mapache after Villa has routed the *federales*, "*Mi general*, with the new guns and ammunition this would never have happened."

Yet the rifles remain to some extent a discriminate and therefore a limited power, whereas the machine gun comes to represent something approaching omnipotence. In a succession of some of the film's subtlest imagery, it acquires a supernatural aura far beyond that of the other machines. When it is placed at last upon its tripod and positioned on a table in the portico, it takes on the characteristic of a shrine or altar. And during the saturnalian revelry in which Mapache's court musicians serenade it, a whore does a dance around it, and the entire regiment celebrate their acquisition of it in drunken debauchery, the whole scene comes to suggest some kind of pagan rite. (As we see yet again, precious little of Peckinpah's biblical training, much of it from the Old Testament, was wasted on him.) After the battle is over, the most prominent figure is Pike's, now dead, sunk to his knees, his hat still on, his fist clenched tightly around the handle of the gun, the barrel cocked high in the air. It is a disturbing image, the figure at once heroic and ominous, his posture both humble and defiant. It alludes to the wish of the Viking warrior to die with a sword in his hand, and it completes the theme of glory basic to this epic, as to all epics: the warrior's decision to live a brief but intense life of violent action in which his senses will be charged to the limits of physical endurance. No film, not even *The Seven Samurai,* has explored this terrain so completely as *The Wild Bunch.*

Probably one of the difficulties that some audiences have had with *The Wild Bunch* stems from Peckinpah's handling of the themes of glory and heroism, especially insofar as he internalizes them by making the very style and technique of his film embody the feelings and sensations his characters experience in action. He does not handle these themes as they have been handled in the Western, but as they have been handled in the epic tradition, where heroism and glory are inseparable from bloodshed, which is, of course, as it should be. It is in the very graphic depiction of the violence that these themes find their artistic validity, their complexity, and their irony. What Peckinpah shares with Homer, with the anonymous poet of *Beowulf,* with the Shakespeare of *Henry V* and the *Henry IV* plays, and with the Kurosawa of *The Seven Samurai* and *Yojimbo* is an ability at once to identify himself with a warrior-hero's sensibility and to stand apart from it. He is thus free to express the various states of feeling—the fierce joy, the excitement—of this kind of life and at the same time to leave us undeceived as to what it also involves—a suicidal passion for glory, a near psychotic reveling in bloodshed. As storytellers none of these poets is a preacher; and while they function as storytellers, they are neither for nor against violence, at least not in such a way that their poems are reducible to a polemic that will please political-ly correct moralists. As poets their point of view is not interested; it is sublimely disinterested. This is why it is a mistake to view *The Wild Bunch* as an antiviolence film or as an anti-Western, as if Peckinpah had made nothing more than an exceptionally beautiful and excit-ing message movie. These magnificent epiphanies of violence and death, with perhaps the most passionately charged images of fighting and killing ever put on film, cannot be reduced to a thesis without diluting the very passion that gives this vision its grandeur and its humanity.

In a famous essay Robert Warshow called violence in the Western violence without cruelty,[50] which is accurate enough and which ap-plies, as we shall see, even to *The Wild Bunch*. However, the conven-tional Western, for all its formulaic and ritualistic beauty, has always been something of a fake with its combination of the excitement of violence, "clean" acts of violence, and an overlay of good versus evil that is somehow supposed to legitimate the appetite for violence that it whets. What most conventional Westerns rarely deal with is the trait of the westerner that Warshow mentions: when the westerner draws his gun, he does so not at all reluctantly. Heroes in the epic tradition like their way of life, they enjoy it, are fiercely, passionately commit-ted to it. What limits their indulgence is not an external or official set of values, but a few codes of conduct, derived from experience and personally held, that ensure some measure of restraint. What makes Peckinpah's violence so disturbing, ambiguous, and subversive is not that he removes the so-called countervailing values of law and order of the conventional Western or that he undercuts the excite-ment of violence by dwelling on its ugliness. It is, rather, that he is able to render the violence so terrifyingly, so sensually, with such raw and unflinching power, yet *still* respond, and make us respond, fully, even exultantly, to the joy, the intensity, and the exhilaration these men experience when fighting, and, further, to display no misgivings about making his film embody these feelings.

It is nevertheless not uncommon to hear people object that, for all the similarities, *The Wild Bunch* is "somehow" different from the great epics of the past. This is both true and untrue, and for some of the same reasons. It is true to the extent that Peckinpah's heroes are outlaws rather than warriors as such. But the values of Pike as a fighting man are not fundamentally different from those of an Achilles or a Beowulf, neither of whose poets leaves us in any doubt as to where his hero really lives and finds his essential being. The real difference lies in the changes that history inevitably brings to artistic conventions. The closer we come to the modern world or, to put it more precisely, the deeper an action story is rooted in a period of transition characterized by increasing complexity of social organization and by increasing technological advancement, the more ambiguous a hero's virtues are likely to appear and the more he will begin to assume the status of a buffoon or a maverick, until eventually he must be made either a real clown or an actual outlaw, or at least a rebel with potentially criminal tendencies. This has been a theme of American literature since the time of Cooper (who, it will be recalled, introduced Natty Bumppo by having him get thrown into jail for violating game laws) and finds its most comprehensive intellectual statement in "The White Negro," where Norman Mailer resurrects the outlaw-hero in the form of the psychopathic Hipster, and its most comprehensive artistic treatment in *The Wild Bunch*, where Sam Peckinpah resurrects the epic warrior in the form of the outlaw-hero. Peckinpah is absolutely aware of the changes time has wrought upon the West (of both fact and fiction) and upon the heroic narrative traditions to which he is drawn. Indeed, these changes are informing themes of his films, and his prodigious sense of irony expresses that awareness.

Still another, perhaps the central, difference between *The Wild Bunch* and past epics has to do with the intensity and vividness of the violence, and this relates to the different mediums in which they exist. Film has so radically altered our notions of just how much immediacy is either possible or desirable in art that it is questionable whether we can ever experience, say, Homer's descriptions of violence with the same impact that earlier generations of readers unfamiliar with film have experienced them. What many people who object to Peckinpah's violence are objecting to is its power and immediacy, and they are thereby paying a lopsided tribute to his command, which is consummate, over the resources of his medium. Peckinpah's usual procedure for depicting violence (and also much action in general) is to film an event with cameras operating at standard speed and at higher speeds (the latter producing the slow-motion effect), then to take the standard footage and intercut it at a few points with very brief inserts from the slow-motion footage. This is a technique that rapidly shifts us from one perspective to another, forcing us to see from two different angles of vision and directing us toward two distinct modes of response; and it produces a curious, contradictory, even somewhat paradoxical effect. The slow-motion intercuts with their hypnotic allure distance us from the action by aestheticizing it, thus intensifying aesthetic feeling as such but ameliorating any vicarious experience we might have of the physical sensations the action produces. The normal-speed shots plunge us much more immediately into the action, making us almost participants by intensifying our vicarious experience of the physical sensations but vitiating any purely aesthetic feeling as such. We find here, then, yet another, though intensely concentrated, manifestation of Peckinpah's favorite formal principle of structural polarities. In a sense, what he is doing is referring us first to a romantic and then to a realistic view of the violence. In the one we are earthbound, right in the thick of bleeding, struggling, fighting humanity; in the other we have an almost Olympian detachment, the slow motion, with its sensual, even voluptuous, appeal, lulling us into a purely aesthetic contemplation. By rapidly cutting these two perspectives together, Peckinpah developed a technique that tends to divorce feeling from sensation (which is what makes his art so seductive, hence disturbing) and that enables him to strike exactly the right balance between an emotional, indeed, an almost palpably physical proximity to the violence and an aesthetic distance from it.

Peckinpah has often been called (in fact, called himself) a romantic, which is usually taken to mean that his films express powerful feelings, that he is sympathetic to individuals as opposed to society, and so forth. But his aesthetics is, properly speaking, classical in at least one respect: it seeks to maintain a dynamic relationship between the formal or decorative aspect of art and the substantive or material aspect. Those who condemn his violence as decadent or immoral are responding wholly to one or the other aspect, and they fail to see that with this director it is always the mixtures, combinations, and conflicts that count. Much of the moralistic cant that has been raised against his films might disappear (or at least turn to the serious issues they raise) once it is understood that what he makes us respond to is neither the matter—violence—nor the manner—aesthetic beauty—exclusively but to both simultaneously. Just about the only critic who seemed to understand this when the film first came out was Stanley Kauffmann, who recognized that Peckinpah's "interest is in the ballet, not the bullet," "and this insistent aesthetics is perhaps the cruelest of all the film's cruelties. The slow-motion snatches are irritating in two ways: first, because they draw our attention to the film as such; second, because Peckinpah is right—right to remind us that more than one prism of vision is possible at every moment of life and that this prism at this moment magnifies the enjoyment of killing."[51] But Peckinpah is also interested in the bullet or, rather, what the bullet does. For the slow-motion shots are almost always held to a particular, often subjective, point of view that is clearly, if implicitly, identified as such in and by the film. If it is necessary to make this explicit, we can say that the point is not that violence is beautiful, but that violence can appear beautiful depending upon the limitations and restrictions involved in the point of view, angle of vision, or perceiving eye. (For Peckinpah even an Olympian view is limited.) In the largest possible terms, then, what Peckinpah does is alternate between a moral and an aesthetic view of the violence, which tends to divorce the moral from the aesthetic response (this is the analog to the separation of sensation and feeling already noted and is another thing that makes his violence so disturbing) and which gives rise to one of his abiding themes: it is only by divorcing the physical sensations, the pain and suffering, from our apprehension of the violence that we can feel the violence as beautiful. This separation can occur in two ways: by our being totally removed from the physical or by our getting so caught up in the physical that we are overwhelmed by it—the bloodletting really coming to seem a ballet, we the dancers at last one with the dance.

When Peckinpah's violence is understood in this way, the whole issue of his so-called excesses is thrown into clearer relief. People who call *The Wild Bunch* excessive are referring to the protraction of the opening and especially the closing gun battles and to the number of bodies that pile up and the amount of blood that is spilled. However, in art excess is rarely a matter of quantity as such (it can be, but it isn't in this film), but has rather to do with uniformity and intensity, or, perhaps more accurately, with uniformity *of* intensity. What keeps Peckinpah's depictions of violence from being uniform is that our slow-motion rapture is constantly being disrupted by the rapid cutting that introduces normal speed, thus jolting us back into reality, only to return us to the trancelike state when another slow-motion shot is cut in, which is then in turn disturbed once again. This technique was devised by Peckinpah—and despite dozens of imitators, no one has been able to use it as intelligently or as effectively as he does—precisely to ensure that the potential excesses of each device would be not neutralized but checked, balanced, and kept in suspension by one another other. This suspension in turn ensures that his depictions of violence remain securely within the purview of art, not extend to provocation, incitement, or mere sensationalism. Which is exactly what he meant when he said, "If I'm so bloody that I drive people out of the theater, then I've failed."

What his imitators don't understand is that the greater effectiveness of his violence depends on two things: first, the brevity of his slow-motion inserts (his imitators drag these out so long that they no longer function as inserts); and second, the relative absence of gore, which keeps our eyes riveted to the screen even as the bloodshed makes a much more appalling effect subliminally. This is what he meant when he said that people want to walk out on his films "but they can't," "they watch, and that makes them mad."[52] This is also why his method is to draw out the buildup and the anticipation, extend the release and reaction, but get over the actual moment of bloodshed, collision, or contact almost in the blink of an eye (as a matter of literal fact, if the viewer were to blink his eyes at the wrong time— even during the notorious moment when Angel's throat is cut—he would miss all that Peckinpah usually shows of the gore, catching only the attendant action). Inasmuch as Peckinpah's films have always shown how the life has to be beaten, bludgeoned, or blasted out of people, the slow-motion footage acquires a significance over and above the psychological, for its purpose is not, as is commonly assumed, to prolong the moment of death but to slow down the last few moments of life, thereby paying an almost elegiac tribute to the peculiar nobility Peckinpah finds in the reluctance of the human animal to give up life, tenaciously clinging to it right down to the last agonizing seconds before letting go. But these images are also infused with a savage irony, for the way the bodies twist and writhe in grotesque spasms suggests a parody of that very grace under pressure that the slow-motion technique appears to confer upon them by way of its aestheticizing function. As always with this director, then, the effect is ambiguous, the meanings deliberately paradoxical: whether parodies or elegies, these blood ballets are bacchanalias of death that express, tragically and ironically, a force and principle of life.

Once we realize the relationship between Peckinpah's artistry and his violent subject matter, we are able to see that he is not glorifying violence. He is instead telling a story about men who find themselves glorified *in* violence. To this end he makes the filmmaking style embody from time to time a sensibility that experiences great fulfillment in violence. However, this is a fulfillment that goes beyond violence as such, and at this point we might profitably return to the idea of Peckinpah's slow motion as an analog to Homer's catalogs. Both devices serve a similar function as regards the dynamics of experiencing the poems involved: they highlight physical detail yet keep it securely yoked to an overall arc of movement or pattern of dramatic action. Cordell Strug, in the essay cited earlier, explained this aspect of Peckinpah's violence better than anyone else has:

> In his best work, Peckinpah is absorbed not so much in violence or gore but in violent action. This may be a spurious distinction, but compare the lopped-off head and the sliced-off breast of *Soldier Blue* with anything in Peckinpah. The former are given to us as ends in themselves, they are stuffed down our throats, we are meant to be disgusted. Peckinpah absorbs the extremely explicit acts of violence into the rhythm of the action. . . . [The] outrageous death, the potentially revolting image, is firmly placed within an action sequence which draws all the aesthetic value to itself and doesn't allow itself to fall apart into outlandish fragments.[53]

This is a distinction that makes it possible to say that for all the ferocity of the Bunch's violence remarkably little of it involves deliberate cruelty. When Dutch says that the Bunch are nothing like Mapache because they don't hang anybody, it is a meaningful distinction within the film's frame of reference. It distinguishes the Bunch from the real fascist mentalities in the film, such as Harrigan, Mapache, and the Germans, all of whom relish the power they wield over others and take real pleasure in causing ridicule and inflicting pain. The Bunch, however, experience as much joy and exhilaration robbing the train as they do fighting; they take as much satisfaction in doing a good job or confronting a powerful adversary (hence Pike's "I wouldn't have it any other way"); they appreciate similar displays of expertise and prowess in others (as when Dutch says of the Indians, "I'd say those fellows know how to handle themselves"); and their killings are tied more closely to necessity, given their line of work, than to sadism as such. Even the Gorch brothers, the most self-indulgent members of the Bunch as Pike is the most restrained, lose their grip on their instincts only in the fury of the final bloodbath. Here is yet another reason that Peckinpah includes all those shots of the Bunch riding across the desert or taking their wagon up and down the windswept, rocky terrain, and why he slows down so many images that are not of violence as such but simply of exciting action. As we have seen, these shots help to unify the narrative. But they also express in the broadest possible terms where the Bunch's real commitment lies, which is not centrally to killing but to a life of sensation, conflict, and collision—in a word, to kinesis at the most powerful and intense physical level where the alternatives are pushed to an extreme at once simple and profound: life and death.

From this perspective it is now possible to see that the best gloss, if one is even necessary, on *The Wild Bunch* is not Robert Ardrey's *African Genesis* (which, though touted by Peckinpah for a while in interviews, he discovered only *after* he had made the film), but Norman Mailer's "The White Negro." Some of the similarities are obvious enough—the Bunch, for example, as representatives of Mailer's Hipster, the psychopath who refuses to conform to a stultifying commercial, mechanistic, and dehumanizing society and becomes thereby a rebel mostly by default and *sans* ideology. This is suggested with great economy in the opening sequence, where, on their way into town, the Bunch pass a man sweeping the railroad tracks, another man in a ready-made suit that seems to squeeze his very shoulders together, the mayor addressing the Temperance Union ("Five cents a glass. Does anyone really think that that is the price of a drink?"), and dozens of citizens in starched collars and tightly buttoned-up dresses. It is also suggested by a really spectacular irony that informs the closing scenes of the film, in which the Bunch's decision to reclaim Angel inadvertently has beneficial consequences for the revolution. The similarities extend to Peckinpah's conception of character, which, like Mailer's, views people not as fixed and limited but as fluid and dynamic, the determinant being the context in which action is taken and the available energy at the moment of decision. They extend further to include the drive one finds in both author and filmmaker to throw themselves and their characters into experience and, more disturbing, to their apparent belief in the creative and redemptive possibilities of violent action. Perhaps most significant, the similarities encompass even language. The single most important word that Mailer found in the vocabulary of Hip is the word "Go," and the most frequent refrain in *The Wild Bunch* is "Let's go." If this is mere coincidence, then it must have been teleologically ordained, for it includes even their fundamental dialectic, which is drawn not between life and death, but between movement and death defined as stasis.

V

We can begin to get a clearer fix on what *The Wild Bunch* is about, its "ideas" as it were, when we realize that basically it is a vision in which concentrations of energy—primarily organic and mechanical or, al-

ternately, human, animal, and technological—act, react, and collide
within the same space. The theme is not of diminishing space, but
of fixed and limited spaces becoming increasingly crowded, which
only multiplies the possibilities for conflict and violence. If, as Kenneth Burke has said, form is the setting up and fulfilling of expecta-
tion, then the opening scene of *The Wild Bunch* is practically a classic demonstration of his thesis. The first collision is minor: Pike and
an old woman accidentally bump into each other, the moment so
keenly shot and composed that when Peckinpah cuts in the reaction
shots it is as if vectors have collided and splintered off in different
directions. From this seemingly inconsequential accident, the sequence builds relentlessly to the moment of outburst when all hell
breaks loose. The sense of mounting tension, of energy barely able
to be contained, is conveyed by the increasing number, brevity, and
intensity (e.g., closer closeups, more setups off the level) of shots
edited together in accelerating tempo, which has the effect of con-
centrating and impacting the various dramatic forces—the Bunch,
the posse, the temperance marchers, the band, the children, the citizens—as they converge in that single, restricted space where the
street bends. The hymn "Shall We Gather at the River?," which the
marchers are singing and the band is playing, gets louder and louder, while, imperceptibly at first, then clearly, the sound of a heartbeat
dislodges itself from the drone of the music and thumps a measured,
then a racing, beat. In a brilliant touch, barely two shots before Pike
shoves the railroad official out into the street, Peckinpah inserts a
zoom-out, as if the camera itself were trying to create more space in
which to accommodate the accumulating energy. But it is too late,
and the first volley of bullets prevents the zoom from completing itself.*

This idea—of energy packed into limited space—is announced
scant seconds into the film by the now-famous image of children huddled around a thatched cage filled with ants swarming over a few scorpions. Like most of the symbols in the film, this is too dense with
allusions for its range of significance to be limited to one and only
one meaning. Of all the symbols, however, this one has the characteristic of a true epic simile inasmuch as the vehicle is detached from
the immediate tenor and ramified metaphorically throughout the rest

---

*Any discussion of *The Wild Bunch* implicitly acknowledges the editing by Lou
Lombardo and Robert Wolfe, so integral is it to the style, meaning, and effect of
the film. Still, one should at least observe that the art and craft of film editing know
no higher peaks than *The Wild Bunch*, and very, very few that are anywhere near its
summit.

of the film. Initially it refers to the opening ambush, where the Bunch and the bounty hunters shoot at each other through the frantic townspeople—a connection Peckinpah makes almost explicit with that great dissolve that superimposes a long shot of the main street littered with bodies over a closeup of the ants and scorpions the children are burning. The simile is later alluded to when the Bunch first enter the main square of Agua Verde, where the final battle will take place. Two sides are enclosed by high walls with barred windows in them; behind some of the lower windows children sit aimlessly tossing pebbles at the passersby, among whom are the Bunch. Peckinpah cuts in a shot of the Bunch from inside a window, looking through the bars, the children's point of view. The area is filled with villagers crowded together, milling, teeming, pulsing with human energy. As the Bunch move toward an available table, the composition of the shot, the way they walk, and the clothes they wear all serve to highlight them against a swarming monotoned background of khaki uniforms. The relationships are cemented: the Bunch become the scorpions on the anthill of *federale* soldiers, the square itself the cage containing them, children presiding over all. Within minutes, Angel will shoot Teresa and almost touch off a gunfight.

These relationships and their volatile capabilities are shifted about, extended, and developed in at least three later scenes. When the bridge explodes with Thornton and the posse on it, the event is witnessed by the Bunch on one side and by "children" in the form of the cavalry of "green recruits" (some of them only adolescents) positioned on the opposite ridge. Shortly before the explosion, TC, idiotically gun-happy, starts firing at the soldiers, killing one of the youngest, as the other bounty hunters join in, before Thornton manages to stop them. When Herrera and a company of Mapache's soldiers try to take the rifles without paying for them, the setting—a canyon flanked by steep cliffs, the Bunch and their wagon load of rifles and ammunition near the middle at the bottom, *federales* positioned at both entrances and on the surrounding cliffs—recalls the cage of insects. When the Bunch uncover the machine gun, one of the soldiers panics and fires. Pike lights the fuse that will blow up both the wagon and themselves, the soldiers cock and aim their rifles, and Lyle says, "Start the ball, Tector," as Tector readies the machine gun for action. As before, we have a restricted space existing within a much larger space, densely packed energies, a fuse racing against time, a world teetering on the edge of explosion. "Cut the fuse," pleads Herrera; the soldiers lower their weapons, Pike complies, and Herrera orders the soldier who panicked executed. This time disaster is averted, but the antagonistic forces converge at the end when the Bunch march through the crowded streets of Agua Verde to reclaim Angel. Mapache pretends to hand him over but cuts Angel's throat at the last minute. As if in reflex all four members of the Bunch fire their weapons, killing the general instantly. There is an electrifying moment of silence in which the very air crackles with immense energies charged for release yet momentarily suspended. Dutch's giggle, followed by Tector's, breaks the air. Pike takes aim, fires at the German commander, and all hell breaks loose once more and for the last time.

We can now see why Peckinpah felt it necessary to reduce the violence in the opening gunfight: this closing one must resolve not only the energy accumulated in the immediate situation but all the energies accumulated from the rest of the film. It also resolves the epic simile, as Pike is brought down by a boy soldier who, lifting a rifle with obvious effort, fires from behind one of the barred windows, bringing the "game" to an end as the children brought their game to an end at the beginning when they tossed straw into the cage and set fire to it.

The ants and the scorpions were first presented to Peckinpah quite literally as a simile. Emilio Fernandez one day told him, "You know, for me, the Wild Bunch is like a scorpion on an anthill." Peckinpah snapped to attention, "Wait a minute, what's that?"[54] Fernandez told him about a game children play in Mexico, filling a cage with ants and dropping some scorpions into it. "And from that point on," Peckinpah said, "that was the way I saw the whole picture."[55] Just how richly and complexly he extended its implications throughout the film may be seen in what he does with children. Shortly after the dissolve from the burning insects to the massacred town, a group of children is seen running down the street and shouting, "Bang, bang! Bang, bang!" as Peckinpah cuts in a ground-level shot from the point of view of one of the dead bodies, the children circling the camera and still firing their make-believe pistols. (This setup is parallel to those used for some of the closeups of the children at the beginning, where it is as if we are looking up at them from inside the cage.) Their voices are momentarily carried over into the next scene, in which a wounded member of the Bunch falls from his horse because, shot in the face during the opening ambush, he can no longer see to ride. The effect is as if the children have dropped him with their "innocent" game, which Pike then joins and completes for real by executing the man (at his own request). Peckinpah repeatedly uses associative editing to link the Bunch, Pike in particular, to the children, as when he frames a tracking shot along several children's faces with closeups of Pike, or, at the very beginning, when he cuts from closeups of the children huddled around the cage to closeups of Pike and Dutch as they ride by.

The association is made explicit at one point, when Don Jose, the old man of Angel's village, tells Pike, "We all dream of being a child again, even the worst of us. Perhaps the worst most of all."* This is a fine example of Peckinpah's writing, for if the Bunch are among the worst of us, they are nevertheless recognizably *of* us. What Peckinpah means to suggest by associating Pike with the children is that Pike's capacities for moral growth and development are not yet completely closed off, that there is more to his character than may be apparent at any given moment. It is this childlike aspect of Pike's sensibility, free from habitual or learned response and conflicting with it, that makes any kind of redemption possible and is thus vital if his decision to reclaim Angel, which is a decision that breaks a pattern in his life up to that point, is to make any sense. By contrast, Peckinpah almost never symbolically associates children with the grown-up children, such as Crazy Lee (whose name tells us what we need to know about him) or the bounty hunters (who forever try to pass the buck for their mistakes) or even Mapache (who exhibits the cruelty yet lacks the excuse of being a child). These characters are "children" with all the power and authority yet none of the sense of responsibility of adults.

We can dispense—once and for all, it is hoped—with the banality that children express Peckinpah's belief that all men are killers, that the children enjoying cruelty and torture and bloodshed indicate the innate evil of mankind. Peckinpah uses children to provide another perspective on the events; they become another sensibility upon which the action is registered, in their case a sensibility that has not yet developed resources for moral evaluation. What they appreciate is spectacle divorced from any evaluative context except the purely aesthetic; they are like prisms that record fact and sensation but not judgment and moral discrimination. Peckinpah himself has said as

---

*Peckinpah considered the sequence in which this line occurs the most important in the film, and regarded the Bunch's exit from Angel's village as the turning point as far as the humanity of the Bunch is concerned. "If you can ride out with them there and feel it," he said, "you can die with them and feel it." This scene also contains the piece of editing that frames the row of children with closeups of Pike, which was removed from Domestic II. It is precisely the loss of this sort of thing—subtleties and nuances—that Peckinpah feared when others tampered with his films, and it is what he meant when he spoke of his films as being "intricately intertwined." When something is cut, the effect is never merely local or discrete, but affects other things elsewhere.

much: "I believe in the complete innocence of children. They have no idea of good and evil. It's an acquired taste."[56] It is too simple to suggest that one must become as a child to find violence beautiful, but a childlike perspective on the violence is woven into the narrative texture of the film, and shifting, colliding perspectives are one of the main things *The Wild Bunch* is all about.

When one reviewer criticized Peckinpah for not being able to do more than one thing at a time in any given shot, he was apparently referring to the restlessness of Peckinpah's editing style.[57] Even a cursory viewing of the film will not support this criticism. As for the editing, surely it would be more productive to inquire whether the style functions positively within the film than to assume it is the result of deficient technique. Such an inquiry leads us first to something we have already noted: that Peckinpah almost never uses an establishing shot as such to open a scene. His method is usually to open out from some significant detail, occasionally with a reverse zoom in the manner of an iris effect (the starving dog at Angel's village; the woman suckling an infant, a bandolier slung over her shoulder, the baby fingering the bullets). We then notice that a good many of the establishing shots he does use after opening a scene are not "objective" but are tied instead to individual characters' points of view. Next we notice that several of the long or full shots are photographed with a telephoto lens. Lucien Ballard, the cinematographer, and Peckinpah pored over all the photographs and newsreels of the Mexican revolution they could lay their hands on.[58] What they noticed in all of them was a prevailing flatness of perspective, and they carefully chose a selection of telephoto lenses to replicate that flatness. The effect of the lenses is to compress the depth of field so that everything is pressed closer together. This is especially true in the Agua Verde setting, where we itch from the congestion of people and animals milling about. When things moves laterally, we often fear a collision (watch, for example, as the camera follows a group of marching soldiers until Angel and Dutch appear in the frame). When they narrowly miss, the point has nevertheless been made subliminally: collision is at all times imminent and possible in this place. The telephoto lenses also have the effect, particularly when used for closeups, of pressing us closer to the surface of the film and thus of subtly reinforcing our sense of congestion.

One significance of both the editing style and the compositions is thus psychological: Peckinpah wants to make us experience event and incident as vividly as possible, from the inside out as it were, more or less as participants, to which end the camera itself becomes less

an observer than a participant in the action, a restless, shifting, wan-
dering avatar that moves through a seemingly limitless number of
points of view. Peckinpah is a master of that most problematic of all
moving-camera devices, the handheld subjective shot, which he in-
tegrates fluidly into the ongoing narrative line by using it in ever-so-
brief inserts that plunge us right into the thick of spectacle: for example, the rapid arc in which the camera spins topsy-turvy when a
nameless member of the Bunch is shot off his horse during the ambush, or the momentary switch to the woman's point of view when
Pike's horse rears above her. It would be tedious to analyze the whole
film in shot-by-shot detail—there are well over 3,600 individual edits, more than any other color film ever made—but it should be noted that an incredible number of the film's shots are visualized in
terms of the characters' impressions or are simply set up as they might
logically see what is being shown. (For example, most of the exit from
Angel's village is composed from two basic points of view, that of the
departing Bunch and that of the serenading villagers.) Except for
when he wants to create an effect of dramatic irony, Peckinpah is
usually concerned with preserving the integrity of the sequence of
the characters' sense impressions as long as he can. This in turn
points toward a larger purpose: making the visual style approximate
the way the characters experience the spaces they inhabit.

In the hands of a genuinely serious artist, style is never a mere
extravagance used to decorate the material. It is determined by the
material, has something of its own to say, and constitutes a kind of
subtext that runs parallel to the main text. If the artist is any good, if
he has mastered the resources of his craft, then it is not unusual to
find that the style is telling us much the same thing as the manifest
content of the artwork seems to be trying to tell us. We have seen that
Peckinpah's rapid editing and telephoto compositions have a psychological import. They also have a thematic import, intimately related
to the psychological. They are the stylistic equivalent to and formal
analog of a world where, as in the cage of ants and scorpions crawl-
ing over each other, everything is so crowded together that it is impossible to concentrate one's attention on any single thing for longer than a few seconds, yet equally impossible to unify more than
provisionally the multiplicity of fact and sensation that invades the
senses. The compositions reveal a congested space, the cutting
records the massive implosion of data upon the receptor. Thus both
the editing and the cinematography grow out of and serve the opening simile; and as this simile is extended and ramified throughout the
entire film, the visual style expands with it, embodying and express-

ing what it feels like to live and move and breathe in a space so crowded that it is like a cage full of insects. At the most concrete level the style demonstrates that if a dozen ants are biting us in a dozen different places at once, it is impossible to divide our attention equally among them. Moving up the scale toward abstraction, the style also has the effect, by way of the camera's restless exploration of new and increasing points of view, of plying perspective upon accumulating perspective until the density of conflicting points of view equals the density of conflicting energies within the film's space. The sense of being crowded eventually becomes so oppressive that implosion leads to explosion, the inevitable consequence of which is violence. Owing to that sense of pleasure we feel almost automatically when a great burden is lifted or an intense pressure is finally relieved, the violence becomes both exhilarating and horrifying, because both liberating and lethal. What the visual style is trying to tell us is what the film itself is trying to show; style becomes thus synonymous with and inseparable from meaning, and what it means is what it feels like to exist in this space from one moment to the next.

Just how subtly and surely Peckinpah can fuse style and substance, and ramify his naturalistic symbolism, may be seen in the significance that dynamite comes to have in the course of the film's development. It is shown just a few times, three or four sticks wrapped in a tight bundle, caught in equally tight closeups or at one point in a rapid zoom that completes itself in a tight closeup. If the caged insects symbolize the space within the film and its human, animal, and mechanical occupants, then the dynamite symbolizes the impacted energy in that space and leads us to consider how vital the basic structure of the film is to its overall effect. That structure is a chase structure, which is a race against time in which time runs out, space becomes more and more restricted, and protagonist and antagonist are brought into closer and closer proximity to one another until they cannot escape collision. It is a structure thus not unlike a flame speeding along a fuse, and it suggests a world in which things (vases, bridges, bodies and sensibilities, perspectives, points of view) explode, shatter, disintegrate on the literal and the figurative levels, the concrete and the abstract planes. It is a world where things really do fall apart and the center does not hold for very long.

In this context the slow-motion footage acquires another meaning. At the most intense moments of violence, which are a consequence of the densest concentrations of energy, space is at such a premium that time itself is forced to take up the slack, which it does by expanding to contain the violent energies released in collision. However, time in this sense is a matter not of measurement but of perception, so the slow-motion images are usually located securely within a given character's point of view. In what is surely one of the film's great moments of cinematic architecture, Peckinpah cuts together shots of a man getting riddled with bullets in normal speed, the man arcing to the ground in slow motion, children watching the spectacle, and bounty hunters aiming and firing their rifles at the man. With the utmost economy he pulls together and concentrates several ways of looking at the same thing and expresses the various states of feeling— the blow of the impact as metal hits flesh, the sensual beauty of the image when divorced from every evaluative context except that of the aesthetic, the thrill of the bounty hunters when their bullets find a mark, the pain of the victim as his body takes the slugs, and the re- luctance with which the body gives up its life. Similarly, the amazing shots of the bridge exploding, the horses and riders suspended in midair as the bottom drops out from under them, then floating grace- fully to the water below, are held mostly to Pike's and Dutch's line of sight. The slow-motion intercuts are thus not mere indulgent displays of pretty pictorialism that interrupt the continuity. They are instead part of an infinitely elastic continuity, and function as true epipha- nies, gestalts realized out of the welter of conflicting sights and sounds. They are moments of equilibrium, dynamic rather than stat- ic—hence, slowed-down rather than stopped motion—always labile, subject to being shattered by the next sensation—hence, the rapid cut into each slow-motion gestalt almost as soon as it has been formed.

Peckinpah's images have an almost unparalleled richness and density of texture, which is mirrored in the way he makes all the shots count, thus managing to do several things *with* each one. For exam- ple, we have already observed how he extends the epic simile to in- clude Agua Verde and how most of the Bunch's entrance into the square is shot from Pike's point of view. At the same time, then, as Peckinpah is developing his simile, he is also establishing a new set- ting and unfolding his central character, making us see what Thorn- ton meant when he called Pike the best and making us feel—through the discrete shots with cuts back to Pike that force us to pause and weigh the strategic implications of each detail just as Pike is doing— what it is like to be on guard every moment.

Another example of how Peckinpah makes style and technique serve meaning is the Bunch's encounter with Herrera on the trail. Most of the scene is shot in long and medium shots until that terri- fying moment when one of Herrera's men panics and fires at the

Bunch, and Pike lights the fuse. At this point the action is seen in a proliferation of extreme closeups (some of them the result of very fast zooms) of the Bunch and the soldiers rapidly cut against one another. The effect this has is to show us the characters' expressions, to pull us into the action, and to jack up the tension as tightly as possible. The paramount effect, however, is to obliterate our sense of the physical space separating the antagonists, which Peckinpah achieves by filling the cinematic space (that is, the space of the screen) with nothing but antagonistic energies—faces tight with anticipation, eyes narrowed and taking aim, weapons raised and triggers cocked. It is as if the filmmaking style had suddenly exploded. Then, as Herrera pleads for Pike to cut the fuse, the tempo of the editing slows down, but the shots remain tight closeups. It is only when Pike finally does cut the fuse and the danger of explosion has passed that the style completely "relaxes," the camera slowly zooming out from closeup to medium distance. It is obvious that if Peckinpah had wanted, he could have filmed this moment with fewer cutaways, inserts, and reactions, but it would have been at the expense of feeling: using longer takes and a more distant camera, the film would have illustrated the tension of the moment but the style would not have embodied it, as a consequence of which we would feel it less immediately, if at all. And in the final analysis, the scene would then mean something else: with the camera farther from the action, the physical space in and around the characters preserved, the world within the film would feel less like one that is always threatening to explode as conflicting energies exhaust the available space, and more like one where destructive energies are held in control.

Except in the most concentrated of art forms or in special cases, it isn't possible to document an absolutely direct relationship between form and content. This is rarely what critics mean when they seek to equate the two. Rather, what is meant is that there is a general correspondence between what is being said or shown and how it is being said or shown, and the correspondence is genuinely organic, usually functional, and sometimes seamless. Having seen, then, how form follows function and manner mediates meaning in this film, we may wish to address ourselves for a moment to the question of whether the style can be said to represent the man, as we are often told an artist's style does or should. We know that Peckinpah was fond of saying that things are always mixed. We also know that he grew up in a family where one parent gave him pious certainties from a "Bible that was very big," while the other parent represented a figure of unquestioned authority. We know too that, as one reporter put it, the

absolutes fed him of law and morality drove him nearly crazy; he started questioning them and, by his own admission, continued to question them throughout his life. This same reporter, who spent some
time with him, wrote, "Like the strained ground in earthquake country, slipping and shearing to adjust to an ever-shifting core, the ambivalences in Sam Peckinpah run deep," and she went on to report
that at the same time that he was mocking his daughter's pacifism,
he was handing out medallions that read, "War is not healthy for
children and other living things."[59] Clearly this is a man who is quite
unclear and very mixed up, and whose artistic style is designed to
express his "mixtures."

It is a style that shatters centers and makes things fall apart, and it
indicates a person who is himself unsure of where he stands, what he
believes, and how he knows. The multiple perspectives that are the
organizing principle of his films suggest a mind dissatisfied with all
absolutes, discontent with all certainties, disinclined to settle upon
any simple explanations. The style has been called, with considerable
accuracy, "prismatic," "kaleidoscopic," and "mosaic." It is prismatic
because it tries to see from as many different points of view as possible; it is kaleidoscopic because it tries to illuminate its subject in as
many different ways as possible; and it is mosaic because the unity of
its effect is a function of quick glimpses, sidelong glances, and dart-
ing impressions caught by people who are often on the run, trying
to avoid or avert collision. The style is expressive of a sensibility that
is likewise restless, searching, and inquisitive and that reveals a man
who was equally intense, alert, and uneasy. In this sense, the style is
enough like the man, or at least like an important aspect of the man,
that it can be said to be the man; and this is why analyzing the style
of his films hastens us back to their meaning and why a discussion of
meaning carried far enough turns into a discussion of style.

In general Peckinpah may be said to have two basic styles: one, seen
primarily in his Western films, that is open, somewhat lyrical, and
expansive; the other, seen primarily in his films with contemporary
settings, that is darker, tenser, and a little more closed in. However,
there are elements of both styles in all of his films; and it can be seen
that the contemporary-settings style is not so much an antithesis as
an extension of the Western style. When the setting gets more contemporary and space is at a greater premium, then the sense of being quite literally crowded intensifies, the flow of images is more often punctuated by competing images, the glimpses of open space are
more sporadic, and the expansions into lyricism are of briefer duration. Similarly, the camera moves closer to the action (in a crowded

setting, even it has less space in which to maneuver), and as a consequence it sees less at any given moment, so the cutaways multiply. In *The Wild Bunch* the two styles are synthesized, because its setting is both savage and civilized, primitive yet recognizably our century—the most transitional of all his settings. His combination of deep focus, telephoto lenses, slow motion, and fast cutting is ideal for weaving the thick, pulsating, protean textures of life he is after and for expressing the psychological effects of living in a world of such density. The longest unbroken shot (nearly a minute in length) occurs in one scene where the Bunch seem to have the whole desert to themselves; strung along in file, giving each other ample space, and nestled in the seemingly infinite expanse of sand and sky, they can afford to relax, to drop their guard for a while. By comparison the tempo of the editing increases as spaces become more crowded with antagonistic energies, and it reaches its peak during the moments of violent outburst in which everything disintegrates and in which, for self-preservation, we must be at our most alert and attentive. It is precisely at such moments, however, that it is most difficult to retain our wits sufficiently to see everything whole and unified, and the quickness of the cutting embodies the difficulty of being involved in something yet trying to remain detached from it. Peckinpah's visual style is thus the logical consequence and expression of an insistent dialectics of forces in collision, which he pursues right down even to the smallest structural unit of his film, the shot-to-shot cut.

VI

Peckinpah has an intuitive grasp not only of the most ancient archetypes and genres—the chase, the hunt, stories of revenge and honor and heroism—but also of the origins of drama in ancient rituals and festivals. His early training was in theater, and he draws upon his theatrical background every bit as much as he uses his knowledge of the Bible. There is something, for example, almost Shakespearean about the way he builds his dramatic structures upon contrasting groups of characters. His materials do not permit the broad range of social types from the highest to the lowest that we find in Shakespeare, but this matters less than the amount of diversification he is able to draw from the materials.* As in Faulkner, there is a rich and

*Peckinpah worked so often in action genres that he has never been recognized as what we clumsily call a "social" or "societal" director. Yet in his best work the observation of social forms and behavior and their implications for character is about as keen as anything in Renoir or Satyajit Ray. In addition to several examples that have

varied assortment within the terms the materials do allow: the outlaw Bunch, the officials of the town, the god-fearing Temperance
Union, the conservative middle-class citizens, the railroad men, the
U.S. cavalry, and the gutter trash and dregs among the posse of bounty hunters. These are paralleled on the Mexican side of the border,
where Peckinpah is able to expand the sociopolitical scale by representing Europe in Mapache's German military advisers and spies and
by immersing us in a peasant culture and then an Indian culture.
Concentrated as it is into a single and restricted dramatic space, this
variegated mixture enables Peckinpah to reap rich dividends of irony and ambiguity and to incorporate yet another of his favorite dialectics, illusion versus reality. In the extraordinary opening, he deliberately upsets and confuses all our standard reference points, as
soldiers turn out to be bandits, law and order are represented by mer-
cenaries, and children engage in games of torture and cruelty. Similarly, in each of the three main groups of the story—Pike and the
Bunch, Thornton and his posse, and Mapache and the *federales*—the
same themes or complex of themes—camaraderie, honor, courage,
loyalty, treachery, betrayal, revenge, discipline, incompetence, and
responsibility—are developed in an endlessly shifting counterpoint,
sometimes mirroring one another, other times setting off contrasts
of irony, romance, comedy, and tragedy.

Peckinpah also likes to incorporate audiences within the dramatic fabric of his stories, and these audiences function somewhat in the
manner of choruses as telltale signs or clues to the desired mode of
response, again either straightforwardly or ironically. When Teresa
presents Mapache with a gift of a horse, the whole gathering bursts
into applause. Elsewhere there is a moment in which Thornton asks
Coffer what is in Agua Verde. "Mexicans, what else?" Coffer answers,
and we join the rest of the posse in laughter. When Thornton glares
at them, cutting their ridicule short, we too feel chastened for laughing at the stupid wisecrack. We are similarly chastened in an earlier
scene. When Crazy Lee drops three men and their bodies happen to
fall into a neat row, it is as if the director were daring us to laugh. If

---

already been adduced incidentally, consider this fine, subtle moment: when Lyle
Gorch demands some women for himself and Tector, Zamorra orders Herrera, the
accountant, to find *las viejas* (meaning, literally, some old ones). Herrera hesitates,
forcing Zamorra to repeat the order, this time shouting, whereupon the accountant
complies, but only reluctantly and with deep revulsion. A whole world of sensibility
is revealed in that hesitation: this odious little man with decaying teeth—who no doubt
holds women in as low esteem as Mapache does—nevertheless doesn't want to give
even some of his country's old whores to these loathsome gringos.

we do—and the bit almost always gets a laugh—the bounty hunters, gleefully shouting things like, "This is better than a hog killing!" remind us of just how obscene our laughter is.

There are also other kinds of internal audiences that proliferate his films and that recall for us elements of opera, song, dance, and festival used both as source music and as score (occasionally at once, as when the Bunch leave Angel's village). This sort of thing also suggests how musical Peckinpah's dramatic constructions are, with their recurring themes, motifs, patterns of action and movement, their contrasting sets of characters and locales, their verbal and visual reiterations and variations, and of course the musical materials themselves. When Mapache gets the first load of rifles, he shouts, "*Musica!*" and his "court" orchestra of singers and guitarists breaks into song. These things are integral to the structure, reinforcing the legendary quality of the story and preparing us for the remarkable gradation of mood and tone in the last twenty minutes, during which the very language of the film is made to undergo a subtle transformation from the representational and symbolic to the iconic and imagistic, as Peckinpah pushes his drama to its final resting place.

The film opens with one kind of language: a desaturated black-and-white still of the Bunch, deceptively dressed in army uniforms, riding toward us. Throughout the front titles, which are accompanied by ominous martial music, the color images are periodically frozen into black-and-white stills, the very alternation of the two kinds of shots "telling" us that the story we are about to see is going to move from the world of history to the world of the imagination. The black-and-white stills, which suggest lithographs, are Peckinpah's way of saying that here our avenue to the past is initially through material of record—old newspaper accounts and photographs, perhaps. This is one kind of truth, available through one kind of language: hard, decidedly fast, cut, and dried. But there is another kind of language, which yields another kind of truth: fluid, tenuous, ambiguous. This is the truth of the imagination, its language the language of art and originating in a mode of reporting quite different from that of the newspaper story. Nobody knows how legends really get started, but it is a respectable enough guess that the process has something to do with a spectator's being on the scene of some extraordinary event. He tells it to someone, who in turn tells it to someone else, perhaps embellishing it here, embroidering it there. Eventually someone may write a song about it, someone else a poem, until the story is well on its way to becoming part of folklore. This is why Peckinpah's films are so replete with songs, with balladeers and instrumentalists, with children, and with so many other kinds of internal audiences. These audiences are bearing witness to events of such stuff as legends are made on, and the import of the events is not lost upon them, but is being recorded in song even as they occur.

When the Bunch strap on their guns and begin their march through the crowded streets of Agua Verde, they are reenacting a Western convention that is so generic it seems to dissolve into ritual before our very eyes. The film is about to move beyond itself, as fact and legend are made to merge: the image, because of the heat, subtly shimmers, and the merger is heralded first in song, sung here by some drunken soldiers the Bunch pass along the way, and then in a reprise of the martial music that accompanied the Bunch's slow ride into Starbuck at the beginning. When they cross a long open stretch and walk through a break in a wall that will lead them to Mapache and Angel, they have come full circle, only now they have chosen to walk back into the cage, undeceived about what lies ahead, with a seriousness of purpose they have never known before.

When the battle is over, the bounty hunters descend upon the village, while vultures fly in and settle on the surrounding walls and rooftops, patiently awaiting their turn at the carnage below. In a quiet moment that seems to set a seal of benediction on all that has happened, Thornton walks up to Pike's body and takes his friend's pistol, a gesture that signals the fulfillment of his word to Harrigan and pays a tribute to his dead comrade, who was killed paying some old debts of his own. Moments later Coffer comes upon Pike's body and says, in hushed tones, "TC, it's him . . . it's Pike." TC is likewise momentarily awestruck, then regains himself and says, "You ain't so damn much now, are you, Mr. Pike?" For the time being, however, it is not the meek or the courageous but the scavengers, human and animal, that will inherit this battle-torn piece of earth. The bounty hunters soon depart, taking with them the lifeless bodies of the Bunch to ensure getting the reward, and ride off into hostile country blithely singing, "I went to the river but I couldn't get across / Singing polly-wolly doodle all the day"—a prophecy that comes true a little later as, victims at last of their own ineptitude, they are ambushed by the Indians of Angel's village. After the bounty hunters have gone, the peasants enter Agua Verde to clear it of supplies for the revolution and to pick up the dead and help the wounded. A woman dressed in black threads her way through the corpses, and the scene becomes appropriately dark, dusky, and windswept. The buzzards, impatient now, circle overhead, while the departing peasants seem to form a kind of processional that suggests a funeral march and file out the gates past Thornton, who sits leaning against the wall, squinting his eyes to keep out the dust, holding the reins of his horse. The last to leave is a man hobbling along on a crutch, and then Thornton is completely alone.

The mood is one of utter desolation. All the elements of the composition—the solitary man and his horse, the two vultures perched like sentinels on either side of the gates, the crumbling wall, the wind blowing up the dust, the darkening sky—seem to reveal the place in the aspect of some ruined monastery temple. After a while Old Sykes rides up, leading the band of Indians who dispatched the posse and among whose number is the old man of Angel's village. There is an exchange that suggests all pledges have been honored and hard feelings forgot, whereupon Thornton mounts up and joins them, he and Sykes companions once more. It is not difficult to see that here is a story if ever there was one—of the Battle of Agua Verde and the four strange gringos who returned for their friend and wound up eliminating an army of oppressors and liberating a village—that will be told for a thousand years around the campfires of these people. And beyond that in whatever form and format the storyteller's imagination dictates—song, dance, drama, novel, poem, and, of course, film.

In *Love and Death in the American Novel* Leslie Fiedler writes:

> The immense barrier of guilt between white man and dark man is no more mitigated in our classic fiction than is the gulf of color and culture itself; both, indeed, are emphasized to the point of melodrama, so that the final reconciliation may seem more tender and miraculous. The archetype makes no attempt to deny the facts of outrage and guilt; it is nurtured by them. It merely portrays them as meaningless in the face of a passion immune to what Melville calls "that climax so fatal to ordinary love." "It's too good for true, honey," Jim says to Huck. "It's too good for true."[60]

This is an insight that applies to all the dialectics and paradoxes, the polarities and contradictions, that animate and inform American literature: love and death, war and peace, savagery and civilization, the machine and the garden, light and dark, man and woman, the one and the many, the whole spiraling, expanding chain of yin and yang that gives our finest products of art and expression their power, their vitality, and their authenticity. "The fact is that many of the best American novels achieve their very being, their energy and their form, from the perception and acceptance not of unities but of radical disunities," Richard Chase has written. "The American novel tends to rest in contradictions and among extreme ranges of experience."[61] When it does reach the occasional moments of stasis and of peace, nothing is truly resolved or reconciled; what synthesis or mutual accord there is has been achieved at the expense of the fiercest, most intense and violent struggle, and is at best provisional, transitory, and equivocal.

It is no different in Peckinpah's work, and when it is understood that his work rests securely in this tradition, the whole matter of his so-called confusion, cynicism, and chaotic thinking is revealed in a different perspective. Peckinpah is not really calling into question our most time-honored conceptions of heroism; he is not really calling into question the whole symbolic idea of the West as a place where genuine liberation, free from the constrictions of society, is possible; he is not really calling into question even the idea of regeneration through violence, however much he may ironize it. The ironies, the ambivalences, the ambiguities, the doubts, the fears, the angers that lace and lacerate his films serve the same purpose they have always served in our art and expression: they give depth and complexity to what might otherwise be complacent simplicities; they make dramatic form and order out of feelings and desires so disruptive and instinctual they would otherwise be chaotic; they plumb a radical diabolism that would otherwise be, in D. H. Lawrence's splendid phrase, "mere childishness."[62] If *The Wild Bunch* is seen as an anti-Western, then it is not seen at all. The whole point of its conflicting perspectives, its explosive polarities and dialectics, is not to "expose" the Western, much less to erode the basis of its heroic virtues, which Peckinpah carries all the way back to their first appearance in the epic tradition. These things are there rather to tighten the screws of the struggle, to make our assent more difficult, indeed, almost impossible, so that when the release comes and the heroic ideal is reclaimed in all its savage beauty and terror, it really is more miraculous than we had ever dreamed or imagined.

The dialectic here, a familiar one announced long ago by Hawthorne, is between the actual and the imaginary, which are but other faces for the tragic and the comic, the realistic and the romantic, the historic and the artistic, the sacred and the profane. Peckinpah takes the actual as far as it can go: what is left in the world of time and circumstance, which is to say the world of history, are two old men, survivors off to fight for a cause they don't believe in because it gives them another chance at something they do believe in, which is to stay on the run, on the move, on the *go*. "It ain't like it used to be," grins Old Sykes, "but it'll do." From this kind of realism, in which memory is already so mixed with desire that it borders on romance, Peckinpah can take his film in only one direction: the camera rises as Thornton and Sykes ride away and their laughter is swept up by the laughter of the other members of the Bunch, lately dead but now miraculously brought back to life again as one by one their laughing faces are faded in and out. Yet still this is not enough, for the device leaves each man isolated from his companions, and all isolated from the environment in which they find their ratification. So the laughter is dissolved into the song the peasants sang when the Bunch left their village, and the leave-taking itself is reprised. The landscape, mostly parched and barren through-out, is now green and lush, the color and mood of springtime; and the Bunch are no longer riding toward us in their false military uniforms, but are instead decked out in their motley outlaw regalia and head-ing toward the eastern sun that shines through the trees, refracting off the morning mist and bathing everything in a nimbus that seems to transfigure and purify. Their destiny is complete and inscribes a way-ward but inevitable odyssey that originated in wildest villainy and end-ed in heroic redemption.

Villains become heroes, yet another turn of the ironic screw? Per-haps, but just as extremes meet, so irony carried far enough turns in upon itself and becomes its opposite. When the Bunch attack a whole army on behalf of their fallen comrade, theirs is a sacrificial gesture of human solidarity not so very different in principle from the prin-ciples for which the revolutionaries are fighting. It may also be insane, but when this kind of insanity instigates and occurs among events of such splendor, magnitude, and complexity, it has a way of masquer-ading as bravery, so that even sophisticates and cynics, to say noth-ing of these primitive peasants, might confuse these very bad men for heroes. Well, who wouldn't be confused? Perhaps heroism and villainy are for Peckinpah very much as love and hate for Hawthorne: philo-sophically considered, the same at bottom, except that one happens to be seen in a celestial radiance, the other in a dusky and lurid glow. Peckinpah doesn't know; and if he thought he did, it would be only his opinion, which, ever the discreet storyteller, he would disdain to impose upon his film or force upon his audience. What he does know is that the perspective is everything, and the perspective to which he shifts in order to bring his turbulent film to rest is a peculiarly inno-cent angle of vision that takes the appearance of things for the real-ity and carries it all the way to celebration. The Bunch's villainy is left to perish in the dusky and lurid glow of the windswept desert when Pike, Dutch, and the Gorch brothers are carried off head down over a saddle as society's outlaws. When they are next seen, it is as heroes of some legendary adventure, illumined by a radiance if not celestial then at least transcendent, emanating from the faithful if factitious folk imagination of the people of Angel's village, who, childlike yet not childish, saw something in these men early on that we, less gullible, more prey to suspicion and cynicism, could not see and that will ensure the Bunch are sent forth in glory whenever the story of the Battle of Agua Verde is told.

The world at the end of *The Wild Bunch* is not the "real" world. Rich with laughter, song, and the great good feeling of brotherhood regained and community reintegrated, it is a festive world, that world of total human intelligibility that Northrop Frye has speculated it is the business of art to reclaim for us. By enclosing myth within ritual and festival and resolving his story therein, Peckinpah takes a dramatic structure that has been tragic for most of its length and at the last possible moment deflects it away from the tragic toward the comic. Order is reinstated, balance is restored, and paradox is resolved in the only way he knows how: through the language of image and metaphor, which is to say through the language of his art. This most volatile of films is thus made to close upon a chord of almost pastoral grace and tranquility, its actions and reactions in perfect harmony, its antitheses synthesized, its kinesis reaching in the end not so much stasis as an animated equilibrium. When horse and rider, leader and followers, liberators and liberated, and song of praise are revealed each in its ordered place, the image is frozen yet it doesn't cease moving. Instead, in a touch that subtly recalls the Quest myth, it is made to recede until it disappears into the redemptive blur of morning sunlight and springlike foliage. The mood is one of celebration and what it now seems to be celebrating is nothing so much as the return of the film itself to that world of romance it had appeared only minutes earlier to have forsaken when the vultures descended upon the ravaged village. This is not a world that we are asked to "believe" in. It is, rather, a world seen through the eyes of some people who do believe in it, a world the Bunch for one brief moment actually did occupy in fact by returning for Angel and so for these peasants may now occupy forever in folklore and fiction. In this world it still ain't like it used to be, but it'll do more than ever because it is like it never was though might and should have been, which is to say that it has become at last too good for true, too good for true.

The Ballad of Cable Hogue for me is an affirmation of life. It's about a man who found water where it wasn't. It's also about God.

—Sam Peckinpah

6
The World Elsewhere

A man's life does not really belong to himself. It belongs to his sons and his daughters, to the rain and the stars, to the voices of the past that live in a man's heart, to God.
—*Pericles on 31st Street*

I

When things become too good for true in America, they die or are banished, ostracized, or otherwise sent away. The most romantic excesses of the American imagination are in this way almost always held in check by a sense of realism that is often equally excessive. The romantic attitude usually expresses itself in visions of idealized and— one wants to say "therefore"—unrealizable love, either amorous or comradely; the realistic attitude usually in visions of violence and death (though even these occasionally reach curiously transcendent moments of suspension). Neither ever really holds full sway; and the formal difficulty our fiction often poses is that the two attitudes are each so imbued with the other, very much like Hawthorne's actual and imaginary when he sits in his moonlit study, that it is often impossible to separate them. For tastes attracted to the traditional European novel or simply to practical-minded folk, the American novel is liable to seem particularly frustrating, often willful, usually a little unbelievable. Of course, the same is true of the American cinema vis-à-vis the European.[1]

It is still not usual to encounter readers who wonder of *The Scarlet Letter* why Dimmesdale and Hester can't just pack their things and get out of town; or who criticize Catherine's death in *A Farewell to Arms* as "unconvincing" or "unrealistic"; or who feel cheated at the end of Henry James's thwarted fairy-tale romance, *The American*. In each case and in others like them (*The Awakening, The Age of Innocence, An American Dream,* and *The Sun Also Rises,* perhaps the bitterest treatment of this theme), what is held out is a possibility for happiness and what happens at the last moment is that the possibility is withheld. An irony and a complication in all of this is that while these endings are often criticized as being unrealistic, their fabricators will defend them precisely on the basis of their realism. Further still, much of what is hard-edged and cynical in American art is itself rather romantic. This is perhaps because realism in our fiction has, despite Hawthorne's famous dictum, not centrally to do with staying close to the ordinary and probable in the course of human events, and romanticism does not always involve the improbable or the fanciful. Rather, the terms become confused, perhaps deliberately, and wind up being aligned with attitudes or feelings: realism tends to express pessimism, romance to express optimism. The underlying dialectic seems to be, on the one hand, a vision of what life could be, and, on the other, a belief—or secret fear—that it always turns out badly in the end.

We are nevertheless likely to feel that there is somehow more truth—emotional truth, in any case—to the "unbelievable" unhappy endings in our fiction than to the happy resolutions in so much of our popular culture; and this no doubt has something to do with our experience of life in America and what we take to be the distance between aspiration and realization. At this time in his career, Sam Peckinpah knew what it was like to have something that seemed just a little too good. We may wonder if he was ever happier than he was during the two years between the summers of 1967 and 1969. He made the first feature film he had been allowed to work on since 1965, he started immediately upon another, and he spoke in the most glowing terms of his new producing associates. But by the end of July 1969 everything was in disarray. First, there was the business of the unauthorized cuts made in *The Wild Bunch,* which as late as March of the following year he was still fighting to get restored. Then in the winter Warner Brothers was indifferent when the film needed its support for Academy consideration. Next, the studio showed an unfinished version of *The Ballad of Cable Hogue* to some distributors without announcing that it was still a work in progress.[2] And finally, after Peckinpah finished the release print, the studio, still wavering and uncertain about how to handle it, having had little faith in it from the outset, eventually did almost nothing at all with it. Within a month of its release, it was difficult to remember whether there had even been such a film; or, if one did remember and wanted to see it, to find a place where it was showing.

It must be admitted, however, that speaking strictly from the studio's point of view the problem of how to promote this film appropriately cannot have been the easiest to solve, for there is nothing quite like *The Ballad* anywhere. It begins as a revenge story when the title character, a middle-aged desert rat and sometime prospector

down on his luck, is left to die by his two partners, Taggart and Bowen, because there's enough water for two but not for three; moves
into comedy and occasional slapstick when, after four days of suffering during which he asks God for relief, he stumbles onto a water hole
("found it where it wasn't") and is joined by a lecherous man of the
cloth who calls himself the Reverend Joshua Duncan Sloane ("preacher to all of eastern Nevada and selected parts of northern Arizona");
becomes a love story when Cable meets a prostitute named Hildy, who
lives with him for a while at his water hole, which he has since turned
into a relief stop for the stage line (he calls the place, after Josh's
suggestion, Cable Springs); and reintroduces its revenge plot (after
having forgotten it for nearly half the story's length) just in time for
one of the damndest endings ever contrived (Cable is run down by
one of the first motorcars in the New-Old West).

If the studio executives had trouble with this mixture, they weren't
alone. Many reviewers couldn't seem to figure it out either, especially since it had come from the notorious director of *The Wild Bunch;*
and though several publications were enthusiastic (*Time, Newsweek,*
the *New York Times, New York Magazine, Village Voice, Rolling Stone*), the
prevailing attitude was neatly summed up by *Esquire's* Jacob Brackman, who wrote, "It was curious to learn that this venomously brilliant director was trying something light," and concluded:

> But the truth is one laughs no longer or louder at *Cable Hogue*
> than at *The Wild Bunch.* Not because one cannot build a comedy
> around the themes of vengeance, deceit, defilement, etc., but be-
> cause of something simply absent from Peckinpah's dark direc-
> torial personality; a lack which seems to make him sensational at
> comic relief and unsuited to extended comedy. There's no sav-
> ing friendliness at the bottom of his vision, no final charity, no
> compassionate interest in why almost everyone turns out so
> messed up. . . . He doesn't despise and laugh at what people do,
> but at people themselves.[3]

Brackman's review—actually, a general essay on Peckinpah's
work—is intelligent, thoughtful, and fair, but it is easy to disagree with
his conclusions. Filmgoers who had kept up with Peckinpah's career
knew that of all his gifts, his gift for comedy was perhaps the least
sufficiently appreciated or even recognized. When the mood was on
him Peckinpah loved to do comedy, which he carried off with his
usual sure touch and customary technical control. It would probably
be more accurate to say that his comic relief in films like *The Wild
Bunch* and *Bring Me the Head of Alfredo Garcia* tends toward the grim

and grotesque and thus falls more easily under the rubric of black humor, which is more acceptable to many contemporary palates, while his comedies often go in for broad, occasionally unsubtle effects that, although usually beautifully directed and expertly timed, may not be to everyone's taste. His comedy is nevertheless genuinely funny and, perhaps harder for many people to believe given his reputation as the "Picasso of violence," full of great good humor and generous feeling. Although some of it (like parts of the three comic episodes he directed for *The Westerner*) is hokey and some more of it (like parts of *The Losers*) does rely on pratfalls and bits of cinematic business, most of the rest of it is altogether wittier, subtler, and more sophisticated than is generally credited. In any case the *Westerner* episodes are early and come out of a time when he was still learning. By the time of *The Ballad,* he had learned something about comedy, just as by the time of *The Wild Bunch* he had learned something about tragedy. For Peckinpah, these were years of both experimentation and mastery.

One way to begin to get a clearer fix on the film is to think of it as a "problem play." This is a play that attempts to deal with some social and political problem, and the term has often been applied to certain comedies of Shakespeare (for example, *Measure for Measure*). In this context, then, it is suggestive that some reviewers have called *The Ballad* an allegory of capitalism and free enterprise, have written of its treatment of the ecology crisis, or have worked out interlocking themes of individualism and mass society. Not too surprisingly, some of these same reviewers have been forced to conclude that the film is a disaster, just as many critics have been forced to find Shakespeare's problem comedies and romances ridiculous if read as sociopolitical allegories. At a juncture like that, we must dismiss the work or, if we happen to enjoy it, find another way of approaching it.

Since few critics or theatergoers take even Shakespeare's so-called problem plays as political or social allegories any more, perhaps therein lies a clue: these plays, the comedies, and the late romances all involve deliberate mixtures of styles, genres, and modes; they undergo radical shifts in mood, tone, and feeling; they do not ask to be judged by the strictures of realism or mere surface consistency; and they intentionally, almost brazenly introduce "artificial" elements that suggest the magical, the miraculous, and the supernatural. What they are about, more than anything else, is themselves and the theatrical traditions their author knew. It may be profitable, then, to trace the genesis of this film that John Huston once affectionately described as "the most wayward film he had ever seen."[4]

Peckinpah once called *The Ballad* "a new version of Sartre's *The Flies*
with a touch of Keystone Cops."⁵ The latter is easy enough to isolate
(the film uses fast motion, and there is a hilarious slapstick set piece
involving a prayer meeting), but the former may not mean much, except perhaps indirectly. Sartre's Zeus is a malicious deity who punishes men if they yield their freedom to him and who punishes them
equally if they arrogate it to themselves, and he thus suggests parallels
with Dostoevsky's Grand Inquisitor (or the God of Melville's Ahab).
Peckinpah's God is, by contrast, "wise and bountiful," as Josh points
out, and exceedingly kind, generous, and benevolent (up to a point).
More than likely, Peckinpah got the idea of introducing God as a stage
character from Sartre's play, where Zeus appears disguised as a stranger
who greets Orpheus and the Tutor upon their arrival in Argos. While
Josh is not, of course, God in disguise, he nevertheless is, as he identifies himself, the man *of* God, his spokesman, and throughout he acts
as the voice of God by quoting appropriate verses from scripture.
Moreover, Cable's sin, like that of Orpheus, is the sin of hubris; and
in *The Flies* Sartre uses one of the classic revenge stories that also happens to involve a thwarted love story. The love story in *The Ballad* isn't
between siblings, but it *is* crossed with a revenge story.

However, there are other sources that may be more illuminating.
The similarities between Peckinpah's work and John Ford's are fewer than many critics like to think, but the one Ford film that Peckinpah named among his favorite films was *My Darling Clementine*,⁶
which is, of all the earlier director's films, his most purely romantic,
an almost fairy-tale vision of Wyatt Earp in Tombstone. Throughout
the first half of the film, we are in an utterly "masculine" world. Then
the title character arrives, and when she steps off the stagecoach, the
whole feel of the town is subtly transformed, infused with a grace,
civility, and beauty that are alien to it and yet that sweep all before
it. It is surely one of the great moments in Ford's work, and it must
have been uppermost in Peckinpah's mind when he conceived the
equally beautiful entrance for Hildy about a third of the way into *The
Ballad*. Dressed in pink and white, seen from Cable's point of view
(as Clementine is seen from Wyatt's), with the soundtrack quietly
playing the melody that is associated with her, she makes the whole
desert bloom with her presence. When she is later threatened by a
group of hatchet-faced, respectable "ladies," they could have been
members of the Women's Law and Order League who drive the prostitute Dallas out of town in an earlier Ford film, *Stagecoach*. Furthermore, both *Clementine* and *Stagecoach* are, like *The Flies*, love stories
arising out of revenge stories; and just as Dallas tries to persuade the

Ringo Kid not to go to Lordsburg to face the Plummer brothers, so
Hildy tries to talk Cable out of waiting at the Springs for his former
partners to show up. *The Ballad* may also have a source in Peckinpah's
first film, *The Deadly Companions,* which is a revenge story about a
saddle bum who falls in love with a prostitute, who in turn tries to
dissuade him from revenge. Inasmuch as Peckinpah was both interested in these themes yet dissatisfied with the resulting film, it is not
unlikely that he thought of this new film as an attempt to do them
again, this time right.

   The inspiration for Cable himself, however, is another matter. Peckinpah derives him in part from *The Treasure of the Sierra Madre,* the
Huston film that he admired and to which he alluded in other films
(not just in *The Wild Bunch,* but in *Bring Me the Head of Alfredo Garcia,*
which itself, in its use of a prostitute heroine and a revenge-obsessed
hero, takes up themes from *The Ballad* and *The Deadly Companions*).
Huston's film was adapted from a novel of the same title by B. Traven,
of whose work Peckinpah once said, "At one time I went through a
whole period of reading everything of his I could find."[7] The main
character of *Treasure* is a bum named Fred C. Dobbs, who is likable
enough at the outset but who becomes so infected with gold fever that
he shoots his partner and makes off with all the gold, saying, "Nobody
ever put anything over on Fred C. Dobbs." It is from this line and from
what might be called the "Fred C. Dobbs" complex that Peckinpah
takes his cue for Cable. But Peckinpah's concerns are ultimately different from those of either Traven or Huston, and he never borrows
except as he recognizes and makes his own. For Huston, Dobbs was
probably an apotheosis of the Sam Spade character from his earlier
film, *The Maltese Falcon* (another of Peckinpah's favorites). As Pauline
Kael has written, "Humphrey Bogart [who played both Dobbs and
Spade for Huston] takes the tough-guy role to its psychological limits:
the man who stands alone goes from depravity through paranoia to
total disintegration."[8] Peckinpah doesn't take Cable into madness, and
in many respects the character is the more complex for it. Unlike
Dobbs, Cable, betrayed and left to die, has some justification for acting the way he does; also unlike Dobbs, Cable is neither insane nor a
killer, and it is because he isn't a killer that he hesitates when he has
the drop on his partners. "You damn fool," says Bowen, after he has
wrested Cable's rifle from him, "you had us"; and Taggart adds, "You
just wouldn't pull the trigger, because you're yellow." Cable has, in
other words, a capacity for trust, a genuine faith in friendship and in
people. It is only after he is betrayed that he becomes defensive, self-
protective, and excessively cautious with everyone he meets.

Peckinpah has always been ambivalent about the so-called codes of the West, the masculine attitudes and gestures by which his heroes often define themselves, and the virtues of extreme and isolate individualism. It is not accurate to call him a critic of the cult of masculinity, because he is not a didactic artist. And those who persist in calling him a proponent of machismo simply haven't been watching his films attentively. His attitudes toward masculinity and individualism are at all times complex, often conflicting, and informed with a profound and abiding sense of their limitations, failings, and excesses. In the way of a really broad generalization, it could be argued that one of the reasons he incorporates contrasting sets of male groups is that one group—Steve and Gil, the Bunch, Cable and Josh—express the more positive, attractive aspects of masculine camaraderie, while the other group—the Hammonds, the bounty hunters, Taggart and Bowen—express the more negative, less appealing aspects. As with so many other themes and subjects, Peckinpah is never content to reveal them in only one aspect; and to male mythology he neither grants nor withholds full consent, preferring instead to examine its states of feeling, its attractions, its justifications, and of course its insufficiencies and inadequacies. In Cable he conceived a character in whom he could explore these further, and a character who is in several ways different from any of his previous heroes. Cable is not only not a killer, he is not an outlaw per se or especially drawn to a life of action, violence, and collision (like the Wild Bunch) or to a life of stoicism, self-denial, and unrewarded service (like Steve Judd). *Straw Dogs* has been called Peckinpah's first film without a hero.[9] However, if that term is used in the strictest sense, the observation applies more accurately to *The Ballad,* for Cable is at once the least heroic and the most recognizably ordinary of Peckinpah's main characters (except Royal Earle Thompson, not coincidentally also played by Jason Robards). Perhaps for this reason he may also be the most easily accessible and appealing.

Cable isn't really a good man, as Josh is careful to point out in his closing eulogy, or really a bad one. He is simply a man ("made out of bad as well as good") and is thus prey to the follies of other men, including a fierce desire to retaliate when his ego is bruised and his illusions are shattered. The first scene of the film not only sets up the revenge story and the Old Testament "eye for an eye" morality; it also characterizes Cable by giving him a subtler, more human motivation, by showing us how vulnerable he is, as any man might be, to assaults on his generosity and courage. Taggart and Bowen don't merely leave him to die, an action that might be defensible according to the log-

ic of better two alive than three dead. Rather, they hit him, as the
saying goes, where he lives, or, more precisely, where he doesn't suspect he lives. He pleads with them to leave him a little water (less than
his share), but as they walk away they only ridicule him for being so
stupid as to spare them when he could have killed them and for being fooled so easily (because they played on his sense of humor). And
then, adding insult to injury, they ridicule him further by making up
a song about what they've just done, praising their prowess and la-
beling him a coward.

> Oh, Cable is yellow, oh, Cable's white,
> Old Cable's dying, but it's all right.
> Taggart and Bowen as slick as you please,
> Took all the water and left for the trees.

Cable mutters to himself, "Call me yellow. Leave me to dry up and
blow away. Sing a song about it. Laugh at old Cable Hogue," and *then*
swears his revenge, "I'll get out, I'll get out! Don't you worry none
about that! You just worry about when I get out." The sequence here
is significant, for in associating Cable's desire to prove himself to
Taggart and Bowen with his desire for revenge, Peckinpah is able to
suggest that he doesn't so much want to get even with them as show
them what he's made of. This is reinforced late in the film when, after
he has turned the tables on them, they remind him that he didn't
kill them the last time he had a chance because he "never did have
no guts." "Well, now, that's a fact," Cable replies. "Care to try your
luck again, fellas?"

With Cable's partners out of the picture, Peckinpah concentrates
his attention on Cable alone, and here the film takes its first unexpected turn. Despite the initial betrayal, things are made to go rather well for Cable. He wanders four days without water and, nearly
dead from thirst, lies down in the middle of a sandstorm and says,
"You call it, Lord, I'm just plain done in. Amen." Whereupon, as if
in answer to his prayers, he sees mud on his boots, gets back up,
scratches frantically around in the sand, and at last finds water. The
next day he notices stagecoach tracks nearby, and soon a stagecoach
appears. When the drivers, Ben and Webb, and the passengers learn
what has happened to him, they offer him free transportation into
town; and when he declines, Ben and Webb give him the rest of their
whiskey and loosen the bags and trunks so they will fall off when the
stage lurches forward and thus provide him with supplies. A few days
later his first customer appears, and when the man refuses to pay the
ten cents for a drink of water and pulls a gun on him, Cable shoots

him. He isn't a coward, and he still hasn't become a killer. He merely defends himself (significantly, he kills only when his life, not his
property, has been threatened), and the act is later sanctioned by the
man of God. "Well said and well done," Josh tells Cable, "defend
thyself with the jawbone of an ass if need be."

But Cable's generosity does not extend to allowing Josh to drink
for free. "Cast thy bread upon the waters and allow this man of God
his just desserts," Josh pleads. "You talk like a man of God," Cable answers, "but I worked like hell for that water." Which is not, strictly
speaking, true. He suffered for it, but the water itself was a gift freely
given to him through the grace of a deity he has already started to
forget. Josh tells Cable that he is "but a poor sinner in need of redemption, I will redeem you," and, appositely, points out that Cable
had better secure his claim. Cable borrows Josh's horse to ride into
town and file a claim, but not before reminding Josh to put ten cents
in the cup every time he takes a drink or "I'll blow your ass into next
Wednesday." It is the beginning of the "Fred C. Dobbs" complex, and
there is a nice, understated moment when Josh first appears that
shows how defensive Cable has become. Josh offers his "hand in all
good fellowship," and Cable tentatively offers his own in return, all
the while glancing around for signs of treachery.

Once in town, Cable, filthy and funny looking, is ridiculed by many
people, and several others are skeptical about his claims to have
found water where everyone knows there isn't any. The owner of the
stage line physically kicks him out into the street after Cable asks for
a grub stake (but this only after making his point graphically by pouring a pitcher of water on the man's britches). However, at the bank
he is treated better. The president asks him if he has any collateral
and Cable answers, "I'm worth something, ain't I?" The president
hesitates a minute, then asks to hear more, and finally gives Cable a
grub stake almost three times the thirty-five dollars he had originally asked for. Sometime later, after the owner of the stage line signs a
contract for water rights, Ben and Webb hand Cable a package.
"What's it going to cost me?" Cable snaps back. Ben says it will cost
him nothing, and it turns out to contain a flag. In a quiet moment
presided over by the man of God, Cable raises the flag above Cable
Springs. In the meantime, the desert has become a strange place, for
in addition to the water, it abounds in animals and vegetation. Indeed, within days after discovering the water hole, Cable has found
all sorts of refuse—pieces of wood, discarded chairs—that he can put
to good use. It would appear, then, that throughout this first part of
the film, Peckinpah is giving us a rather free rendition of the Job

story—a man is inexplicably made to suffer and is thereafter rewarded by being allowed to prosper—and the story becomes a kind of trial of faith and belief.* In addition to his material prosperity, Cable acquires a widening circle of new friends and acquaintances who are, all things considered, very nice to him and who admire him for what he has managed to achieve with such limited resources.

But God's generosity doesn't end with the gifts of (local) fame, fortune, and good fellowship. Given what Peckinpah is up to in this film, he couldn't very well achieve it without a major woman character, and he found a splendid one in Hildy. It is doubtless no accident that those who label him a misogynist and who complain that his women characters are soft, compliant, and attracted to the most efficient killer always conveniently leave *The Ballad* out of their considerations.[10] To be sure, Hildy is a prostitute, but there are several reasons for that. Among other things, Peckinpah has never made any attempt to hide his feelings for or his experiences with prostitutes: "I've never thought of these women as objects to be used. I put a lot of the relationships I've had with whores into the love story of Cable Hogue and his whore, Hildy. They had a relationship that was truer and more tender than that between most husbands and wives. The fact that she was a whore and went to bed with men for money didn't change anything."[11] There is no doubt a sentimental streak in him a mile wide when he gets on this subject; but, then, it can't be denied that it is a subject he knows something about. Hildy exists as one of the most fully imagined characters in all his work, and not the least of her significance when it comes to understanding Peckinpah on the matter of men and women in love with one another is that her love for Cable has nothing to do with any of Cable's machismo. (The same is true, incidentally, of Kit in *The Deadly Companions* and Elita in *Bring Me the Head of Alfredo Garcia* with respect to the men they love.) Indeed, her love for him exists not because of but in spite of his desire for vengeance. The real reasons she loves him lie elsewhere. He doesn't judge her, as the "good people of Deaddog" do, he has been good to her, and he treats her "like a real lady." In one of the best

---

*It is unlikely that this is coincidental. *Job* was Peckinpah's father's favorite book of the Bible, and Sam remembered him referring to it often. In a *Rifleman* episode called "The Home Ranch," which has a powerful cattle baron trying to drive the McCains off their new spread, burning down their house in the process, Peckinpah wrote a long scene in which the father tells the son the story of Job and how, despite his trials and misfortunes, his confusion, and his great though apparently undeserved suffering he never lost his faith. Yet again we see that artistically speaking there was very little in the life and world of Sam Peckinpah that he left unexploited.

scenes in the film, there is this exchange, on the first night she stays at Cable Springs:

> *Hildy:* You've been awful nice to me, Hogue. Ain't it never both-
> ered you none, what I am?
> *Cable:* No, it never bothered me. I enjoyed it. Well, what the hell
> are you? A human being. We try the best we can. We all got our
> own ways of living.
> *Hildy:* And loving?
> *Cable:* Gets mighty lonesome without it.

And when Hildy appears at the doorway in her nightgown:

> *Cable:* Now that is a picture.
> *Hildy:* You've seen it before, Hogue.
> *Cable:* Lady, nobody's ever seen you before.

From here the film goes into its loveliest sequence, the beautiful "Butterfly Mornings" interlude in which Hildy and Cable sing of their love for each other in a succession of images that takes them from their morning chores to their afternoon walks to their evening plea-suring of each other. If Peckinpah were only the misogynist he has been called, scenes like this would be inconceivable. Equally incon-ceivable would be the way he handles the revenge theme and plays it off against the love affair. "It ain't worth it, Hogue," Hildy tells Cable. "Revenge always turns sour. Why don't you just forget them?" When Cable answers, "There are some things a man just can't forget. I've got me two of them, Taggart and Bowen," it's clear enough that he's not acting for Hildy, he's acting for himself. And when she says, "You couldn't handle them the last time. Next time you'll probably just get yourself killed," it is also clear that she wants nothing to do with his vengeance, that he doesn't have to prove he's a man to her, and that she is above all afraid for him because she loves him and wants to preserve their life together.

Josh says pretty much the same thing, and it is mostly through him that Peckinpah unifies this rather unlikely pairing of story types. Just as Josh reminds Cable of the blessings of love, so too does he warn him against the folly of revenge. When Cable won't admit to ever having had a passion, Josh is quick to ask, "What do you call that vengeance that gnaws at the very walls of your soul? That's the pas-sion that'll nurture the dandelions above your grave":

> *Cable:* Taggart and Bowen left me out there to die. . . . I aim to kill
> them for it. I don't call that a passion.
> *Josh:* Vengeance is mine, saith the Lord.

> *Cable:* That's fair enough with me, just as long as he don't take too
> long and I can watch.

Similarly, from time to time Josh is on hand to express Cable's feelings
about Hildy when he himself is too guarded to admit to them. When
Cable says, "Hildy ain't mine, nobody owns Hildy. She's got her life and
I've got mine. Right here, right where I want to be," Josh quietly cor-
rects him, "That's not exactly true, Cable. You love that girl." And when
Cable says, "You can't convince Hildy with anything but hard cash," Josh
answers, "We'll see about that, Cable." In both cases Josh is proved
right. Cable is at the Springs only because he is awaiting Taggart and
Bowen; and he does manage to convince Hildy with something other
than hard cash—with love, kindness, and generosity.

Set against Cable's dream of vengeance, which is really a nightmare, is Hildy's dream of going to San Francisco, marrying rich, and
living in style, "like a lady." At first she tries to talk Cable into coming with her, but after three weeks at the Springs, during which their
love for each other deepens, she is ready to give all that up and remain with him there. The point is contrast: whether they stay or go,
Hildy wants to be with Cable because she loves him, whereas Cable
wants to stay at the Springs only out of hatred for Taggart and Bowen. The thirst for vengeance eventually infects his relationship with
Hildy. One night Josh joins them at dinner, and Cable demands fifty
cents payment from him for the food. "That's hardly fair," Hildy says,
"you never charged me nothing." Cable snaps back, "That's because
you never charged me nothing." He is not at first aware of the effect
the remark has on her, but Josh comments dryly, "Oh, brother, you
are a true samaritan." Hildy bursts into tears, and announces she will
be leaving in the morning. When Cable asks if it is because he hasn't
been good enough to her, she replies, "Maybe too good, I don't know.
I just can't handle it. Thank you very much for everything, but I'm
leaving." What she can't handle is not, of course, Cable's goodness
and kindness but his meanness and pettiness, which is a function of
what Taggart and Bowen did to him. Hildy understands this, yet when
he of all people can say that he doesn't charge her for room and
board only because she doesn't charge him for lovemaking, it is too
much even for her to bear. It matters little that Cable doesn't really
"mean" what he has just said. What matters is that he said it almost
as if by reflex, and it serves to show us how much he has fallen into
the "nobody ever put anything over on Fred C. Dobbs" kind of thinking, how little disposed he is to leave himself vulnerable to anyone,
even the woman he loves. As much as he might want to—and it is

obvious that he desperately wants to—he can't even bring himself to apologize, much less beg her not to leave him. We realize too that she is right to tell him it is unfair to charge Josh, for we are reminded of the days during which Josh had kept Cable company, helped him hunt for supplies, helped him build his house, helped him wait on customers—all without, so far as we are able to tell, apparent consideration for material gain and without any motive save that in which he first offered Cable a hand in all good fellowship.

Yet, as small as Cable has become at this point, the beneficence of Josh and his God is not finished. Early in the film, by way of seducing a townsman's wife, Josh said, "The Lord works in many strange ways. Sometimes when he has dealt a blow too much for one to bear, he sends a messenger to comfort and to love." After the Lord had made Cable suffer almost beyond endurance, he sent him comfort in the form of water, friendship (and counsel) in the form of Josh, and love in the form of Hildy. So for one last time he sends Hildy to Cable. If Cable can't bring himself to apologize, then at least Hildy is capable of making a gesture toward reconciliation. In the middle of the night, she walks quietly out to where the two men are sleeping, takes Cable by the hand, and leads him off to a secluded spot where they make love. It is one of the film's tenderest scenes, and also one of the most subtly tense, for we wish here more than ever that Cable would forget his revenge and realize what happiness he has found. But come morning Hildy rides away alone as Cable goes about his business at the Springs. He affects nonchalance, but Josh puts things in the right perspective once again by pointing out, "Funny thing. It doesn't matter how much or how little you've wandered around, how many women you've been with. Every once in a while one of them cuts right through, right straight into you." Confused, his armor pierced again, Cable asks, "Well, what do you do about it?"; to which Josh answers, "I suppose, maybe, when you die you get over it." When Cable makes no move to follow Hildy, Josh realizes his work is finished. He has made the point, issued the warning for one last time, and indicated to Cable the way to salvation. And so he bids the desert rat farewell.

The unification of the two separate stories is complete: just as Cable's former partners have cut straight into him with hatred, so Hildy has cut straight into him with love. If Cable elects to satisfy the former rather than to follow the latter, he can never say that he hasn't known both and been warned of the consequences. It hardly needs to be said here that Peckinpah has a lot of the preacher in him. But he remains first and foremost the dedicated storyteller, and perhaps it is because he doesn't make more of a "point" about the issues involved that some critics miss the point. What he is "saying" here is that love is to be preferred to hatred, kindness to meanness, generosity to stinginess, and charity to vengeance. He is saying that the conditions for love are so fragile, the opportunities for happiness so rare, and the possibilities for good fortune so few that if these things come a man's way, it ill behooves him to let them get away, particularly when his motives are so base as vengeance and so hollow as ego. But Cable does let them get away and he becomes, as a consequence, fate's fool, which is made clear in the film's most ironic encounter. When Taggart and Bowen show up three years later and are amazed at how Cable has prospered, Cable says, "I owe it all to you boys"— which from an admittedly odd perspective is true. But three years is a long time, long enough for Cable to plan a reprisal worse than the offense. He orders them to shed themselves of all their clothes except their longjohns ("boots, too") and head out back through the hills with no water. Taggart refuses and goes for his gun, and Cable shoots him dead. Bowen starts to flee, then turns and says, "Cable, I just can't go it out there." Pathetic, weeping, he drops to his knees and cries, "I'm sorry, Cable. You know how it was with Taggart." Bowen's attitude here is not unlike that of Josh, who had dropped to his knees and begged Cable for sanctuary from the woman's irate husband, saying, "To err is human, to forgive is divine." Cable capitulated and helped Josh. Ever responsive to the sight of human weakness, he spares Bowen now.

The Ballad becomes thus a peculiarly thwarted revenge story; and Cable is revealed at the last in a light that places him closer to several of Peckinpah's other main characters. He makes a discovery he is not prepared to make: believing that he is living for one thing, he finds out, too late, that all along he has been living for something else. With Taggart dead and buried, Bowen forgiven and become a partner again, Cable's thoughts turn to Hildy. As if by magic, Hildy reappears, in a brand new automobile, driven by a chauffeur. But it is only a final trick of that very fate to which Cable still has some debts to pay. "Vengeance is mine, saith the Lord," Josh had warned him early on; and Hildy had told him, "Next time you'll probably just get yourself killed." And so, just when everything seems about as wonderful as it can be for Cable, when it seems, really, too wonderful, the fatal accident occurs. The emergency brake is accidentally tripped by Cable when he tosses a bag of belongings onto the seat, and the automobile starts to coast down the slope toward Bowen. Cable pushes him aside, tries to halt the car's progress himself, and is run over. It is the final retribution by which Cable unwittingly makes the prophecy in the song that is associated with him throughout come true: "Whatever debts I owe to fate I'll make fate pay." By the time he is ready to die, Josh has turned up, driving of all things a motorcycle, and his black attire now makes him seem a minister of death arrived just in time to preside over Cable's funeral. By the time Cable has been buried, all the rest of his friends, acquaintances, and business partners—Quittner, the stage line owner; Cushing, the bank president; and Ben and Webb—are on the scene to hear Josh's eulogy, which is worth quoting in full:

> We are gathered here in the sight of God and all His glory to lay to rest Cable Hogue. Now most funeral orations, Lord, lie about a man, compare him to the angels, whitewash him with a really wide brush. But you know, Lord, and I know that it just is not true. Now a man is made out of bad as well as good, all of them. Cable Hogue was born into this world nobody knows when or where. He came stumbling out of the wilderness like a prophet of old. Out of the barren wastes he carved himself a one-man kingdom.
> Some said he was ruthless, but you could do worse, Lord, than to take to your bosom Cable Hogue. He wasn't really a good man, he wasn't a bad man. But, Lord, he was a man!
> He charged too much, he was as stingy as they come. Yes, he might have cheated, but he was square about it. Rich or poor, he gouged them all the same. When Cable Hogue died, there wasn't an animal in the desert he didn't know, there wasn't a star in the firmament he hadn't named, there wasn't a man he was afraid of.
> Now the sand he fought and loved so long has covered him at last. Now he has gone into the whole torrent of the years, of the souls that pass and never stop. In some ways he was your dim reflection, Lord; and right or wrong, I feel he is worth consideration. But if you feel he is not, you should know that Hogue lived and died here in the desert, and I'm sure Hell will never be too hot for him.
> He never went to church, he didn't need to. The whole desert was his cathedral. Hogue loved the desert, loved it deeper than he'd ever say. He built his empire, but was man enough to give it up for love when the time came. Lord, as the day draws toward evening, this life comes to an end for us all. We say, "*adieu*," to our friend. Take him, Lord, but knowing Cable, I suggest you do not take him lightly. Amen.

Early in the film an anonymous stagecoach passenger had tried to silence his complaining wife by invoking a passage from the Bible that ends, "My judgment is just." The same might be said for Josh's eulo-

gy, which endeavors at all points to be fair and accurate. It might also
be said for God's judgment, which, though harsh, is not unjust. Fame
(if only locally), fortune, fellowship, and love were all placed within
Cable's easy grasp. But they were not enough, he had to have his
pound of flesh too. Still, it is not our business to cast judgment on
that. If we think to blame Cable too much for his faults and sins, the
eulogy is there to remind us of his virtues and accomplishments. We
may recall as well, in the course of giving him consideration, that in
the end he forgave at least one of his partners, saving the man's life
while sacrificing his own. And we are led to admire the ease, good
grace, and great humor with which Cable accepted fate's decision
against him. If we wish that he had loved a little more and hated a
little less, been a little wiser and a lot less foolish, and gone with Hildy
when he had the chance, we are nevertheless made to understand
why he could not do these things. Indeed, given the extremity of the
betrayal, perhaps the wonder is that he loved and laughed as much
as he did. Meanwhile, Peckinpah himself remains mute on the subject, declining, as one of his apprentices once said, to judge his characters. They have lives of their own, and how they go about living
them is something over which, once having set them in motion, he
has no final control. We may suspect, however, that he concurs in
Josh's evaluation (the film he made supports it, after all), and in so
doing we may wonder if there isn't more in the way of "saving friend-
liness," "final charity," and "compassionate interest" at the bottom of
his vision than some critics tell us we should expect to find.

II

The most illuminating insight as to what Peckinpah is up to in *The
Ballad* comes Richard Poirier's *A World Elsewhere,* a literary study that
doesn't mention this or any other film. Poirier argues that a distinctive characteristic of American literature is the attempt by our writers to create, through the means of style, language, and art, "environments radically different from those supported by economic,
political, and social systems," environments "*designed* to make the
reader feel that his ordinary world has been acknowledged, even
exhaustively, only to be dispensed with as a source of moral or psychological standards."[12] Discarding the generic distinction between
the novel and the romance (or between a work of realism and a work
of fancy), Poirier offers in its place a distinction between "two kinds
of fictional environment": "the provided environment," which mirrors "one already accredited by history and society," and "the invent-

ed environment," which is essentially an imaginative one created for the hero. Works in which the artist gives us an invented environment are not intended to reproduce the familiar world around us; they are intended ultimately to displace it with another, thoroughly self-contained world. These environments are invented, moreover, so as finally *not* to be translatable into the terms of the provided environments; "and their extravagances of languages are an exultation in the exercise of consciousness momentarily set free."

However much Peckinpah's films may seem to lend themselves to interpretation as allegories, fables, or parables, what they are fundamentally about are his attempts to envision through the language of his medium environments quite different from those to which we are accustomed, and to fill dramatic spaces and order dramatic time according to laws equally different from those that obtain outside the theater. This is what in his own way Peckinpah kept trying to tell interviewers when he insisted that he is a storyteller; and it is what he meant when, invidiously comparing the lot of the director to that of the writer, he once said that as a writer "you only have to deal with yourself; you can escape into your fantasies and be a king."[13] But it is clear enough that he looked upon filmmaking in much the same way (which is why he fought so hard to keep films intact), and in *The Ballad* he found himself an ideal vehicle, a story of a hero who "out of the barren wastes carved himself a one-man kingdom."

Poirier calls attention to the obsession that American writers often have with building things (Thoreau at Walden, the Pyncheon seven-gabled house, Sutpen's Hundred, and so forth), where the hero's construction of a dwelling place becomes a metaphor for the artist's construction of an artwork, and the hero himself comes to seem a surrogate for the artist.[14] In *The Ballad* the first thing that Cable does after he discovers the water hole is to start building a house for himself and getting his way station in shape for business. It is always risky to push the parallels between artist and artwork too far, but it is nevertheless difficult to escape the suspicion that Peckinpah deliberately set himself the most difficult task he could imagine: take the unlikeliest, the least promising and most hackneyed set of materials—a prostitute with a heart of gold, a lecherous preacher, an irascible if lovable old desert rat—and put them in the emptiest space he could find, an actual desert, and then see what could be done with them. Not the least of his accomplishments is the tacit demonstration that there is no such thing as a cliché, only a clichéd treatment.

It is equally difficult to resist the feeling that *The Ballad* was for him an especially personal undertaking. He thought enough of the script to purchase it during a time when he was broke, had to borrow the money for it, and couldn't even be certain he would ever be allowed to direct it; he revised it on and off for the better part of the next two years, despite work on other projects; it was the first feature film on which he acted as his own producer; and he called it, more than once, his favorite among his films.[15] This does not mean that it is his best, or even that he necessarily considered it so (he didn't), only that he looked upon it as something special during its making and regarded it the rest of his life with special favor. Just how special, and just how preoccupied Peckinpah was personally with the building metaphor Poirier has identified as a recurring pattern in our art and expression, is suggested by a remark the director once dropped, with characteristic laconism, into an interview: "I can't live it, so I remake it."[16] The observation is almost too self-aware (it's the kind of thing—like Hemingway's saying that his analyst is "Portable Corona No. 3"—that an artist is supposed to wait for a critic to say about him), but it locates exactly his real commitment, which is to the environments that he invents as opposed to those that are provided him.

One ramification of this commitment is stylistic. As Poirier observes:

> To make an environment in language that thwarts any attempts to translate that language into the terms of conventional environments is to write with a complexity that few even now are willing to allow to the novel or to any kind of prose. Indeed it is significant that most adverse criticism of, say, Melville or James, displays a marked failure to give requisite attention to the demanding styles by which these writers create an imaginary environment that excludes the standards of that "real" one to which most critics subscribe.[17]

Substitute "film" for "novel" and "filmmaking" for "prose," and we have here a remarkably accurate capsule description of much of the adverse criticism that has been leveled against Peckinpah. But it is not uncommon to hear even some of his admirers wondering with whom among his opposing characters he means for us to side or asking such questions as, "Is he a realist or a romantic?" To the extent that this can be taken seriously, the only possible answer is "yes," since with this director it is always the mixtures that matter most.

But the terms of the question itself are responsible for some of the confusion because they set up a comparison that may be invalid and is certainly misleading. Properly speaking, romance is a type or genre of storytelling, which means that it is a structure. Realism, however, is a technique; it is a formal cause of storytelling that has to do with

matters of scene setting, details of observation, preciseness of description—in other words, with how the subject is rendered. It is only when
realism is treated as a final cause that it becomes the "inept term"
Northrop Frye once called it, in a moment of uncharacteristic testi-
ness. In its place Frye offered "irony" because it implies the kind of
distance and detachment usually required to observe the world at its
most quotidian.[18] More than mere semantics is at issue here. In Peckinpah's films there is so much foreground irony in the textural density, the wealth of observation, the multiplicity of authentic detail, and
the depiction of teeming humanity in all its tragically flawed beauty
that it is perhaps easy to understand how some viewers might lose
sight altogether of the background romance and myth. (It is necessary to go beyond the medium to find storytellers who get as much
tension as this one does from the contrary pulls of irony and myth.)
Seen this way the function of realism in Peckinpah's art is not to
undercut myth and romance toward the end of an obvious and easy
ridicule or cynicism—that is, irony as it is commonly understood.
Rather to the contrary, in fact: he uses realism to counter the tendency of myth and romance toward abstraction, his purpose to invest
them with a flesh-and-blood reality that will make them all the more
compelling by the very lifelikeness of the presentation.

Of all Peckinpah's formal devices and techniques, the epiphanies
are most to the point here, for it is in them that he dissolves the
boundaries between foreground and background and allows irony to
flow momentarily into myth and vice-versa. The key word is "momentarily." One of the things that Peckinpah's style has in common with
those of the classic American writers who make up Poirier's study is
a tendency for the narrative line periodically to be extended into
moments of lyric expansion, interior revelation, and epiphany. Poirier writes that often what "we remember about a book—and this is
notably true in American literature—is often the smallest, momentary revelations that nonetheless carry, like the mystical experience
to which William James alludes, an enormous sense of inner authority."[19] At the same time, however, "the rest of life, like the rest of a
book, 'tends to contradict them more than it confirms them.'"

As a case in point Poirier cites *Adventures of Huckleberry Finn*, from
which we are most likely to remember the raft scenes only to discover that they "constitute less than a tenth of the whole." By the same
token, *The Wild Bunch* is famous for its violence, but if we were to
splice together all the violent footage, it might total fifteen, perhaps
twenty minutes out of a 145-minute film. The apparent contradiction
is to be accounted for by the intensity of feeling during the moments

of revelation, in which our consciousness is raised to such a heightened state of awareness that we seem to burst through one kind of
existence into another where time ceases to exist and an instant can
seem, as Pauline Kael once remarked of the exploded bridge in *The
Wild Bunch,* "extended to eternity."[20] However, it is only a trick of
perception, and the instant passes quickly enough. If it is to have any
longer existence it will have to be by way of art. To all the other structural polarities we have identified in Peckinpah's films, then, we can
add still another, and a fundamental one: a continual interplay between a pair of distinct and radically opposed worlds of being. At the
very end of *The Wild Bunch* he moved effortlessly from one of these
to the other. In *The Ballad* he makes their opposition his organizing
principle.

Perhaps the best way to move into the environment of *The Ballad*
is through both its title and those techniques of deliberate artifice
that have been the bones of so much critical contention. The realism is obvious enough: the grimy, weatherbeaten clothes; countless
details of *mise-en-scène;* the tremendous depth and clarity with which
the desert is seen; the look and feel of life, human and animal, moving in the Western landscape. These distinguish all of Peckinpah's
Western films. The most ostentatious techniques of deliberate artifice
are, however, apparently something new: the fast-motion cinematography, the animation of the face of an Indian on a dollar bill into a
lascivious grin as Cable contemplates spending part of his grub stake
on a prostitute, and the split-screen business used during the opening credits and sometime later when Cable gathers refuse from the
desert and starts building his house. It is curious that Peckinpah's
slow-motion, which is equally artificial, should find, all things considered, a fairly quick and easy acceptance, while devices like these
should cause some discomfort. Let us grant, before going further, that
the smiling Indian (however much it can be justified as a point-of-
view shot) is a bit much (though it *is* funny), and that the director
may, as some critics have charged, get a little overly playful here and
there with fast motion (in particular, the moment when Josh sprints
away from the snakes, though this too is funny).

After granting these things, however, we may notice, especially in
view of the hint Peckinpah dropped about Keystone Cops, that the
fast-motion refers us back to the era of silent films and has therefore
an archaizing effect. Frye has written of the "archaizing tendencies
in Shakespeare," which "establish contact with a universal and worldwide dramatic tradition" and which are seen in Shakespeare's appro-
priation of such rudimentary or primitive forms of theater as the

masque, the processional, the dance as rite, and various kinds of ceremonies (like weddings).[21] In much the same way the world of the silent film is something out of the childhood of the medium. This is not to ignore the great films made then; but their achievement notwithstanding, when we think of the silent film we are apt to think first of slapstick comedy, and then of such primitive forms of storytelling and drama as the chase and the mime. We think too of people who move in a funny way, and who are also strange because of the way they *don't* sound, their "speech" being limited to a variant of the comic strip's balloon. If we think of sound at all, what comes to mind is music, in particular a lone piano tinkling away in a pastiche of melodies lifted from such warhorses of the romantic period as the *Pathétique* symphony or the *Peer Gynt* suites. It matters relatively little that these impressions are often misleading, that, for example, the jerky, mechanical quality of movement is a function in most cases of running these films through modern projectors not equipped with the correct speed. What matters is that the effect has stuck and has acquired nearly the status of a convention. When Peckinpah employs fast motion here, he is employing the most widely recognized characteristic of the silent film, and it is simply for him one more instance of the archaizing tendencies we have already identified in some of his other films with their songs, dances, and festivals.

Music is always an important element in Peckinpah's work, but here it is given a much greater expressive role to play than usual. He calls the film a ballad, which is itself a rather archaic form and, like films, plays, and operas, a bastardized one, drawing upon literature and music. He is not, of course, trying to create a literal ballad any more than in *The Wild Bunch* he was trying to create a literal legend. What he is doing is giving us a ballad more or less in the making, which is one reason that he has his characters express themselves in song from time to time. Taggart and Bowen are not even out of earshot before they make up a song about what they've done to Cable and start singing it; and sometime later, as Cable prepares to set a trap for them, he sings, to the same tune, "Taggart and Bowen as quick as you please / Took all the money and left for the trees." Peckinpah also had songs written for each of the three main characters, and each song tells us something significant about the character's situation: Cable's "Tomorrow Is the Song I Sing," Hildy's "Butterfly Mornings," and Josh's "Wait for Me, Sunrise." Each character is introduced while his or her song is played on the soundtrack; and in the most unabashedly romantic scene—the montage sequence that records the idyll Cable and Hildy enjoy at the Springs—Peckinpah does exactly what

he did in *The Wild Bunch* when the Bunch left Angel's village: he simultaneously uses song as both source music and score. Songs are,
of course, a stylized or heightened form of expression, and when they
are incorporated into a dramatic structure the effect is often to sev-
er its ties with the "real" world and usher in another kind of world
where people are blessed with a curious gift of eloquence that gives
them the power to express their deepest feelings instantaneously in
verse to the accompaniment of an imaginary collection of instruments that has no existence except on the soundtrack (or, in the
theater, in the orchestra pit).

In such a world it should not be too difficult to accept the convention that people might, in moments of stress or excitement, move a
little faster than normal (particularly when it is deployed as chastely
as here, in just four scenes, never for more than a few seconds each
time). What could be more natural, in any case, than Cable's eager-
ness to prepare a room when his lady love pays him an unexpected
visit just as he finishes his day's work; and how better to dress it to
advantage than to speed up the camera a little, as his heart races
slightly in anticipation of the coming night of pleasure? The fast-
motion business is used again a short while later. As Cable bathes
Hildy one morning while they sing of their love for each other, the
stagecoach, filled with passengers, arrives. Cable starts rushing around
to find Hildy a robe, and when he isn't fast enough, she hops out of
the tub and rushes toward the house. What has happened here is that
one world has intruded upon another; and inasmuch as they operate according to different tempos, when they clash there are a few
moments of lurching back and forth before they get into sync with
one another. This in turn directs our attention to how carefully Peckinpah has made the geography of the film's space serve as metaphor.
The towns of Deaddog and Gila are separated by forty miles of desert
and joined only by a highway that is scarcely more than some grooves
worn into the sand by stagecoach and wagon wheels. Exactly midway
between the two towns is nestled Cable Springs, not quite on the road,
but a short distance away from it: a little oasis or, as Josh calls it, a
"cactus Eden," which the outside world passes, stopping there only
for refreshment and renewal before resuming its business.

The more ostentatious techniques of deliberate artifice may also
lead us to wonder if Peckinpah isn't using other, similar business
throughout, though in subtler ways. For example, just how playful he
allows himself to become with the revenge story is indicated by how,
after the initial betrayal, he lets the audience forget completely about
it for awhile. When it is next referred to—Josh reminding Cable of

Cable's passion for vengeance—it comes as a slight shock to us. This is obviously the intended effect, for by allowing us to become so preoccupied with Cable's increasing prosperity and general good fortune that we forget about his vengeance, Peckinpah is able to impress more forcibly upon us how little Cable is allowing himself to forget and how resolutely he fails to heed the counsel of the song that is associated with him:

> Let tomorrow be the song you sing.
> And yesterday won't mean a thing.
> Make today your next day's dawn,
> And you'll still be here grinning when the sun goes down.

Much later, when Taggart and Bowen show up, Peckinpah resolutely declines to make a "big" scene of it, even though, by any conventional rules of dramatic construction, it is the moment toward which the film has been building. Instead, they no sooner get off the stagecoach than Peckinpah slyly upstages the whole confrontation by having a couple of the other passengers rush up to Cable and inquire as to the whereabouts of the outhouse. It is a brilliant touch, because it has the effect of throwing Cable's passion into a much larger frame of reference and underscoring how insignificant it really is as far as the rest of the world is concerned. Once we are adjusted to Peckinpah's general method and approach in this film, even some of what has been criticized as clumsy or faltering begins to function positively and appear as design. This is particularly true of the last scene, where coincidence after outrageous coincidence piles up; yet, somehow, the improbabilities seem an integral part of the scene's total effect, much the same as, say, the inability of an actress to hold herself *absolutely* still in the statue scene from *The Winter's Tale* is undeniably a part of the scene's total effect (indeed, without which the scene as a whole could not and would not work on the stage).

Although one critic has already invoked *The Winter's Tale* as a means of helping to explain *The Ballad*,[22] a more likely source for so unlikely a combination of story types and genres may be *The Tempest*. To begin with, Peckinpah uses one device so familiar from that play— the storm near the beginning of the story—that it seems to amount to quotation. There are many other similarities as well, notably in the use of a hero who makes a one-man kingdom for himself, has a personal vendetta, and eventually brings his enemies totally under his control in a situation where he exerts a godlike power of life and death. But the similarity that concerns us most immediately is the storm and its implications as a convention. In stories like this, storms are natural catastrophes that throw the characters from one world into another. As devices, then, the tempest in the play and the sand-storm in this film at once symbolize a world in disorder (where kin betrays kin, friends betray friend) and have the effect of disorienting both the audience and the characters. (It is partly by way of preparation that Peckinpah records Cable's four days of "suffering time" on a split screen, which has a slightly disorienting effect and which therefore adumbrates the more radical dislocation we undergo in the sandstorm.) When the storms subside, the characters find they have been taken to a strange and distant place that often has, by contrast to the world from which they were removed, an archaic, pastoral quality. Inasmuch, then, as the storm separates, defines, and substitutes a world of peace, order, and happiness for one of violence, disorder, and sadness, the passage through it assumes the characteristic of a deliverance, which in turn suggests providential intervention. In most of the Shakespearean comedies and romances there is either an actual deity (like Apollo) or a person (some figure of high royalty) who functions more or less as a deity by proxy or by analogy, and this deity is eventually seen to be ordering the events of the play. Just how closely attuned Peckinpah was to this convention and its traditions while he was working on the film is suggested by a remark he made shortly after its completion: "*The Ballad of Cable Hogue* is about a man who found water where it wasn't . . . it's also about God."[23] At two key points in the film Peckinpah positions his camera so as to imply the actual presence of God. Immediately before Cable discovers the water hole, there is an extremely high overhead shot looking directly down upon him. And later there is another high-angle shot suggesting the same point of view, this time of Josh walking toward his horse on the morning he leaves Cable Springs—which is, of course, the same morning Hildy leaves and the morning Josh, alluding to God's generosity, subtly tries to persuade Cable to follow her.

Providential agency is central to the mechanism of stories of this kind for a number of reasons: it refers us to an overriding cosmic order of which the initial act of betrayal constitutes a violation, it accounts for the prodigious number of coincidences in the plot, and it introduces another convention, that of prayer. In these stories prayer has a power to affect and effect quite at variance with what it usually seems to have in life. One reviewer has called attention to the Lord's answering Cable's third prayer and to Cable's being run over by the third automobile he has ever seen (actually, the film is not specific on the latter number).[24] However, the number matters to Peckinpah less than the manner in which Cable offers his first two prayers, which is belligerent, sarcastic, and arrogant. In the middle of the sandstorm, almost dead, he shouts, "Careful, you're about to get my dander up," at which point the wind suddenly blows more fiercely than ever. It is not until Cable rolls over on his back and says, "Lord, you call it. I'm just plain done in"—not, in other words, until, humbled, he is ready to give up his life—that the Lord gives it back to him and produces the water hole.

This is the last time that Cable prays, but there are nevertheless other prayers. Just after Cable makes his mean remark at the dinner table, Hildy says grace, asking the Lord to "bless this house"; a short time later, the Lord sends her out to Cable. And both Josh and Bowen fall on their knees before Cable, who in turn gives the one sanctuary and the other reprieve. It would seem, then, that the power of prayer has something to do with both the attitude and the posture that the person assumes while praying, which suggest both humility and faith. The attitude thus implicitly acknowledges that cosmic order which was originally violated, and the posture puts a person in his ordained place within that order (subservient to God). Furthermore, prayer, more or less as a matter of course, implies trust in providence; and equally as a matter of course in a world plainly seen to be magical and miraculous, such trust is rewarded.

Just about everything else in the film relates to and derives from the basic division of the dramatic space into a world on this side of the storm and a world on the other side of the storm. Frye calls these two worlds the objective or the real (that is, the world of the spectator) and the created or the illusory (that is, the world of the play).[25] This distinction is analogous to Poirier's invented and provided environments; and since we are dealing with drama, perhaps it is a more appropriate one. The enchanted quality of the world of illusion is often a function of who is looking, or for what. In *The Tempest* the island appears to Prospero's enemies as both barren and deserted and to his friends as lush and verdant (where the very clothes they wear have never looked better). When Taggart and Bowen go looking for water, all they find is "fifty thousand gallons of sand," while Cable finds water, something few people in town will believe. When the stagecoach company digs for water on land adjoining Cable's, its efforts come to nothing, and Quittner is forced to sign Cable's contract. Similarly, early in the film when Cable finds old pieces of wood, discarded furniture, and other rubbish lying around, it is easy enough to explain these things as having been thrown away by people traveling the road. However, these things can also be thought of as having appeared more or less magically, put there by a benevolent deity for

Cable to use as need dictates, which may be why, in addition to its value as narrative economy, Peckinpah uses the split-screen business again. He also reinforces the theme of perspectivism, as Cable sees value and worth where others saw only waste and rubbish. The very first shot of the film shows a gila monster swelling itself as Cable approaches with a knife, but by the time Cable has passed through the storm, there seems hardly any need for the knife. In one scene, he captures some snakes with his bare hands, and in another some customers enjoy a stew he has concocted from the snakes and from toads, grasshoppers, rabbits, squirrels, gophers, and prairie dogs.* This is, indeed, a plentiful desert put there by a wise and bountiful God for the use of those who know how to find what riches it contains.

As the area around the Springs becomes more self-contained, its characteristic subtly changes. Rather than using the techniques of realism to make the desert itself look different, more often than not Peckinpah registers the changes with language, song, and music, deploying only a very few visual clues or physical indications (a single wildflower that Cable picks for Hildy, a butterfly, a few domestic birds and animals). The transformations in the environment are significant, for, in a species of pathetic fallacy, stories like this almost always evoke their contrasting worlds in terms of contrasting natural imagery. The real world, prey to death, decay, and dissolution, is aligned with fall and winter; the invented world, abundant in life, rebirth, and renewal, is aligned with spring and summer. Since he set his film in the actual desert (it was shot in Nevada's Valley of Fire), Peckinpah would have had a difficult time showing seasonal changes even if he had wanted to. This is, however, less of a problem than it might seem. For example, given what we know about the paucity of means and the limited technical resources of the Elizabethan theater, it couldn't have happened much in early productions of Shakespeare either. And when contemporary directors use the considerably more sophisticated stagecraft of the modern theater to "illustrate" the imagery of the poetry, however much the effects may charm us, at the same time they are liable to strike us as just a little cloyingly literal minded. This is because Shakespeare does not use human mood and emotion as metaphors for the seasonal cycle, he uses the seasonal

---

*When informed what is in the stew, the customers bolt from the table and throw up. This is a touch one wishes Peckinpah had avoided or thought more about. He is again playing different perspectives off one another: free from their habitual associations, the customers enjoy the stew; told what is in it, they get sick. (A child—played by Peckinpah's son, Matthew—keeps right on eating.) Yet as rendered the scene smacks too much of stock Western-humor where the fall guys are always city slickers.

cycle to supply metaphors for human mood and emotion. (It is a case, as Emerson once put it, of nature always wearing the colors of the spirit, not the spirit wearing the colors of nature.) It is thus to some an extent an integral part of Peckinpah's method that the externals of scene and setting remain more or less constant throughout. Cable Springs does not so much come to look different from the desert at large as to *feel* different, and this has to do with the power of suggestion and with what Peckinpah allows the place to be invested with as it becomes increasingly like a pastoral idyll. This is most apparent when Hildy joins Cable, for she completes his life at the Springs and her influence effects the most radical and romantic transformation of the environment. Indeed, it turns the provided environment into the invented environment.

Before Hildy arrives Cable Springs is a masculine world, comprised of Cable and Josh, and it has been developed about as much as a society of men is capable: the house is built, the corral is finished, the business is underway, and the place is well supplied. Yet it lacks grace, civility, and charm, which in this place are to be classified not as adornments but as essentials. It lacks, in a word, femininity, and all that femininity implies. In romantic comedy, the heroine is, by convention, supposed to be chaste, a convention that has become somewhat outmoded or, rather, the terms of which have changed. In view of this, although it is perhaps stretching a point to say so, it is possible to see Hildy's role as prostitute as a way of keeping her chaste for Cable. The concept is doubtless paradoxical, but then comedy is built upon paradox. When Cable says, "You can't convince Hildy with anything but hard cash," it is another way of saying that however much men may be able to buy her body, they cannot buy her soul, which must be convinced, as Cable convinces it, with kindness, charity, and love. Moreover, Hildy's profession is absorbed within the twin themes of perspectivism and double environments, for she is a prostitute only by society's lights, that is, only in the world on this side of the sandstorm. In the world on the other side, and to Cable, she is perfectly chaste (hence, his sigh of relief when she tells him that she wasn't ready to be saved by Josh's ministrations, and Josh's unsuccessful attempt later on to seduce her).

In any case, what is significant is what happens to Cable Springs after she gets there, which is, more than anything else, that it is metamorphosed into what its name implies. It is surely no accident that for all the talk of Cable's water, Hildy is the character with whom the film imagistically associates water most of the time. We don't really see much of it (what we see is a hole in the ground) until she arrives, after which it is seen in abundance and put to uses other than quenching thirst. There is a lovely shot in which the camera tracks along a trough down which the water flows into a bucket held by Hildy, an equally lovely one of Cable bringing her breakfast in bed, and a real beauty that has them unloading a crate of chickens (the first domestic animals seen at the Springs), the crate falling and breaking open, the couple chasing after the chickens. These are set to the music of Hildy's song, the lyrics of which associate her with an iconography new to the film and suggestive of fertility, rebirth, and recreative potential: butterflies, wildflowers, sunflowers, dandelions, cantaloupes, and seeds. Inasmuch as the musical interlude concludes with Cable's giving Hildy a bath (which recalls the earlier scene in which she bathed him), the interlude assumes the function of a passage, parallel to but different from Cable's passage through the storm, not violent and disruptive, but gentle, persuasive, and sweet. The storm brought Cable to the Springs, but it is Hildy's presence and influence as a redemptive power both of and for nature that makes it the world elsewhere. As a consequence, the musical interlude signifies arrival as well, and it is possible to mark the exact moment of arrival: when Cable joins Hildy for the second verse, the alignment of natural and spiritual regeneration is complete, and the sequence draws together, focuses, and climaxes the motifs of rebirth and starting fresh that are implied by these lines from the song: "On the wings of a butterfly I woke to my morning / On the beams of a sunflower, on the day I was born in." It is the final displacement whereby Cable Springs is cut loose, set free, and left to drift "in butterfly mornings and wildflower afternoons," and, as such, constitutes the dramatic and symbolic center of the film and the resolution of its comic action. All the rest is, in a very real sense, falling action, a return from the world elsewhere to the world right here.

This romantic idyll, in which the film seems suspended forever yet which ends almost before we know it, is destroyed only when Cable reintroduces the outside world by reminding Hildy of what she is back there and by reminding us of what he is and of the vengeance that continues to gnaw at the walls of his soul. Cable's failure to forget— which is, after all, the real basis for any kind of new life—symbolizes his inability to renounce hatred for love, death for life. When this is clear once and for all, Hildy has nowhere to go except back into the world, and the whole idyll is dissolved. She can't take it with her, yet without her it isn't what it was, and so it dies. The death is only figurative, but when something so fragile ceases to be an article of faith, it leaves itself vulnerable to the decaying cycle of nature. Consequently, even as the landscape continues to look pretty much the same, there is throughout the rest of the film a corresponding shift of the iconography, as rabbits, flowers, and chickens are supplanted by snakes and finally by a coyote, whose appearance at the end of the film is reminiscent of the scavengers near the end of *The Wild Bunch*. In this context it is doubtless no accident that on the night when Cable insults Hildy, a coyote howls ever so faintly in the distance or that in the early scenes snakes were part of the sustenance Cable could count on in the desert, while in the last scene they are used as weapons.

In comedy it is never easy to pass from one kind of world to another. What is required is some natural event of sufficiently catastrophic proportions to disrupt the continuity of existence and obliterate most of our reference points. This is, as we have seen, the function of the storm. After Hildy and Josh leave the Springs, Peckinpah uses another device that suggests an analog to the storm. This is the montage sequence, composed of a succession of overlapping images, which is used to condense three years of time. That Peckinpah wants us to think of this as the analog to the opening storm is reinforced by two repetitions: he reprises Cable's song, "Tomorrow Is the Song I Sing," which led into the storm and leads into the montage sequence, and Cable is heard saying the same things in both scenes. Immediately after he has discovered the water, while the storm still rages about him, he shouts: "Told you I was going to live. This is Cable Hogue talking! Hogue, me, Cable Hogue. Me. I found it. Me." During the montage sequence, he shouts: "Me. Cable Hogue! Right here! Waiting. Right here. Waiting!" But there is a difference in imagery, as the montage sequence consists of shots of Cable over which are superimposed shots of the stagecoach riding back and forth, arriving at and leaving the Springs. It is a sequence in which a long period of time is compressed into a short narrative interlude, and the primary symbol both of time passing and of the outside world coming and going becomes the stagecoach itself. Equally telling is how the stagecoach moves. During the earlier parts of the film, it never moved at full tilt; during the montage sequence and thereafter, the team hardly ever moves at less than full gallop (at least while en route). Meanwhile, Cable is seen fixed in one spot, and the sequence ends with a subtle superimposition that leaves his tiny figure at the hub of a spinning stagecoach wheel. The overall impression is that a world is passing Cable by and is swallowing up the Springs as we remember it when Hildy was there to vitalize it.

Critics have often remarked upon Peckinpah's gift for manipulating and organizing filmic space. What is never mentioned, however, is the extraordinary leverage he gets from time. This is not just a matter of controlling tempo and dynamics, which he does supremely; it is more a matter of his juxtapositions of various kinds of time. At once the subtlest and the most potent tension set up in this film is the contrast between dramatic time and real time, which underscores the most profound difference between the world on this side of the sandstorm and the world on the other. What characterizes the romantic idyll of Cable and Hildy is its composition as a series of many brief scenes that follow one another in fairly rapid succession. Often a scene will consist of no more than a single exchange of dialogue, and eventually the scenes consist of only half an exchange, with the other half provided in the next scene occurring later that day or on some other day, we aren't sure which. Yet the effect of this organization is paradoxically the opposite of frenetic. Time turns in upon itself, each moment seems extended to eternity, and all the moments melt together into a continuous present in which there are both world and time enough for anything that we might wish or desire. It is not quite the same as a timeless world; but it is a world where time does not prey upon the consciousness, where existence seems absolved from the pressures of time, where time is subordinated to other rhythms—emotional, sensual, natural, mythical—as opposed to being the controlling rhythm. At the very center of this world is the musical interlude, the prismatic axis on which the entire film spins.

But when the montage sequence, a storm of onrushing time, takes us back into the world of ordinary experience, time seems to be all there is yet there never seems to be enough of it. The last quarter of the film consists of exactly one scene; and from the moment when Taggart and Bowen have dug themselves into the pit to the end of the film, there are only three time lapses (that is, cuts or dissolves that indicate a jump over a period of time), and these cover at most a few minutes to an hour or so of time. In other words, for one-fourth of the film's length, dramatic time and real time are made synonymous, yet, ironically, more is made to occur and at a more bewildering pace than anywhere else in the film. Taggart and Bowen reappear, Taggart is shot, Bowen is forgiven, Taggart is buried, an automobile roars by the Springs, the stagecoach arrives at a frantic pace, Hildy reappears, Cable is run down, Josh reappears, Cable dies, is buried, and eulogized, and the film ends. And toward the end, time is racing so fast that there isn't time to show everything, such as the arrival from Deaddog of Quittner and Cushing, Hildy's change into mourning clothes, Bowen's too, and the actual digging of the grave and the lowering of Cable into it. What kind of crazy world is this? Or, to ask the question that Cable asks when the stagecoach arrives, "What kind of a cockeyed schedule is this?"

No cockeyed schedule, just a mail run, and business as usual in a world that has already begun to move at a faster tempo than Cable is accustomed to. This is, of course, because of its contrast with the idyll, in which time seemed held in abeyance and to which we are briefly referred when Cable has a pensive moment as some images of him and Hildy as they were in days past are faded in and out to the sound of Hildy's voice, softly now, as if in whisper, singing, "Butterfly mornings, butterfly mornings, butterfly mornings, and wildflower afternoons." In the here and now, however, everybody and everything seem in a hurry, and time is an oppressive force that sweeps all before it. Not surprisingly, the characters themselves become conscious of it. When Cable tells Hildy he is ready to leave with her, she says, "We've got nothing but time, Hogue, nothing but time"; and a few minutes later, when Cable is dying, he urges Josh to get on with the eulogy because "I ain't got any time." The eulogy itself contains an ironic allusion to the storm, which brings the film full circle. At the beginning the storm was a localized event that ushered forth a new and different world; but when Josh reminds us that Cable has gone "into the whole torrent of the years," we realize that the storm becomes the informing metaphor for the world itself, where all existence falls victim to the implacable advance of time.

When Peckinpah called *The Ballad* a new version of *The Flies,* he must, then, have been thinking primarily of the last part of the film, where even God is back to his old familiar ways, is become again a god of wrath and vengeance. His harshness is most evident in the sardonic trick of fate and illusion that he plays on Cable by putting happiness once more within his grasp only to snatch it away all the more violently at the last possible moment. When Hildy steps out of her automobile, she is dressed in a long flowing gown of green and gold brocade, her hair done in elaborate graceful swirls under a broad-brimmed hat with an immense feather adorning it. And when she tosses the hat aside, opens her arms, and runs toward Cable, her cape billowing, she becomes the butterfly of the song, as the music swells to crescendo and she and Cable embrace. It is the most effusively romantic moment Peckinpah ever directed and so it is also, as we might fear, too good to be true. The final joke that God plays is to have Hildy's automobile, which is the same color as her dress, be responsible for Cable's death, for when she left the Springs, she too was absorbed into the world that passed Cable by and that in the end

will quite literally run over him. In this world the automobile supplants the stagecoach as the primary symbol of time as a destructive
force and reminds us that Josh's early prophecy is already beginning
to come true—"I foresee a great community springing out of the
desert, busy thoroughfares, alabaster buildings"—though in a typically ironic way. It occurs to us that perhaps the basic reason that time
wields such power here is that the one thing we do not believe in is
the inevitable consequence of its passing, which is death. This is why
Peckinpah draws out the lead-up to Cable's death for so long, with
the bad jokes and the awkward reassurances and the disbelief of everyone present. Only Cable believes that he is really about to die; and
Peckinpah skips over the actual moment of expiration because death
is a certainty that nobody, ourselves included, believes can happen
until after it happens. It happened here during the last time lapse
of the film, a split-second cut, like the blink of an eye, which takes
us from the party gathered around Cable's bed listening to a mock
eulogy to the party gathered around Cable's grave listening to a real
eulogy. Consequently, Josh's initial attempts to be eloquent are hollow and flat, lacking as they do a suitable occasion; later, the eulogy
becomes genuinely eloquent because he is by then suitably inspired.
This, then, suggests that for all the similarities between Cable and
Prospero, there is one power, perhaps the most important, that Peckinpah withholds from Cable and turns instead over to Josh—the
power of language, a vehicle both of prayer and of art.

In addition to its function as convention, prayer comes to have a
metaphoric significance that refers to nothing outside the story, but
to the story itself. Art like this doesn't so much force as ask us to suspend disbelief; indeed, it has no power to force us, because it lacks
the safety nets of the ordinary and the familiar, drawing its power
instead from the strange and wonderful, the deliberately artificial and
make-believe. As such, the film and our relationship to it mirror Cable
Springs and Cable's relationship to it, and the filmmaker is asking
from us only what Shakespeare is asking from his audience and what
God is asking from Cable: give me some faith, a little imagination,
and a willingness to suspend disbelief (which is to say, to renounce
the world you know), and in return I will give you beauty, pleasure,
and more freedom than you have ever dreamed possible. I will place,
in sum, a whole alternate world at your disposal to do with what you
will. This is, of course, a totally imaginary world, a world of illusion
and vision, existing only within the confines of the story, play, or film.
This being the case, we may wish to ask the question that Frye asks
of Shakespearean comedy and romance: "What is the value, as en-

tertainment, of a story like this?"[26] His answer is that the world within the story is identified, through the language of simile, metaphor, and myth, with the paradise that, we are assured, we once inhabited, from which we subsequently fell, and to which we are referred by such names as Eden, the Golden Age, and Arcadia or by such metaphors as spring, morning, and festival.

In this context, then, there is one other symbol in *The Ballad* to which we might want to devote some attention, and this is the flag that Cable raises above the Springs as the man of God looks on, apparently with approval. The favored interpretation of the flag relates it to the views of the film as either an elegy for or a criticism of laissez-faire capitalism, and one critic has already chastised audiences for remaining "so respectfully and ludicrously silent those times that Hogue raises and lowers Old Glory at Cable Springs, which was founded on nothing more noble than murder, greed, and betrayal!"[27] But this leaves too much unexplained and much else covered over or merely ignored. The betrayal is *of*, not *by*, Cable, his killings are out of self-defense (in more ways than one), and his greed is in part a protective reaction against the very generosity and good humor that left him vulnerable to betrayal in the first place. This interpretation also fails to account for the emotional tenor of the scenes involving the flag, which are suffused with such genuine, appealing, and straightforward warmth of feeling as to invite the audience's silence, which more than likely indicates shared affection rather than sentimental reverence. It fails as well to explain why it is that the flag is, if anything, more conspicuous by its absence in the world beyond the Springs, particularly in Deaddog. Finally, it doesn't take into consideration that Peckinpah associates the flag nearly as much with Hildy as with Cable, and, more important still, with the two of them as a couple. When she arrives at the Springs, Cable is lowering the flag; seeing her he quickly hoists it back up again and turns his attentions to her. Later on, in one of the film's most beautifully shot and composed images, the two of them are seen lowering the flag at sunset, the sky pink and auburn, the wind whipping lightly at their hair. In other words, it is the world of the idyll, not the world at large, in which Peckinpah locates the flag, thus incorporating it into the whole network of images, symbols, and metaphors of rebirth, renewal, and regeneration that is drawn around the Springs when Hildy joins Cable and they begin to build a new life together. The flag is associated with the aspect of Cable Springs that Josh likens to a "cactus Eden" and that becomes, in due time, more like a traditional Eden, with butterfly mornings and wildflower afternoons.

We may wonder, then, if Cable does not in the end rest in the long line of American Adams that R. W. B. Lewis has documented so thoroughly,[28] and if Hildy is not therefore his Eve and the Springs their garden. Certainly much of Josh's eulogy, to say nothing of the prevailing imagery throughout the film, touches off the mythic reverberations. Cable was born into this world nobody knows when or where; he came stumbling out of the wilderness like a prophet of old and was reborn, so it would seem, out of the very dust and sand of a desert storm; he is the Lord's dim reflection; and he is courageous, resourceful, and fiercely independent—"an individual" (the words now belong to Lewis) "emancipated from history, happily bereft of ancestry, untouched and undefiled by the usual inheritances of family and race; an individual standing alone, self-reliant and self-propelling, ready to confront whatever awaited him with the aid of his own unique and inherent resources." In the beginning, of course, Cable, lusting for vengeance, is not innocent, and in the end he is victim both to history and to progress; but then the same is true of many another American Adam, the way the archetype is shaded, colored, or shaped owing largely to the party to which his creator belongs. Lewis, taking a cue from Emerson, describes two: the party of hope (or the future), those who celebrate America's lack of a past as the firmest basis on which to secure its glorious future; and the party of despair (or the past), those who bemoan America's lack of a past as the surest indication that it will repeat the mistakes of history. Between these two extremes, Lewis describes a third party, the party of irony, the membership of which is comprised mostly of artists; and it is surely the one in which, extending his categories to twentieth-century art and expression, we would have to include Peckinpah, "characterized," as it is, "by a tragic optimism: by a sense of the tragic collisions to which innocence was liable (something unthinkable among the hopeful), and equally by an awareness of the heightened perception and humanity which suffering made possible (something unthinkable among the nostalgic)."

"Tragic optimism" also happens to be a remarkably accurate, if oblique description of the comic sensibility, at least in its structural aspect, which takes its characters into a visionary world of heightened human order only after plunging them into darkness, despair, and chaos. In *The Wild Bunch* Peckinpah made a tragedy, but at the last moment he directed the structure toward the comic and the romantic; in *The Ballad*, by contrast, he has made a comedy and a romance, but at the very end he deflects the structure toward the tragic. The terms are being employed here in their technical, that is, structural sense; but much of the excitement and pleasure of these two films derives from the tension between mood and structure, the variations that Peckinpah is playing upon familiar patterns of drama, and the extremes to which he pushes and then transforms them. *The Ballad* does not in any literal way imitate *The Tempest,* either in plot or in character types: Cable is like Prospero only up to a point; in other ways Josh bears a closer resemblance. And in *The Tempest* the love story is developed with a pair of young lovers and ends well. Most of all, the endings of play and film differ radically. When Shakespeare separates the illusory from the real, we are left in the illusion, while time ceases to be a continuum and becomes instead a circle that is completed when the brave new world of the future is identified with the great golden age of the past. When this same separation occurs in *The Ballad,* the film is only half over, and by its end we have been deposited back into the real world and made to witness under a darkening sky an event that dramatizes the ravages of time.

Such differences may indicate nothing more than different sensibilities at work at different times in similar forms; but they may also point to the changes that history and culture must inevitably wring from even so indestructible a structure as comedy. If, as Leo Marx has argued, *The Tempest* really is Shakespeare's "American fable,"[29] then perhaps we can understand why it could end as it does and equally why Peckinpah's cannot end in any other way than it does. The new world was a strange and wonderful place, rich with the terror of the unknown but richer still with potential and possibility, a world where it made sense to make of Caliban a savage force of nature in need of enlightenment and to locate the visionary world in the future. Two and a half centuries later, it was still possible for Emerson, Thoreau, and Whitman to place their dream of what might be in the future, and even to employ a vocabulary that implied a future, for there was still continent enough and time. Almost a century and a half later, with the country covering the whole continent and the continent itself on the verge of depletion, we are no longer so sure; and our artists really have no more cause to end their works with a return home than Shakespeare had cause not to. There no longer is any home, the dream has not been realized, its vocabulary has become "what might have been," and every fact of our lives testifies to the reality, however frantic its pace and preposterous its complexity, of the environment we have provided for ourselves. And so when Caliban gets around to putting in his belated appearance, it is a brief but decisive one. He is no longer a monster, half-human and half-animal, but a grotesque, comically absurd contraption, bastard offspring of human ingenuity and Satanic technology, and already, even in so early a stage of his development, beginning to get a little out of hand. And, of course, there is more than one of him. "What in hell is that?" asks Cable when the first motorcar roars by the Springs; "Ugly looking damn thing, ain't it?" says Webb when the next one comes along, with Ben adding, "Kinda strange, a moving all by itself"; and, as Josh pulls up on his motorcycle, Cable remarks, "It sure is an ugly thing." In one of the last images of the film, the automobile and the stagecoach cross paths, one ushering in the future, the other closing off the past.

While many reviewers concede that it is formally and emotionally right for Cable to die at the end, the manner of his death—at the most literal level an instance of *deus ex machina*—continues to strike some as problematic. We may here be dealing with one of those edgy situations in art where response is so subjective that analysis is of little avail to persuade one way or another. Both Cable's death and the manner of it are implicit in the structure of the film: they are carefully built up and foreshadowed (note, for one example, the sermon at the revival meeting, where a preacher shouts, "The devil seeks to destroy you with machines!" or how several times Cable is almost run over by horses in town), and they are a function of everything from Cable's stubbornness to the director's manipulation of time and space. Yet problematic they remain, and the problem is an integral part of the total effect. Perhaps the most telling observation came from *Newsweek's* Joseph Morgenstern, who said: "The main thing about the movie is pleasure, and it's even a great pleasure to watch Peckinpah play with his ending and go farther and farther into fantasy as he gets deeper and deeper into the literal problems of a resolution. Endings bother us all, after all. This one leaves the sharp aftertaste of life."[30] That aftertaste has to do with, among other things, how successfully Peckinpah has integrated the love story with the revenge story and related both to a pattern about as old as any in our fiction, at least since the time of Hawthorne, who had Hester Prynne, dreaming of the future, return to the place of both her joys and her sorrows. With eyes fixed on the future, our heroes and heroines, victims each one of time, are borne ceaselessly to the past.

The quest for the world elsewhere often takes the form of an attempt to start the American experiment, which failed or fell short in life, over again. But the same happens in our art too—Thoreau in the end leaves Walden; Huck Finn lights out for the territory, one step ahead of "sivilization"; Ike McCaslin, for all the grandeur of his relinquishing family and fortune, lives to see his forest grow smaller and smaller and recede farther and farther; Sutpen's Hundred lies in ruins; Gatsby is shot; Cable is run down; and Rip Van Winkle returns from what he thought a catnap only to discover a new country he hardly recognizes. "If there is such a thing as an American tragedy," Pauline Kael once observed, "it must be funny."[31] Why this should be so, at least why it often *is* so, was suggested by Philip Young when he tried to give voice to those "subliminal murmurs in an unintelligible tongue" that he heard in "Rip Van Winkle." If we mock Rip for what he has missed, "we do it tenderly—partly because it is something hidden in ourselves we mock. . . . It is all our own lost lives and roles, the lives and roles that once seemed possible and are possible no more. In twenty years all springs are over; without mockery it might be too sad to bear. Today would grieve, and tomorrow would grieve; best cover it over lightly."[32]

It is Peckinpah's special synthesis in this film that he takes a subject more properly that of tragedy than of comedy and romance— the failure of love—and associates it with the failure of a dream; and his method is to make his film straddle the section of the circle of dramatic structures that moves from comedy to tragedy. But the mood remains comic, not grim, and the tone affectionate rather than bitter. How could it be otherwise? Loss of love and loss of opportunity are too commonplace for tragedy, and an automobile accident, however predestined it seems, is not the stuff of "high seriousness." Best to render it lightly. When Cable allows Hildy to leave, the dream is dissolved, or, rather, it ceases to be an actuality and becomes only a dream, which Peckinpah makes explicit with those few shots of Hildy that he fades in moments before her reappearance.

Still, the dream continues to exert a pull on our imagination that no passage of time or contingency of circumstance seems strong enough to weaken. Somehow we believe, or at least want ourselves to believe, it will be possible to start all over again, to recover not so much the actual past, which is but the record of our mistakes, as that single instant of self-origination when it seemed for all the world as if there were an alternative and that the alternative contained within itself the seeds of infinite potential and possibility. When the brave new world, once a firm prediction, becomes instead a lost opportunity, our art and expression undergo a corresponding shift in tone, direction, and emphasis, and begin to be concerned less with projecting than with recollecting the visionary gleam. The myth of the garden is a myth that dies hard, many of our artists have been telling us since the turn of the century, if not before; but should it be allowed to die, it will die just once and then for good. Their art exists to keep it alive; but the power of art has its limitations too, and often the message is of the impotence of art in the absence of sustaining faith.

An aesthetics of deliberate artifice, drawing upon a long tradition of convention, type, and archetype, tends to result in the most objective kind of art. But in the right hands it can be equally subjective and, however disguised, quite personal. Even so nonbiographical a critic as Frye was willing to concede that it is not altogether improper to think of *The Tempest* as in some sense Shakespeare's special play;[33] and we know that, likewise, *The Ballad* occupies a favored position in Peckinpah's affections. It may be, then, that in the final analysis the closing scene of this film can be read as a statement of the limitations of art in much the same way that Prospero's closing speech has been read and the source of its power is identical and equally ironic: for the finest art that the artist is capable of has been necessary to express the inadequacy of his art to do more than set forth a model of desire that, it is hoped, will be sufficiently inviting to awaken desire and in turn sufficiently pleasing to make us want to satisfy it. At the furthest reaches of this kind of art there is a profound stillness that is a suspension, for the circle of hope finds its completion in our assent and therefore is and can only ever be but partially inscribed by the artist. The rest depends upon our willingness to entertain the offered fantasy. As Josh finishes his prayer with the words, "Take him, Lord, but knowing Cable, I suggest you do not take him lightly," all the director's charms really are overthrown and what strength he has left is most faint enough, so faint that, the resources of his craft nearly exhausted, all he can do is align himself with the character through whom he permits himself a voice, the character blessed with the gift of language: the preacher begging indulgence of God on behalf of his friend the desert rat suggests the director begging indulgence of us on behalf of his film.

The response of the twin deities, both of them audiences demanding to be pleased, is withheld, as it is not at the outset when Cable's prayers are answered with life-renewing water. Instead, the sky begins to darken, and for one last time the director will marshal all the forces of his art. He reprises the song about seeing what tomorrow will bring, yet what we see is a coyote picking about the remains of Cable's shack; he pulls back the camera to let in more light and air, but it reveals only more of the advancing darkness that is fast enclosing Cable Springs. And when he finally freezes the frame, the cinema's last resource to halt the inevitable, we realize that the whole scene comes to stand as the formal equivalent to his unwillingness to let time devour the world of his film. Yet the credits roll on, the song draws to its close, and the words "The End" appear on the screen. The film is thus left, even as the lights are coming on, frozen in its own reluctance to end itself, which is but an analog to the director's hope that we will share his dream and thereby grant it some measure of existence. He lacks, as any artist lacks, the means and resources to answer his own prayers; so, for that matter, does the critic, except as he may be one voice of assent. But if we do answer them, and if the dream is taken, then knowing Peckinpah, I suggest you do not take it lightly.

Rudy Wurlitzer's screenplay of *Pat Garrett and Billy the Kid* was a real epic confrontation with a great lyric quality to it. I brought it down some but I attempted to retain its lyricism and I was really pleased with it—proud of it. Then those emotional eunuchs at MGM cut all of the character and humor and drama out, leaving, or at least trying to leave, only the shoot-outs. And it didn't work.
—Sam Peckinpah

7
Two Killers Elite

Once it has been discovered that the true theme of the Western movie is not the freedom and expansiveness of frontier life, but its limitations, its material bareness, the pressures of obligation, then even the landscape itself ceases to be quite the arena of free movement it once was, but becomes instead a great empty waste, cutting down more often than it exaggerates the stature of the horseman who rides across it.
—Robert Warshow

I

"Men who have lived out of their times, *et cetera,* I've played that out," Sam Peckinpah said in late 1969. "That's a thing that ends with me with *Cable Hogue.*"[1] When he made this statement he could not have known that in fewer than four years he would be at work on *Pat Garrett and Billy the Kid,* another Western film. Since the Western film and the theme of anachronistic men have become virtually synonymous in Peckinpah's career, it may be necessary to point out that there is less contradiction here than meets the eye, for *Pat Garrett* is not centrally about men who have lived beyond their time. With its interlocking themes of casual violence and naturalistic determinism, it is as close as Peckinpah ever came to making a film that is a thoroughly ironic treatment of those "good" old days to which his characters often nostalgically refer. It also marked for him the completion of business that had been left unfinished for a decade and a half.

One of the first full-length screenplays Peckinpah ever wrote was an adaptation of *The Authentic Death of Hendry Jones,* a novel by Charles Neider, published in 1956 and based on the lives of Pat Garrett and Billy the Kid. Neider spent a great deal of time in New Mexico researching the history and trying to get a feel for that part of the country, then he moved to Northern California and decided to set the story there and change the names of the protagonists to Dad Longworth (Garrett) and Hendry Jones (Billy). The title is an ironic allusion to *The Authentic Life of Billy the Kid,* Garrett's book, which Neider used as a source for several incidents and even some dialogue. In 1957 Peckinpah wrote his adaptation, which eventually became the basis for the 1960 film *One-Eyed Jacks*. By then, however, he had been long gone from the project—he never even made it to the beginning of shooting—and his screenplay had been by turns scrapped or revised until it was unrecognizable. The project appears to have been nothing but a headache for all concerned. Among other things, it went through as many as six directors (one of whom was Stanley Kubrick) before the star, Marlon Brando, took over and finished the job himself—in more senses than one, Peckinpah always felt. But he so admired the novel that he considered himself "lucky enough at least" to have written a screenplay of it.[2]

We may imagine, then, the enthusiasm with which he jumped at the chance to direct *Pat Garrett and Billy the Kid* when it was offered to him in 1972 by the producer Gordon Carroll. What sweetened Carroll's offer even more was that the author of the screenplay was Rudolph Wurlitzer, a young novelist who had written *Two-Lane Blacktop*, a film Peckinpah admired. Though Wurlitzer was familiar with Neider's novel, he based his screenplay almost entirely on his own research in New Mexico. The similarities that now exist between the novel and the final shooting script owe chiefly to their derivation from common source materials (in particular Garrett's account) and by portions of Peckinpah's early adaptation that he interpolated into Wurlitzer's screenplay during shooting. It appeared, then, as if the collaboration of the young writer and the older director would be an especially productive one, and Carroll felt he had made the right choice.

The project began under what appeared to be the brightest possible circumstances, and at the outset there was every reason to share Carroll's high hopes that "we were going to make a fabulous picture." But then at the outset no one had reckoned with MGM's new investments in Las Vegas, which led the studio's president, James Aubrey, to put construction of the new MGM Grand Hotel ahead of filmmaking on the company's list of priorities and which in turn eventually resulted in the film's being shorn of sixteen minutes of material. Aubrey had the dubious distinction of being perhaps the most thoroughly hated studio chief of his day. Nicknamed "the smiling cobra," he would be the deadliest companion of Peckinpah's career, relishing the thought of becoming the one man in a suit to bring the most unruly director in the world under control. Perhaps the best way to telescope the course of events from Carroll's initial optimism to the end of production is by quoting Peckinpah on the occasion of the film's release: "It was my worst experience since *Major Dundee*."[3] He did not choose the comparison lightly, as *Pat Garrett* received worse treatment from a studio than any film of his since *Major Dundee* and was equally fraught with conflicting aims and cross-purposes.[4] And thereby hangs the rather long tale that follows . . .

II

"I would not say that the picture was anything but a battleground," recalls Gordon Carroll, "from two to three weeks before we started shooting until thirteen weeks after we finished." No one seems to remember exactly how the battle started or when and where, but (perhaps needless to say) Peckinpah was at the center of it and fighting several fronts at once. As good a place as any to begin is with one of the bigger bones of contention, the shooting schedule. According to Carroll, there was never a schedule upon which everyone was in agreement, even once production commenced. The studio insisted the film could be shot in thirty-six days, a ludicrous estimate. Peckinpah spent what he described as three hopeless months trying to persuade the corporate heads that at least fifty-eight days were necessary, and even this was a risky figure that allowed for almost nothing in the way of even the most routine of delays (inclement weather, for example, or equipment failures) that beset all location production. Peckinpah was especially concerned with having adequate rehearsal time: one of his stars, Kris Kristofferson as Billy, had little acting experience, and one of his costars, Bob Dylan, had none; and equally inexperienced local people were to be used as bit players and extras. The studio grudgingly capitulated to the extent of scheduling fifty days, all the while insisting that the original thirty-six were more than adequate. A week into production Peckinpah told a reporter, "It's definitely under-scheduled. It'll be almost impossible. . . . Altogether, there's more pressure than I expected. Do I anticipate any severe crisis with the company? Always there's a severe crisis with the company."[5]

The first was not long in coming. Since the film was being shot on location, the footage of each day's shooting had to be sent back to MGM's laboratories in Los Angeles for developing and then returned to Durango, where Peckinpah and his editors could watch it. This is standard procedure for location films, but it has the disadvantage of involving about a week's delay or longer between the shooting of film and its first viewing by the director and his crew. Shortly after receiving the first batch of footage, the lab telephoned Peckinpah with the

news that although the film looked wonderful it was also out of focus. This immediately threw the entire set into what one of the editors called a "mass panic" that didn't abate for days. The special
difficulty in such a situation is not only that footage already shot may
be unusable but also that footage presently being shot or about to
be shot may be equally unusable. When checks and rechecks of the
cameras revealed nothing, Peckinpah had no choice but to continue shooting and hope for the best. (Reports from lab were most of
the time useless, as the footage was screened at high speed, which
made it virtually impossible to spot problems with focus or anything
else.)

    The first batch of dailies to arrive back in Durango relieved every-
one; they looked sensational and there were no focus problems.
Unfortunately, the next shipment contained soft footage, and a new
investigation revealed that one camera had a bent mounting flange,
a defect that necessitated the reshooting of a few scenes and of parts
of several others. All of this could have been avoided if MGM had
listened to Peckinpah from the beginning. He had wanted to shoot
the film in New Mexico, as much as possible in or near the historical
sites Garrett and the Kid roamed, but MGM preferred Mexico as a
way of saving money. Peckinpah agreed but then asked that a Panavision repairman be on the set throughout the production just in case
the cameras developed problems. The director had worked in Durango before, where the climate is exceptionally dusty and windy, and
he knew how time-consuming equipment repairs in Mexico could be.
Once more, the studio, operating on its penny-wise, pound-foolish
thinking, refused. Peckinpah stated flatly that it was as a direct consequence of those decisions that the production company accumulated almost two weeks of downtime, which was what really drove the
picture way over budget.

    Aubrey, meanwhile, forbade any and all reshooting, ordering Peck-
inpah to have his editors quickly assemble the footage and then pick
up only what was absolutely necessary to get something that would
enable them to cut a coherent scene. From the standpoint of budget Aubrey's edict was puzzling, as insurance covered the costs of the
reshoots; and in any case it was impossible to obey as too many master shots were out of focus. Peckinpah managed to reshoot everything
he needed but only on the sly and sometimes by having his second-
unit and assistant directors do the actual filming while he worked on
new scenes.

    In addition to defective equipment, there was incessant illness. A
virulent influenza epidemic swept through Mexico during the shoot-

ing, which lasted from mid-November 1972 through the end of January 1973. "Everybody got very sick," recalls James Coburn, who plays Garrett. "Sam and I got so sick that we shot a scene that neither one of us remembered shooting."[6] According to the producer, almost everyone on location fell seriously ill at least once, Peckinpah evidently throughout. "Sam was puking every day," Kristofferson said.[7] By the end of the first week in December the director was so weak he was bedridden with a temperature of 104.[8]

Peckinpah's illnesses were exacerbated by his drinking, which was worse by an order of magnitude on *Pat Garrett and Billy the Kid* than ever before. "What it did for him, I guess, was close out all of the shit going on around him, all the problems and chaos," James Coburn said, "so he could just focus on the scene."[9] Which might have worked for part of the day, but only part. "He was a genius for about four hours," Coburn added, "then it was all down hill." This was doubtless an exaggeration—a film like *Pat Garrett and Billy the Kid* does not get directed on only four good hours a day, even by a genius. Peckinpah's increased drinking owed to many things, not least the necessary fights with MGM. But there were also the *un*necessary ones. Because of his volatile history with moneymen, Peckinpah was already the victim of snide accusations to the effect that he had engineered "safety valves" into some of his projects—that is, "problems" ostensibly caused by others beyond his control on which or on whom he could then blame his failures. (John Huston and Orson Welles have been similarly accused.) This was never a fair assessment, and it had little basis in reality on his previous films. But his behavior here appeared at times so aggressively self-destructive, especially during postproduction, that more than a few of his friends and colleagues thought it, and a few even said it openly.

A particularly public instance of his sheer outrageousness was the notorious *Hollywood Reporter* announcement, which strained the sympathies of even his closest friends The studio brass had been blaming the delays on his drinking, and the word got around town. This was utter opportunism on the part of the executives, who knew that only a relatively small number of the delays and cost overruns were in fact the result of Peckinpah's drinking, while a lot of money was saved by his ability to shoot quickly and well when necessary.[10] And a whole lot more was saved when he had the courage to defy Aubrey and reshoot the out-of-focus scenes. Without this footage there would have been no film to release because a complete film would have been impossible to cut together. If that had been the case, the amount of money required to reconvene cast and crew back in Mexico to get the necessary footage would have been vast, to say the least. Yet rather than point this out or just ignore the charges and get on with things, Peckinpah instead secured a gurney, climbed aboard it, surrounding himself with some cast and crew, and rigged a bottle of Johnny Walker to look as if it were being administered to him intravenously. This "scene" was then photographed, printed on official MGM Memorandum stationery with a directive to "the boys at the Thalberg Building," and sent to the *Hollywood Reporter,* where it was run full page. "Dear Sirs," the caption read, "With reference to the rumors that seem to be spreading around Hollywood that on numerous occasions Sam Peckinpah has been carried off the set, taken with drink, this is to inform you that those rumors are totally unfounded. However, there have been mornings . . ." It also featured the signatures of Coburn, Kristofferson, and Dylan, among others.

The pressures of the film itself also contributed to Peckinpah's drinking. Once the deal was made, the news blazed through the film community: a new Western by Sam Peckinpah, about Pat Garrett and Billy the Kid. Among serious filmgoers and critics, few films were more eagerly anticipated the following year, and there was even talk of another *Wild Bunch.* Peckinpah began to fear the project, to fear, that is, his own ability to meet expectations. Carroll says that during preproduction the director begged to be let go. When he wasn't, the accumulating pressures became almost unbearable. He was overwhelmed, not least by his concerns about the screenplay. He had first read it, quickly, while he was busy finishing *The Getaway,* loved it, and agreed immediately to do it. A year later, the contracts signed, he read it again and was stunned. He was completely unmoved, realizing that Wurlitzer's script was booby-trapped: it read wonderfully, but when it was broken down with a mind to filming, it was resolutely, almost defiantly, undramatic. "What the hell am I going to do with this thing?" he asked his close friend, Jim Silke. "Maybe this is the way it really happened in Lincoln County in 1881, maybe this is really the way these men were, but who gives a damn?"[11] Peckinpah eventually addressed most of the problems, including this fundamental one, but not before fighting with almost everyone from the writer to the producer to the studio chief about it.

As it became clear that the film would exceed both schedule and budget, Aubrey took a closer look at the screenplay to see what might be expendable. He lighted upon the raft episode as an easy candidate. While this scene, one of the most hauntingly beautiful in all Peckinpah's work, is not strictly necessary to the plot, it is important to both story and theme. Aubrey, however, could see in it only a di-

gression, and he absolutely forbade Peckinpah to film it. As a consequence, it became, according Roger Spottiswoode, the chief editor,
"*the* big test of wills," not only between the studio head and the director but also between the studio head and the entire cast and crew,
who were prepared to quit en masse if it were eliminated. Although
Aubrey remained intractable, Peckinpah, in what must have been a
virtuoso display of sheer filmmaking, managed to get the thing shot
in a single afternoon as the cast and crew were in transit from one
location to another. (This was actually the second time he shot it; the
first was in the soft-focus footage.) At the time, of course, few of them
believed MGM would allow it into the completed film, but at least they
had it on film.

Unfortunately, the closed ranks the production company displayed
in disputes with the studio provide a deceptive picture of its internal
unity. The two biggest aesthetic issues concerned the script and the
music score, and involved Peckinpah in numerous disputes with
Carroll, Wurlitzer, and Bob Dylan. To take these in order, as a filmmaking project *Pat Garrett and Billy the Kid* began with Carroll's desire to produce a Western that would have "some contemporary relevance, but without its being forced or strained." Specifically, he was
fascinated by some parallels between rock stars and outlaw heroes,
"the idea that someone could have his life and have it all between the
ages of nineteen and twenty-five" and "the question of what it must
be like to live all your life at one incandescent point, then it's over."
As it happened, although Carroll had not yet thought about using
the story of Garrett and the Kid, he had unwittingly lighted upon the
same theme that informs Neider's novel, where the Billy character
is already ever so slightly past his prime and beginning to feel the
burden of his reputation. By the time Carroll decided upon the Billy the Kid legend, he had been introduced to Wurlitzer, who quite
independently had already been researching the raw materials pur-
suant to writing a screenplay about this very legend.

Wurlitzer chose to confine his original screenplay to the last three
months of Billy's life because they offered him the freest area for
invention and imagination: no one knows what Billy did then, only
that he left the territory and then returned. The script opened with
Billy awaiting execution in the Lincoln County jail, from which he
manages to escape, in the process killing two of Garrett's deputies,
J. W. Bell and Bob Ollinger.[12] The manhunt then begins and is struc-
tured as a series of scenes alternating between Garrett and Billy, who
never meet until their final confrontation. To this screenplay Peckinpah added much new material at the beginning and deleted some

scenes (including a digressive frontier roof-raising party) and made numerous smaller changes, deletions, and additions. The most significant of these is the death of the old sheriff, Cullen Baker, which Peckinpah made into an extended elegiac reverie that completely transformed what is in the original script.

The first of Peckinpah's major additions was the frame story, which came from a suggestion by Carroll: Peckinpah opened the film with the assassination of Garrett in 1908 by some of his former associates (notably Poe, his deputy, whom Peckinpah makes a lackey of the vested interests who are putting up the reward money for the Kid).[13] At the end of the film there is a brief reprise to the assassination, thus transforming the whole manhunt into one long flashback. Peckinpah then added a new opening to the flashback, a scene in which Garrett arrives in Old Fort Sumner to ask Billy to clear out. Following this, Peckinpah added the shoot-out at Stinking Springs, showing Garrett capturing the Kid. Finally, he added Garrett to what was Wurlitzer's original opening, the card game in the Lincoln County jail as Billy awaits execution.

The changes were not made all at once but were added individually throughout the shooting schedule, sometimes by Peckinpah himself, sometimes by Wurlitzer, and sometimes by Wurlitzer acting on Peckinpah's instructions. It is difficult to figure out with much greater precision how much actual writing Peckinpah himself did, because reports vary, as do memories. Peckinpah recalled that the prologue and epilogue (i.e., the frame) are entirely his, that about half the first scene is his, and that the new jailhouse scene is probably more Wurlitzer's than his. Early in the production Wurlitzer said he was "thrilled" to have Peckinpah directing the script, and seemed not at all displeased with the changes the director was making.[14] But as the demands for more and more changes mounted, Wurlitzer became less and less pleased, and once complained to a reporter, "There's no script left." ("Then it's not a Wurlitzer?" the reporter asked. "It's a Peckinpah," Wurlitzer replied, "Sam makes the changes mostly.")[15] Wurlitzer finally vented his spleen once and for all in the preface to a published version of the screenplay, accusing Peckinpah of having become

> suddenly thrilled by his own collaborative gifts. In the writer's version, Billy and Garrett never met until the final scene, when Garrett killed him. The director wanted their relationship in front, so that everyone would know they were old buddies. Rewriting was imposed with the added inspirational help of some of the director's old TV scripts. The beginning was changed completely. Ex-

traordinary lines about male camaraderie made a soggy entrance into the body of the script. The writer suspected that the script (not to mention himself) had been reduced to its most simplistic components.[16]

While Wurlitzer's attitude here is not difficult to understand—what writer enjoys having his work changed?—he was not an experienced writer of screenplays at the time he wrote this one, and it shows. Much of the dialogue, for example, is good, but much of it is also stilted and inauthentic. As for those lines about masculine camaraderie that supposedly made a "late" entrance into the script, perhaps Wurlitzer became so confused that he forgot who wrote what and when. Some of the stickier such lines—the exchange, for example, between Billy and the dying Alamosa Bill—come straight from his original. On the other hand, the new opening, in which Garrett arrives in Old Fort Sumner to meet with the Kid, deals most explicitly with their camaraderie; yet far from being soggy, it is one of the best and best-written scenes in the film, and is attributed by Wurlitzer totally to Peckinpah. Perhaps the best way to evaluate the validity of Wurlitzer's criticisms is to consider them in light of this scene and the benefits that accrue from it to the film as a whole.

Wurlitzer to the contrary, the inspiration for the scene (and for some of the other additions) came not from Peckinpah's old television scripts but from his early adaptation of *The Authentic Death of Hendry Jones,* where there is a brief meeting that has Dad Longworth warn Hendry to leave the county. But what in Neider's book is only a short exchange of dialogue was expanded and elaborated by Peckinpah into an opening scene that would truly generate the drama to follow. Garrett arrives in Old Fort Sumner to find Billy and his gang sitting around a fountain shooting the heads off chickens buried in the sand. The sheriff-elect dismounts, takes aim, and fires at one of the chickens himself, surprising Billy, who welcomes him, saying, "That's pretty fair shooting for an old married man." Garrett offers to buy him a drink—the last drink they will share as friends, a motif that is woven into the rest of the film—and they trade small talk:

> *Garrett:* Jesus, don't you get *stale* around here, Bill? Maybe a year or so down in Mexico'll do you some good.
> *Billy:* I didn't figure you'd bother to make a ride out here.
> *Garrett:* You know me better than that.
> *Billy:* You heard about Eben? He drowned . . . in the Rio Grande, trying to get back to that old Mex you're talking about. Took two of the posse with him.

> *Garrett:* I'm sorry to hear that. I always liked old Eben. At least he
> knew when it was the right time to leave.
> *Billy:* We did have some times, didn't we? It's going to be pretty hard
> to turn your back on all that, ain't it?

Then they get down to business:

> *Garrett:* You want it straight?
> *Billy:* If that's what you're here for.
> *Garrett:* The electorate wants you gone, out of the country.
> *Billy:* Well, are they telling me or are they asking me?
> *Garrett:* I'm asking you, but in five days I'm making you, when I take
> over as sheriff of Lincoln County.
> *Billy:* Old Pat . . . Sheriff Pat Garrett. Sold out to the Santa Fe Ring.
> How does it feel?
> *Garrett:* It feels . . . like times have changed.
> *Billy:* Times maybe, but not me.

Quoting the dialogue is enough to suggest some of the sense of
the scene, but little of its ambience, its dramatic charge, its emotional
texture and tensions, or the feeling it conveys of an inseparable gulf
opening up between these two men, lately friends, soon to become
enemies. We can see it in the way the Kid subtly needles Garrett about
his having gotten married; in the way both of them circle around the
real reason for Garrett's visit; in the way they test and prod one another, knowing they are evenly matched, each reluctant to draw first
blood. Nor does the dialogue alone indicate how the scene is
played—the pause, filled with a deep breath Garrett takes when he
tells Billy that times have changed, suggesting the weariness with
which he is about to assume a burden he neither desires nor yet can
avoid. And in the way the point of the scene, the farewell and the
challenge,

> *Billy: Adios,* Pat.
> *Garrett: Adios,* Bill.
> *Billy:* Don't press your luck.
> *Garrett:* I'm not worried about my luck.

is forestalled until the last possible moment, the scene not only gen-
erates but embodies in microcosm both the form and the meaning
of the drama to follow: a chase in which Garrett, trying to put off the
inevitable, uses every diversion open to him to give the Kid every
opportunity to escape.

Wurlitzer believes that his plan of not having them meet until the
last scene is more "daring" and "existential."[17] But the making of a

film that has a story to tell is much more than the working out of concept, however daring, or the development of a theme, however relevant. It is the telling of a story in dramatic terms; and if something doesn't work dramatically, then it doesn't work at all. Peckinpah's disappointment the second time he read the script stemmed from his realization that what was lacking was a true germinal scene, a scene in which there is a sense of promise and implicit fulfillment, of direction and implicit destination, of forces being set into motion that must inevitably and unavoidably collide in the way they finally do. The new scene accomplishes all of this and also infuses the story with something else lacking in Wurlitzer's script: a central or grounding tonality against which contrasting tonalities can be played. In the completed film, the pursuit, which has Garrett and Billy disparate, is the tonal foil to the first scene, which has them together. The greatest improvement wrought by the new opening is to make the relationship between Garrett and Billy a flesh-and-blood reality, so that when the Kid lies dead on the porch of Pete Maxwell's house and Garrett stands over him, we feel with Garrett the stab of loss and dissolution.

In all fairness, though, Wurlitzer's patience was sorely tried by the director, who demanded rewrites and revisions on what became by the end of shooting almost a daily basis. (The rewrites were not always coherent ones at that—once while drunk Peckinpah angrily demanded a new scene involving a character who had been already been killed off *before* the scene's chronological place in the story.) Yet Peckinpah always spoke highly of the screenplay, calling it "an epic confrontation with a great lyric quality," both of which he sought, mostly successfully, to realize on the screen.[18] And inasmuch as more than half (closer to two-thirds) of what remains is there as Wurlitzer wrote it, the completed film must be called a genuine collaboration. Among other things, the sense that this is a chase involving reluctant antagonists—in which, to use Carroll's excellent description, "a man who doesn't want to run is being pursued by a man who doesn't want to catch him"—is right there in the original screenplay, as are many of the elegiac tones and autumnal colors usually associated with Peckinpah. Such vital scenes as the argument between Garrett and his wife, the meeting with Chisum, and the killing of Holly are directed essentially as Wurlitzer conceived them, with most of his dialogue left intact. Moreover, sometimes Peckinpah's changes were not for the better, and in a few instances were downright preposterous, as in the addition of three more whores to a scene that already had Garrett bedding with two. (Almost everyone on the production tried to dissuade the director from that; but, uncharacteristically for him, at least as regards his relationships with casts and crews, he refused to listen, and it soon became what Spottiswoode described as "a non-discussible point.")

Nor was Peckinpah always so wise in the deletion of dialogue—for example, this passage, spoken by one of the big-shot investors in the scene at Governor Wallace's mansion in Santa Fe: "You people are obsolete, Sheriff. Oh, the Chisums will hang on for a while, and a few of them might survive, but you and the Kid have only a few plays left." According to Carroll, this was cut because Peckinpah absolutely forbade the use of the word "obsolete" here or anywhere else in the film. When asked about this, Peckinpah replied that for the life of him he could not remember having forbidden the word, "unless it was simply because of the way somebody played it in one particular take or something." Whatever the reason, by allowing its removal Peckinpah lost an important point of irony: although Chisum and Billy are now antagonists, and Chisum and Garrett uneasy allies, all three of them— the cocky gunslinger, the aging sheriff, and the self-made cattle baron—will soon be swept aside by the larger economic and social forces of history. Even with this dialogue deleted, it is difficult to understand how so many reviewers could have assumed that Chisum is the controlling political and financial power, for the dialogue that Peckinpah substituted, which remains in the film, has the investor say: "I can assure you, Mr. Garrett, that Chisum and the others have been advised to recognize their position, and in this particular game there are only a few plays left." While the idea of Chisum's obsolescence is lost, what nevertheless remains with unmistakable clarity is his position in the power struggle, which is that he too is caught in the same squeeze, faces the same choices, as Garrett and the Kid do. The real source of power remains the collusion of monied and political interests represented by Santa Fe.

In the disputes over the screenplay Peckinpah was able to exert a large degree of control, as he was not over the music score, which he did not like and which remained a touchy subject with him the rest of his life. This is understandable given the care with which he customarily applies music to his films, particularly when he works with Jerry Fielding, who shares the same ideas about what how a score should work. Unfortunately, these could not be more at variance with those of Bob Dylan, who at the time simply didn't know how to write music that exists to serve some other end than itself. (*Pat Garrett* was Dylan's first film score, and it really shows in a cue like the one for the prologue/first-scene montage, where his soporifically repetitive guitar-strumming, which ambles monotonously along for over six minutes, makes an already long sequence feel much longer than it is.) Neither the director nor the singer enjoyed the most harmonious relationship working with one another. Years later Peckinpah said that he objected less to the music Dylan wrote for the film than to the use to which it was put in the film. As if the conflicting aesthetic principles weren't enough, Peckinpah faced a conflict of loyalty that placed an even greater burden on the situation. He had originally hired Fielding, the idea being that Fielding would use a couple of Dylan's songs as unifying threads in a score that would otherwise be his own. But Fielding found he could not work with Dylan and eventually he left the project, complaining, as Peckinpah later would, that Dylan's songs were being used too prevalently and at all sorts of inappropriate moments.

Dylan was thus left to finish the scoring alone, which he did with Carroll's blessing and encouragement. It was probably this that provoked Peckinpah's charge that the music score came out as it did because "Gordon Carroll obviously wants to sell a lot of Bobby Dylan albums."[19] Peckinpah was rarely unfair, even to those he disliked. But he was here. Carroll really believed Dylan's music to be an asset. One can disagree, but the producer didn't sell anybody out for the sake of an album (which Dylan dedicated to Peckinpah). The whole matter was, in any case, more complicated than Peckinpah later let on. Garth Craven, the coeditor, believes that the director simply had so many things to contend with that he neglected to take a firm enough stand on the issue of the music until it was too late to do much more than minimize the damage. This is easy to believe, for by that time far more worrisome was the damage the studio was doing to the film.

Despite all the setbacks, delays, illnesses, and equipment failures, Peckinpah brought the picture in by late January 1973, twenty days behind schedule and $1.5 million over the original $3 million budget, with, says Spottiswoode, "surprisingly little wasted footage." As editing had been going on during shooting, it wasn't too difficult to get a first cut together in time for a mid-February screening in Mexico City for the producer and MGM. This cut ran about two hours and forty minutes, much too long. Yet the screening proceeded amicably, and Peckinpah, Spottiswoode, and Craven left eager to begin preparing the final cut, the release date a comfortable five to six months away. Within a few days, however, MGM asked that the release date be moved up to the last week in May. Management had driven the studio so far into debt over construction of the MGM Grand in Las Vegas that its cash reserves were almost depleted, and Aubrey wanted to show some cash on the books by the July stockholders' meeting. He planned to accomplish that by getting as many pictures then in production out to the theaters as fast as possible, which in the case of *Pat Garrett and Billy the Kid* left only a little over two and a half months to complete editing, scoring, and dubbing. What Aubrey was asking for constituted a violation of contract and required the approval of the producer. After some thought, Carroll decided to grant it, first, because he felt the extra time would not result in a significantly better film given the footage there was to work with; second, because he believed that this one major concession would buy complete freedom from subsequent studio interference. (From Peckinpah he won a consent, though a grudging one, for, as the director remembered, no one had much choice in the matter anyway, as the studio was going to do what the studio was going to do, contracts be damned.)

Carroll's was a calculated risk in a difficult situation; and in the end the producer, who has since thought twice about his decision, was proved half right, half wrong. Once the new release date was final, Spottiswoode and Craven asked that Robert Wolfe, with whom they had worked on previous Peckinpah films, be hired to help with the editing. The editors worked in shifts, around the clock, seven days a week, and managed to prepare a cut in time for the first of the previews. This version came out to 124 minutes in length. In overall form and structure, it was, those who saw it seem to agree, the best film that could be made from the footage that had been shot, though additional trimming, tightening, and fine tuning remained to be done. In this sense, then, Carroll was not mistaken. Where he went wrong was in underestimating Aubrey's ill will: what no one realized until fairly late was that there were never any plans to release a version prepared by Peckinpah. Aubrey by then so hated Peckinpah that he was ordering scenes cut for no other reason than that he knew the director especially wanted them in the picture.[20]* And the sales

*Aubrey seems to have made life miserable for practically every director who worked at the studio during his regime, among them Blake Edwards, whose *Carey Treatment* was thoroughly trashed. James Coburn, who also starred in that film, said that Aubrey's "particular evil nature, I mean the thing that he got his kicks off of, is destroying films that other people made. You can't imagine, you really can't imagine the kind of ability that this cocksucker has! For a man to deliberately destroy a film, for the justification of saying, 'The people are stupid! The people are dumb! They don't want to see that, they won't understand what that is! Just give them the straight down-the-line thing like that! We'll get them in the theaters on the names of the thing!' And what happens is that we all take the blame for it. He doesn't care" (quoted in Leydon, p. 8).

department knew that the only way to guarantee a quick cash turn-over was to provide exhibitors with a film that could be booked into as many theaters and for as many showings per day as possible, preferably at the easy-to-remember two-hour interval. Allowing for short subjects, coming attractions, selling popcorn, and moving audiences in and out of the theaters, this translates into a film of ninety to a hundred minutes' length.

Aubrey's real plans became evident when the director's cut was shown at the two previews stipulated for him by contract, which were unusual in that they were held at the studio, not in theaters for the equivalent to a paying audience. (Only two critics—Pauline Kael and Jay Cocks—ever saw an early cut of the film, and that because Peckinpah managed to sneak them into a projection room where a rough, unscored version was being shown.) Instead, Peckinpah charged, the previews were held "by invitation only" at MGM, where the studio executives had "more armed guards . . . than Watergate." "They allowed me to bring twenty-two people, members of my family only," he said. "They wouldn't allow me to bring my crew or Jason Robards or Henry Fonda."[21] That these previews were granted merely to fulfill the letter of the contract while sidestepping its spirit was made apparent when Peckinpah discovered that behind his back Aubrey, using as cover the confusion generated by the rapidly approaching deadline, had ordered a dupe made of the work print and hired another editor to prepare a release cut. This cut of the film ran only ninety-six minutes and reduced everything except the violence, the action, and the barest minimum of exposition sufficient to get from one bloody outburst to the next. For a day or so Peckinpah actually considered approving the release of this version to dramatize for public and critics alike in no uncertain terms just how pernicious the practices of the Aubrey regime really were. He soon changed his mind, but only to insist upon the release of his unmodified preview version. Aubrey refused.

When it became clear that Peckinpah and beyond him the film would be the losers in this standoff, Spottiswoode and Wolfe, on the assumption that three-quarters of a loaf are better than half, sat down to the bargaining table with Aubrey while Carroll and Daniel Melnick, who had left independent producing to become MGM's production chief, tried to mediate.* Aubrey wanted just another horse opera,

---

*Melnick's involvement caused a rift with Peckinpah that wasn't healed for a few years. Melnick despised Aubrey; but he was also working for the studio and felt put in an impossible position by the director, who didn't attend the first preview and whose cutting notes consisted in removing about ten seconds from one shot.

while the editors tried to retain as much of what they knew Peckinpah wanted and to polish the rest of it. For example, the raft episode, to which Aubrey had so vehemently objected during production, was allowed to remain, but only in exchange for the frame story, which was removed. And so it went, day in, day out, this traded for that, until the film was eventually whittled down to the 106-minute version that went into release.

Shortly thereafter Peckinpah brought suit against MGM on four counts—breach of contract, unfair competition, invasion of privacy, and false attribution—in an amount that has variously been reported as $1.5 to $2.5-million. Among other things, the suit demanded either that the cuts be restored or that the director's name be removed from above the title both in advertisements and on the film proper, as he no longer considered the released version his own. For the studio it was an easy victory of attrition simply to meet neither condition; after several years the suit just trailed away into some sunset or other. As for Aubrey, his four-year reign at MGM was a disaster on every conceivable level. The hotel was never finished under his management, though he raped, pillaged, and broke the studio trying, selling off every holding and asset he possibly could (including Ben Hur's chariot). Between the pictures he canceled (Fred Zinneman's adaptation of *Man's Fate,* for one) and the pictures he destroyed trying to rush them to market, the company's box office declined so steeply he was let go about six months after *Pat Garrett and Billy the Kid* came and went in theaters.

III

Some of the more sympathetic critics have suggested that whatever material the cuts involved, *Pat Garrett and Billy the Kid* seems to have suffered remarkably little from them.[22] There is a small validity to this claim: Spottiswoode and Wolfe did do their best to guide the picture through the bargaining sessions with its dramatic sense and unity preserved. And since what was cut are those scenes in which character motivation, social pressure, and personal and professional obligation are seen to generate action, incident, and decision, the released version has, to be sure, a "ritualistic," "mythic," rather "existential" "purity" that is not without a certain hypnotic power, beauty, and fascination. All the same, that purity remains a pretty sporadic, because largely serendipitous, affair, and it is of no help whatever toward filling in the narrative lacuna.

To do that it will be necessary to review what was cut and how it affects the tone, theme, and structure of the whole film. The major cuts consist of the frame story, showing the assassination of Garrett many years after the events of the main story; a meeting between Garrett and his wife, Ida; a visit by Garrett and Poe to Chisum's ranch; a couple of scenes and pieces of scenes dramatizing Billy's courtship of Maria, the girl with whom he makes love before he dies (these scenes establish that Maria is not a prostitute); an interlude between Garrett and several prostitutes (which was replaced by the single shot in the theatrical version); and a long, drawn-out scene in a place called Tuckerman's Hotel (it looks more like a stable or a flop house) where Poe learns of the Kid's whereabouts.

These last two scenes are easily the weakest and most expendable. The frolicking with the whores is ridiculously overdone, but Peckinpah was perhaps trying to point up Garrett's isolation vis-à-vis the gregariousness of Billy and his gang, most of whose women are camp followers. As for Tuckerman's Hotel, it is wholly expendable. As the only scene with neither of the title characters present, its effect is primarily to break the spine of the structure, or would be if the scene had any real effect at all. But it is dismally played and written, its only plot function to show how Poe and Garrett find out that the Kid is in Fort Sumner, which is covered in the scene where Garrett gets the same information by slapping around one of the whores (not in the preview, but of necessity in the theatrical version once the hotel scene was removed).

There is also one scene that is unusual inasmuch as the visual component remains in the film but the dialogue is different from what was both written and shot. On his way to Mexico, Billy comes upon his friend Paco, an old Mexican shepherd who has been fatally beaten by some of Chisum's men. As originally written by Wurlitzer and directed by Peckinpah, Paco's death-bed speech consists of his last delirious thoughts as his mind wanders off in a reverie about a house he plans to build in Mexico from adobe bricks he will make with his own hands and which will have a veranda with three chairs, the middle one reserved for himself, and anyone who doesn't do right, he will blow his head off. As rewritten and looped into the film during postproduction, the speech now takes the form of a cautionary little sermon that Paco delivers to Billy, advising him to continue south. Paco even indulges in a little psychology: "You will say you go back because of what they did to me. But it is really because you are afraid to change." The reason for the new speech—which was patched into the theatrical release, according to Spottiswoode, "over Sam's stiffening body"—was that several persons on the project believed that the script failed to account for Billy's decision to return from Mexico. The new material, written by Wurlitzer on instructions from Carroll, was intended to supply the missing motivation. In fact both script and film—as Peckinpah knew, hence his opposition to the change—provide more than sufficient motivation for Billy's return. Carroll, who accepts full responsibility for the decision (and takes full blame for its result), says that at the time the problem really did seem to loom larger than he now feels it does in retrospect, and the rewrite-*cum*-loop seemed the most viable solution.*

It is the other cuts, however, that cause the most problems, and the first area of damage is to the structure of the film. Many of the scenes are interlocked with Peckinpah's usual intricacy so that, as with *The Wild Bunch,* removing something in one place usually means something else falling out or failing to cohere fifteen pages or minutes later. For example, the scene between Garrett and Chisum reveals that Garrett has borrowed money from Chisum to purchase some land; it is a dispute over this land that in the frame story gets Garrett killed. The scene also has Chisum subtly putting the pressure on Garrett to apprehend the Kid faster, which at once lends urgency to Garrett's earlier remark to his wife, "There's too much riding on it for me not to," and helps to motivate Garrett's killing of Holly. Or, take the scene in which Garrett goes to the barber shop. Dirty, unshaven, having just returned from a few days on the trail collecting taxes, he orders a bath prepared and tells the barber, "Do me up good this time." Then, hair trimmed, cleanly shaved, freshly bathed, he leaves the shop and goes directly home to see Ida. Yet now that the scene with her is missing, and with it all mention of going to see her, the contradistinction implied by the words, "this time," makes no sense.

*Carroll may be too kind in taking all the blame upon himself. According to Spottiswoode, Peckinpah allowed Emilio Fernandez, who plays Paco, to read the original speech so melodramatically as to be ludicrous. Craven, however, feels that the reading was not quite that bad and that it was in any case preferable to the substitution. In the end no solution was satisfactory. The weather was abysmally hot the day of filming; after several takes Fernandez was sweating so profusely that the cosmetic blood had smeared all over his body. The staging is also uninspired, as is the filmmaking, too much of it done with long-range lenses. And in one respect it is difficult to imagine what Peckinpah could possibly have been thinking: Billy has just prevented Paco's daughter or wife (the film is not clear which she is) from being raped. Yet after Paco dies, Billy just mounts up and rides off, leaving the girl to do what—bury him herself or load his (very large) body onto the wagon and leave, again by herself? The film is arguably better off without the scene, except that Billy would not be shown turning back at all. (As it happened, owing to some nudity the scene was removed from the television version, with surprisingly little harm.)

Similarly, consider how the gossip Ida relates—"They're all complaining about you," "probably repeating those stories about being a friend of his"—prepares us for the snide insinuation by the Santa Fe businessmen to the effect that Garrett's friendship with the Kid is keeping him from performing his duties as sheriff as diligently as he might. The argument between Garrett and his wife also advances a motif already introduced when Garrett had told the Kid, "The electorate wants you gone." But, as Ida, who is Mexican, tells her husband, "My people don't talk to me. They say you're getting to be too much of a gringo since you been sheriff, that you make deals with Chisum." Inasmuch as Garrett was originally elected sheriff because he garnered a large portion of the Mexican vote, another point of irony is lost. And to give the scene at Tuckerman's Hotel its small due, it does show that many more people among the electorate than the Mexicans fail to support Garrett's position, as Poe has to knock an old man senseless in order to "persuade" the man's friends to reveal some information about the Kid. This bit of business is paralleled in an adjacent scene that has Garrett doing nearly the same thing to a prostitute for the same reason. Both scenes show how pervasive loyalty toward the Kid is among the populace and, indirectly, how antipathy for him seems to be confined mostly to the vested interests and the well-to-do.

There are also many small cuts, trims, and clips too numerous to detail. No single one of these is, of itself, vital to the exposition (though some of them smooth a few abrupt transitions); but collectively they serve to alter the overall mood of the film, making it, according to Spottiswoode, "less elegiac and more violent." In fact, Spottiswoode recalls,

> Sam's version is much less violent than the studio's, despite, or maybe because of, the fact that his is longer. What was cut were the things that made the action work and that gave sense to the violence. By taking out eight to ten minutes of dialogue in five or six scenes, the studio made that action come much quicker and made the violence seem senseless. Although the film was quite episodic, with each scene playing at greater length, it got its power from that length and from the episodic structure, which contained the violence and gave it validity.

What makes MGM's interference in this regard especially pernicious is that it militates against—but does not destroy—one of the subtlest yet most impressive of Peckinpah's and Wurlitzer's achievements: the depiction of the casualness of frontier violence and of its ready acceptance by its perpetrators, victims, and spectators alike as a fact of their lives. It is difficult to indicate any particular scene, either in the theatrical release or the preview, as a way of demonstrating this quality, because it depends for its full effect upon the gradual, almost leisurely accumulation of one act of violence after another and upon the curious nonchalance with which the violence is both rendered and performed and which differentiates it from the violence in Peckinpah's previous films. Little of the violence is sprung upon the viewer without warning; rather, it is carefully built up at a fairly slow and steady tempo, with plenty of tension but little suspense as such. One is left with the impression that some of these people at once realize and relish the inevitability of its outburst, as when Billy tells some bounty hunters a story, each pause and point in the plot a silent cue to his pals to get set; while other characters simply resign themselves to it, calmly preparing for its consequences, as when a trading-post keeper begins to dismantle a door for coffin wood as two men face each other off. Critics who have complained that the violence in this film is senseless have gotten the point and missed it too. This senselessness is part of the thematic meaning of the violence.

Equally obscured are the psychological aspects of the violence, a matter best approached by a fuller description of the frame story. Processed in sepia tones like an old newsreel, it consists of a prologue and an epilogue, both set in 1909 and enclosing the rest of the film, which in turn is set in 1881.[23] The epilogue is a brief reprise of the prologue, which opens on an old, embittered Garrett riding across his land in a buggy. Seated beside him is a friend of Poe's, and Poe himself rides alongside on horseback. Poe's sheep can be seen off in the distance grazing, while Garrett orders them to be removed.

> *Poe:* It's my land, Garrett, it became mine when I signed the lease.
> *Garrett:* I'm paying you off when we get back and I'm breaking that goddamn lease.
> *Poe:* I don't allow the law will agree to that.
> *Garrett:* What law? That Santa Fe Ring law? That goddamn law's ruining the country.
> *Poe:* Ain't you still part of that law? . . . I believe they elected you and paid you good wages for killing the Kid.

Garrett calls Poe a son of a bitch and reaches for his rifle. By this time the driver, on the pretense that something is wrong with the harness, has stopped and climbed down. At the sound of Garrett's words, another man appears from cover some distance away with rifle raised and fires. Poe and the driver draw their weapons and do the same.

Garrett falls to the ground and as he tries to get up is shot several more times. Filmed in slow motion from a ground-level setup, this is intercut with similar slow motion, ground-level flash inserts of chickens getting their heads blown off and with additional inserts of Billy and his gang and of Garrett himself firing at the chickens.

It is not difficult to see how Peckinpah uses the frame story both to introduce and to resolve several thematic strains, or to guess at how much is lost by its removal. Lost first of all is the whole larger dimension of history, of how people are duped, exploited, and finally swallowed up by forces beyond their control. Along with this goes a reduction by half of the theme of determinism. This is not just in how Garrett is shown to be trapped by the unforeseen consequences of his actions, but in how the very structure of the film, which lets us know in advance how each of the title characters will die, confers a powerful dramatic irony upon the action to follow: no matter what these men do or say, no matter what decisions they make or efforts they expend, no one and nothing can prevent them from ending up in that dark room at Pete Maxwell's house where Garrett will shoot and kill Billy, or many years later prevent Garrett from meeting an even more violent death at the hands of his partners. This in turn points up another loss. Poe, whom Garrett loathes, has ironically become a business partner. The prologue thus contains in miniature the plot of the film at large; one man being killed by another man who is, or was, a partner. Of course, the similarities between the partnerships end there, but the differences are equally important to Peckinpah: history repeats itself, but in ironic and unpredictable ways. Finally, and chiefly, lost was the point of view, which in the original belonged wholly, and rightly, to Garrett. And in a touch that recalls Ambrose Bierce's "Occurrence at Owl Creek Bridge," when the last part of the prologue returns by way of epilogue to complete the frame, the enclosed story is revealed to have been the last, fleeting memories that raced through Garrett's mind seconds before his death.

Peckinpah was principally driven to tap the psychological vein of these materials and explore the complexities, contradictions, and confusions that rest in Garrett. James Coburn, who plays Garrett, once said of Peckinpah, "He's got the violence of man against man, and man against the System, but he hasn't got man against himself yet."[24] This was spoken not long after Coburn had finished the picture; and since he is usually quite insightful on the subject of Peckinpah (who was a close friend as well as a sometime colleague), we may suppose that in the case of this particular film he missed the point simply because he had played so large a part in its making, and also because, like the rest of the cast, he had been barred from the two previews and so never saw the director's version from start to finish. In any case, his observation was doubtless based mostly on Peckinpah's earlier Western films, to which it applies with considerable accuracy. Even so, the idea of man against himself has always been latent in those films, the two halves of the embattled partnerships suggesting, on the purely abstract as opposed to the dramatic level, conflicting sides of single but divided and of course quite hypothetical personalities.

In *Pat Garrett and Billy the Kid,* however, Peckinpah makes this idea of a single personality considerably less hypothetical, for the title characters are seen to share a closeness unlike that of, say, Pike Bishop and Deke Thornton or Steve Judd and Gil Westrum, a closeness made explicit when a grizzled old saloon keeper tells Garrett, "You used to be just like a daddy to that boy." Psychologically, of course, they are even closer than that: immediately after shooting Billy, Garrett turns and fires at a reflection of himself, the bullet striking the mirror image in the heart, the same relative spot where his first bullet struck Billy. The killing thus assumes the aspect of a suicide, and there is an ironic reversal of roles. While Billy remains, even in death, curiously unmarked save for the small spot of blood where the bullet went in, Garrett survives only to be left psychically scarred for life. Staring into the mirror, shattered now by the second bullet, he finds himself face to face with a mocking, Dorian Gray–like distortion, grotesquely disfigured by a hole in the reflecting surface but nevertheless a true picture of his innermost being and the violence he has done to himself there.

Peckinpah means, then, for us to think of Garrett and Billy as being identified with one another in a deeper, more thoroughgoing way than such terms as "symbolic" or even "filial" and "fatherly" are able to suggest. Just how close may be seen by looking at the several associations Peckinpah draws between Billy and Christ. The first of these is at his capture at Stinking Springs, where he emerges from the cabin, holster and gun in full view, his arms outstretched, a smile on his face, as he moves toward Garrett. Later, shotgun in hand, he faces the Bible-beating Ollinger and asks, smiling once again, "How's Jesus look to you now, Bob?" and blasts him; and later still, he surprises one of Chisum's men, who exclaims, "Jesus Christ!" as Billy shoots him dead. This is all so uncharacteristically heavy-handed that one suspects—hopes—the intent is irony, even a bit of joke: a "redeemer" who dies for no one's sins, instead dispatching people with a seraphic smile on his face.

But at one point there is no ironic intent, at least not in any jocu-lar way, and that is in the final scene where Garrett climbs the porch of Pete Maxwell's house and passes the room in which Billy, whisper-ing, "Jesus, Jesus," and Maria are making love. He pauses at the open window, then, recognizing who they are, turns, walks over to the swing, and sits down. When they finish, he gets up, slips into the house, and moves quietly down the hallway to an opposite bedroom, where he seats himself beside the bed. In the meantime Billy has gone for something to eat. Seeing two of Garrett's deputies, he backs into the room, turns around, and, recognizing his friend, smiles. The sheriff rises up and fires. There is an explosion, a blinding flash of light, and, as the bullet slams into Billy's heart, the sensual, undulat-ing, almost exquisitely graceful recoil of his body. Then Peckinpah's staging produces one of the strangest, even spookiest, compositions anywhere in his work. Billy lies on his back, dead, outside the bed-room door, his arms outstretched as in a crucifixion, the faintest hint of a smile on his face. Garrett walks through the doorway and paus-es to regard the Kid's body for a moment before carefully stepping over it, moving toward the swing, and slumping down upon it, spent and exhausted.

Not since *Straw Dogs* has Peckinpah's slow-motion violence been so charged with an ambiguous erotic energy. The erotic undertone of this scene—the most thickly allusive, richly suggestive in the film—cannot help but make us wonder if the earlier moment in which Bil-ly confronted Garrett with outstretched arms is not open to alternate interpretations—say, a son going to hug his father or, to bring it closer to the last scene, a lover moving to embrace his partner. The latter finds some reinforcement in the way Peckinpah cuts away from Billy and Maria before they've reached a climax, which has the effect of displacing it quite literally to the moment of Billy's death, the flash of Garrett's revolver.

One way to begin to unravel this ambiguous thicket of sexual, re-ligious, and violent imagery is to note that the scene is visualized al-most wholly from Garrett's point of view. This makes it the most thor-oughly subjective scene in a film that is all subjective anyhow, and what it dramatizes is the moment in Garrett's life when he is at once his most determined and his most confused. Peckinpah does not mean to suggest that Billy is any sort of Christ figure, but rather that Garrett has sacrificed his past self, that part of himself which Billy symbolizes. In a sense Billy *is* Garrett by this point in the film; or, to put it another way, he is perceived by Garrett as being so thoroughly and oppressively a part of himself that Garrett must kill him in order to be free from him and to secure for himself a place in society and a piece of the future. But that part of himself will not die so easily, and the effect of Peckinpah's cutting together the prologue and the first scene is to dissolve the twenty-seven years actually separating the events they depict, suggesting thereby how close together they are in Garrett's mind and how alive they are to him.

Yet in killing the Kid, Garrett does not succeed in setting himself free; on the contrary, he succeeds only in wedding himself all the more inextricably to the Kid and, by implication, freezing himself in the past he so desperately wants to put behind him. The sexual imagery does not imply latent homosexuality, but is there to suggest the seductive power the past and the wild continue to exert upon Garrett. And inasmuch as Billy is a close friend and represents that power at its most potent, theirs is to Garrett a dangerous and finally a deadly relationship because it threatens the very autonomy of identity itself. The full measure of the Kid's destructiveness is seen in how, by forcing Garrett to confront him and ultimately to kill him, he effects Garrett's death as surely as he does his own.

In death Billy is resurrected by way of legend, but, in contrast to what happens in *The Wild Bunch*, Peckinpah lets all the mythmaking devolve to the background presence of Bob Dylan as Alias. The resurrection that really interests the director is the absorption of Billy into Garrett's personality where, once internalized, he poses a greater threat than he ever did while alive, as the personality of the outlaw begins to erode the personality of the lawman. This is a process that will take the rest of Garrett's life, but it starts almost immediately with a gesture that indicates the first characteristic of Billy's that Garrett assumes, the Kid's loyalty (perhaps his paramount virtue). When the cowardly Poe rushes onto the porch to cut off the Kid's trigger finger, Garrett lets out a long, agonized scream of protest, and kicks the deputy away. (For all the killing, this is the most violent single moment in the film.) Though Garrett has killed Billy, he will not allow the Kid's image to be tarnished, even as the fatal bullet seems hardly to have marred his body. The completion and consequence of the process are shown in the prologue, where the cool, composed, calculating temperament of Garrett's middle years is no longer in evidence. Instead, full of rage, impetuous, inclined to shoot first, he seems more like the old man Billy would have become, reaching for his gun because of an insult from Poe, someone he had once considered so beneath contempt that he would hardly acknowledge his presence, let alone give him the satisfaction of answering a wisecrack. The idea of role reversal is foreshadowed here: openly hostile to the law, threatening to break the law, then finally breaking it, Garrett becomes an outlaw. It is less significant that he had once been an outlaw. What matters is that this is the role the Kid died playing, that Garrett killed him for playing, and that Garrett himself—the process of internalization complete—is about to die playing.

It is fitting that Garrett's executioner should be Poe. Approximately the same age, Poe and Billy are antipodes to Garrett that represent his own conflicting selves and social alternatives: the life of the lawman versus the life of the outlaw. As Poe tells Garrett, "This country's got to make a choice. The time's over for drifters and outlaws and them that's got no backbone." Garrett's reply suggests why his hatred of Poe is so scathing: "I'm going to tell you this just once, and I don't want to have to say it again. This country's getting old and I aim to get old with it. Now the Kid don't want it that way. He might be a better man for it, I ain't judging. But I don't want you explaining nothing to me and I don't want you saying nothing about the Kid or nobody else in my county." Garrett sees in Poe everything he loathes about himself and the decisions he has recently made. For Poe likewise aims to get old with the country, and by essentially the same means—latching onto that "winning hand" offered by the big shots in Santa Fe, where the sheriff first lays eyes on the deputy. They each have different reasons: Poe an opportunistic young man on the rise, Garrett a weary middle-aged one looking to settle down. But they are nevertheless doing the same thing. When Poe says he's a special deputy answerable only to Santa Fe, Garrett knows how trivial the distinction between himself and Poe really is, for he too is answerable to the same authority, since that is where the purse strings are pulled.

At a still deeper level Garrett resents Poe's self-confidence, resents how utterly without shame, irony, or reservation the younger man is able to pursue his ambitions and accept the values of the society, while Garrett himself is wracked by guilt, self-doubt, and self-contempt. Poe represents what Garrett would be like if he did not have Billy as an equal and countervailing influence; if, in other words, he had not experienced something of friendship and fellowship to shore against the temptations of money and materialism. At the conceptual level, Poe's function is in part not unlike that of the mirror image Garrett faces at the end, serving as a kind of distorted reflection of what he will do to himself if he kills Billy. It comes as little surprise, then, to find in the prologue that just as Garrett seems to have been taken over by Billy's personality, so Poe appears to have absorbed the "official" side of Garrett's. And since Poe is a Garrett who has never known genuine camaraderie, he is also a Garrett who will not dispatch his

Billy gently into the night. The manner of Garrett's death, his body riddled with bullets, writhing in agony as it tries to pick itself up off the ground, contrasts markedly with that of Billy, who seems to float downward, his head coming to rest serenely on the porch, as if lovingly cushioned from impact.

If these shifting roles and slippery identities seem confusing, then that confusion may not be so far from the point. It is the overriding note that Peckinpah sounds in the prologue. By juxtaposing in rapid succession images of Garrett getting shot and the chickens exploding, Peckinpah immediately plants the suggestion of suicide, because we soon see that a couple of the chickens are blown apart with bullets fired by the younger Garrett. At the same time, the director deliberately obliterates all temporal reference points. Owing to the quickness of the cutting, it is impossible for us to tell where the gunshots are coming from; do they originate in 1909 or 1881? It doesn't matter, for to the mind all time exists as space. To Garrett's mind, which is where the structure of the film locates these and the other events of the story, his murder by Poe is merely the completion of the suicide begun twenty-seven years before. Peckinpah strengthens the connection with some visual motifs common to both the prologue and the opening scene. The bright-colored blanket that Garrett has draped over his lap in the buggy turns out to be the overcoat he is wearing when he rides into Old Fort Sumner; and shots of the 1881 Garrett firing at the chickens are cut against shots of the 1909 Garrett dying on the ground. Garrett's sense of confusion is echoed in the last scene by way of the odd little appearance by Peckinpah himself as a coffinmaker named Will. Working, not inappositely, on a child's coffin as Garrett passes on his way to find the Kid, Will asks, "You finally figured it out, huh? Go on, get it over with." But Garrett hasn't figured it out, and it won't be over for the better part of three decades. Even then, after years of turning it over and around and upside down, he still can't figure it out, still can't make it come any clearer or better or straighter. And when it passes before him for one last time as the bullets tear through his body, the most he might achieve is a burgeoning awareness that he has been an unwitting accomplice to his own death, a dim, tragic recognition that he was a link in the chain of causality that has brought his life to this dying fall.

As the prologue depicts a Garrett considerably older than the actual Garrett was at the time of his death, this may be the appropriate place to take up the matter of the casting, especially since Peckinpah received so much flak from some reviewers for choosing the then thirty-six-year-old Kristofferson to play Billy the Kid, who actually died when he was twenty-one. In the first place, one cannot help wondering how many critics would have carped if they had not known Kristofferson's age. In the film he doesn't look thirty-six, looks rather closer to thirty, and can easily pass for late twenties. In the second place, Peckinpah and his collaborators were not writing history; and these materials, which are not well documented and enjoy a tremendously vital existence in legend and folklore, gave them considerable artistic license. The anonymous contributors to folklore had already taken advantage of that license many years before the first, let alone this, Billy the Kid film. There is little real evidence to support the view that Billy and Garrett were ever partners in crime before they became antagonists, or that they ever palled around together in the "old days." If those old days refer only as far back as five or ten years before Billy's death, then he must have been between ten and fifteen years old the whole while he and Garrett were supposed to be doing all that whoring, boozing, robbing, and rustling—clearly ludicrous even for the "wild" West.

There are thus good dramatic reasons for making the Kid older, and good historical reasons as well, at least as regards the history of the legend. The Kid's body was hardly even cold before stories began to circulate to the effect that the sheriff had gunned down his old friend. In other words, history, in the form of gossip, had already begun to imagine Billy as older—say twenty-five, the age of Neider's Hendry Jones, from whom Peckinpah took his cue. Neider advanced Billy's age because he wanted a gunslinger hero who was just a shade beyond his peak years as a fast draw. Peckinpah clearly saw in Kristofferson the slightly used look, just a touch fat and soft, of a star who was burning himself out fast and young, exactly the right look that novelist, writer, producer, and director all regarded as essential to the meaning of the story. If the same reviewers who were so quick to jump on Peckinpah had paused to consider what he was obviously doing, his casting of Kristofferson, far from seeming a mistake, would be seen as further evidence of the care with which he customarily matches actor to role. Peckinpah wanted Kristofferson's persona as a self-destructive folk-rock star just beyond his peak years to infuse his performance as Billy, for it becomes a way—like William Holden in *The Wild Bunch* or Joel McCrea and Randolph Scott in *Ride the High Country*—of giving the character an appropriate history even before he makes his first appearance: this is a Billy who has already spent far too many Sunday mornings coming down.

Once Billy becomes older, so too must Garrett. In 1881 Garrett was, at thirty-one, only ten years older than Billy, an age difference more suggestive of a brotherly than a fatherly companionship. But the same popular imagination that made them the partners in crime they probably never were also felt the need for theirs to be a father-son relationship and saw no more reason to let the facts stand in the way on that account than on any other. One explanation for this, no doubt, is that the Kid was called, after all, a *kid*. Another, probably better, is that the sheriff killed the outlaw at exactly the right moment in history, when New Mexico, not yet a state, was going through a period of violent transition trying to forge a going economic concern out of a wild, sprawling territory. The legend of Pat Garrett and Billy the Kid became in response an ambiguous allegory of progress. Scratched deep enough such allegories often turn out to be fables about growing up, getting old, and accepting responsibilities. At least this one does. So as gossip hardened into legend, the Garrett of 1881 was advanced in age to his middle or late forties, as in this film, which then obligated Peckinpah to put him past seventy when he is killed (though his actual age was only fifty-seven). This was an obligation that was hardly met reluctantly, for in the preproduction stages, when the characters were closer to their historical ages, Peckinpah alone seems to have realized that the only way the story makes sense— emotionally, symbolically, and dramatically—is if it takes up with Garrett just as he has reached that "age in a man's life when he don't want to spend time figuring what's coming next."

IV

When Sheriff-elect Pat Garrett rides into Old Fort Sumner, dismounts, and takes a shot at one of the chickens, it is a moment equally of reunion and union, for in rejoining the Kid and playing a familiar game with him, Garrett has briefly recaptured the past and it is become like old times once again. But it is a moment only, and its very brevity serves to underscore the truth of what Garrett soon tells the Kid, that times have changed. There is as well an unstated corollary to what Garrett is saying, for Peckinpah knows that the sheriff is wrestling with problems far more complicated than that.

In Wurlitzer's original screenplay the only reason posited for Garrett's hunting of the Kid is that the sheriff has borrowed money from Chisum to buy some land. In other words, Garrett is portrayed as little more than a corrupt official who has "sold out." But what interested Peckinpah is *that* Garrett turned away from the past and toward the future; and in the new opening scene the director laid the groundwork for a deeper, richer, psychologically more plausible motivation or, rather, matrix of motivations that exists parallel and prior to the loan and is suggested by what Garrett finds when he arrives in Old Fort Sumner. The chicken shoot is only a surface manifestation, and the "fun" of his joining in merely points toward a deep and pervasive malaise that is only hinted at by his first remark to the Kid when they sit down for a drink—"Jesus, don't you get *stale* around here, Bill?" Garrett's story is the story of a man undergoing a belated process of maturation. What he really finds when he arrives in Old Fort Sumner is not his *compañeros* of days past. What he finds is a bunch of feckless youths so bored and so unimaginative in their boredom that they can't think of anything better to do on a hot afternoon than bury some chickens in the sand and shoot their heads off to the amusement of still younger boys who rush up to claim the dead birds. We are left to ask, as Garrett has doubtless asked and by then answered himself, how long a man can go on living the kind of life Billy represents. It is clear that these games have lost all interest for Garrett, and what amusement there might have been in them has by and large evaporated. Nor does he find much comfort in the old gang. Except for the Kid, none of them likes him much, which would bother him more than it does if the feeling were not mutual. Garrett has become tired of this life, their life, his former life, because there simply isn't enough to sustain him in it. And whether times have changed matters relatively little as far as his personal problems are concerned, for what he really means to be saying is that, getting older, he is beginning to see things differently and feels the need for a change himself.

The pursuit proper has been called Garrett's journey into his past. It is not, however, a nostalgic journey. The places he visits and the familiar faces he meets up with serve only to deepen his sense of how essentially estranged he is from them. His friend Sheriff McKinney has to be reminded of all he owes Garrett before he will accompany him into Old Fort Sumner after the Kid. And earlier he had to bribe his old friend Sheriff Baker into helping raid Black Harris's camp to get some information on the Kid; although the older man returns the coins, the demand itself still cuts a deep disappointment. "One of these days when I get my boat built, I'm going to drift out of this damn territory," Baker says, and goes in to talk to his wife about helping Garrett. Peckinpah stays outside with Garrett, who walks around the unfinished boat. It is seen in a hand-held shot, from Garrett's point of view, that Spottiswoode recalls was very difficult to cut in, but that "Sam was insistent on using." It is one of the most insightful single shots in the entire film, the boat, its hull still only a skeleton, evoking an almost childishly pathetic dream of flight and escape that will soon be dashed when Baker is shot and staggers off and sits beside the river, dying as his wife looks on, helpless and weeping.

The unfinished boat is another of Peckinpah's naturalistic symbols that ramifies in meaning as the film progresses. Isolated within Garrett's point of view, it represents his dreams of escape too, which will likewise remain incomplete and in a far more miserable way than those of Baker, who at least dies his own man and in the company of his devoted wife. As it is explicitly associated with drifting, the boat also anticipates the raft episode, with its family floating down river, and pulls together and concentrates all the movement throughout the film into an image of humanity carried inexorably along by forces of nature and history much larger and more powerful than itself. And its various associations with dying and with dreams of leaving the past behind and starting over are recalled and resolved in the scene with the coffinmaker, who says that he's going to put everything he owns into the child's coffin he's constructing and "I'm going to bury it in the ground, and then I'm going to leave the territory."

In Peckinpah's original version these scenes are juxtaposed against other scenes that show Garrett's new associates and places of business, thereby making the pursuit a journey through his future as well as through his past. One of these is the scene with Chisum, which shows how subservient Garrett must be to the man who holds his loan. Another is the remarkable scene between Garrett and his wife. Though they've only recently married, already their marriage shows signs of strife. When he visits her after being away from home, he doesn't say he's happy to see her, offers no pleasantries, and soon fabricates a story about an unruly drunk as an excuse to leave, telling her he doubts he'll be back in time for dinner. When she cries, "You don't touch me. You are dead inside," he turns and silences her by literally putting his foot down, hard and loud on the floor. "We'll deal with this when it's over," he says on his way out the door. It is clear that this marriage is a loveless one; that Garrett married because it is more or less expected of him in his new lifestyle; and that his wife spends most of her time alone without even the company of her own people, who ignore her because her husband has become too much of a gringo, siding with the powerful landowners. The power behind these landowners figures in the next scene, the meeting with the businessmen in Santa Fe, which has Garrett trying to regain some of the pride he lost in the exchange with Chisum, as they too urge him to clear the territory of the Kid and his gang. The sheriff holds himself in, unable, probably not even wanting, to tell them that his reasons for going after the Kid are considerably different from theirs. The most he manages to do by way of salving his self-respect is to tell them in no uncertain terms where they can stick their reward money.

What Peckinpah is presenting is a fairly complete picture of the paucity of options the environment opens for Garrett. Caught between a life that has lost even the meaning that pleasure might confer upon it and a life devoted to making the territory safe for the very entrepreneurs he despises, Garrett is the only fully alienated character in the story, his situation the only tragic one. But it is not the tragedy of a man who has lived beyond his time. After all, the year is only 1881; if Garrett really wanted to go on living the kind of life he had been living, he could always take off for Mexico, California, or other points south and west, as he advises the Kid to do. Rather, his tragedy is that he has come to a realization of how impoverished, restricted, and limited his way of life is, and now that he is ready to become a responsible citizen, all that he has made himself fit for is to become a legal gunman, sheriffing for wealthy landowners and speculators.

The full measure of Garrett's alienation is not revealed until the very last scene, in which his departure from Old Fort Sumner the morning after he has killed Billy is set up, shot, and composed so as to recall the departure of the hero from the small Wyoming town in George Stevens's *Shane*. But the allusion is ironic: Shane rides alongside the wooden walkway of the town, Garrett alongside the wooden porch of Pete Maxwell's house; at their respective corners, the riders continue on out into the prairie, a small boy chasing after Shane, shouting, "Come back, Shane, come back," a slightly older one running after Garrett, pelting his horse with stones to hasten him faster away. At the last moment Stevens cuts to an alternate angle so that he can magnify Shane's stature against the verdant Wyoming range; Peckinpah, by contrast, holds us to the shot of the disillusioned boy, who turns and walks back toward town while Garrett's figure recedes in the distance as the arid New Mexico desert begins to swallow it up. Surely there is in effect and implication no bleaker, blacker, bitterer ending to any Western film. The reverberations that Peckinpah sounds by alluding to what is probably the most well-known conventional Western in the history of motion pictures only intensifies the dominant tones of irony and despair.

This irony and also the sense of anger and disgust Garrett feels with his life infuse the film as a whole with a quieter, less romantic and flamboyant mood than his other Western films. There is much drinking, some whoring, and a lot of killing, but most of it is seen to exist as a desperate reaction against a boredom that might be—and in Garrett's case perhaps is—literally suicidal in its consequences. This is the only Peckinpah Western that contains nothing of the hilarity and bawdiness that the others break into from time to time, and none of the excitement and exhilaration that a life of action lived close to the edge provides, say, the Wild Bunch when they pull a good score. Horses are seen at a gallop just once, framed in such a way as to preclude any stirring or romantic effect. And although there are some beautifully composed images, they have little of the kinetic charge and energy of those in *The Wild Bunch* or *Major Dundee*. Instead, the riders are seen picking their way slowly through a rocky, sparsely shrubbed terrain, crisscrossed by barbed wire. There is a pall of hopelessness and desolation that seems to hang over everything and to infect everyone. In *Straw Dogs* Peckinpah gave us a world nearly as joyless as this one, but there he was working, however brilliantly, with an aesthetics of asceticism and reductionism. Here his textures are as rich and pulsating as ever, but the expansiveness brings only expanded possibilities for death and destruction because these people are shown to be too limited, too narrow, too unenlightened to resolve their disputes by any means other than violence. This is particularly brought to the fore in the strange scene where the Kid kills Alamosa Bill by cheating in a duel because neither of them can think of any other way to handle their chance encounter at a trading post. Meanwhile, some children watch the contest, learning all the wrong lessons from it.*

Nor are they the only children seen witnessing acts of violence. Children are on hand at the beginning to pick up the dead chickens; they play, rather too obviously, on the gallows built for Billy's execution; and they figure in the much-argued-over raft episode. At dusk Garrett, camped on a riverbank, hears gunfire, looks upriver, and sees a raft moving with the current, a family on board, the father taking potshots at a bottle floating some distance ahead, the wife and children watching. As he did at the beginning when he rode into Old Fort Sumner, Garrett aims and fires at the target, only here the man fires back and nearly hits him. The sheriff ducks, takes aim again, then smiles and lowers his rifle. The current continues to pull the raft down river, the man staring back in Garrett's direction. In conventional terms the scene is unnecessary and can even be said to retard

---

*In response to a comment that the children respond too uniformly, Peckinpah said he directed them that way "because they know what is coming: not long before they had seen their brother killed" (a reference to which is made in the scene), so they've already lost a bit of their innocence.

the progress of the narrative. But this is a criticism that places plot above story in order of importance. The scene pulls together and crystallizes so much, and so richly augments theme, texture, and atmosphere, that Peckinpah and his crew were right to fight for it as hard as they did. It shows how quickly the people in this environment resort to their weapons; how the weapons themselves function alternately as instruments of amusement and aggression; how easily chance encounters can flare into violence; how surely Garrett is becoming alienated from the world he used to inhabit. Most of all, the scene extends the range of life the film opens onto, the raft and the family it carries suggesting something of the oppressive squalor that was much of frontier life.

In view of such scenes, it is difficult to understand how so many reviewers, whatever their persuasion as to the film's merits, could have taken it as "still another of those elegies for the Old West; the two heroes, posed nonchalantly against a variety of Mexican landscapes, lament the good old days when gunslingers lived the free life."[25] If there is one thing that *Pat Garrett and Billy the Kid* is not, it is *another* of anything. Set three decades before *The Wild Bunch* and two decades before *Ride the High Country,* the film deposits us into just precisely the time to which the protagonists of those earlier films refer when they are speaking lyrically of the ways things used to be. Yet once back there, we find not a simpler, nobler way of life, but a grosser, dirtier, more violent and shabby one, where, ironically, the people are talking about the better times that existed even farther back in the past. It is difficult to understand how Peckinpah could more clearly demonstrate that the "glory" of the "Old West" exists not in fact but in fancy, specifically in the characters' memories.

This was always more or less implicit in the earlier films. In *The Wild Bunch,* for example, the flashbacks—which show us Pike deserting a friend, leaving behind a member of the Bunch, and through carelessness allowing the woman he loves to be killed—serve only to give the lie to any sentimental talk about the old days. By the same token, in *Pat Garrett* what the characters reminisce about contrasts markedly with the mood and manner in which the reminiscence is recalled. In one of the best-written and best-played of these moments, Pete Maxwell, so old and toothless he eats only soup, loses himself in this bit of nostalgia: "Recollect the time Toddy Sparks got his horse stole. Jace Sommers stole it. Just up and stole it! Was up by del Rio. Old Toddy got even, though. He sure did. Put a rattler in Jace's blanket. Bit him through the neck. Buried him in a thunderstorm. Summer of seventy-one, it was." Nearly every time a character recalls something from the past, what it concerns is some violent incident, some death, some killing—as when Billy asks Bell if he knows how Carlyle died, then tells him, "I shot him three times in the back, blew his goddamn head off." And the killings rarely owe to principle, sense of mission, or devotion to a dying way of life, certainly not to the moral imperatives dictated by codes of honor or outmoded chivalry. Mostly they owe to greed, happenstance, thoughtlessness, stupidity, or plain hellishness ("Just up and stole him!"). The cumulative effect is as if romantic preconceptions and illusions are being stripped away, as if the patina of memory itself is being scraped off the past.

If Peckinpah is here using the legend so that he may work against it, then the function of Alias, the character played by Bob Dylan, is to suggest how the legend got started in folklore and popular culture. Alias is introduced working in a newspaper office; after Billy escapes, Alias is shown with pad and pencil in hand, taking notes and questioning bystanders. This suggests that one of his jobs at the newspaper is gathering information, perhaps even actual reporting. When he hears that a posse is being formed to track the Kid, he quits his job and takes off to warn him, eventually joining up with Billy's gang. Thereafter he remains mostly on the periphery of the action, yet he is always around when important things are happening. It seems clear that he represents the chronicler and storyteller, and he becomes more or less the stand-in for all the anonymous contributors to the legend of Billy the Kid. Even his name—"Alias who?" "Alias anything you please"—reinforces this notion, suggesting that while the individual person or persons telling the story change as the years go by, each and all are nevertheless doing the same thing: remembering and by extension mythmaking. (This character type, particularly in the role of reporter, is a convention in many Western stories, and is prominent in one of the rare other good films made about Billy the Kid, Arthur Penn's *The Left-Handed Gun*.) By allowing Dylan's folk singer persona to spill over into the role of Alias, much as Kristofferson's does into Billy, Peckinpah strengthens the connections between the Bob Dylan playing Alias, the Bob Dylan singing the theme song of the film ("Billy, they don't like you to be so free"), and the Bob Dylan who made his reputation during the sixties romantically chronicling outlaws in albums like *John Wesley Harding*. (Alias has, of course, his equivalents in Peckinpah's previous films: Mapache's retinue of musicians; the Mexican peasants who serenade the Wild Bunch and Dundee's troop; and Corporal Ryan, whose diary contains the record of Major Dundee's punitive expedition.)[26]

But if Alias romanticizes Billy, it is not an invitation for us to do the same. Some critics have done exactly that, however, investing Billy with the qualities of a doomed, romantic outlaw hero or, worse still, a "knight-errant," in blithe defiance of all the contradictory evidence that Peckinpah everywhere places on the screen.[27] Virtually nothing Billy does is heroic, noble, or honorable. When he kills people, it is almost always from the back, out of ambush, or by surprise. One of his killings is even shown to be gratuitous, for when he shoots his friend Bell in the back it accomplishes exactly what it is intended to prevent, as the sound of Billy's gun and Bell's body crashing through the jailhouse window alert the townspeople to the impending escape every bit as fast as Bell himself would have if left alive. At other times Billy is merely irresponsible, but the price is still death, albeit someone else's, as when he and Alias leave their friend Sylvus to guard some cattle they've just rustled from Chisum while they take off after some wild turkeys. While they're away, Chisum's men return, swarm down upon Sylvus, and kill him. Or take the shootout at Stinking Springs, where Billy lets his friends get cut to ribbons before he decides to surrender. "You're in poor company, Pat," he says. "Yeah, I'm alive though," Garrett replies. "So am I," smirks Billy. Though Garrett is often called the pragmatic survivor and Billy his hapless victim, in fact Billy is not without a certain craftiness of his own that enables him to get out of scrapes even as his pals are killed one by one. In this context, the meaning of the Alamosa Bill duel is doubly illuminating. Billy not only cheats first, but in so doing demonstrates how well he has learned the lessons of his elders: you don't play fair, you play to win, that is, to survive. (Peckinpah's disinclination to glamorize or otherwise idealize the old days is again confirmed.) Nor will Peckinpah reveal Billy in the aspect of a cowboy Robin Hood. This Billy has no desire to become rich, but that is chiefly because he has no ambitions at all.

Peckinpah once complained that Marlon Brando made a mess of *One-Eyed Jacks* because "in those days he had to end up as a hero and that's not the point of the story. Billy the Kid was no hero. He was a gunfighter, a real killer."[28] Not surprisingly, in Peckinpah's hands Billy becomes something of a sociopath who dispatches people with a smile on his face and hardly a backward glance. He is a likable—even charming—sociopath, which is perhaps one reason why the subject of this Billy remains so confusing. Another is that the character is never fully developed, is always a little remote and impenetrable, which certainly has some historical basis. Amazingly little is known for certain about William Bonney, and what testimony there is by those who knew him tends to be inconclusive and rather contradictory. But this is a weak justification for what is either a scar across the film or a serious flaw in a story that is otherwise principally about Garrett. As regards this latter, Billy's thematic function is to suggest the wild, antisocial side of Garrett's personality: a more individuated Billy would not necessarily weaken this story, but it would certainly make it a different one.

A third possibility is that the character's very amorphousness operates positively within the overall design. From the initial conception, before Peckinpah was involved, the Kid was seen as a man who is far from fully developed, whose development has rather been arrested at the stage of his first notoriety. There is about him an aura of ambiguous, unresolved adolescence that is constantly pulling him back toward childhood even as the forces around him are insisting upon his obligations and responsibilities. When Billy returns from his aborted flight to Mexico, Eno, speaking for the whole gang, tells him, "You just give us the word, there's enough of us left"; and Billy replies, "Nobody's running us off." Our first impulse is to think, yes, now he will assume the burden of consciousness and act. Instead, he becomes even more desultory and dilatory. He target shoots some tin cans as Alias and some kids applaud; and in one extended moment that seems to be about nothing but that perfectly captures the essence of his lethargic ambivalence, he has a drink with Alias as the gang looks on, just waiting, waiting, waiting. When Alias leaves the table to join the others, Billy just turns away and looks enigmatically off in the distance. His reasons for not acting can only be guessed at, and he remains a remote, mysterious figure, his very elusiveness the basis perhaps of his fecundity as a symbolic figure in storytelling and myth-making.

From this perspective the suggestion that *Pat Garrett and Billy the Kid* is maybe the best film ever made about the decline of the sixties rock-culture is less farfetched than it may seem. The genesis of the project consisted in its parallels with self-destructive rock stars, while the casting of Kristofferson, Rita Coolidge (then married to Kristofferson), Bob Dylan, and members of Kristofferson's band practically guaranteed the connections. As someone who really *has* lived his whole life at one incandescent point, and then it's over, Billy can be seen as a kind of passive suicide. He *wants* it to be over and awaits only a suitable finish, which it is the fated duty of Garrett to provide. By the time Peckinpah made this film, he had been, though through no special ministrations of his own, sort of adopted by the counter-culture. Beginning in the early seventies he and his work were several times featured in publications like *Rolling Stone,* the *Berkeley Barb,* and the *Los Angeles Free Press,* including a famous article by the late respected journalist Grover Lewis.[29] Peckinpah seldom missed much of what was going on around him. And in this film, which ended the counterculture's infatuation with him, there is no mistaking in Billy and his gang the sense of lives played out and dissipated, and behind them a world ebbing away.

Since so many of Peckinpah's films, and all of the Western films, feature a pair of protagonists, there has been a tendency among critics to treat both the pairs and the issues to which their conflicts refer as identical from film to film. Thus Billy, owing to his resistance to change, is likened to Pike Bishop and Steve Judd; while Garrett, the alleged sellout, is associated with Deke Thornton and Gil Westrum. The trouble with neat little formulations like these, however, is not so much that they are grossly generalized and that they distort the films in question (although they are and they do) as that they appear to be a lot more insightful than they really are, and here they break down almost immediately. Surely the values embodied in this Billy are not those of an obsolescent heroism. He suggests nothing of the Pike Bishop who wouldn't have his foes any way other than ready, willing, and able to meet him at the peak of their powers; or of the Steve Judd who would rather fight face to face in the traditional Western showdown, clean and straight-up. When Billy engages in such a duel it is dirty and lowdown, the chief "value" he displays being the requisite cynicism to cheat first. However, the largest dissimilarity that renders the identification of Billy with Steve and Pike invalid is to be found in comparing their respective responses to change, a comparison that reveals both the older men as being considerably more mutable than they are customarily taken to be. Pike realizes that the old "days are closing fast," so he leads the Bunch into Mexico where, the pickings being lean, he hires out to the renegade Mapache, thus sacrificing a measure of his former independence. Furthermore, he is actually looking for a change and wants to pull one last job to try to effect it. Similarly, Steve is saddened to find himself passed over and nearly forgotten by the very society he had helped to establish; but if his decision to hire himself out to a bank as a mere guard represents anything, it is precisely his flexibility, his realization that if he is to retain his self-respect he must accept jobs less auspicious than his marshaling of days past. In the cases of both men, what is being shown is their resilience and their awareness of the inevitability of change. These are just the qualities that Billy lacks. When Garrett tells him that Old Eben, who was killed while crossing the Rio Grande in flight from a posse, at least knew when it was the right time to leave,

Billy doesn't get the point, instead muttering only that times change but "not me."

It would appear that Billy doesn't even believe that times change. He tells Alias, "Maybe Mexico won't be so bad for a couple of months," a remark that ought to silence those who complain that his decision to return isn't motivated. Manifestly, he was planning before he left to come back soon enough, believing, as he seems to, that in a little while the trouble will blow over and things will be just like they used to be. There might even be an implication that he thinks Garrett will come to his senses and rejoin the old gang. After killing Holly, Garrett pauses on his way out the door and tells Alias, "When you see Billy, tell him we had a little drink together." Alias does tell Billy, and tells him also that Garrett is still in pursuit. And when Billy, his face breaking into a strange smile, replies, "Yeah, I reckon. Maybe he wants to have a drink with me," we are not sure he doesn't really believe that is what Garrett will do. We are still left wondering in that splendidly ambiguous moment when his face breaks into the same strange smile as, turning, he sees Garrett sitting beside the bed in the shadows.

The obtuseness that Billy periodically displays has its roots in the fundamental polarity that separates him and Garrett, the difference in their ages, which is also what primarily distinguishes their friendship from the friendships of the male pairs in the earlier films. Steve and Gil, Pike and Deke, these men go back decades together; even Dundee and Tyreen have a past that is substantially shared. Garrett and Billy, by comparison, have hung around together only for about five years, give or take a couple (and they haven't seen much of each other during the year immediately preceding the events of the story), so they haven't developed that solidarity that can come only from long and deep association. This is more or less what is suggested by Holly's cryptic remark to Garrett, "Ever since you and the Kid have been together, you been just a little short of supplies." How little comprehension Billy has of the changes that time and circumstance have wrought upon his friend, and how simplistic is his assessment of Garrett's actions, is suggested in an early exchange with Bell, one that recalls the famous "It isn't that simple, is it?" dialogue between Steve Judd and Elsa:

> *Billy:* You know, I think Pat's lost his sand. Won't come on a person.
> *Bell:* You hadn't ought to run him down, Billy. You and him used to be pretty close.
> *Billy:* He ain't the same man. He's store-bought and womanized. Signed himself over to Chisum and every other goddamn land-

owner that's trying to put a fence around this country. Hell, but that's what you been doing, ain't it, Bell, selling us out and getting fat?
Bell: It ain't that easy, Billy.

The friendship between Garrett and Billy is thus revealed to be a peculiarly tenuous, even labile one, obliquely suggestive of the hostilities that exist in *The Wild Bunch* between Pike, Dutch, and Old Sykes on the one hand and the Gorch brothers on the other—a division that is also traceable to differences in age. And if the jibes Billy occasionally directs toward Garrett about getting old and settling down recall the insults the Gorches hurl at the older members of the Bunch, so too does Billy's remark, "I ain't shut of this country yet," suggest a parallel to the Gorches' talk about getting a stake so they can begin robbing banks and trains elsewhere, despite Pike's warning that they have to start thinking beyond their guns. In both cases, Billy and the Gorches, there is a failure to perceive the large changes that are going on everywhere around them.

From this perspective it is apparent that Garrett is a lot more like Pike than Billy is, as Garrett too knows when it is the right time to leave or to change, has opted for the latter, and is eventually fatally entrapped by unforeseen consequences that follow upon his decision. This is identical to what befalls Pike and, for that matter, Steve Judd and even Ben Tyreen, although each of theirs is a heroic death while Garrett's is not. Neither, however, is Billy's, which is a crucial point that Peckinpah, in one of those startling moments of black humor that from time to time turn up in his films, drives home by way of an ironic allusion to the Western cliché about a man's wanting to die with his boots on. Billy dies not while engaged on some mission (like Tyreen), returning to save a fallen friend (like Pike), or upholding a point of honor (like Steve). Instead, he is killed while getting himself a postcoital snack, and our last glimpse of him is a closeup of his bare feet sticking out from under the blanket that covers his corpse.

That closeup is also Peckinpah's way of suggesting that Billy is, figuratively speaking, not quite a man when he dies, for he has not learned, in Deke Thornton's words from *The Wild Bunch*, "what it's all about." This is precisely what Garrett has endeavored to teach him; and it can be argued that still another reason for the prolonged, circular strategy of his pursuit is that he is trying to impress upon Billy the seriousness of his enterprise, to show him that the decision to marry, become sheriff, and settle down was not made lightly and is not about to be revoked. Perhaps equally, it is Garrett's attempt to fulfill his role as surrogate father more responsibly than he did in the past. This aspect of their relationship is indicated in a subtle but consistent touch: everyone refers to the Kid as "Billy," except Garrett, who usually calls him "Bill." But Garrett's efforts are both belated and futile, as the opposition sounded from the outset between Garrett's responsibility and Billy's playfulness demonstrates. "C'mon out, Bill. Game's over!" Garrett shouts after the shoot-out at Stinking Springs. But when Billy appears, that smile on his face, his arms outstretched in mocking imitation of Christ, it is clear that for him the game has just begun. "I never figured to hear you brag on being a working man," he tells Garrett a little later. "It's just a way of staying alive," Garrett replies, and then announces he has to leave for a couple of days to collect taxes. Not long afterward Billy goes to the outhouse and discovers a pistol there, the proximity of the two events suggesting that Garrett has given him another chance to stay alive too. But it doesn't take, and the opposition between work and play reverberates throughout the rest of the film as scenes of Billy horsing around are juxtaposed against scenes of Garrett doing his job. The effect of the cutting is always to wrap Garrett's scenes around Billy's, like a noose that is slowly tightening, right down to that fatal evening when Garrett's movements—passing by the window, crossing through the doorway, stealing down the hallway—inscribe a circle around the heedless Kid, who, obtuse and unregenerate to the end, continues in his lovemaking.

But if Billy is not quite an adult, neither is he quite a child. To put it another way, he is a grown-up child, or an adult who has learned to shoot, steal, and kill but who has failed to develop a commensurate moral sensibility or capacity for judgment. In this sense, then, his real progenitors in the earlier films are to be found not in the main characters but in such secondary characters, also grown-up children, as the Hammond brothers or Crazy Lee, the wild, unpredictable psychopath who also kills with a grin on his face and whose dying remark to the man who shoots him is, "Well, now, how'd you just like to kiss my sister's black cat's ass?" And like Crazy Lee, Billy, too, "ain't exactly predictable," as Garrett points out. Nor is he much more responsible or less dangerous, because, again like Crazy Lee, he has little self-awareness and less control of his lethal skills. During his escape from the jail in Lincoln, the townspeople are so scared all they do is smile accommodatingly, give him what he asks for, and clear a wide path for him to ride through so he can be gone as fast as possible. He rides a few days to his hideout where he surprises his men, who are of course glad to see him, but not before there is a moment's hesitation in which everyone looks around cautiously. One of them then offers Billy the woman he is with, remarking as he crawls out of bed, "Like I said, sure is good to have you back again, Kid," the irony of his tone giving the lie to how little choice he really has in the offer.

Scenes like this tend to cement the similarities between Billy and some of the less savory secondary characters in the earlier films, for in the gross, filthy way they live, Billy's gang, including to a large extent Billy himself, bear a far greater physical resemblance to the Hammond brothers and to the egg-sucking, chicken-stealing, gutter-trash pack of bounty hunters that Thornton is forced to lead than they do to the Wild Bunch. Since in Peckinpah's work resemblances on the physical level often imply similarities on other levels, Billy is revealed as less an exemplar of Western freedom and individualism than a product of the very unrestraint and homogeneity of frontier society that necessitates marshals like Steve Judd and drives Garrett to seek something different. The visual scheme sets this forth clearly enough: Garrett is outfitted in a suit of austere, rather ominous black and white, which usually throws him into relief against the background, and he is often framed in such a way as to heighten our sense of his isolation and alienation. Billy, by contrast, is dressed so that he is frequently indistinguishable from his gang, and in long shots the lot of them often blend right into the setting (the first shot of Old Fort Sumner, an overview of the fountain, is a telling example). The effect is as if Billy simply emerges from the environment. In this respect he recalls Poe once again, and together they introduce another polarity: Poe has been shaped by Santa Fe, which represents the New West with its impersonal, businesslike violence; and Billy has been shaped by Old Fort Sumner, which represents the Old West with its random, casual violence. And since neither character has been able to develop an ironic attitude toward or distance from his experience, he is revealed as not only the product but the prisoner of his environment.

Those who continue to see Billy as an "existential" hero who "chooses" to become "Billy the Kid"—that is, to live and die according to the legend he has made for himself—miss the point of the age difference between the title characters. As a consequence they miss as well the enlarged perspective this film provides on the twin themes of aging and change so prominent in the earlier Western films, where it begins to appear in retrospect that the closing of the frontier is not the main concern. If this is doubted, then we should remember that only three of those films—*Ride the High Country*, *The Wild Bunch*, and

The Ballad of Cable Hogue—are set after 1895, the date that Frederick Jackson Turner "officially" assigned to the closing of the frontier, a date that has stuck both in history and in art and legend. Two of the other films—*The Deadly Companions* and *Major Dundee*—are set in or within a decade of the Civil War, when there was still frontier left; and *Pat Garrett and Billy the Kid*, disregarding the frame story, is set shortly after the Lincoln County cattle wars, when there was also frontier left. What all of these films share, however, is settings that are marked by times of transition and, except for *The Deadly Companions*, feature aging men of action in collision with changing times. But since Peckinpah's paramount interest is and always has been in character, he has developed his themes of aging and change primarily in their personal and psychological aspects, only secondarily in their sociohistorical aspects. Viewed this way, then, it can be seen that the transitional settings function chiefly as backgrounds or objective correlatives for the interior transitions that have long since beset his aging protagonists.

Once this is understood it puts into sharper focus an irony that informs Peckinpah's use of both young and old protagonists in the same stories. The younger characters—the Hammond brothers and the Gorches, some of the more youthful members of Dundee's command, Heck throughout the journey to Coarsegold (and part of the way back), to some extent Angel, and of course Billy and his gang— are considerably more conservative than the older characters, not in the political sense, but simply in their being less flexible in the way that young people in their youth and inexperience often are. Contrary to what is often assumed about Peckinpah's work, they are thus more stubborn than the older characters, and also correspondingly less heroic. This irony has been latent since the very first films, but it did not become fully apparent until Peckinpah made age differences as such the central conflict of a story, as he did in *Pat Garrett and Billy the Kid*. Billy, given his age and the circumstances that have formed him, is no more capable of walking away from his life-style than Garrett, given his age and the circumstances that have formed him, is capable of remaining in it.

Taking a backward glance toward the earlier Western films, we can see that what separates the two sets of characters is the greater resilience of the older men, the greater stubbornness of the younger men. This is because the young men have not yet learned the necessity for making adjustments, accommodations, and sacrifices. Nor do such compromises necessarily involve a loss of honor or a breach of integrity, for that is an assessment made by such as the inexperienced Billy. On the contrary, these virtues are only thrown into fuller relief by the compromises the older men have made. Steve, contemptuous though he may be of the bank and its owners, will nevertheless honor his contract as tenaciously as if he were on some marshaling mission of days past instead of merely delivering a small shipment of gold, most of which belongs to a whorehouse anyway. Pike, however loathsome Mapache and his German advisers may be, will do the same, and will even at the end resist the temptation (as he had not always before) to run out on a friend, though that friend may be a pain in the ass and more than half responsible for the fix he has got himself into. And Tyreen will keep his word to the Major even after the Apache has been taken and destroyed because by then the lives of his Union colleagues mean as much to him as those of his Confederate colleagues. Even Cable—the most stubborn of the older protagonists—is ready to leave the desert and give up his fortune for love, even if too late.

Most of these men change too late. Some, like Garrett, change too little. But that matters less than their ability to change at all, which in turn demonstrates that they've learned something from their experience. What they have learned is how to face the world and what it has to offer unflinchingly, the rock-bottom fact of that reality being the ceaselessness of change itself, the basic imperative to roll with it with as much style, grace, and humor as the situation will allow. When Old Sykes says, "It ain't like it used to be, but it'll do," and Thornton laughs in assent, they are candidates as fit for redemption as the rest of the Wild Bunch, and the remark can stand as an epitaph for all of Peckinpah's aging heroes. What he salutes is their courage to reconcile themselves to the way things are without succumbing to despair or betraying their deepest ideals and convictions. In the end, what they learn is that the frontier can remain wild or become tame as the case may be, the world can stay the same or change as it chooses—these matter little, being external changes only and mere emblems of those deeper, more personal and abiding changes over which no man can exert choice or power to halt. After all, new frontiers, literal and figurative, continually open up, and social changes often resemble pendulums in their movements. But should a person grow old, even half a lifetime is enough to witness the irreversible taming of his wildness, and in the process he will have given up youth, possibility, and life itself, acquiring in return a backlog of memory, a storehouse of experience, and with any luck a measure of wisdom sufficient to help him realize—if we may paraphrase Milton's Satan—that "Myself am change." Something like this must

have been what Peckinpah had in mind when a friend once asked
him if there were any villains in his films. "All of the seven deadlies,"
the director replied, "plus age and stupidity."

Epilogue

There is an odd, disturbing scene in *Cross of Iron,* Peckinpah's film
about German soldiers on the Russian front in World War II. Sergeant
Steiner is ordered by his superior, Captain Stransky, to execute a
Russian prisoner who is only a boy. Steiner refuses, telling Stransky
that if he wants the boy shot, do it himself. Stransky begins to draw
his pistol, Steiner stands by impassively, making no move to prevent
him, whereupon Schnurrbart, an enlisted man, says he'll take the boy
away and carry out the order himself in a less public place. (He
doesn't, but for the time being the ruse saves the boy's life.) Steiner
is supposed to be the hero, and yet, for all that we can see, he appears perfectly willing to let the boy be shot in order to save his own
honor and force Stransky prove a point about himself.

Substitute Peckinpah for Steiner, James Aubrey for Stransky, and
Pat Garrett and Billy the Kid for the boy, and you have a remarkably
accurate picture of what seems to have happened during the final
stages of postproduction. Both men so hated each other that neither
seemed to care that the picture was being destroyed, provided they
got their licks in. Roger Spottiswoode fought often with Peckinpah
about this very issue, "because Sam was so much smarter than Aubrey.
He could have finessed and outmaneuvered him and got much of
what he wanted on the screen. Instead, all he did was fight to prove
he was right and Aubrey was wrong, and all that happened was that
the film was lost along the way."

The versions of *Pat Garrett* and their claims to directorial authority
are more confusing than those of *The Wild Bunch.* Over the years the
long version has acquired something of the same mystique as the European version of the earlier film, but this is misleading and undeserved. No matter which version of *The Wild Bunch* one sees, it is a film
that the director spent the better part of a year putting into fine cut,
whereas the long version of *Pat Garrett* was never fine cut at all. This is
not to disparage the work of the editors, who did a nearly miraculous
job preparing the preview in the time they had. But they prepared it
in a month, and you cannot fine cut a feature film and you absolutely
cannot fine cut a Peckinpah film, with its massive coverage and multiplicity of choices, in a month. This in turn raises the question of whether there ever existed a version of the film that can in any meaningful
sense of the word be said to represent Peckinpah's final thoughts.

There are three basic versions of *Pat Garrett*. The first, longest, and best is the studio preview that runs about 124 minutes. The second is the original theatrical release, 106 minutes long. The third version—the only one currently available—is a relatively new one shown theatrically in 1989 at the Directors Guild of America in Los Angeles and issued soon thereafter as a widescreen laserdisc by Turner Entertainment, which had acquired the MGM library some years before. Turner advertised this as "the director's cut" and issued a lot of self-congratulatory puffery about the effort and expense required to restore the film. In fact, despite a commendably superb transfer from a gorgeous print, Turner botched the job by failing to include the scene with Garrett's wife, which is why this version runs some two minutes shorter than the preview.* But even if the scene had been included, the Turner version would still be only one more version of a film that was never properly completed. There is no question that the preview cut of *Pat Garrett* is too long, with a few scenes that don't work at all and several others that go on long after their ships have sailed. Too many moments play like parodies of vintage Peckinpah: rhythms sometimes go slack; pauses sag like loose elastic, with little of the charged intensity of his famous silences; and some of the line-readings are dismayingly listless.

Did Peckinpah notice? It's hard to say. Spottiswoode's recollection is that the director never once watched the film all the way through at any time during postproduction. He didn't attend screenings or fell asleep drunk when he did; or else he arrived late, again drunk, and then fell asleep.† The first preview he skipped entirely, which sandbagged everyone who was trying to support him at the studio, including Dan Melnick. Garth Craven remembers things differently,

---

*Years earlier when MGM sold the film to network television, so much violence was removed that in order to fill out the time slot some of the cut footage had to be restored, including the wife scene. It is likely the scene is now stored with the elements that were used to prepare the film for broadcast. Yet though Turner and MGM were explicitly told (by Spottiswoode and others) that this scene was missing and were even told where they might find it, no one bothered to look or to allocate the quite small amount of money necessary to restore it. Bureaucracy—a frequent enemy on both sides of Peckinpah's camera—triumphed once again.

†After one screening a furious Peckinpah called the editors front and center and yelled at them for putting in a shot of Garrett and another rider leaving Old Fort Sumner at the end. Where had they found this footage, he demanded, because he certainly hadn't shot it. Didn't they read the script? Doesn't the script state that Garrett rides out alone? Doesn't this prove that people are out to sabotage the picture? He ordered the proper shot put back in. The next morning they showed him the scene, completely unchanged, and he left satisfied. The explanation? He was so drunk the night before that he was seeing double, including another horseman leaving with Garrett.

as did Robert Wolfe, both believing that Peckinpah attended at least one screening through which he stayed awake and sober. Alas, the one testimony is as damning as the other, and neither makes it easy to escape David Weddle's conclusion that just "when Sam needed to be in peak form, he was dropping the ball."[30] It was this sort of thing that started his friends wondering if he weren't deliberately doing the film in just to save his reputation. The only trouble with this reasoning is that Peckinpah cared very deeply about the film. Despite his troublesome behavior, which was concentrated more toward the end of postproduction than the beginning, he worked extremely hard with his editors all the way up to the preview. And in the years to follow he often showed, without apology, the preview print, which he had secured for his private collection.[31]* Yet he remained so angry that he spurned an offer by Melnick, made some months later after Aubrey was gone, to prepare a new version of the film. Nothing came of it, says Melnick, because "it needed Sam to put the picture into shape, and he just wouldn't make himself available."[32]

To the question, then, of whether any of these versions can be equated to the 1995 restoration of *The Wild Bunch*—which represents Peckinpah's final intentions and efforts—the answer is at best equivocal because the choice is Hobson's. The Turner gives us basically the preview, minus the wife scene and without benefit of thorough fine cutting; the theatrical version loses several important scenes, but the vast majority of those it shares with the preview and the Turner are far better cut, tuned, and timed. If the theatrical version betrays Peckinpah's vision, the Turner and the preview compromise his artistry.

It would be tedious to go through the entire film scene by scene, but two examples, one from the beginning and one from the end, illustrate the superior editing of the theatrical version and suggest why more than craftsmanship is at stake. In the fine cut of the first scene in Old Fort Sumner, when Garrett leaves, Holly asks, "Why don't you kill him?" "Why? He's my friend," Billy replies, and the scene ends, as it should. In the Turner/preview versions there are

---

*Secured indeed: when it became clear that Aubrey was bent on destroying the film, the editors remembered that the preview print was still in the projection booth. Peckinpah's driver obligingly removed it. Unfortunately, he did not take the soundtrack—the print was not a composite—which led Spottiswoode to place an urgent call to the director, saying that a terrible thing had happened, the preview print had been stolen, but the thief made a mistake and forgot to take the sound units. He reported that the studio had ordered that the cutting rooms be cleared out, but if the thief returned real soon, there would still be time to carry his mission to successful conclusion.

several more beats, and J. W. Bell says, "You boys are playing a losing game. I figure on staying alive," then walks out, very slowly. A few more beats and Black Harris says, "Well, he sure ain't your friend no more," turns, and walks away so slowly he seems to be moving in slow motion (though he is filmed at normal speed).

It is easy to see why all of this had to go. For one thing, the scene has made its point, peaking naturally on Billy's reply to Holly. For another, the additional dialogue is misleading: we still have almost two hours in which the story will unfold, letting us decide for ourselves whether Garrett remains Billy's friend and showing us the kind of friendship they have. Yet much has nevertheless been made of this additional material in arguments that tend to be strained and rather insensitive to the film as story and drama.[33] One area where "high" academic criticism joins hands with the "low" enthusiasm of fans is in the matter of texts: both tend to equate more with better. Scenes in Peckinpah's films always function on many levels, but not so many as to become bloated and impede the forward motion. This director was ruthlessly disciplined when it came to story. Spottiswoode, who had cut two previous films for him, and Wolfe, who had cut four, knew this, and knew also his style and approach. They realized that the function of this scene is to establish the world of the film, to make us feel the kind of the friendship Garrett and the Kid have so that it will resonate throughout the rest of the film, and to get the plot moving. The main reason to go out on the exchange between Holly and Billy is that it's the right emotional moment. But it also serves to characterize the difference between Billy's feelings for Garrett and those of the rest of his gang—they don't give a damn about the new sheriff. Then too the people who hired Garrett in the first place have doubtless asked him the same question Holly asks Billy, and though Garrett probably wouldn't dignify them with an answer, his ride to Fort Sumner demonstrates that his answer is in effect the same as Billy's. The scene thus ends by putting both men pretty much in the same position with respect to each other as the story begins: neither will make the first move. Dispensing with the extraneous material also strengthens the impression of fatalism that darkens the entire film. The very reluctance of either man to force the issue suggests an acceptance of that very destiny which no one can alter, and reinforces the almost Elizabethan sense of time in this film as both prime mover and final arbiter.

The second example is from the climax. However uneven a work *Pat Garrett and Billy the Kid* is, the whole last sequence is beautifully sustained and among Peckinpah's finest achievements. Yet the pow-

er of one small but important moment is diminished in the Turner/
preview by comparison to the theatrical version: Garrett's great cry
of "*Nooooooo!*" as Poe goes to cut off the Kid's trigger finger. At once
enraged protest and anguished denial, Garrett's scream feels like
something torn from his very viscera. But in the Turner/preview, after
the scream Garrett hisses, "What you want and what you get are two
different things." What is *this?* Well, one thing it may be, Michael
Sragow has suggested, is "a forced, pallid re-rendering" of Thornton's
"What I want and what I need are two different things" from *The Wild
Bunch.*[34] But to give Peckinpah, or maybe it was Coburn, the benefit
of the doubt, perhaps they did in the filming feel that Garrett should
say *something* here, so they shot it just in case. But as cut together, it's
pretty obvious that the prolonged "No!" really says it all and certainly doesn't need this bathetic homily (even Coburn's line reading is
unconvincing and suffers especially coming immediately upon the
supreme conviction of the scream).

It is always a risky business to speculate about what might have
been. But with *Pat Garrett and Billy the Kid,* it is unavoidable. As a final
example of the uncompleted state of this film, consider that between
them Peckinpah and the studio came up with at least four different
versions of the end titles, and each of them was eventually dubbed
and put into composite. The worst ending is unquestionably the one
in the theatrical version, a smiling two-shot of Pat and Billy from the
first Fort Sumner scene, which, Spottiswoode says, was personally
ordered by Aubrey over the protests of the director and the editors.
It is maudlin and works against the entire dramatic, thematic, and
psychological movement of the structure, which has been toward
disunity, dissolution, and decay. Another ending, also to the theatrical version, was seen in a print shown in the early 1980s at the University of Southern California: it dispenses with the two-shot and rolls
the credits instead over the image of Garrett disappearing into the
desert. A third ending, part of the Turner, reprises the murder as the
credits roll over a shot of the buggy wheel freezing just as the falling
Garrett clears frame. Still a fourth ending, to be seen only in the
preview print that was in Peckinpah's private collection, is identical
to the Turner except for a legend that Peckinpah personally wrote
and had superimposed on the freeze-frame at the top of the credit-
roll, informing us that Albert Fall defended Garrett's murderers, got
them acquitted, and then went on to become Secretary of the Interior in the Harding administration, where he was eventually involved
in the Teapot Dome scandal. The last line of the legend asks, "What
else is new?" and is signed by a symbol that resembles a figure on a

branding iron, ∕S, a combined S and P, which was how Peckinpah wrote his initials. This legend is happily out of the Turner laserdisc. But the reason Peckinpah tried it in the first place was by way of alluding to conspiracies in two administrations he despised, Aubrey's at MGM and Nixon's in the White House.* It was a sophomoric thing to do, that mostly just blemished the film. But it was a pretty clear indication of where his priorities were in the final stages of postproduction. It also suggests why the rubric "director's cut" must be applied cautiously, if at all, to any known version of the film.

Peckinpah's drinking and forcing those around him into you're-either-for-me-or-against-me positions were way out of control and the film suffers for it. Yet, paradoxically, both the drinking and the either/or extremism remain issues about which it is difficult to take a clear position: because in the end they do manage to find their way into the film where they function, however sporadically, with real artistic purpose. The urgency of Garrett's interior struggle between the two sides of his personality, which he cannot mediate and which results in death, is obviously related to and informed by the conflicts that were going on behind the camera between the director and his crew, the director and the studio, and the director and himself. About this last he was as explicit as he would ever get in a film (or, almost, in any other public utterance). When Garrett starts to walk away from the coffinmaker's shed, the director, now inside his film *as* the coffinmaker, shouts after him, "When are you going to learn you can't trust anybody, not even yourself, Garrett?"

Just before he starts to leave, Garrett offers the coffinmaker a drink, which is refused—an inside joke, as Peckinpah hardly ever turned down a drink. Yet more alcohol is consumed in this film than in any of his previous work, and one of the things the film embodies is that haze, that peculiar kind of edgelessness that alcohol induces and is in part consumed to induce. This is not to suggest that Peckinpah drank deliberately to get this effect; more than likely the drinking itself produced it. It hardly matters, as Peckinpah tended to work closer to his instincts, intuitions, and feelings than almost any other director. The previous criticisms of pace and performance notwith-

---

*All his life Peckinpah harbored a fierce animus toward Richard Nixon, and never forgave him the pardon of William Calley after My Lai. "It is not really the question of what he felt he should do," Peckinpah wrote in a telegram to the White House (4 Apr. 1971). "The fact is what he did and there is no form of patriotism to justify the wanton killing of women and children outside of Nazi Germany." He was also outraged over the pardon of Nixon, cabling President Ford that it was "a disgrace to the nation and to our system of law and order" (9 Sept. 1974).

standing, the distended rhythms, the utter lethargy with which everyone moves, the slowness with which they speak, the swollen pauses,
the faces that come wearily into focus before the replies, the overall
sense of drifting, of languor, apathy, and melancholy—over the course
of the film these gradually develop into a style and bring into focus
a vision that is unique and almost nakedly expressive of Peckinpah's
condition and state of mind at this time in his life.* This is why he
shot and included the long sequence involving the prostitutes. However ludicrous it looks, he had been there; and he meant *Pat Garrett,*
as film and as character, to be as scathingly honest a self-portrait as
he was capable of painting.

At times Peckinpah's identification with his protagonist was so intimate it frightened him. Sometime after *The Wild Bunch* he was given
the gift of a set of knives, which he took to throwing, mostly for theatrical effect, too often while drunk. When the shock value of the knives
wore off, he took to firing a pistol, which he carried around all the time
on the set of *Pat Garrett.* To the Mexicans this wasn't that big a deal, as
it is apparently fairly common there for men to fire guns, especially
when they're happy. But the American and English crew members were
not amused, were in fact often truly scared, and with good reason:
Peckinpah was seldom happy on this project. There were days off when
he never left his hacienda, staying in bed for hours on end, drinking
and shooting up the room. Once he was found "in bed with a half-
empty bottle of Vodka between his legs and a revolver in his hand,"
firing at his own reflection in a mirror.[35] When Coburn, who knew of
the incident, saw a mirror on the set, he immediately wanted to have
Garrett shoot at his reflection after killing the Kid. Peckinpah refused
and remained adamant throughout the rehearsal and all the next day.
It wasn't until the first night's actual filming that he relented and let
Coburn do as he wished. "That's what you want to do, isn't it?" Peckinpah asked, the presence of the mirror on the set in the first place
suggesting that the actor discovered what his director, perhaps only
subconsciously, put there to *be* discovered.

In this context, to say nothing of the broader one of Peckinpah's

---

*It is precisely this quality—that is, an embodiment in the very style of the narra-
tive of what it is like to be continuously drunk—that is absent from John Huston's
rather lame adaptation of *Under the Volcano.* Richard Burton, no stranger to the abuse
of alcohol, once told Peckinpah that if he ever directed *Under the Volcano,* he, Burton, would play the part of the consul for nothing. Hearing this, a friend wrote Peckinpah, "It should be directed by someone who's had that experience of having one
aim for several weeks at a time—getting another drink and who's woke up one morning wondering why he's still alive after a night in a cantina" (Joe Bernhard to Sam
Peckinpah, letter, 12 Jan. 1973 [Peckinpah Collection]).

subsequent life and career, the joke of refusing the drink is feeble indeed, and casting himself as a coffinmaker working on a child's coffin looks far more disturbing in retrospect than it appeared at the time. His identification with Garrett seems to indicate an awareness of his own self-destructiveness, identifying it as suicidal and admitting to helplessness in being able to halt its fated outcome. He then moves beyond his surrogate when he actually steps into the film and assumes a role that shows him on screen literally *directing* Garrett to go in and get it over with. Like the sheriff, he is killing the child in himself. But as the coffinmaker, he appears to be not just directing, but presiding over and positively hastening his own destruction. He is even, he seems to be saying, building the coffin—all of which begins to suggest pathology rather than art, and calls for analysis of a different sort.

If so, then Peckinpah's friend James Hamilton (who would do a rewrite on the *Cross of Iron* screenplay) diagnosed the illness: "That's the movie where, if you studied Sam's work, you knew that the game was over and that the fatigue and melancholy set in. It's one of the most fatigue-ridden movies ever made, you can feel it running off of the screen. But what Sam does is make all these wonderful images for the last time, like the wonderful death scene with Slim Pickens. Sam must have known: 'This is all I've got left.' He was finished with the genre."[36] It has been said that every scene in the film is a farewell scene. Quite a number surely are (we meet Paco when he's saying goodbye); and those that aren't often consist in leave takings of other kinds, usually dying (the film opens with the death of the Garrett). And the casting—someone once quipped that the film features every Western character-actor who ever lived—only reinforces the feeling of remorse and doom. Like Garrett, Peckinpah kills these people off one by one. Yet several of them are *his* people, and they are all reminiscent of the kinds of characters and presences he spent his entire career creating and building up. So it is difficult to escape the feeling that, also like Garrett, he would rather destroy his past than go on repeating it, leave it rather than sentimentalize it. This picture is the longest, saddest, most anguished goodbye from a director who was, Sragow has written, "the master of the long goodbye."[37] No wonder he was so wracked and tortured throughout its making.

A decade later Peckinpah wrote to a correspondent, "All I know is that someone once told me that nostalgia is the cancer of the soul."[38] To the end of his life there were several Western projects he worked on or otherwise talked about doing, but somehow they never came together. Perhaps he sensed that the exhaustion of *Pat Gar-*

rett and Billy the Kid was honestly come by because it was a hard-won and *expressed* exhaustion, articulated and almost heroically transformed into art—admittedly problematic art in some scenes, but the real right thing all the same. Not meretriciously nostalgic, but authentically elegiac, the film stands honorably as his last word on the genre that he was most closely associated with. It marks the end of a line that begins with a more or less realistic Western series about a likable cowboy, courses through romance, epic, and comedy, and here winds down into intrigue, betrayal, and murder.

From this perspective we can give Peckinpah's appearance as the coffinmaker just one more turn. Coming near the end and at a crucial juncture, it suggests that he was pulling away from a total identification with Garrett. He always believed he had other artistic lives to live, and some pretty accomplished non-Western films exist to prove it, including a couple that came after this one. For all his self-destructiveness, which didn't abate and in some respects got much worse, suicide was never really an option for him. Ten years earlier on *Major Dundee* Coburn wanted to know what it was about the title character that made Peckinpah want to do the film. The director's answer was a declaration, and it rang throughout the twenty years that were left him: "Because he continues. I mean through all the shit, through all the lies, through all the drunkenness and the bullshit that Major Dundee goes through, he survives and continues!"[39]

There was something indomitable at the very core of Sam Peckinpah's being. It was this something, or, rather, its extension or equivalent in his imagination, that—despite the flaws, mistakes, and weaknesses of *Pat Garrett and Billy the Kid*—managed to survive, intact and unbroken, the whole long, agonized year of fear, anger, booze, infighting, and desperate self-destructiveness. It is the thing that we call—imprecisely but exactly—vision, and it sweeps all before it. This is one of the few films, and perhaps the only Western film apart from *The Wild Bunch*, in which the effect of tragedy is felt and sustained. Yet *The Wild Bunch* is a triumphant tragedy, and it culminates in transfiguration and redemption. No such light illumines the bleak horizons of *Pat Garrett and Billy the Kid*. When the sun goes down on the dusky, godforsaken world of this Western, it seems also to go out, and the sense of finality is shattering.

I regard everything with irony, including the face I see
in the mirror when I wake up in the morning.
—Sam Peckinpah

8

The Masculine Principle in American Art and Expression

How much is there anyhow, to the young men of These States, in a parcel of helpless dandies, who can neither fight, work, shoot, ride, run, command—some of them devout, some quite insane, some castrated . . .—waited upon by waiters, putting not this land first, but always other lands first, talking of art, doing the most ridiculous things for fear of being called ridiculous, smirking and skipping along, continually taking off their hats—no one behaving, dressing, writing, talking, loving, out of any natural and manly tastes of his own, but each one looking cautiously to see how the rest behave, dress, write, talk, love . . .—favoring no poets, philosophs, literats here, but dog-like danglers at the heels of the poets, philosophs, literats, of enemies' lands—favoring mental expressions, models of gentlemen and ladies, social habitudes in These States, to grow up in sneaking defiance of the popular substratums of The States? . . . in the scanned lives of men and women most of them appear to have been for some time past of the neuter gender; and also the stinging fact [is] that in orthodox society today, if the dresses were changed, the men might easily pass for women and the women for men.
—Whitman to Emerson

Emerson never gave up deploring the want of male principle in our literature.
—F. O. Matthiessen

I

In 1836, ten years after being licensed to the ministry, a New England clergyman—thirty-three years of age, rather undistinguished academically, his chief claim to anything like fame being his appointment as minister of the prestigious Second Church in Boston (a tenure that ended with his controversial resignation) and a friendship with Carlyle after a trip to Europe—published a little book on and called *Nature*. In form the book was an essay, an attempt and exploration; in genre it belonged to what may be the first American literary genre after the travel sketch, the jeremiad. What all jeremiads, which were basically a kind of sermon, shared was an invidious comparison of the present by way of an invocation of the past.[1] It mattered little that the past most jeremiads invoked never existed except in the fancy—or, better still, the conscience—for the purpose of the sermon was to awaken listeners to the insufficiencies of the present by contrasting them to the glories of the past. The theme invariably engendered was that most ancient theme of religious literature, the fall from grace; and the corrective proffered was that most indigenously American of all reform correctives, instruction from example and inspiration rather than from dogma.

Ernest Hemingway once made the claim that "all modern American literature comes from one book by Mark Twain called *Huckleberry Finn*." He might have cited also or instead this "little" book by Emerson, which is perhaps the most comprehensive single statement we have of the general intents and purposes, the animating impulses and generating assumptions, of virtually every important American artist from Anne Bradstreet and Jonathan Edwards near the beginning to Norman Mailer and Sam Peckinpah in our own day. Hemingway might have cited in particular the question Emerson posed near the opening of the essay: "Why should not we also enjoy an original relationship to the universe?"

The more overt causes for the Transcendental Movement and for the larger revolt that contained it, the American Renaissance, are easy enough to identify. Several members of the then younger generation, with Emerson their first fully articulate spokesman, were disturbed by the commercialism of American society; were dissatisfied with the stultifying rationalism of Unitarianism, the religion of their elders, a religion once radical but by then already well ensconced among the wealthy and the well-to-do; and were equally dissatisfied with most forms of ritual, dogma, habit, and any other kind of intermediary that attempted to insert itself between the mind and a direct confrontation with the world. Rightly or wrongly, a great many American artists, including the most important ones, came to associate much of what was stultifying, prosaic, and materialistic in American culture with women, in youth the mother, in maturity the wife. We tend to think of the Victorian Age as confined largely to England, but Victoria ruled as strongly in America; and it isn't necessary to search very far in our literature to discover the full extent to which many of our artists established an opposition between themselves and wife and mother, however much they may have tried to veil, cloak, symbolize, or otherwise disguise their feelings by indirection or euphemism.

Writing about Cooper's Leatherstocking Tales, Leslie Fiedler identified the duplicity:

> The clue is here, the revelation that the very end of the pure love
> of male for male is to outwit woman, that is, to keep her from trap-
> ping the male through marriage into civilization and Christianity.
> The wilderness Eros is, in short, not merely an anti-cultural, but an
> anti-Christian, a Satanic Eros; and yet it is proffered by
> Cooper . . . and accepted by his readers as innocent. To believe this
> one must become as a boy, to whom neither sex nor violence is real,
> and to whom mother is the secret enemy, to be evaded even as she
> is loved.[2]

One good indication of just how extreme feminine gentility was
may be seen by looking at Sophia Peabody's editing of her husband
Nathaniel Hawthorne's journals after his death. As Frederick Crews
has pointed out:

> Wherever Hawthorne had expressed skepticism about marriage,
> womanhood, America, or Christianity, Sophia improved the text by
> deletion or revision. References to smoking and drinking were gen-
> erally suppressed, as were, of course, all passages of sexual inter-
> est. She could not admit the comparison of some pond lilies to "vir-
> gins of tainted fame," and still less could she allow posterity to learn
> of her forty-six-year-old husband's fancy, which had struck him while
> he was peering into the lighted window of a Boston boarding
> house, that a beautiful damsel might be disrobing within. Of great-
> er interest, because of greater imaginative subtlety, are many of
> Sophia's apparently trivial revisions of phrasing. For Hawthorne's
> "animal desires" she substituted "temperament"; for "baggage,"
> "luggage"; for "itch, "fancy"; for "vent," "utterance"; and for "caught
> an idea by the tail," "caught an idea by the skirts." This, I submit,
> is the work of a dirty mind.[3]

Hardly surprising, since, as Crews himself suggests, "in the age of the
draped piano leg," virtually everything "was covertly sexualized."
Meanwhile, Hawthorne's friend Melville, in one of his more puckish
tales, "I and My Chimney," posits his thinly disguised self as carrying
on a reverie with the grand, stately chimney in his house, the chimney that his wife wants torn down. At one point, contrasting his lazi-
ness with his wife's industriousness, the narrator remarks:

> No danger of my spouse dying of torpor. The longest night in the
> year I've known her lie awake, planning her next campaign for the
> morrow. She is a natural projector. The maxim, "Whatever is, is

right," is not hers. Her maxim is, Whatever is, is wrong; and what
is more, must be altered; and what is still more, must be altered
right away. Dreadful maxim for the wife of a dozy old dreamer like
me, who dotes on seventh days as days of rest, and, out of a sabbat-
ical horror of industry, will, on a week-day, go out of my road a
quarter of a mile, to avoid the sight of a man at work.

Melville may here have had in mind that grown-up child Rip Van
Winkle, who wandered off into the mountains and fell into his twen-
ty-year nap because he was evading an equally industrious wife who
wanted him to work and make money, while all he wanted to do was
hunt, fish, and walk the forests with his dog. (Irving's crowning touch,
designed to undercut the last vestiges of sympathy for the wife, is to
have Rip's dog be as terrified of her as Rip himself is.)

From Irving to Mark Twain, who substituted one Mrs. Clemens for
another, keeping himself yoked to gentility his whole life, yet fighting
it all the way in his writings (which, in turn, he allowed his wife to
edit). He recalls, for example, how his mother was so gentle that she
warmed the water before she drowned kittens. In a famous thesis, still
generally sound, Van Wyck Brooks has argued that the "ordeal" of
Mark Twain consisted precisely in the conflict between the values his
mother and later his wife believed in and the values that his experience and his imagination drew him toward.[4] Twain and Hawthorne
are not writers we might ordinarily think of comparing, but in the
influence their wives exerted upon their work we might find some
common ground—the conflict between the artist's (necessarily) rebellious imagination and the man's desperate need for approval from
his wife (who in turn is a synecdoche for the society at large). In both
cases the wives (and, alas, their husbands too) preferred the artists'
less impressive work. And then there is the case of Hemingway, of
whose rebellion Philip Young has written:

> It is hard to realize today how great was the *need* for rebellion—how
> preposterous were things *At the Hemingways*, the name of Marcel-
> line's affectionate book. Home was a Victorian matriarchy, and it
> has been said more than once that Hemingway was the only man
> in the world who really hated his mother. She had considerable pre-
> tensions to the arts; she sang, composed, and later painted. Her re-
> sponse to *The Sun Also Rises* was "I can't stand filth!" Her husband,
> though a busy doctor, kept house far more than she did. ("Dr.
> Hemingway did most of the cooking. He'd fix the kids' breakfast
> and then take the Mrs. her breakfast in bed.") She raised Ernest
> as closely as possible, as a twin, a twin girl, to Marcelline. They

looked alike, and were "dressed alike," his sister writes, in "ging-
ham dresses and in little fluffy lace-tucked dresses. . . . We wore our
hair exactly alike in bangs." (Harold Loeb, Robert Cohn in *The Sun
Also Rises,* traces the source of Hemingway's insistence on his masculinity to this. It was as if he were forever saying "Damn it, I'm
male.")[5]

If, then, a harsh, repressive gentility was the prevailing culture of
American society even well into the twentieth century, it is perhaps
little wonder that Emerson was given to lament the absence in American culture of a strong masculine principle, and even less wonder
that many of our artists in the nineteenth century are curiously schiz-
oid, or, to use the more up-to-date terminology, possessors of disso-
ciative personalities, mouthing genteel pieties yet creating works in
which there is, in Melville's words, a blackness ten times black. On
the one side they have, from figures of authority, teachings of home
and hearth, pieties of doing good and being good; on the other side
they see in the world around them so much that contradicts what they
have been taught to think and feel. Young Sam Clemens bore witness
to more poverty, hardship, and violence than he could comprehend;
Hemingway ran away from a suffocating middle-class home only to
fall into the horrors of the first modern war; Hawthorne, less mobile,
turned his sights inward and was equally horrified by what he saw, the
human heart, that "foul cavern," as he called it. The theme of innocence lost is old enough and common to the art and expression of
many countries, but in America it tends to be rendered with a bitterness and anger unparalleled elsewhere. This must have something to
do with an early education that, our artists feel, does not endeavor
to teach us much about the world we are going to find once we leave
home. "If it could only be like what they told us it would be like when
we were kids," Peckinpah once said.[6]

Now there are a lot of reasons why American society was like this,
and at their most sane and rational most of our artists, however much
they may identify women with a state of affairs they secretly detest,
rarely blame them for it. Moreover, Hawthorne and others implicated men in this state of affairs, too. If sickeningly sweet light-ladies-
as-saints-and-saviors are an all too recognizable type in our fiction and
films, then equally recognizable is the stern, severe, draconian patri-
arch to be seen in Hawthorne's judges, preachers, and scientists, who
survive still in characters like Peckinpah's Joshua Knudsen. At the end
of *The Scarlet Letter* Hester is left dreaming of "some brighter period"
to come when the whole relation between men and women would

be established on a surer ground of mutual happiness. And Haw-thorne himself once remarked, "We certainly do need a new revela-tion—a new system—for there seems to be no life in the old one."

Insofar as many of our artists can be said to be limited, it consists perhaps mostly in their failure to imagine what that new system might be. This could be called a failure of imagination and, less sympathet-ically, a failure of nerve; but it suggests as well a generalized failure in American culture and society to face realistically "the facts of life." What we get instead are expressions of dissatisfaction with the way things are; and when we get intimations of what they could be, they often take the form of the most idealized aspects of masculine cama-raderie (Natty and Chingachgook, Huck and Tom or Huck and Nig-ger Jim, Ike McCaslin and Sam Fathers, Steve Judd and Gil Westrum); or else they conjure up, as Hawthorne liked to, an Arcadian society (a mythic preserve still viable well into the twentieth century—for ex-ample, "The Last Good Country," an unfinished Hemingway story exhumed for the posthumously published *Nick Adams Stories,* which has Nick as a youngster on the lam from a game warden and fleeing with his sister into the woods, where the boy and the girl make a camp and play at being married). Whatever the complaint sounded or the vision proffered, all of these artists are revolting against the prevail-ing official culture, and the revolt usually consists in an escape from a place they don't like to someplace elsewhere.

That world elsewhere can take many forms: sometimes, as in our own century, it takes the form of Europe or simply of an outside, often metropolitan, world that exists beyond the local community (in *A Walker in the City* Alfred Kazin goes from Brooklyn to Manhattan, in *Look Homeward, Angel* Thomas Wolfe takes his autobiographical hero from small town to college and later to big city). In most instances, however, the artist's journey at least crosses through some kind of wilderness, and that also takes many forms: Emerson's strolls through the Concord countryside, where he could feel "the currents of be-ing" flowing through him; Thoreau's experiment at Walden Pond; Ike McCaslin's hunting trips; Nick Adams fishing in Michigan or Jake Barnes in the mountains of Spain with old Bill; Melville at sea; and Peckinpah returning to Mexico for "rest and refreshment."[7] What do they find beyond the frontier—or now, let us say simply, in nature? Emerson gives us the first clue when he says in *Nature* that to know nature is to know yourself, by which he means that there is a corre-spondence between what is found in nature and what can be found in the mind, the point of transcendence being to liberate yourself from the constrictions imposed by habit, routine, dogma, education, in other words, by society, so that the hidden self, the true self, buried beneath all that, can emerge. In his later work ("Experience," for example), Emerson supplants the concept of transcendence with an injunction to acquire broader and broader ranges of experience. But this is a less radical change than it might appear: early or late, Emerson recognized the necessity for shedding one self as a prerequisite for acquiring another self and thus preventing the atrophy of sensibility. The point in both cases is to get out and beyond.

Emerson's central idea, then, is ever to continue to get outside a limited frame of reference to a wider frame of reference, and every American writer after him took it up in one way or another. The ocean, for example, became Melville's in fact and in fiction; hunting and later Europe became Hemingway's, and, to some extent, Twain's and Crane's; Europe alone became Henry James's (and when he needed then a broader perspective on that he turned his sights once again to America). The necessity for a wider or higher perspective is to be seen, for example, in a book like *Adventures of Huckleberry Finn,* which remains our most trenchant attack upon American gentility and its mores. One of the beautiful ironies of the story is that Twain leaves Huck fully believing he will burn in hell for helping his friend Nigger Jim to escape—a scene that takes us to the very core of American conceptions of masculinity. Out in the wilderness or on the raft, away from civilization, Huck recognizes Jim for the friend he is, and the actual, palpable feeling of friendship undermines the abstract, moralistic teachings that are revealed as the real source of corruption.

In this sense, then, it is easy enough to understand why Hemingway said what he did about *Huckleberry Finn:* an abiding theme of his own work is the disparity between what he was taught and what he came to know through experience. The lesson ultimately is to derive values from experience, not to force them on experience, to test them in experience, not to expect experience to conform to them. This is more or less why Frederick Henry in *A Farewell to Arms* says, "Abstract words such as glory, honor, courage or hallow were obscene beside the concrete names of villages, the numbers of roads, the names of rivers, the numbers of regiments, and the dates." In *The Sun Also Rises* Jake Barnes is contemptuous of Robert Cohn because Cohn gets all his ideas from books. And in *Death in the Afternoon,* the first book in which Hemingway moves himself as self to center stage, he enunciates his famous credo: moral is what makes you feel good afterward and immoral is what makes you feel bad afterward. In the same section Hemingway identifies the three most difficult problems of writing as "knowing truly what you really felt, rather than what you were supposed to feel, and had been taught to feel"; putting "down what really happened in action," "what the actual things were which produced the emotion that you experienced"; and then finding "the real thing, the sequence of motion and fact which made the emotion." Hemingway went on to observe that when people "have learned to appreciate values through experience what they seek is honesty and true, not tricked, emotion and always classicism and the purity of execution." Near the beginning of *The Wild Bunch*, there is a seemingly innocuous line, spoken by an anonymous character, which goes, "It's not what you meant to do, it's what you did I don't like"—a line that is, in many ways, a paraphrase of Hemingway's credo. And Norman Mailer in *The Armies of the Night* says that what he learned from both Hemingway and Dwight Macdonald was to look to the feel of the phenomenon—if it feels bad, it is bad.[8] Which brings us full circle to the Emerson who advised men to trust their instincts: "the only right is what is after my constitution; the only wrong what is against it."

Women come to be identified, at least in the form of wife and mother, or, more generally, family, as the force that says no, that tries to make one suppress one's deepest feelings and substitute ersatz or false feelings. If in a single sentence one had to identify the masculine principle in American art and expression, it would be this: the insistence by the American artist that knowledge be gained absolutely firsthand, without any kind of mediation, to the end of having the courage to risk self-knowledge in the fullest sense. This risk-taking has several ramifications. First, it results in an art that is drawn to the extremes of experience, where our artists can find sufficient energy and action to break the strangleholds of habit and learned response and to reconstitute the self in some crucible of experience. Second, it results in an ethos in which the worst failure becomes synonymous with the failure to take on new experience, a failure associated with complacency, with conformity, and ultimately with death. That is what Mailer means when he says, "A man can hardly ever assume he has become a man—in the instant of such complacency he may be on the way to becoming less masculine";[9] and it is what Peckinpah had in mind when he described his heroes as "individuals looking for something besides security."[10] Third, in the rebellion against official culture, which says that the forbidden is bad and will lead to damnation, there is the sneaking suspicion that hell and damnation may not be all that bad. Hemingway must have had something like this in mind when, in one of his few humorous episodes, he has Nick Adams, who learned that Caruso was arrested for mashing, ask his father what mashing is. "'It is one of the most heinous of crimes,' his father answered. Nick's imagination pictured the great tenor doing something strange, bizarre, and heinous with a potato masher to a beautiful lady who looked like the pictures of Anna Held on the inside of cigar boxes. He resolved, with considerable horror, that when he was old enough he would try mashing at least once."

At the same time, however, our artists often find in their rebellion another damnation, far worse and more comprehensive than they had ever been led to expect: the damnation that is the loss of innocence, a loss that has fairly little to do with sexual initiation and mostly to do with violence. "In America violence is daily," Nathanael West once said. At the extremes of experience the American artist discovers more knowledge than he is prepared for. He discovers, as Huck Finn did, that what people are capable of doing to one another is enough to make a body sick of the damned human race; he discovers, as Nick Adams did, that courage doesn't come easy, and that he must drink and tighten his chin strap to keep his lips from trembling as he goes into battle; he discovers that nothing he learned at home, from mother or from defeated father, does him any good in dealing with the world. A greater irony still is his discovery that what Peckinpah has called "the worst of us" may have something far more useful to teach him than do the best of us. At least the worst seem to fight back, and they offer both a style of conduct and a set of codes, however limited, that help us to cope. Confronting life directly, which is what Emerson is urging when he counsels establishing an original relationship with the universe, means more than anything else that if everything you have been taught is false or a distortion, then what you are left with is self, and to find values you must create them out of some reservoir of character and personality that is formed at least in part by new experience. You are forced, in short, back upon your feelings; and feelings, however transitory they may be, do not lie. At any given moment, whether good or bad, they are the truest part of you. This is why Hemingway, in one of the make-believe "press conferences" in *Death in the Afternoon,* told the man who confessed to not liking bullfights that his response is okay but he can't have his money back—knowledge about himself is his reward. In "The White Negro" Mailer puts it this way: "Truth is not what one has felt yesterday or what one expects to feel tomorrow but rather truth is no more nor less than what one feels at each instant in the perpetual climax of the present."[11]

We find here in a different version the same idea that Emerson voiced when he advised filling up the present moment to the very brim. What Mailer has found in the masculine ethos—the life of the senses, of action and assertion—is a way of creating and opening up new possibilities for experience. The reason that both he and Peckinpah are drawn to the fringe areas of experience, to violence and sexuality, is simply that there and there alone they can find dramatized those moments of self-discovery, where the self is poised on what Mailer likes to call the existential edge—the edge between life and death. The issue for both these men is not between violence and nonviolence, but between personal violence, which contains redemptive possibilities, and impersonal, or state and mechanized, violence, which does not. The implicit dialectic is between conforming to a mechanized, bureaucratized society or else cutting oneself off and existing, in Mailer's words, "without roots, to set out on that uncharted journey with the rebellious imperatives of the self." Even the justification that Mailer uses is not different from that of Emerson, who in "Experience" said that death is at least the one reality that will not dodge us.

But death in our century, after the concentration camps and the bomb, means, as Mailer says, that "our collective condition is to live with instant death by atomic war, relatively quick death by the State as *l'univers concentrationnaire*, or with a slow death by conformity with every creative and rebellious instinct stifled." It was in the aftermath of the McCarthy period that Mailer wrote: "A stench of fear has come out of every pore of American life, and we suffer from a collective failure of nerve. The only courage, with rare exceptions, that we have been witness to, has been the isolated courage of isolated people." The hero becomes, then, the outlaw, the loner, the individualist. When Peckinpah was trying to explain his attraction to these types, he used a vocabulary not unlike Mailer's: "Look, unless you conform, give in completely, you're going to be alone in this world. But by giving in, you lose your independence as a human being."[12] And "I find color and vitality and meaning in the loser. The outcast is the individualist. I'm not concerned with Everyman. I see color, conflict, a wish for something better, in the man who strikes out for himself."[13] Similarly, when Mailer got around to explaining the "heart of Hip," he said that the courage of the Hipster "contains within itself . . . some glimpse of the necessity of life to become more than it has been."[14]

"That is," Emerson says, "every man believes that he has a greater possibility." Neither Mailer nor Peckinpah is content to define the self in terms of what it has already achieved, but in terms of what it has yet to achieve; and in the largest possible terms this translates into what it has yet to discover about itself. One of the most important sections of "The White Negro" is Mailer's conception of character as being not fixed but fluid. Hip, Mailer tells us, does not concern itself with whether men are good or bad; Hip assumes that they are good and bad as a matter of course and simply views each man as a collection of possibilities. What dominates character is context, and what in turn dominates context is the amount of energy available at each moment of conflict between self and society. Here it should be pointed out that for Mailer energy is more or less the equivalent to God, it is quite literally that influx of being which Emerson talks about. Events, contexts, and consequences make hash of good intentions, and what we find in this view of character is one of the most basic struggles that goes all the way back to the beginning of American life, the conflict between grace and works, between what one is and what one does, between piety and moralism. Character is thus not synonymous with action, but it is nevertheless revealed in action, and the emphasis is placed upon what one does as the only real way to discover who one is.

Mailer makes this explicit in several parts of *The Armies of the Night;* and it is implicit in Peckinpah's theme—seen first in *Ride the High Country,* continued in *Major Dundee,* and most fully developed in *The Wild Bunch*—of heroes obsessed with their own best image of themselves, repeatedly failing to live up to that image, and finally succeeding in one heroic assertion that they nevertheless stumble into almost by accident. The immersion into experience becomes a way of recreating oneself at any given moment, and it is what Mailer has in mind when he calls himself an existential man, by which he means a man who makes himself as he goes along. The preoccupation with violence is to be explained only in part by the enormity of the society against which the self is posited; the rest of it has to do with the difficulty of recreating a new self, the prerequisite being experiences violent, even apocalyptic, enough to destroy the old self and the old nervous system. Violence thus becomes a provisional means of creation, is seen as the prelude to spiritual and moral growth, and presupposes what Mailer calls a "literal faith in the creative possibilities of the human being." Similarly Peckinpah often talked about the necessity of releasing pent-up violence as the prerequisite for any kind of constructive use of the same energies.

It is difficult to say whether a preoccupation with violence springs from a preoccupation with death or simply leads to it. Whichever the case, Peckinpah was referring to Hemingway when he said: "What he did, he laid it out the way it was. He stood and looked it in the face."[15] "It" is death, about which Peckinpah has also said: "I suspect it's inevitable. I'm not afraid of it. What I am afraid of is stupid, useless, horrible death. An automobile accident. A violent death for no purpose."[16] Or, as Mailer puts it, dying "as a cipher in some vast statistical operation," a death "which could not follow with dignity as a possible consequence to serious actions we had chosen."[17] Given these terms—which is rebel and live or conform and die, Macomber's short happy life as opposed to Prufrock's long moribund one—it was perhaps inevitable that the metaphor these two artists should light upon to express their rebelliousness belongs to a dialectic about as old as our history, the dialectic between civilization and savagery. That dialectic is, of course, implicit in Peckinpah's use of the Western, while Mailer, characterizing his Hip outlaw and that outlaw's sphere of activity, called him "a frontiersman in the Wild West of American night life." Equally inevitable, given such terms, is their failure adequately to effect a satisfactory synthesis. But then in this they are not different from most of our artists, past or present, and the question we are forced to ask ourselves is this: in the dialectic between civilization and savagery, is it a failure of imagination on the part of our artists to conceive of civilization in terms other than those of an emasculated, devitalized domesticity on the one hand and a rapacious, materialistic technocracy on the other, or is it a failure of our entire society to give them other terms? Or are they all just sociopathic? If this last is the case, then even our more "civilized" artists like James, Kate Chopin, and Edith Wharton suffer from the same affliction, for in a very real sense they short-circuit the problem of synthesis with suicide, either actual or symbolic. When Isabel Archer elects duty over desire and stays in a lifeless marriage, it is not unlike Claire de Cintré in that convent at the end of The American; when Ellen Olenska in The Age of Innocence takes off for Europe without her lover, it is the equivalent to Hester Prynne living on the outskirts of Salem for the rest of her life; and when Edna Pontellier takes that swim in The Awakening, she literally kills herself.

But these are all just so many forms of suicide and serve to remind us that the status of misfits, loners, and rebels both in our art and in our society is often that of pariahs. Inasmuch as this implies a rejection of our most indigenous hero—the frontier scout or westerner—and our most alluring heroine—the dark woman—it symbolizes our rejection as well of the wild, the natural, and the erotic. For the official culture there is a wilderness to be tamed, an economy to get started, and a society to get organized. Part of the method involves a suppression of all that is potentially destructive of those goals. But Emerson, anticipating Freud, enunciated the great law of compensation; and we have only to look to our finest products of art and expression to see the psychic consequences of "sublimation." In this sense one of the things that separates the work of many important twentieth-century American artists—Hemingway, Faulkner, Williams, Crane, Mailer, Huston, and Peckinpah—from their nineteenth-century forebears is that their work is no longer duplicitous in the way Hawthorne's could be or ironic in quite the way Melville might have had in mind when he said of *Moby-Dick*, "I have written a wicked book, and feel spotless as the lamb." It no longer embodies what Frederick Crews has described as that method of compromise, euphemism, and innuendo by which a Hawthorne could preach official pieties and undermine them at the same time, that "intricately developed vocabulary of high motives and moral comforts to clothe latently titillating situations."[18]

What happens in our century, beginning with Dreiser and Hemingway, is that the tension between official and unofficial is no longer latent, and the artist's attraction for the latter is undisguised. With the attitudes no longer duplicitous, the vocabulary is no longer duplicitous, and the sense of rebellion is open and scathingly candid. As a consequence there is a resurrection of the romantic impulse, a renewed attention to the problem of the one and the many, and an art and expression driven ever further to extremes and fringe areas of experience and sensation. The works themselves appear to be less controlled mostly because, in the absence of externally imposed restraints (that is, genteel proprieties), they are volatile and explosive. The exploration of new states of feeling, awareness, and consciousness is unimpeded by the necessity to sprout what Hawthorne calls "sweet moral blossoms," and the call of wild and wilderness, the lure of the savage, is answered unashamedly, indeed enthusiastically and without apology. At the same time, however, there is a new moral imperative toward self-restraint (there being no other kind save conformity to a lifeless technocracy); and the search for what Mailer calls a new nervous system goes hand in hand with what Peckinpah called "the old cry for identity and purpose."[19] This quest is the twentieth-century equivalent to Emerson's retreat to nature in search of the self, but now the villain that Emerson called society is much larger, more inclusive, and by several orders of magnitude more powerful—just how powerful and how deadly Hemingway was among the first to realize when he had Nick Adams and Frederick Henry, after their respective woundings, declare "a separate peace." Given, then, such a quest in such a world, it is little wonder that Mailer found in Hemingway's "categorical imperative" of "The Good" the "viable philosophy" that fitted most of the facts of the Hipster's life;[20] or that Peckinpah, more laconically, should have said of Hemingway, "That man was my bible."[21]

II

According to D. H. Lawrence, one of the reasons there is so much violence and terror in American literature is that the country began old, began European, and then became progressively younger, in the process shedding an old identity and acquiring a new one. People came to America, Lawrence tells us, for two reasons: "1) To slough the old European consciousness completely. 2) To grow a new skin underneath, a new form. This second is a hidden process."[22] In our century, as we have seen, the process is no longer so hidden, but it nevertheless remains difficult enough to need "a real desperate recklessness to burst your old skin at last. You simply don't care what happens to you, if you rip yourself in two, so long as you do get out." That desperate need to get out, start anew, see for oneself is where the rebellion originates. From this perspective it is relatively easy to account for the so-called "cult of masculinity" that one finds in American culture, even at the highest levels. Europe was conceived not only as old but as somehow feminine; to the extent that official American society was seen as Europeanized, that was only further evidence of our culture's essential emasculation.

It follows that if one is rebelling against a society seen as feminine, then one's rebellion, almost as a matter of course, is going to take a masculine form (and too that one's associates are likely to be other men, hence the theme of masculine camaraderie so prevalent in our fiction and films). Nor did our society have to await the bomb or McCarthy to begin to reek of that stench of fear Mailer identifies, and Peckinpah was far from the first to place his faith in the solitary human being. As in so much else, Emerson got there before anyone else and in his famous address of 1837 to the Harvard College Phi Beta Kappa Society articulated most of the concerns, sometimes in more or less the same terms, of later artists: "We have listened too long to the courtly muses of Europe. The spirit of the American freeman is already suspected to be timid, imitative, tame. Public and private avarice make the air we breathe thick and fat. The scholar is decent, indolent, complacent." Timid, imitative, tame, decent, indolent, complacent. It takes no great powers of divination to infer that Emerson is here calling upon the American people and the American scholar, as he would later call upon the American poet, to develop exact-

ly the opposite qualities and to make themselves courageous, original, wild, subversive, active, and enthusiastic. Some of these virtues
are, of course, traditionally masculine virtues, being derived from the
martial arts. If Emerson's invocation of them tends to be rather more
"metaphoric" than that of some later artists who have been drawn to
them, his message is still the same and equally urgent: let "the single
man plant himself indomitably upon his instincts and there abide,"
until "the huge world will come round to him." For, after all, "it is
not the chief disgrace in the world, not to be an unit."

The artistic revolt in America has thus always been masculine in
character, with its emphasis on hardness, clarity, simplicity, boldness,
difficulty, exploration, independence, and rebelliousness. Such an
aesthetics reaches its culmination in Charles Ives, who, writing in the
teens of this century, when gentility was in its prime and about ready
for collapse, defined the enemies of art as the "ladies," the "sissies,"
and the "conservatives." Ives provides another clue for the cult of
masculinity and its attractiveness: the relationship in America between
the arts and women. Women not only represented gentility, but they
cultivated the arts, and so in rebelling against the official culture an
artist is necessarily going to find himself betraying or at least suppress-
ing some of his deepest leanings toward art and expression. That is
a contradiction bound to confuse anyone, especially a young boy
growing up and searching for models and modes of behavior. Hemingway's extreme insistence upon his masculinity must have had at
least part of its origin in that contradiction, for this mother, whom
he hated, was the artist figure in his family, while his father (however meek or emasculated Hemingway may have considered him)
taught him how to hunt and fish. This pattern was paralleled to an
amazing degree in the Peckinpah household, and with predictably
similar consequences for the son who became the artist.

Richard Poirier has speculated that Norman Mailer's selection of
masculine topics is a compensation for what Mailer regards as a basically feminine exercise—writing itself.[23] Peckinpah too appears
locked into this dialectic, at least to judge from remarks like the one
he made after MGM had mutilated *Pat Garrett and Billy the Kid*—"They
maimed my baby."[24] When Peckinpah took to calling himself a good
whore who goes where she's kicked, what he was really trying to say
is what it felt like to work for the kinds of people and institutions
wealthy enough to finance films. He was also referring to the number of times his films have suffered at the hands of the moneymen.
His metaphor allowed him at once to preserve his feminine identity
as an artist yet to affect a masculine toughness of attitude that seemed

to be his way of saying, "So you ruined the picture, you really haven't hurt *me*, it was only a *job*." Privately he was hurt very much indeed, as remarks like this suggest: "Before I started on *Straw Dogs*, I had five pictures in the can, not one of which was visible anywhere in this country either at all or in anything like the form I wanted it to be in. What I'd done had been butchered or thrown away."[25] It was Hemingway who showed us how an excessive display of one characteristic can be compensation for an equal and opposing feeling of another characteristic, how the hero's outward reserve, even callousness, is only a front adopted precisely to protect himself from his own sensitivity and fear of further hurt and betrayal. That sense of hurt and betrayal is one of Peckinpah's themes, and it helps to explain why, in interviews and public appearances, he felt compelled to take on the characteristics of the worst of us. At some level it was his way of protecting himself, of defending the best of us that lies within. This too is a theme that Mailer cultivates in what Poirier calls his "resolute practice . . . to find in the apparent majority the characteristics of a minority."[26]

The problem of women, then, who and what they are and represent, becomes considerably more complicated, for even as they may be seen as the secret enemy, they are also associated with what the artist in his rebellion himself associates with—the wilderness in particular, artistic activity and creativity in general. It is not for nothing that Natty Bumppo identifies the forest as his lover, or that Ike McCaslin, his marriage failed, takes the wilderness as his mistress and his wife. Our artists' attitudes toward women are divided and varied and so are their attitudes toward men and masculinity. If the powerful allure of the virgin land is evoked in imagery that is frankly erotic, then it is usually the worst form of masculinity—controlling, heartless, brutal, greedy—that is seen to be destroying that landscape. Technology is always associated with masculinity—Ishmael Bush and his axes, the bulldozer in *Junior Bonner*, the train in "The Bear"—and is drawn in imagery that often suggests rape. Attitudes this divided help, in turn, to explain why we often find several contrasting male types in our fiction and films. For example, there is a heroic figure like Natty, Sam Fathers, Steve Judd, or Pike Bishop, who is tall, silent, moral, tragic, solemn, and restrained; and against him are juxtaposed other figures, like Ishmael Bush, Boon Hogganbeck, the Hammond brothers, and Harrigan, who represent a more extreme, obsessive, single-minded kind of masculinity that knows none of the checks and balances, none of the reverence and dignity, none of the grace and sensitivity of the heroes.

The biggest mistake that most critics make in treating the cult of masculinity in American art and expression is failing to see that it doesn't exist as some sort of block conception that is undifferentiated from artist to artist or from work to work by the same artist. Whatever the reasons, the fact remains that Mark Twain was impelled to create not just Huck Finn but Tom Sawyer and Pap, Hemingway to create not just the Hemingway Hero but the Code Hero, Cooper to create not just Natty Bumppo but Ishmael Bush, Hawthorne not just Dimmesdale but Chillingworth, and Peckinpah not just Pike and Thornton but Harrigan and Mapache. Contrasting characters like these—and they just begin to suggest how richly varied, stratified, and ramified are the conceptions of masculinity in our fiction—serve to remind us of the artist's divided loyalties, conflicting attitudes, and doubts and ambivalences. They also serve to remind us that the so-called ideal life of men without women is everywhere seriously qualified, and that what it often signifies is men without grace, sensibility, and compassion.

When Perry Miller once tried to establish a connection between Jonathan Edwards and Emerson, he said that the latter might be defined as the former without the concept of original sin. But that didn't really satisfy Miller, because, "true though it be," it "leaves out the basic continuance: the incessant drive of the Puritan to learn how, and how most ecstatically, he can hold any sort of communion with the environing wilderness."[27] Though the line from Edwards to Emerson to Hemingway, Mailer, and Peckinpah is apt to seem rather thin, it has been said more than once and by many that we remain as a nation sons and daughters of the Puritans, many of whom began as reformers and ended as pioneers and explorers. Peckinpah was shaped by both strains, for if he can be said to know anything, it is the Bible and the wilderness: "We were always close to the mountains, always going back to them. When my grandfather was dying, almost his last words were about the mountains. We'd summer in them and some winters I ran trap lines in the snow. We loved that country, all of us."[28] Given his feelings in this regard, one may wonder why Peckinpah should have chosen Hemingway as his spiritual father instead of, say, Faulkner, whom as an artist he resembles (temperamentally and aesthetically) to a far greater degree, and whose *Go Down, Moses* would seem to have had more to say to him? Better to approach that question by way of another: what are we to think of a man who, following Emerson's counsel, makes an errand into the wilderness where in discovering nature he discovers himself only to be scared to death by what he sees?

In their different ways Hawthorne and Melville were at times almost shrill in trying to warn Emerson that this sort of thing was bound
to happen, that an ecstasy of communion with the wild can all too
easily become a mania of unrestraint. Hemingway discovered much
the same thing in his exposures to violence. Originally he was terrified
and revulsed, but in summoning forth the courage to "look it in the
face," he eventually came to develop a peculiar kind of love affair with
it until, in *Death in the Afternoon,* he aestheticized, codified, and glorified it. It is clear enough that what Peckinpah and Mailer drew from
Hemingway is both a style of conduct and a code ("grace under pressure," quoted by both of them on many occasions) designed to allow
them to face the most horrifying aspects of self without going crazy.
They learned too how style can impose order and how restraint can
and must originate from within. But also like Hemingway, they began to fall a little bit in love with all the violence. Freud once said,
"No one who, like me, conjures up the most evil of those half-tamed
demons that inhabit the human breast, and seeks to wrestle with
them, can expect to come through the struggle unscathed." This is
a theme worthy of tragedy: the man who fights corruption only to
become corrupted by it. In America, however, it seems to have a new
twist, for our artists begin to be rather protective of their pathology,
to court it, to preserve it, to anticipate wrestling with it again and
again.

"I wanted to show the motion-picture audiences a mirror into their
own insides," Peckinpah said of *The Wild Bunch;* but later on he added an important qualification: "I'm defining my own problems; obviously I'm up on the screen. In a film, you lay yourself out, whoever
you are. The one nice thing is that my own problems seem to involve
other people as well."[29] But if they really are problems, why not try
to cure them? When asked if he would take the road to peace and
salvation if someone indicated the way, Peckinpah replied, "No. In
my family we kill our own dogs."[30] This sounds like the Hemingway
who said that he didn't need a psychiatrist because he had his type-
writer, and like the Mailer who, for all his talk about God and the
Devil and his own private demons, makes psychoanalysis one of the
Hipster's enemies. The Hipster is searching for the apocalyptic or-
gasm (which Mailer evokes in terms that recall Emerson's widening
circles of being), while the shrink—never has the epithet been so
appropriate—is only an "educated ball-shrinker who diagnoses all joys
not his own as too puny."[31] Mailer may actually believe that, but it is
difficult to escape the feeling that he is being a little self-serving too,

especially when, as in *The Armies of the Night,* he tells us how hard he
worked to conquer the nice, modest Jewish boy in him and become
the confident, strutting, aggressive egoist that is his legend. He likes
his legend, worked hard for it, and is loathe to give it up.[32]

But this is not to derogate from Mailer. Like any artist he has a
personal mythology that he believes in and from which he works. But
when a personal mythology appears over and over again in the works
of artists who belong to the same country, we may wonder if we
haven't discovered a significant pattern. Few people were more
amazed or horrified by the demons his imagination called forth than
Hawthorne himself was. He could never understand how he of all
people could have written so "hell-fired" a book as *The Scarlet Letter,*
and he used to speak of his tales and sketches as "blasted." It was,
however, this same Hawthorne who turned to his terrible Puritan
ancestors because he didn't find a great deal to interest him in contemporary Salem. D. H. Lawrence spotted the duplicity, and remarked of the end of *The House of the Seven Gables:* "Oh Nathaniel,
you savage ironist! Ugh, how you'd have hated it if you'd had nothing but the prosperous, 'dear' young couple to write about! If you'd
lived to the day when America was nothing but a Main Street."[33] Similarly, James went to Europe because America was too provincial to
write about, Faulkner locked himself up in a gothic South, and in our
own day Mailer courts the life of crime and Peckinpah made films
about a Western past.

There is in American art and expression a fascination—bordering,
some might argue, on the pathological—with the exotic, the foreign,
the criminal, and the wild. This fascination in turn results in a fiction
that rarely moves very far from escapist genres. The reasons our artists give for this fascination almost always reduce to the same one
when we cut through the rhetoric of individualism and freedom: the
insufficiency of mainstream American life to vitalize the imagination.
Dig deep enough and we find a common ground where the unlikeliest of companions join hands, a Melville with an Emerson, a Twain
with a James, even a Dreiser with a Howells. For what in their various ways a Hawthorne or a Mailer or a Peckinpah is saying is not quite
that he doesn't want to be cured—else why keep working, turning out
books or films?—but that he is afraid of being cured. What they are
telling us is something at once sadder and more appalling about
American life than any of the didactic novelists like John Steinbeck,
dramatists like Arthur Miller, or filmmakers like Oliver Stone are
telling us. They are saying that Main Street is so boring, stultifying,

and unexciting that if their personal problems were cured their imaginations would be left with nothing to feed on and their creativity would as a consequence quite literally starve. The most hell-fired demons, the most savage and ruthless killers, the most dreaded underworlds of crime and corruption are, it would seem, preferable to Main Street. This, more than anything else, is what Peckinpah and Mailer may at the deepest level have recognized in Hemingway, which is also what Philip Young discovered when he got around to asking himself what Hemingway conspicuously left out of the Nick Adams stories. "The answer," Young said, "is so obvious that it might never dawn on us": Oak Park, Hemingway's and Nick's middle-class home.

> Almost nothing Hemingway ever wrote could be set in Oak Park; it is extremely doubtful that he could have written a "wonderful novel" about the place. What he could write about happens "out there"—an exact equivalent for what, departing "sivilization" for the last time, Huck called "the territory."
>
> In the overall adventure, life becomes an escape to reality. No reward whatever is promised, and the cost in comfort and security is high. Out there can kill you, and nearly did. But it beats "home," which is a meaner death, as Ernest tried to tell Marcelline.[34]

Or, for that matter, as Elsa tried to tell her father in *Ride the High Country*.

The underlying theme is the theme of education, not sentimental, nor yet academic, though along the way it might involve both, but personal and therefore almost by definition quite original. In Peckinpah it acquires an added poignance, because his heroes are usually older men who, like Steve and Gil or Pike or Tyreen, still have something to learn and still act upon the influx of new experience, converting it into principle, though the cost may be, as it so often is, death. Inasmuch too as this education takes from time to time the form of what has been called the cult of masculinity, it is a cult that Peckinpah applies indiscriminately—or should we say, "democratically?"—to men and women alike. Of the films that Peckinpah made beginning with *Straw Dogs*, four have women as central characters, and in at least two (*Straw Dogs* and *The Getaway*), he ran them through an initiation process as ruthless as that of the men. When he found in them a courage equally worthy of admiration, he didn't hesitate to grant it. In this sense, then, "masculinity," as a code and as a conduct, exists for him, as for our best artists who have been attracted to it, as a kind of metaphor for dealing with a world that Hemingway called *nada* and that we tend to find simply absurd. And the bedrock injunction of this metaphor, despite the limitations necessarily imposed by the terms, is to pursue experience to the furthest frontiers of feeling, where feeling itself comes to be seen as revealed truth and the domain is that of self-discovery and moral necessity.

I detest machines. The problem started when they discovered the wheel. You're not going to tell me the camera is a machine; it is the most marvelous piece of divinity ever created.
—Sam Peckinpah

9
World of Our Fathers:
An American Artist and
His Traditions

David Weddle: You know, Peckinpah had a tendency to exaggerate.
   He didn't always tell—

James Dickey: What you're saying is that the man was a hell of a liar.
   Well, I like that. He was a man of imagination. He *should* have
   been a good liar!

I

It is now fairly well known that Sam Peckinpah overstated his actual
experience of the Old West. Most artists who reach celebrity status
do a certain amount of making themselves up as they go along, including rewriting history to suit their persona of the moment. Peckinpah was no exception. He may have been strapped in a saddle at
the age of two for a ride up into the high country, as he liked to claim,
but he never visited Coarsegold while it was a functioning mining
town. He was not part Indian, although he did have an *adopted* great
Aunt Jane who was half Sierra Mono (the other half was German).
And though he worked his grandfather's ranch many a summer and
could ride adequately, he was only at best a competent cowhand, and
never aspired to becoming a better one.

But when all the facts are said and the corrections done, we may
wonder if they've really told us much as they seemed at first to promise. Perhaps the artist himself, with his half-truths and semi-fictions,
even his "lies," brings us closer after all to the truth about his imagination and his art than any neat sorting and careful accounting of
the facts. For Peckinpah was truly a westerner, in his very bones and
marrow. If it is argued that he grew up mostly in town without spending all that much time leading a cowboy's life, then that is to miss the
point that the Western experience, especially as it is refracted into
works of art, is by its very essence fleeting. And if Peckinpah came

along almost too late to see even the end of Old West, merely the ends of some lives that were once part of it, well, that too is in the nature of the very idea of the frontier. It was a time that, measured against the vast expanse of time, existed only for an instant, and seemed the stuff of memory, fiction, and myth even as it was going on. It is little wonder that in the critical literature on the Western film, perhaps the single most epigraphed line is the newspaperman's observation in John Ford's *The Man Who Shot Liberty Valance:* "When the legend becomes fact, print the legend."

The ancestors on both sides of Peckinpah's family were pioneers. The name first turns up in America in Uniontown, Pennsylvania, where a farmer, George Peter Peckinpaugh, as it was then spelled, settled with his family in the late eighteenth century, having emigrated from the Rhine Valley in Germany. (The name is a derivation from "Beckenbaugh," and some forty-six different variants have been traced.) Within two generations the family had moved through Kentucky (in the wake of Daniel Boone) and Indiana into Illinois, where Thadius Rice (the director's great grandfather) and his wife Elizabeth settled in Mercer County in 1841.[1] They too raised crops and dairy cattle, and a brood that eventually numbered fourteen. One day Rice decided the family name used too much ink, so he shortened it to its present spelling, which also preserved the original pronunciation. In the spring of 1853 the family pulled up stakes and headed west along the Central Overland Trail in wagons drawn by oxen. This was early enough for them to have come across the great herds of buffalo that still roamed the plains, and they also encountered several different Indian tribes, all friendly. Apparently the only hostile encounter came when the wagonmaster of a larger train ordered the Peckinpahs off an attractive campsite beside a river in Nevada. Rice held his ground, and the dispute was soon settled with fists, and then some. The wagonmaster was having the better of it when Rice's eleven-year-old daughter jumped on his opponent's back and started pulling at the man's handlebar mustache, all the while yelling for her brother to run for the bullwhip. When the boy returned, the wagonmaster was persuaded that there were probably easier folks to push around than the Peckinpahs and cleared out.

The family entered California through the Beckwourth Pass in October 1853, six months and 2,500 miles from whence they started. They continued west until they reached the Pacific Ocean off Bodega Bay, near where they soon settled on a farm. The four youngest children went to school, while the older ones scattered and took up various trades: cook, printer, seamstress, harnessmaker, gunsmith, policeman, schoolmaster. One of them, John William, a self-taught dentist, must have been a distant model for the Rifleman. Born deaf and with a speech impediment, he made himself so expert a marksman that in competitions he would often handicap himself by holding his rifle upside down or holding it upside down over his shoulder as he looked at the target in a mirror (no matter how he shot, most of the time he hit the bullseye).

When Charles Mortimer, the twelfth born and eighth son (and the director's grandfather), finished school he went north to Humboldt County and with his brothers opened a sawmill, which was quite successful until the lumber famine of the 1870s drove him into bankruptcy. Charley apprenticed himself to a wagonmaker, built two wagons, borrowed some cash to buy a good team of horses, and in 1875 headed for the borax fields in Death Valley. He rented his wagons out while he himself worked as a carpenter. Within eighteen months he was made a foreman and over the next several years managed to save enough money to pay off his debts. He moved to the Fresno area in 1883 where, with his brother Edgar, he built the Peckinpah Lumber Company on a mountain in the foothills of the Sierra that was soon to be known as Peckinpah Mountain (it still is). They also built a cabin each to live in and to establish ownership of their land claims. By 1885 the mill was turning out over a million board feet of sugar pine a year.

A successful entrepreneur once again, Charley, then forty-two, decided he wanted a wife and family. In San Francisco he had met and courted Isobel Toner, a young Catholic from County Tyrone. They must have made a curious couple: Belle, as she was aptly called, a beautiful city girl in lace and crinoline, and Charley over twenty years older, a logger and a packer with a glass eye (from a timber accident). For all his lack of refinement, however, Charley was a splendid dancer and a self-taught musician, as was Belle. He was also an ardent and solicitous lover, his letters to her beautifully written, very romantic and even rather poetic (as would be those of both his son, David, and David's son, Sam, to their respective wives). Charley figured Belle would not want to leave San Francisco, but was surprised to discover that a life in the mountains very much intrigued her.

They were married in 1890 and headed for Peckinpah Mountain. On the third night of their trip Belle had an experience that her grandson almost certainly drew upon for the wedding-night sequence in *Ride the High Country*. The newlyweds were forced to stop for repairs in Fine Gold. The only room they could find was a lean-to adjoining the local saloon. The common wall had cracks so large that Charley could have thrown his hat through some of them. "I have heard my mother tell us many times about that night," wrote Mort, the couple's oldest son.

> How afraid, actually scared and nervous she was all night long. She would tell how rough the bed was and she could not get to sleep, her Charley was mixing with the men and leaving her alone. . . . She told us how she would peek through the cracks from her bed and watch those ugly old timers, miners and lumberjacks and long line skinners drinking their whiskey and raising old Ned until long after midnight. . . . Charley came to bed around midnight and went right to sleep. . . . Father admitted that it was a tough ordeal that could not be helped.[2]

That seems to have been the worst of it. Home on Peckinpah Mountain turned out to be a brand new log cabin with large rooms, sealed with new lumber, and furnished with new hand-made furniture. The couple eventually had three children: Edgar Mortimer ("Mort"), David Edward (Sam's father), and Charles Lincoln. Later they also adopted two Indian girls, Jane Visher and Lena Long (both were mixed-blood) and raised them as sisters to their sons. The Peckinpah boys grew up with Indians all around them. Out of thirty students at the local grammar school, three were white, the rest Indian—"some of whom," Mort said, "turned out to be our playmates and lifelong friends": "we had to learn to talk the Indian language and fight Indian style."[3]

Charley and his brother had ten good years of logging before another timber famine forced them to sell the company in 1903. With the proceeds Charley built a general store, with a dance hall upstairs, in South Fork, where in 1900 he had already bought some property and moved the family so that the children would have a place to go to school. A few years later, at Belle's urging, they moved to Fresno, so that the children would get a better high school education.

Fresno was the Churches' town. The first in the area was Moses J. Church, whose family was also from Pennsylvania. He and his wife left for California a year earlier than the Peckinpahs and traveled along much of the same route. Moses was something of a jack-of-all trades, "medicine show huckster, blacksmith, and self-taught engineer who supervised the construction of cotton and paper mills."[4] He acquired a reputation as a canal builder after designing a system of irrigation ditches for some miners and farmers in Diamond Springs, and was invited by a land speculator and developer named A. Y. Easterly to come to Fresno to plant wheat and irrigate the grain fields.[5] Moses and his family arrived in 1868 with some two thousand head of sheep and were promptly driven off their land. In an incident that almost a century later inspired the "Home Ranch" episode on *The Rifleman,* they watched helpless as the most powerful of the local cattleman, William "Yank" Hazelton, burned their house, tore down their corral, and scattered their herd. Church moved his family down to the flats and rebuilt his sheep ranch on government land. Surveying the area, he realized that water could be brought in from the nearby Kings River into the dry Fancher Creek, from which the entire flatlands could be irrigated. Before long Moses had got himself appointed deputy land agent with the responsibility of recruiting new farmers into the area. When Yank Hazelton stampeded his cattle over the new crops, Moses fought for legislation to fence off the fields with barbed wire. The cattlemen tried four times to assassinate him, but he never wavered in his resolve. The farmers won. By the 1880s Moses, then a promoter as well as an engineer, had engineered over a thousand miles of canals, which for a time constituted the largest irrigation system in the world. A plaque commemorating his accomplishments is on the office building of the Fresno Irrigation District.

In 1875 Moses took in his thirteen-year-old nephew, Denver Samuel Church (the director's maternal grandfather). The boy's family was dirt poor; he had been born in a cave near Folsom and when he was three lost both his mother and his sister to tuberculosis. By the time his uncle took him in he had already learned hunting and tracking from his father and was an expert shot. He also displayed an extraordinary memory and a gift for oratory, both of which he put to effective use at the Seventh Day Adventist meetings he attended with his uncle's family. An aptitude for drama, however parallel the field, clearly ran in the genes. After an attempt at a medical career, Denver became a lawyer in 1895. He had married Louise Derrick, a schoolteacher, and they had three children: Earle, Fern Louise (the director's mother), and another son whom they named after his father. When Denver developed a cough he couldn't shake, he became convinced he was the next victim to the family illness. Thinking fresh air would help him, he traveled to Salt Lake City, where his family joined him within the year. The cough turned out to be a false alarm, but in 1898, a year after the family had joined him, the baby boy succumbed to the illness. The couple buried him in Salt Lake; no more sons were born to them. Perhaps that is one reason why they so readily took to their daughter's first born—that and the boy's name, Denver, after his grandfather, but also the name of the infant Denver and Louise had lost in Utah.

Denver and his family left Salt Lake and traveled as far north as

Montana, living out of their wagon and selling potato peelers and other kitchen utensils before coming back to Fresno. (It was while they were itinerant that they met Calamity Jane, described by the director's grandmother as a "dirty drunken woman" who "smelled bad," and "your grandfather spent too much time with her!")[6] In less than a year Denver was aboard a ship ready to depart for Alaska and the latest gold rush. Sitting in his cabin late at night, the ship set to leave at four the next morning, he was delivered a message from his wife: the district attorney had finally responded to his application and the position of assistant district attorney was Denver's if he still wanted it. Denver disembarked and entered his lifelong career in the legal profession: assistant district attorney, district attorney, lawyer, judge, and congressman. But in his heart he was still a nineteenth-century backwoodsman and would-be cattle baron. He bought a ranch from an Indian named Dunlap, and over the years added to it until he owned 4,100 acres situated near Bass Lake and the Crane Valley in the foothills of the Sierra, within a few miles of the mountain named after the family who would soon be his in-laws.

On 21 February 1925 David Samuel Peckinpah was born to David and Fern Peckinpah.[7] He grew up in a middle-class suburb of Fresno called Clovis. Though not wealthy, the family was quite well off. Sam never wanted for anything material. He was known as a "spoiled kid," but the rubric does not seem to have been applied hostilely. Coming from a prestigious, financially secure family, it was assumed as a matter of course that he got what he wanted. He was among the best dressed kids in high school, and even had his own car (very unusual for the time). The family hardly felt the effects of the Depression. Toward the end of it they built a new house, which became a Fresno landmark: over four thousand square feet, a good ten years ahead of its time in design and construction, with hand-hewn beam ceilings, pumice-stone walls, ceramic floor-tiles, an indoor fountain, and three fireplaces made from stone gathered from the creek bed near the family's cabin in Bass Lake.[8]* But though David provided for his family and was generous, he did not display his wealth conspicuously (the home was a model of understated elegance and the use of plain native materials). "Why don't you buy a Cadillac?" his daughter Fern Lea once demanded of her father, who replied, "It would be throwing my wealth around and putting on the dog, and that's not something I do."[9]

*The home was torn down to make room for a commercial complex—a year after Peckinpah finished *Junior Bonner*, in which the title character's father's shack is razed by bulldozers.

James Hamilton has commented upon an unmistakable "air of breeding and courtliness that seems built into the blood"; and with this seems to have come a nascent sense of *noblesse oblige*.[10] David was a community leader. He did a fair amount of *pro bono* work in his practice, and it was not uncommon for him to accept payment in goods and services. But rarely was anyone, however poor, turned away who was in need of legal representation. Fresno was by this time a solidly WASP community, yet with a large population of Indians, Mexicans, and Armenians, who always knew they could get a fair hearing from anyone with the name of Peckinpah or Church. Throughout most of his public life, David honored the principles of his childhood hero, Abraham Lincoln.

Sam's boyhood was not exceptional. He loved reading. When very young he enjoyed a series of children's books that retold classic stories (*Moby-Dick*, the Three Musketeers, Knights of the Round Table). When he was seven he learned Tennyson's *Charge of the Light Brigade* by heart and started staging it with his friends. "By the time I was eleven," he said, "we must have had fifty kids weekly reenacting that famous battle."[11] When he and his sister, Fern Lea, listened to their favorite radio shows, he would turn out all the lights the better to embellish the announcers' stage and scene descriptions in elaborate and vivid detail, including sound effects and ad libs. He always read fiction and watched films, Fern Lea recalls, with the eye and sensibility of a dramatist and a storyteller. He also loved playing at his grandfather's ranch. At the age of five or six he excitedly watched his first roundup. But when a cowhand clipped a steer's ear and the blood spurted out, young Sam fainted dead away. (Peckinpah was his whole life somewhat squeamish before the sight of blood, which may be one more reason why his depictions of violence are rarely gory.)

All those years of listening to dinner-table discussions of the law and the Bible eventually took their toll.* He became the most overt-

---

*Peckinpah's relationship to religion is as conflicted as his relationships to most things he felt strongly about, and mapping its exact contours might easily warrant an essay of its own. Aggressively antidoctrinaire and anti-ideological, he was hostile to its organized manifestations and ridiculed most forms of Puritanical thinking. But he also said that *Ride the High Country* is about salvation and *The Ballad of Cable Hogue* is about God. One of the things he admired about his father was that he was "deeply religious"; and one of the things he valued from his youth was his biblical upbringing, which he never disowned. Indeed, Peckinpah often carried a Bible with him. At a gathering in the late seventies, for example, he emptied his bag in search of a cigarette. Out tumbled a script, a pen and notes, loose change, some personal items, and a very well-thumbed Bible. His first wife was a Protestant; his second and third wives were Catholic and Jewish respectively. Already well versed

ly rebellious of the four children (though Fern Lea was not far behind). His grades inevitably suffered. After he was caught late one night doing wheelies in his father's truck (which he had borrowed without asking permission), his parents decided he might be better off in military school and enrolled him in the San Rafael Military Academy. It wasn't much of a military academy, but it seemed to serve the purpose: Sam apparently did knuckle down to his studies and would have graduated *cum laude* except that he had managed to accumulate more demerits than any other student in the history of the institution. (Reports vary as to whether he liked it there; perhaps the final word is to be found in *The Wild Bunch,* where one of the names of the town shot up in the opening robbery is San Rafael.)

Once out of high school Sam joined the marines. After basic training he was stationed first in Arizona, then in Louisiana. Though he had become bored with high school, Peckinpah long read and often studied wherever he went. He enrolled in local colleges near the bases, taking courses in mathematics and engineering. In 1945 he was dispatched to China, where he did a year's tour of duty disarming and repatriating Japanese soldiers. He saw no action, except once, traveling on a train that was shot at by the Communists. Two bullets tore through the car, one of them killing a Chinese passenger. "I noticed that time slowed down," Peckinpah later said; it was "one of the longest split seconds in my life."[12]

Like most servicemen stationed in China, Peckinpah frequented Tientsin's bars and whorehouses. But he was also different. He read much more than most of them, for one thing. And he became far more involved with the Chinese. He once told of another marine who had boasted

> that he'd thrown a Chinese woman down on a concrete platform and raped her, hit her head against the pavement, and after he was done she didn't move. I'd been practically adopted by a Chinese family. I actually decided I was going to kill him. I went out and stole a gun, a Russian gun, and offered to sell it to him. You know, the

---

in Protestantism from childhood, he studied Catholicism and Judaism when he became involved with the other two women. He told his buddies this was only because the women wanted him to, but close friends and family knew better. "You've got the cursed Jesuit strain in you," Mulligan tells Dedalus, "only it's injected all the wrong way." The same could be said of Peckinpah's religious sense. His films suggest he was religious in one of the few ways a thinking person can be religious in the second half of the twentieth century: he had an unshakable belief in something beyond the solitary and isolate individual, from which the individual takes his meaning and to which he is answerable.

souvenir mentality. When I sold it to him, I was going to kill him. Put the barrel of the gun right under his chin and pull the trigger. The night before our meeting, I saw him standing there, completely blind. Permanently blind. He'd drunk some bad whiskey. If it hadn't been for that, I might be in prison today.[13]

The family he was referring to belonged to a young Chinese woman, a Communist, with whom he had fallen in love. He stopped going to the brothels altogether, and started reading politics and a bit of Zen. He wanted to marry her, but U.S. policy forbade it, and the marines turned down his request for a discharge.

When Peckinpah was returned home, he was still less certain about what he wanted to do than about what he didn't want to do, which was go into law. "I'm the only Peckinpah in four generations," he once pointed out with what appeared to be no little pride, "who has not gone into law."[14]* Like many another young person in a similar situation, Peckinpah decided to go back to school, mostly because he "had nothing better to do." He applied to the history department at nearby Fresno State College, where, owing to the course work he had done elsewhere, he was admitted with advanced standing. There he met his first wife, Marie Selland, "who wanted to be an actress. Fresno State had a small but active theater department and I tagged along . . . one day into a directing class. It turned me on right away."[15] There was considerable resistance from the other students, because he had absolutely no formal theatrical training. His talents soon emerged, however. Marie recalls her future husband's first assignment vividly:

> He had been assigned to prepare the scene from *Of Mice and Men* when Lenny starts fondling the girl's hair and winds up killing her. The class met at the end of the day in a little room and there were windows at the back of the small stage area. Sam not only got the performances—and the actors were just inexperienced students— but—and this is what amazes me—he made the light that was already there, that late afternoon light, work as part of the scene. The effect was stunning.

Between his junior and senior years in college Peckinpah spent a summer south of the border, which marked the beginning of his life-long love affair with Mexico. He often likened it to his experiences in China, which was also a country torn by revolution where advanced

---

*As his father was the first Peckinpah to go into law, this is untrue by double. Even on his mother's side the lawyers go back only three generations.

powers were in collision with a peasant culture. As usual he seems to have spent a fair portion of the time reading books, which included John Reed's *Insurgent Mexico* and most of the major plays of Shakespeare. He also served as the assistant director in a theatrical production of Maxwell Anderson's *Joan of Lorraine*. When he returned home he told his father that he was changing his major from history to theater.

Back in school Peckinpah so impressed the faculty that he became the first undergraduate in the history of Fresno State to be given a major production to direct. (The play was *Guest in the House*.) His first love was for the plays of Tennessee Williams, a production of whose *Glass Menagerie* he did for his senior project. At the time Williams was still a new and controversial playwright. His plays were considered obscene by the chairman of the drama department, who wanted them banned, along with those of William Saroyan (a fellow Fresnoian whose work Peckinpah admired) and O'Neill.* Peckinpah and some other students fought that kind of thinking all the way.

He received his baccalaureate degree from Fresno in 1948, and enrolled immediately as a drama major at the University of Southern California in Los Angeles. He completed most of his course work there during the fall of 1948 through the summer of 1949, acquiring (according to one of his professors) a fairly comprehensive background in theatrical theory, a familiarity with all the most important modern playwrights (though here too were conservative faculty who opposed some of these and whom "Sam bucked"). In the workshops and productions in USC's small experimental theater, Peckinpah did plays or cuttings by Chekhov, Strindberg, Brecht (whom he was to quote in *Cross of Iron*), Coward, and Sophocles, and also original plays by the students. Throughout all this activity his reading continued unabated. Like many serious readers he developed fast enthusiasms, getting hooked on a particular author for a while and devouring a number of his books, then moving on to another and another. Marie recalls,

---

*O'Neill's plays always struck Peckinpah as ponderous and turgid, which is ironic inasmuch as the director's good friend Jason Robards is the O'Neill actor *par excellence*. Robards always believed that James Tyrone's story was Peckinpah's own, and felt he could change his friend's mind about the playwright. The actor nearly succeeded with *A Moon for the Misbegotten:* Peckinpah loved both Robards *and* the play. One of the more fascinating "ifs" of Peckinpah's career had he lived longer is whether he would have come round completely. For it is certainly hard to imagine another director whose personal experience and family history made him fitter to do *Long Day's Journey into Night*, *The Iceman Cometh*, and *A Moon for the Misbegotten* than this one.

He really had a Hemingway crush, then Scott Fitzgerald, and Thoreau, and Faulkner was another that really impressed him. And
there was a lot of Dickens too. Sam was really an avid reader. Our
bed would be stacked with books. We both read a lot, but he read
like a crazy person, and was interested in a wide variety of books.
He was always interested in history, particularly the history of the
Old West. And because of the time he spent in China, he was really interested in Chinese history. But he was also interested in the
Greeks, philosophy—he read a lot of Plato and Aristotle too. Aristotle's *Poetics* was something that seemed to grab him and he was
constantly referring to it. We both became interested in Camus at
the same time, especially *The Stranger, The Rebel* too, and also that
collection of essays—*The Myth of Sisyphus.* You know, it always
seemed amazing, because he'd have his Greeks and the others in
one hand and his cowboy books and detective stories in the other.

Peckinpah generally did excellent work in his courses. But he was
also impatient with them because he was mostly biding his time to
direct. He had played a small role in a university production of *Oedi-
pus the King* and had directed Saroyan's *Hello Out There* as a curtain
raiser for a fellow student's show, but these experiences only intensified his desire to get into the real thing himself. James Butler, the
professor who was his adviser, remembered him as

> one of these fellows who has a burning ambition to go into the the-
> ater. Once in a while you get students like this. He had a feeling
> for directing that few students have. Sam was a very meticulous di-
> rector. And one of the things that stands out with him is his ability
> to handle actors, and I think he showed this in his days when he
> was directing college kids. He had a great rapport with actors. He
> gives his actors, even today in his movies, a good deal of leeway, and
> I think this goes back to his early days as a theatrical director.

So in 1949, with most of his course work finished but without his
degree, Peckinpah left school and spent the next two and a half years
in professional and semiprofessional theater. This included a summer
of stock in Albuquerque and some odd jobs around Los Angeles (including directing Williams's *27 Wagons Full of Cotton*). But his main job,
also his first theatrical job, was with the Huntington Park Civic Theater in a suburb of Los Angeles, where he spent two seasons directing
plays and conducting workshops in acting and directing. Among the
plays he did were *Only an Orphan Girl, Our Town, South Pacific, The Man
Who Came to Dinner,* and *Guest in the House,* and in the workshops he
did Pirandello, Molière, Congreve, Saroyan, and Ibsen (Penelope Gil-

liatt wrote that the exchanges between Thornton and Harrigan in *The Wild Bunch* are "like listening to characters in Ibsen: when we meet them, they are a long way into their lives together").[16]

When he returned to USC in 1952 for more course work, a professor who hadn't seen him in the intervening years was shocked by his appearance—absolutely emaciated (and "Sam was always a skinny kid to begin with"), exhausted looking, yet obviously driven to (and by) achievement. Peckinpah began to think seriously about finishing his degree, which meant finding a thesis topic. He said that originally he wanted to write about some aspect of the theory and practice of tragedy from Aristotle to the moderns, and he recollected having gotten as far as Ibsen in his notes and some drafts before more professional work intervened and eventually forced him to do a practical thesis. In the end this was just as well, for the project he did became an important stepping-stone for more than just the obvious reason of its getting him graduated. The task he set himself was to design a production of a play that would answer at once the requirements of both theatrical performance and television showing, especially on educational television, then in its infancy. He turned to his first love and selected Williams's one-act *Portrait of a Madonna* (he also turned to Marie to act the role of the lead). The project is in two parts, a written commentary and a film. The play was performed on 8 July 1953 at USC's Stop Gap Theater, then filmed one night about three weeks later after hours at KLAC-TV where Peckinpah was working part time as a stagehand. He set up an area to replicate the stage at USC and used one semifixed and two fixed cameras to triangulate the stage area and give himself as much selection of shot, position, and angle as possible under the circumstances.

In his evaluation of the film one can already hear the voice of an eager and frustrated filmmaker. The biggest problems, he felt, were two. First, "far too much stage technique motivated shot selection," the result being that the pace of the television production was slow, especially as compared to that of the theatrical production.[17]

> The second problem, and one that was not evident during production, was that the positions of the cameras on the set made the audience orientation difficult. As each camera covered a separate third of the set, the cuts and dissolves had a tendency to make the viewer lose the relative position of the off-scene characters. This could have been alleviated by tying in the cutting with more definite and continuing action. As an example, any action toward the camera to be used next would serve as an unconscious point of reference for the viewer.

All in all, he concluded, praising his cast and crew while reserving the criticism for himself, "full use was not made of potential dramatic coverage inherent in the three-camera method." Those words are about as prophetic a statement as he was ever to make about himself, since much later, in the shifting, colliding perspectives that inform his feature films, he does realize the full potential of the method, often employing more than one camera (on a couple of occasions he has used as many as seven). But that method began here in what is, for all practical purposes, his first "real" film. Up to this occasion his work had been almost entirely in the theater, but here he conceived, produced, and directed a production that was simultaneously theater and film. By his own evaluation theater won out—this time—and he was awarded his Master of Fine Arts degree on 12 June 1954. However, the real rite of passage the thesis commemorated was the effective end of one career, the beginning of another: he left USC that summer as a filmmaker.

Determined to break into films, Peckinpah took any job that would get him into a studio. He liked to say that he was fired for refusing to wear a suit on the *Liberace* show, though he was only a floorsweep. There is no evidence to support this claim. The more prosaic truth seems to be that he left for the same reason he left his other jobs: he had learned what he could and they had become dead ends. His first big break came through his brother Denny, who had been Pat Brown's campaign manager in Fresno. Denny told the governor about Sam's ambitions. Brown met with Sam, was impressed, and telephoned Walter Wanger (then at United Artists), who in turn asked the director Don Siegel if he could use anyone on his new picture, *Riot in Cell Block Eleven*. Peckinpah was hired as Siegel's "fourth assistant casting director. A gopher really; you know, go for this, go for that. Then I got upped to dialogue director."[18] He also joined Siegel on *Invasion of the Body Snatchers,* where "I played four different parts. . . . Peckinpah, man of a thousand faces. I was also stunt man on the picture. Let me think. I was a meter reader, a pod man, and a member of the posse. In addition, Don also had me on it as a writer." From there the story can be brought rapidly to the point at which this study takes it up—how he went from Siegel to Charles Marquis Warren and *Gunsmoke* to Dick Powell, Four Star, and *The Westerner.*

During his early years in television, and before that in college, Peckinpah was something of a dandy in his dress and accoutrements. He wore ascots and slacks, sported a cigarette holder, and kept his hair short and neat. His face was so boyish looking that he grew a moustache, which he trimmed to an elegant pencil-thin line. Though he brought all this off with considerable flair and dash, there was an air about him during these years that suggests a young man trying on, then rejecting, identities. Fern Lea believes that after he read Peter Viertel's *White Hunter, Black Heart,* a fictionalized account of the making of *The African Queen,* he made a conscious decision to model himself on the novel's protagonist, a thinly disguised portrait of John Huston.[19]* Perhaps, but by the time of *The Wild Bunch* he seems to have settled into the look that he maintained with few variations the rest of his life. Bearing no resemblances to Huston or any other director, it consisted in the bandana tied across the forehead, the mirrored sunglasses pushed up or dangling from his neck (though this may have been for the photographs), occasionally a Western-style hat, the buckskin jacket, the jeans (usually white instead of blue), the hair sometimes unkempt but rarely long, always the moustache (though fuller now), sometimes the beard (that he once admitted was after Hemingway and that in some photographs gives him a startling resemblance to the author). When he felt he had to dress up, it was usually in a black suit and cowboy boots, an open-collared shirt with a bandana or a Western string-tie around his neck.

If this image, or complex of images, seemed to fit him—and he did carry it off with style and conviction—there was no doubt something cultivated about it as well. On *The Getaway* Joie Gould, his third wife, observed that when he dressed in the mornings to go on the set, carefully adjusting the bandana, it was as if he were donning wardrobe for a performance he was required to give in a part he had to play.[20] As the years went on more friends and family came to feel

---

*Peckinpah's personality, like Huston's, was a rich source for other storytellers. Taking a cue from Viertel, Rudolph Wurlitzer wrote up his own impressions of a maverick director in a novel called *Slow Fade.* Peckinpah also figured obliquely in two major motion pictures. Peter O'Toole said that the director was one of four on whom he patterned his portrayal of the director-hero in Richard Rush's *The Stunt Man* (the other three were Huston, David Lean, and Rush himself). And Ron Shelton (a great admirer of Peckinpah's work) said that while he was writing the screenplay for his 1994 film *Cobb,* he kept a pair of notes attached to his computer screen for inspiration. On one of them was written, "Remember, *Richard III* is a comedy"; on the other, simply, "Sam Peckinpah." Several people who knew Peckinpah, including family members and working associates, remarked on how truthfully—not in any literal sense, but emotionally and psychologically—Shelton's protagonist suggests Peckinpah.

While Peckinpah was still alive he was also the subject of a sketch on *Monty Python's Flying Circus,* which he thought so hilarious he kept a copy for himself and would occasionally run it for people who hadn't seen it (Jesse Graham to P.S., 1996).

the same way, and several were concerned that he seemed to be spending far too much energy trying to be the man the journalists called Sam Peckinpah.

II

The foregoing sketch is an incomplete picture of a complex and complicated man, but it tells us something of where he comes from, indicates more than a little of what goes into his art, and allows us to put a few things about each into clearer perspective. One thing it immediately helps to place is the matter of his so-called anti-intellectualism. There is still a small though rather vocal contingent that objects to any suggestion that Peckinpah was an intelligent, thoughtful man who might actually have had some idea of what he was doing in his films. Some of this originates from universities, where an odd and rather contradictory form of anti-intellectualism—call it an infatuation with the primitive—is very much alive. An artist like Peckinpah winds up being doubly damned. He worked so closely from his instincts and feelings that even some of his most ardent admirers want to protect him from the scourge of intellect, as if films of the complexity and difficulty of *The Wild Bunch, Ride the High Country,* and *Pat Garrett and Billy the Kid* could have been made with only half a brain—the right one. Yet when he provokes these same admirers (and others) in ways they find discomfiting, the first thing they will attack is what they perceive as his "wrong" thinking and bad ideas.

Peckinpah's art is among the most passionate, sensual, and visceral of all filmmakers', and his film sense was equaled by few and surpassed by none. He was no intellectual, to be sure, because he did not for the most part dwell in the abstract, the theoretical, and the conceptual. But he was nevertheless well educated, widely if unsystematically read in everything from the Greeks to Shakespeare to the classics of nineteenth-century American and some British literature right up to Hemingway, Fitzgerald, Faulkner, Sartre, Camus, Artaud, Brecht, Cela, Williams, Beckett, Ionesco, and Pirandello (to say nothing of the popular fiction) of the century he was born in. Nor did he just plow through this stuff. He studied much of it, absorbing what he could use, setting aside or discarding what he couldn't. He knew Aristotle's *Poetics* cold; and he could hold his own in a scholarly discussion of the Bible, which he read all the way through, committing parts of it to memory. He also had a taste for poetry—late romantic and early twentieth century in particular, Edna St. Vincent Millay and

Rupert Brooke especial favorites—and even wrote some. Plainly, this was a thinking as well as a feeling man.*

The anti-intellectual posture also has another basis. "I make it a point," he once said, "of not trying to explain my films."[21] It isn't that he didn't want them discussed. It is rather that he believed their meanings consisted not in some neatly paraphrasable theme or idea but in the experiencing of the films themselves, which every filmgoer has to do on his or her own. His attitude is not dissimilar to that of Hawthorne, who writes in the preface to *The House of the Seven Gables* that when stories "do really teach anything, or produce any effective operation, it is usually through a far more subtle process than the ostensible one" of supplying "some definite moral purpose." Peckinpah *hated* to talk about the meaning of his films, which is one of the reasons why he got so feisty in interviews and why he was given to so many outrageous remarks. One of the very few journalists ever to understand the purpose of this behavior is P. F. Kluge, who, in a 1972 profile in *Life*, observed, "You have to go through this, have to get through the jokes, the snorts, the vulgarity, all have to be gotten through before Sam Peckinpah begins to take his own words seriously."[22] Kluge noticed that when Peckinpah did finally offer some interpretations of his work, they were delivered in "half-hearted tones"; and even when he appeared "enthusiastic" discussing Robert Ardrey, it was "as if to deflect direct analysis of his own work." Or at least so that he himself would not have to do the analyzing. In this Peckinpah had a far more sophisticated grasp of the relationship among artist, artist's intention, artwork, and audience than the majority of his critics do.

Another thing that is put into perspective is the Hemingway influence. The filmmaker certainly didn't need the writer to find a context for his rebelliousness. He found plenty of context right at home. When he talked about his parents' absolutes having driven him nearly crazy, it is clear that his family formed a nucleus of moralism, authority, and respectability that left him feeling constrained, dis-

---

*It is difficult to know what to make of a *cul de sac* of primitivism that embraces the man who breaks wind in public but rejects the same man when he reads poetry in private, as if the former were more "real" than the latter. (Surely the lesson of the great American revolt against the Genteel Tradition is that both must be recognized.) What is worse, when some of these neoprimitivist academics get around to revealing their ideas of Peckinpah's importance, it usually winds up having to do with how the theories of Robert Ardrey's *African Genesis* are supposedly dramatized in *The Wild Bunch* and *Straw Dogs*, which for sheer reductionism may surpass in absurdity even those early reviewers who could see only blood lust and slaughter (at least they were responding to something palpable *in* the films, not pasting a thesis upon them).

satisfied, and disaffected. This is no doubt one way to account for the ridicule to which temperance marchers, preachers, politicians, policemen, and other figures of authority are subjected in his films; and certainly the military academy and the marines have something to do with the outright derision heaped upon both the military and military authority in *Major Dundee, The Wild Bunch,* and *Cross of Iron.** His identification with outlaws, loners, and individualists no doubt began to take shape back then as well, for by his own admission he felt like an outsider during those dinner-table conversations when he raised what was apparently the sole voice of protest; and at least one of his high school friends says that "Sam was always something of a loner, always tended to keep to himself."[23] This may also help to explain the rather extraordinary praise he bestowed upon Chaplin, whom he declined to put on any list of favorite or best film directors "not because of his morals or politics, about which I know nothing and couldn't care less, but because I feel that there must be separation between state and church and his vision is so unique and so splendid it would be ridiculous to list him with filmmakers who I feel work in another world."[24] As far as identifying specific sources for his work goes, this remark doesn't take us very far. But as an indirect declaration of empathy, it makes a lot of sense: given Peckinpah's confessed "sneaky affection for all the misfits and drifters in the world," he could hardly have helped but recognize a fellow traveler in the Tramp, for whom things often go amiss and who most emphatically does not fit into any of society's well-oiled grooves.

For all his admiration of Hemingway, Peckinpah's favorite novel was Camus's *The Stranger;* and he once told Paul Schrader that if he wanted to know about *The Wild Bunch,* he should read Camilo José

---

*The influence of the marines upon Peckinpah's development, like that of religion, is far from simple. He was proud to be a marine, and once he was through basic training he felt he had gained admission to an elite society. This is, of course, the guiding philosophy behind boot camp: destroy the identity the recruits come with and replace it with another that finds its sole ratification in the corps. Weddle speculates that Peckinpah later adapted this philosophy to his film sets, trying to forge his crews into units that owed their allegiance only to him and his film, never to the studio (Weddle, p. 209). Moreover, if we take Peckinpah at his word that he felt like an outsider at home, then it may also be true, as he himself admitted, that the marine corps for a while made him feel as if he were part of a family. Making films performed pretty much the same function. Someone once said that people who work in films come either from close families or from disparate ones. The former are looking to replicate their good experience of family life, the latter to find it. "The end of a picture," Peckinpah once said, "is always an end of a life" (Sam Peckinpah to Paul Staniford, letter, 8 July 1971 [Peckinpah Collection]).

Cela's *Family of Pascual Duarte*.[25] Cela is generally regarded as the most important Spanish novelist of the twentieth century. Originally published in 1942 and set in modern rural Spain, the novel shows how poverty and deprivation are breeding grounds for frustration and violence. It is written more or less as a confessional (though without a confessional tone) by the title character, a latter-day *picaro* who describes his gruesome crimes with appalling vividness and passion but otherwise without much in the way of comment or remorse. Therein lies one of its significances for Peckinpah: Cela, like Hemingway (by whom the Spaniard was almost certainly influenced), keeps himself *out* of the story by using a narrative style that is an embodiment of the sensibility that the story is chiefly about. A greater significance may consist in its possible effect on Peckinpah's depiction of the Mexican people and settings in *Major Dundee* and *The Wild Bunch*, where social turmoil and unrest in the one and outright revolution in the other are likewise functions of poverty and deprivation, as well as of oppression and a population too densely crowded together and impacted with energy for anyone's good. Peckinpah also admired a 1951 film by the great Spanish director Luis Buñuel: *Los Olvidados* (literally, "the forgotten ones"), which views juvenile delinquency in modern-day Mexico in terms not unlike Cela's. (Buñuel's *L'Age d'Or*, made in 1930, opens on a tortured scorpion, similar to the famous symbol from *The Wild Bunch*, but Peckinpah never saw the film.)[26] In addition, his thinking can hardly *not* have been shaped by Camus's treatments of violence and revolution in *The Stranger* and *The Rebel*. (According to one of his assistants, Peckinpah was greatly pleased when he read of *The Rebel* being used as a way to explicate some of the underlying ideas that are dramatized in *The Wild Bunch*.)[27]

His feeling for Tennessee Williams's work was probably best expressed in the interpretive section of his master's thesis where, as regards *Portrait of a Madonna*, he made the connection between the heroine's status as a pariah and the damage wrought upon her by social and religious prejudice. He also found in Williams a reflection of his own weakness for all the misfits, drifters, and outsiders in the world. Nor is it insignificant that Williams's central characters are often women victimized by society, for we find in them early, quite distant, yet unmistakable relatives of such later heroines as Miss Jenny, Jeff, Suzy, Sal, Mrs. Kennedy, Kit, Elsa, Hildy, Ellie (from *Junior Bonner*), and Elita (from *Bring Me the Head of Alfredo Garcia*)—victims, outcasts, misfits each and all. Peckinpah's heroines, victimized though they may be, are tougher, smarter, more resilient than Williams's spin-

sters, and are much less willing to accept society's judgments against
them. They also suggest few similarities to Hemingway's rather idealized, excessively romanticized heroines, being altogether freer,
more assertive, independent, and individualistic.

Peckinpah once said that "any film director should be a writer, and
if you're going to be a writer, you have to have spent some time, someplace, besides that camera."[28] Inasmuch as quite a bit of directing
consists in getting performances from actors, a logical place is the
stage, and it is here that Peckinpah's formal education served him
throughout his career. To start with, it formed the foundation of his
directorial experience with actors, both practically and theoretical-
ly. As is not the case with most filmmakers (particularly in the generations following Peckinpah's), all of his early directing was in theater,
and much of that was in college productions. Even his professional
work with the Huntington Park Civic Theater came during a two-year
hiatus from graduate school. He acquired this experience when the
acting school known as the "Method" was arguably the most favored
style among serious American actors (e.g., Marlon Brando, Montgom-
ery Clift, Kim Stanley, Julie Harris, James Dean). He studied acting
theory pretty thoroughly, including the great Russian teacher-theo-
rist Konstantin Stanislavski, from whom American Method acting
largely derives. Williams's development is inconceivable without the
Method; and one of Peckinpah's favorite directors was Elia Kazan, an
important member of the Group Theater, a founding member of the
Actors Studio, and easily the most widely known and influential
"Method" director ever to make films.

Difficult to define but relatively easy to recognize, the Method
aimed for greater psychological and emotional verisimilitude through
a more interior, introspective, and intuitive approach from the actor
than classical styles and techniques encouraged.[29] It also strove for
greater naturalism. Actors were encouraged to draw upon their own
emotional resources, especially their personalities, their personal
(even private) experiences, and their memories. It would be an exaggeration to say that Peckinpah's whole approach to performance
was conditioned by the Method. But his principal purpose was always
to get his actors to the emotional and psychological core of the characters they played, and this usually led him along the same paths and
toward several of the same destinations as the Method. He once said
that the movie camera and the movieola are the two greatest machines in the world because "with the one you can create people, all
types. With the other, you can make them beautiful or smash them
in the ground."[30] As a thumbnail description of how he worked with

actors, this is not far off the mark: he would resort to whatever means he deemed necessary, fair or foul, in the pursuit of a character's authenticity—his or her look, feel, and expression.

A striking example as regards both means and ends is available in Olivia de Havilland's performance in *Noon Wine,* which some observers believe to be the finest of her career.[31] De Havilland arrived on the set made up according to what was customary for the kind of old-fashioned movie star that she is. The first thing Peckinpah did was muss up her hair and order her makeup removed. The character is a farm wife, he explained, and he helped her feel comfortable going before the cameras plain and unadorned. Jason Robards remembers that within a few days "she gave in to Sam" completely and "was just as loose as she could be, she was wonderful."[32] A crisis came on the very last day. According to the producer Daniel Melnick, "Sam could not get Olivia to give him a truthful moment for the last close-up. Everything she did was too much, it was all 'Acting.' We were in despair."[33] *Noon Wine* was filmed in continuity; by then the production was five hours over schedule. After numerous takes, with everyone's nerves frayed to the limits, Peckinpah announced another take, but he took the cameraman aside and whispered, "Keep rolling after I say, 'Cut. That's a wrap.' Just keep rolling." The take was no better than the others. Peckinpah cut it, called for a wrap, and then went over to the actress. According to Melnick, "Sam proceeded to tell her that she was terrible, that she ruined the picture. I don't remember his exact words, but he went on and on, he kept at it until she was devastated. Meanwhile, the camera is running all this time. And that's how we got that final shot."

Auteur studies rarely take into account the importance of actors to a director's style. Yet to mention only the most obvious example, the style of John Ford's films is in some literal sense almost inconceivable apart from his stock company of players, paramountly John Wayne; likewise Kurosawa without Toshiro Mifune; Bergman without Max von Sydow, Liv Ullmann, and Bibi Andersson; Griffith without Gish; and, perhaps most famous of all, Chaplin without Chaplin. And though, unlike these directors, Peckinpah is associated less with stars and leading players than with character actors, as early as his first year of television directing he had begun to acquire what has since come to be known as his stock company, that marvelous collection of actors he would use so often they became almost as much a part of his style as high-speed cameras and prismatic cutting: Strother Martin, Warren Oates, L. Q. Jones, R. G. Armstrong, Ben Johnson, Slim Pickens, Dub Taylor, Chill Wills, and John Davis Chandler. As a dramatist Peckinpah sensed early on the crucial importance of the actor to a full realization of what he had written and what he could see and hear in his imagination. He learned how to be flexible about, remain open to, and then actively encourage the actors' own contributions to their roles, including even new dialogue if they were so inclined (sometimes he would order them to come up with new lines for the next day's shooting).

It can be argued that this is essentially no different from the way all directors use their actors. True enough, except that when a director like Peckinpah—a genuine auteur who often wrote his own material or so changed the material given him that it became his own—uses the same group of actors again and again, then the actors, their personalities, their styles and techniques must inevitably condition the conception and development of the characters. And when character is as central as it is in Peckinpah's films, then by definition and extension the actors must also affect theme, structure, even story itself. This process cannot help but force the actor into an unusually intimate relationship with the role he is playing. Once this intimacy was established (usually in rehearsal), Peckinpah did whatever was necessary to preserve it, as, given the right actor in the right role, he believed the rewards in psychological insight, emotional truth, and plain vitality were tremendous.

In *The Wild Bunch,* for example, the psychologies of the two principal bounty hunters, Coffer and TC, are based in no small measure on the actors who play them, Strother Martin and L. Q. Jones, respectively, whom Peckinpah had by then known personally, professionally, and socially for years. Throughout the shooting he abused Martin in more or less the same way that Deke Thornton abuses Coffer in the story: he can't do anything right, he's a complete screwup, he's stupid, witless, and worthless. "But don't get the wrong idea," Martin pointed out years later. Peckinpah "was keeping me in this frenetic state for a purpose: he wanted me to portray this psychotic character as if I were on the edge of a nervous breakdown. . . . Sam is like a dirty psychiatrist—he gets inside your head and probes around with a scalpel. . . . But when I saw the final product, somehow it was all worthwhile."[34] Or take R. G. Armstrong, who plays the Bible-beating Joshua Knudsen in *Ride the High Country* and similar roles in *Major Dundee* and *Pat Garrett and Billy the Kid.* Armstrong grew up in the Deep South with a mother who was a fanatical Christian fundamentalist and a father who was terrifyingly violent. "Sam saw the depth of my hostility," Armstrong recalls. "Sam said, 'You're a real killer.' He recognized the struggle I had with my religion, and the violence I held within myself."[35]

This is not the only way to get performances in filmmaking, nor is it right for all actors. But it was often Peckinpah's way and he seemed to have an unerring sense of when it was called for. It certainly played a large part in giving the performances in his films that special vitality and volatility that are in the very best and most original sense unmistakably recognizable as the Peckinpah style.

Beginning in high school and continuing through college and graduate school, Peckinpah watched films as enthusiastically and attentively as he read books. Marie remembers that they often went on movie orgies, seeing virtually everything that was worth seeing, from the famous Olivier Shakespeare adaptations to the Italian neorealists to reworkings of genre films by Ford, Hawks, Wellman, Wilder, Stevens, Zinneman, Kurosawa, and Clouzot. Yet it has always been difficult to find much filmic influence upon Peckinpah's work. There are, of course, sources for specific moments, scenes, and sequences, and these have been noted in the previous chapters on the individual films. But even from his favorite directors—probably Kurosawa, Huston, and Bergman—it is hard to discern a great deal in the way of real *shaping* influence. As for the two filmmakers with whom Peckinpah has been most closely associated in criticism and commentary, Ford and Huston, he is very different from them and they from him and from each other.

The differences can be most readily seen from the perspective of Northrop Frye's observation that irony "begins in realism and dispassionate observation. But as it does so, it moves steadily towards myth, and the dim outlines of sacrificial rituals and dying gods begin to reappear in it."[36] Peckinpah's imagination is a contextualizing imagination, that is, he continually reveals his stories, themes, and characters in ever larger perspectives, usually pushing them toward some form of mythic transcendence, and his path is that of irony as Frye here uses the term. Huston, however, stays pretty close to the quotidian worlds of his stories. The respective endings of their most famous films illustrate the differences handily enough. The closing image of *The Treasure of the Sierra Madre* is a push-in to a tight closeup of a torn-open sack of gold caught on the thorns of a cactus, the once valuable dust now blown back into the desert sand from whence it came. Despite the setting amid old, windswept ruins, the effect is insistently to exclude myth in favor of an almost pure irony: our faces are almost literally rubbed in the dirt. In *The Wild Bunch,* by contrast, we rise from the ironic world, where Thornton and Old Sykes ride off with their neo-Bunch, to the realm of myth as the dim outlines of the dead heroes now reappear as the laughing faces of the

Bunch, only to be supplanted by the reprise of their departure from Angel's village. The effect here, for all the realism of the trappings, is pure myth. Even the camera movements are diametrically opposite to each other yet splendidly to their respective points: Huston's descending and zeroing in, Peckinpah's ascending and opening out.

As for Ford, his two most famous early Westerns, *Stagecoach* and *My Darling Clementine*, are throughout romances. But by the time of *The Searchers* and *The Man Who Shot Liberty Valance*, he has come as close to irony as he ever would, only from the opposite direction. If Peckinpah could ascend to myth only through irony, Ford could reach irony only by descending from myth. *Liberty Valance* especially demonstrates this movement: despite the famous pronouncement of its newspaperman, the film actually begins with the invocation of myth and moves toward irony as a legend is dismantled before our very eyes.

Peckinpah's most distinctive stylistic synthesis, his combination of fast cutting and slow motion to render action and violence, was anticipated by another director entirely. This is George Stevens, whose *Shane* Peckinpah once called "the best Western ever made,"[37] to which remark he some years later added, "Killing used to be fun-and-games in Apache land. Violence wasn't shown well. You fired a shot and three Indians fell down. You always expected them to get up again. But when Jack Palance shot Elisha Cook Jr. in *Shane*, things started to change."[38] Nobody seems to have paid much attention to this statement, perhaps on the not unreasonable assumption that a filmmaker as temperamentally and stylistically dissimilar as Stevens couldn't possibly have had much real effect on Peckinpah. But more than a few dissimilar directors have claimed influence from Stevens (Kurosawa, for one); and Peckinpah was here acknowledging a real and present debt. In the showdown that climaxes *Shane* there is a moment of violence that appears, from our present vantage point, to be a remarkable adumbration of Peckinpah. When Shane draws and fires at the gunslinger Wilson, it is with lightning speed and over in a split second. The recoil, however, is protracted, as Wilson's body takes the bullet, is thrown across the length of the barroom, crashes through some tables and chairs, and lands in the corner dead. Now if it were possible to insert a brief, slow-motion shot of Wilson recoiling, the result would be a depiction of violence startlingly similar to those of Peckinpah. In fact, when Garrett kills Holly in *Pat Garrett and Billy the Kid*, it is not unlike Shane's killing of Wilson: the draw lightning quick, the recoil relatively slow, Peckinpah's slower still due to the slow-motion insert, which suspends the recoil of Holly's body before it too crashes through some tables and chairs and lands in the corner dead.

Peckinpah developed this technique and used it with enormous sophistication; but it appears in embryo in this scene from *Shane,* where he saw how the instant of violence itself—the moment of bloodshed, collision, or contact—can go by so fast that one almost misses it, recollecting only one's anticipation and one's reaction. Peckinpah used to tell his editors that the only reason to film something in slow motion is when it happens so fast you can't see it otherwise.[39] Although in practice he used slow motion for many other reasons, his remark provides a clue as to why he kept his slow-motion shots so brief. It is the build-up and the release that he wanted to capture, because perception and feeling, violence as psychological effect, are what chiefly interest him. In moments of great trauma, of physical and emotional excitement, time paradoxically contracts and expands, as when a bullet flying through a passenger train becomes the longest split second of one's life. And for reasons having to do with the way the human mind operates, our memories seem to retain images longer when their duration is shorter, which is another reason why Peckinpah's depictions of violence are so unsettling: the effects are made subliminally, where they stay with us for a long time.*

Peckinpah wanted more than anything else to find a way of fluidly incorporating slow motion into the "ongoingness" of filmic narrative. In *The Seven Samurai* Kurosawa virtually stops the show for the high-speed shots. In *Bonnie and Clyde,* a film Peckinpah loved, Arthur Penn comes much closer to Peckinpah's ideal in the climactic dance of death; but even there, slow motion becomes a device that segregates the climax as a kind of set-piece. Prior to Penn's film, Peckinpah had provided a glimpse of what he had in mind in the two instances of slow motion he used in *The Losers* and *That Lady Is My Wife* on television. Before these, the film Peckinpah named as coming closest to the way he eventually used slow motion is Clouzot's *The Wages of Fear.*[40] When the truck careens off the road down the side of the mountain, it is seen from a several angles, some of them in slow motion. According to Lou Lombardo, the first cut of the opening massacre in *The Wild Bunch,* which went on over twenty minutes, was very linear. Lom-

---

*About nine months before his death Peckinpah talked about this aspect of his editing style: "It's all tied in with retinal retention factor of the eye, which then evolved into slow motion for me. I spent about a thousand hours, it seems, trying to find the psychological reasons for this. . . . It comes down to the fact that, as I think Pauline Kael said [in her review of *Straw Dogs*], we have a kind of archaic memory still happening. Say that it's the aesthetic combined with the immediate. I just say, as I've said before, because it works" ("Sam Peckinpah Retrospective").

bardo said he would shorten it, but Peckinpah told him not to cut it down just yet, "See if you can't mesh it together."[41] "So that's what I did," Lombardo said, "I intercut all the separate pieces of action." It was montage somewhat after the manner of Eisenstein but freed from ideological pointmaking and inflected with a disturbing new psychological expressiveness and emotional intensity. It was also an authentic stylistic innovation that left few films that came in its wake untouched by its influence.

Peckinpah only ever named two other Westerns among his favorite films: *My Darling Clementine* and *High Noon.* The significance of the former is detailed in the chapter on *The Ballad of Cable Hogue,* while that of *High Noon* appears to be slight except as its theme—a man standing alone against almost impossible odds for what he believes—reminded Peckinpah of something his father once told him: "When the time comes, he used to say, you stand up and you're counted. For the right thing. For something that matters. It's the ultimate test."[42] This is precisely the test to which Peckinpah subjects the main characters in *Ride the High Country* and *The Wild Bunch* (after a screening of which his sister remarked, "I can see his father through the whole film").[43] Beyond these Peckinpah was remarkably uninfluenced by Westerns. He didn't care for the Westerns of Budd Boetticher (who made a number of films with Randolph Scott) or Jacques Tourneur (in whose 1955 *Wichita* he played a bit part opposite Joel McCrea). He limited the Ford influence to Ford's early work, where he learned (more than likely from *Stagecoach*) how the dissolve can confer unity, fluidity, and continuity upon a large, disparate, and sprawling narrative, though Peckinpah extends the device into metaphor and symbol, taking it far beyond the merely transitional device it was for Ford. Otherwise, he didn't like such later Ford as *The Searchers* ("one of his worst films") and *The Man Who Short Liberty Valance.*[44]

This doesn't necessarily mean there wasn't influence, and professional jealousy could always account for his disclaimers. But neither supposition is likely. In the first place, Peckinpah was always fairly well aware of what he took or learned from whom and from where; and if he was ever too covetous of his own originality to name the sources, then he did a good job of hiding it in interviews, where he was generous to the point of loquacity in acknowledging debts and paying tributes. Thus, while not uncritical of Ford, Huston, and Kurosawa, he nevertheless still revered the first and numbered himself among the greatest admirers of the other two.[45]*

---

*When Peckinpah was introduced to another of his favorites, Fellini (a touch of whose influence can be discerned in Kate, the fat madam from *Ride the High Coun-*

In the second place, there are many stylistic dissimilarities between Peckinpah and Ford, not least among them being that Ford's West is simply less crowded than Peckinpah's. As Ford got older he lost interest in montage and his style became more theatrical and static. He turned Monument Valley into a kind of "natural" theater, and one of his most famous recurring compositions—framing solitary riders or groups of riders with buttes that flank the screen—gives us the sense of a proscenium. Even when the buttes are not seen on the screen at the same time, as when Ford, following a rider, pans from one to the other and then halts the motion of the camera, the theatrical effect is maintained, as they are still contained within the same integral space, the shot remaining unbroken until the pan is completed. Furthermore, the deep-focus photography that he was so fond of merely intensifies our sense of being in a gigantic theatrical stage, which in turn is reinforced by Ford's reduction of the number of elements and materials he placed in that stage. By the time of *The Man Who Shot Liberty Valance* this reductionism is almost embarrassing: studio sets have replaced exteriors, and when the camera does go outdoors the only things that remind us of the West are a few cactuses that actually look as if they had been obligatorily punched into the ground for the sake of the camera. By contrast, Peckinpah's West kept getting fuller, and his style remained to the end a mosaic, prismatic style that depends centrally upon the cut and operates basically according to the structural principles of montage.

III

The truth is that rummaging around old films in search of source material for Peckinpah's work is a trail that dries up pretty fast.[46] The primary sources of his films were identified by the director himself on several occasions, never more succinctly than in his response to an interviewer who asked if he like "doing Westerns, because the West is almost the only mythology we have." "Hell, no," Peckinpah answered. "I came by it naturally. My earliest memory is of being strapped into a saddle when I was two for a ride up into the high country."[47] He eventually worked that memory into *Ride the High Coun-*

---

try), the American director paid him what is apparently the highest compliment one director can pay another: "I'll shoot second-unit for you anytime." On another occasion, a friend, after seeing *The Wild Bunch,* said, "Sam, there is nobody better than you are," to which Peckinpah replied, "No, there's still that damn Swede" (Don Levy to P.S., 1978).

try, as he did other memories into other films. But his Western past shaped his vision in a much more basic, central, and comprehensive way than that of merely providing local color for his art. Peckinpah grew up just at the right time to see the last vestiges of the Old West disappearing: "My brother Denny and I were in on the last of it. Denny and I rode and fished and hunted all over the country. We thought we'd always be a part of it." For an extremely brief moment, he *was* part of it, helping out on the family ranch, learning something about the wilderness, first from his grandfather, then on his own. But—and this is what is crucial to an understanding of his films—his imagination was stirred not by a direct experience of the Old West, for which he arrived too late, but by the recollections of the old people who survived it. Speaking of *The Westerner*, for example, Peckinpah once said that the character was based on many people: "Al Petit, a cowboy; Uncle Wes Qualls, a Madera County cattleman; Brian Keith, me and Bill Dillon. . . . Bill, when I knew him, was in his sixties."[48] The prostitute on whom "Jeff" is based was much older than that.

Then there were the cowhands who worked the ranch or were simply local characters—carryovers, hangers-on, survivors who "dated back to when the place had been the domain of hunters and trappers, Indians, gold-miners—all the drifters and hustlers. All that's left now are the names to remind you, and *what* names: towns like Coarsegold and Fine Gold, Shuteye Peak, Dead Man Mountain, Wild Horse Ridge, Slick Rock. And the old-timers had their stories to tell, too."[49] And there is his own family: his maternal grandmother, for example, whom he called "one of the great ladies of the world," and his Great Aunt Jane, who when she was over a hundred still took a daily walk through the woods around her home.[50] The pasts of both the Peckinpahs and the Churches are virtually synonymous with the histories of Madera County, by extension of the Far West at large, and beyond that of the Old West in general. Not only do the family histories overlap those other histories, but, as we have seen, they helped shape them.

Peckinpah's father was the real cowboy in the family. He was foreman of Denver Church's ranch and drove the stagecoach between North Fork and South Fork. But the family member who seems to have exerted the strongest influence upon the director's imagination is his maternal grandfather. "Old Denver went broke thirteen times," Peckinpah once recalled, "not that it bothered him any; cattleman, superior court judge, district attorney, congressman, he had quite a life."[51] Peckinpah once said in reference to the Old West, "I can't live it, so I remake it."[52] His grandfather might have said the same thing

Sam (age seven or eight) at the family's cabin near Bass Lake, California (circa 1933).

I remember riding my horse up around the pines in Crane Valley. Her name was Nellie, and I'd only have a rope around her nose for a rein—a handmade hackamore. . . . It was the finest time of my life. There will never be another time like that again.

—Sam Peckinpah

about Dunlap's ranch, which was his retreat from the twentieth century and thus his way of making for himself a life he too couldn't live. It also formed the nucleus of most of what Peckinpah would ever experience directly about the Old West. In this old man and his relationship to both the nineteenth century he was born in and the twentieth century he would die in, there rested contradictions and complexities a lifetime might contemplate. His gifted, impressionable grandson certainly spent a fair portion of his own doing just that. Old Denver was a man with the soul of a poet, who actually *wrote* poetry but had nothing but contempt for any man who would read it. He was a congressman who voted against prohibition, though he was himself a lifelong abstainer; he was a Democrat yet hated Franklin Roosevelt and was fearful of most government intervention. As regards the things that he cared most deeply about, his integrity was cast from iron. Elected to his third term of Congress as an antiwar candidate, he vowed he would not seek reelection if Congress voted the country into the First World War; it did and he didn't.

In old age, fearful that he was losing his eye for shooting, he set up a target a hundred feet away, aimed, and fired, missing the bullseye only slightly but by any standard a respectable hit—any standard, that is, except his own. In younger days he had hit that target dead center; if he could not function at the top of his form, he would not function at all. He put his rifle away and never shot or hunted again. During his last years he was beset by strokes that left him physically impaired. Once when he was having difficulty getting out of a car, Sam went to assist him, only to be shoved violently out of the way: stroke or no, Denver would accept help from no man. Sam's feelings were hurt, but he must also have been impressed by the old man's fierce pride and intransigence, his rude, stubborn refusal to let illness keep him from playing his string right out to the end. Equally impressive, but far more horrible, was the end itself, so ungentle it seemed to be enacting a Welsh poet's exhortation with a vengeance. His mind completely gone, Old Denver was bedridden but in a constant rage. When his wife approached him, he ripped nearly all her clothes off. Soon no one except his beloved Denny, the grandchild he practically raised, could come close to him, and by the time death took him he had become so violent a cage had to be built around the sick bed.

It is hardly necessary to look much further to discover why, even fairly early in his career, Peckinpah should display such a special affinity for old people or why so many of his films have transitional settings, so many of his protagonists are men who lived beyond one era into another, and so many of his moods and colors are by turns angry and violent or autumnal and elegiac. As far back as he remembered, he was exposed to an oral tradition of storytelling: he heard his family, their friends, the ranch hands and cowboys *talking* about the old days. Inasmuch as such talk is never exactly factual nor yet quite fiction, but that strange amalgam of the two we tend to call folklore or legend, the stories he heard must have impressed him with the same incongruity to which he gave expression in *Pat Garrett and Billy the Kid:* the incongruity between what is being recollected and the tones in which it is being recollected. This in turn suggests the origin of his divided attitudes toward the Old West. Those mixtures of romance and realism, idealism and cynicism, optimism and pessimism, fact and fancy, history and myth, which he suspends in such delicate and precarious balance, are the source of many of his polarized structural motifs, and inform all his ironies and ambiguities.[53]

Although Peckinpah was born too late to know the Old West directly, he did arrive in time to develop a real attachment to the wilderness. If he was never much of a cowboy, he really took to the hunting experience. "I was twenty years old before I knew there was such a thing as a hunting season or a game warden," he once said, doubtless with considerable exaggeration, "and I was thirty before I began paying any attention to it."[54] Not only did he hunt, fish, trap, and ride the high country when it was still somewhat free and wild, but he watched it recede, getting pushed back and aside by urbanization, industrialization, and commercialization, those very forces of conformity, mechanization, and materialism that threaten the westerners in his films.* It was to these forces that he was alluding when he said that he didn't return home much: "It's mostly all gone now. Fresno's like a little L.A. today, and the country around it is chopped up with new roads and resort facilities and overrun with all these shit-ass tourists and campers."

The dim outlines of a familiar pattern begin to emerge here, for in the collision of a natural wilderness with a manifest economic destiny we find a conflict that has shaped a good many American artists for the last century and a half or so. What Peckinpah experienced in his own youth was the loss—seen through his family, the old people, nature itself—of one way of life and its replacement by an-

---

*Peckinpah was understandably proud of his ancestors, but he must have had many mixed feelings. For example, though his great uncle Moses was surely on the "right" side in his fight against the cattlemen over fencing off the crops, when the same barbed wire crisscrosses the landscape in *Pat Garrett and the Billy the Kid,* the implications are tragic.

other way of life, the values of the one inimical to those of the other. "I grew up on a ranch," he once said, "but that world is all gone now. I feel rootless." Also gone, or at least "outmoded," are the "codes like courage, loyalty, friendship, grace under pressure, all the simple virtues that have become clichés" and that are embodied in his westerners to show what is needed to withstand the vices of a corporate world run by businessmen and politicians (some of whom he once likened to "killer apes right out of the caves, all dressed up in suits and talking and walking around with death in their eyes"), and governed by a system of values in which money talks most and loudest. In the specific terms of his career, the entertainment industry became for him both the fact and the symbol of such a corporate America. Television is the expression of a vast and pervasive boredom that it compounds by leading to mass conformity. "McLuhan was right," Peckinpah once said, "the medium is the massage. You turn on that box; you're programmed."[55]

> And now, with cable TV and video cassettes coming in, no one will ever have to get off his ass, even to go to the corner for a movie. It's awful. One of the great things about going to a movie or the theater is the act itself—the getting out, the buying of the tickets, the sharing of the experience with a lot of other people. Eighty per cent of the people who watch television watch it in groups of three or less, and one of those three is half stoned. Most people come home at night after work, have a couple of knocks before dinner and settle down in their living-death rooms. The way our society is evolving . . . has been very carefully thought out. It's not accidental. We're all being programmed, and I bitterly resent it.[56]

And filmmaking supplied him with his metaphor of prostitution: "My basic job is dealing with talent in terms of a story. . . . I wish it were that simple. But there's all the shit that comes before and after." All the shit refers to the "wheeling and dealing that's poisoning us," to "hustling products and people, making no distinction between the two," and to "money," which is "what it's all about": "When you're dealing in millions, you're dealing with people at their meanest. Christ, a showdown in the Old West is nothing compared with the infighting that goes on over money. To get my films made, especially at the beginning, I always had to lie and cheat and steal. It was the only way I could cope with all the muscle that stood behind the weight of the money. And even then I couldn't win." It is easy to see why the conflicts in his films are so often reducible to friendship or love or loyalty in opposition to gold or greed or any other kind of purely personal gain in the materialistic sense: like his obsession with whoring, these subjects weren't discovered by Peckinpah, they were thrust upon him. And the virtues he found in a heroic mythology answered both a private desperation and an artistic need: "If I get sucked into this consumer-oriented society, then I can't make the pictures about it that I want to make."

In a remark like that we can begin to see how close Peckinpah's concerns remain to those of the jeremiad. He made this more or less explicit in his famous observation, delivered at a press conference following an early preview of *The Wild Bunch,* in response to a question asking why he didn't make a film about Vietnam if he really wanted to make a statement about violence: "The Western is a universal frame within which it is possible to comment on today."[57] Peckinpah's Western films have always, it seems by now superfluous to point out, been more about "today" than about yesterday, the means and methods he employs "to comment" suggesting a parallel to Norman Mailer's "The White Negro." For even as Mailer, in a world almost oppressively defined by the three great modern determinisms of Marx, Darwin, and Freud, would like to raise man once again to "a neo-medieval summit" in order to restore to him some measure of control over his own destiny, so Peckinpah resurrects an old, essentially antique mode of heroism that originates in the epic in order to indicate something of what he feels has both gone out of and is needed to withstand contemporary life. At the same time, both author and filmmaker realize that a fixation on the past *qua* past is often nothing more than sentimentality and even primitivism, that the hard facts of the past are scarcely less grim than those of the present, and that the actual past does not always offer the most admirable models for emulation. So they refer us to a mythic past and direct their visions toward a future they hope will be possible.

In any and all of this there is little that is new and nothing that is wholly unfamiliar. If we don't see that both Emerson and Thoreau were worried about the replacement of "higher laws" by the mean, grubbing, and avaricious ambitions of a business ethos, then we need to take a closer look at their writings; if we don't realize that the virtues they asked their countrymen to develop in order to combat that ethos recall the heroic ideal of a mythic past rooted in the epics of antiquity, then we do not know all of Emerson's representative men and have forgotten some of the books Thoreau read for inspiration those mornings at Walden Pond; if we are not aware that Emerson and Thoreau, and Hawthorne, Melville, and Whitman, in their several ways cast the most profound and cynical aspersions on what their country confidently regarded as its "progress," then we have fallen prey to many of the same delusions they directed their energies toward exposing; and if we have forgotten that they regarded nature in one of its aspects as furnishing a place where the citizen could go to cleanse himself of society's dross, returning as a true individual, pure, refreshed, and fortified to do battle once again with civilization and its discontents, then the impact of the loss of the wilderness upon our national psyche is greater than the subsequent artists in this tradition have warned us it would be.

Even the very idea of transcendence, a theme of Peckinpah's that has not received much attention, is never far from his concerns, and nowhere does he give it greater or more powerful expression that at the ends of his films: the mountains that, as they witness and ratify the death of Steve Judd, seem to absorb his very spirit and being; the release of the Wild Bunch into folklore, legend, and myth; the moving of Cable Hogue into the whole torrent of the years, his joining the souls that pass and never stop. Nor is the idea of transcendence limited to its metaphysical aspect. At least as often it takes the form of facing and then freeing oneself from the prison of the past, as Pike Bishop does, or simply of going beyond the limitations of any moment in life by staying in motion, acquiring more experience, literally more of life itself, so that the old habit or habit of thought can be broken in the collision of self and society. And the great archetype that we so often find at the center of American art and expression, the archetype that Emerson imagined as the single man planted indomitably upon his instincts against the huge world, has several times been visualized by Peckinpah in compositions and stagings, but nowhere so purely, so profoundly, or so essentially as in the scene that concludes with what may yet come to be regarded as the single most beautiful image in any of his films: Pike on his horse riding away from us into a limitless expanse of sand, sky, and sunlight—an image of the frontier and of our relationship to it that, in its richness of implication, suggestion, and significance, can stand with Fitzgerald's evocation of that new world which put us face to face for the last time in history with something commensurate to our capacity for wonder.

If Peckinpah's work is most richly illuminated by being placed within a tradition of American art and expression that goes at least as far back as the period that has come to be known as the American Renaissance, it is because his life, his career, and his art have been shaped by circumstances and conditions that are parallel, analogous, or nearly identical to those that shaped the earlier period. As a consequence they have given rise to the development in his films of sim-

ilar or corresponding concerns, subjects, and themes. Of course, his
voice and his art are his own because his relationship to the world is
original in the Emersonian sense. But his work is fully understood
only against the backdrop of this tradition, and as an extension and
development of it. "When I was five or six years old," Peckinpah once
told Garner Simmons, "I remember riding my horse up around the
pines in Crane Valley. Her name was Nellie, and I'd only have a rope
around her nose for a rein—a handmade hackamore. It was where
my grandfather, Denver Church, ran his cattle. And a couple of miles
away, my Grandfather Peckinpah had built his sawmill. It was the
finest time of my life. There will never be another time like that
again."[58] This is no exaggeration. What is being recollected here is
an experience, spiritual in its implications, that impressed itself indelibly upon the boy and to the end of his life never deserted the
man. If we dismiss it as mere nostalgia, then there is a fair amount
of the American experience as captured and expressed in our literature and culture that we would have to throw out as well. To call this
early memory "transcendental" may be an overstatement, but an
Emerson or a Thoreau would have had no trouble recognizing the
conditions, and would have been pleased that all the important conventions are observed and satisfied. It takes place in the wilderness
and is characterized by an intimacy with the landscape that we know
only as children—perhaps the closest equivalent in life to Emerson's
ideal of experiencing nature without any mediator whatsoever.
Though the experience is solitary, there is a great feeling of oneness
with the world and a sense of being connected to something beyond
and much larger than the self that is nevertheless continuous with
the self—hence, the awareness of the two grandfathers and the currents of history that flow through them. The intensity of the experience is matched only by its equally intense evanescence, and the very
brevity is part of what gives it, in Richard Poirier's words, that "enormous sense of inner authority," almost as if it were a revelation and
thus religious in its significance. This in turn is reinforced by the
subtext, which recalls once again the jeremiad: all the rest of life is
held up against it and judged wanting in the comparison.

    Just as the same patterns turn up again and again in the work of
many different American artists, sometimes the forces that operate
on one artist's career reconjoin with almost uncanny exactitude to
affect another's in a similar way. Inasmuch as Peckinpah always insisted he was a storyteller first, and a most personal one at that, it is
appropriate that the figure about to be introduced is America's first
great "personal" storyteller. It will be recalled that in "The Custom

House," the *quasi*-autobiographical preface to *The Scarlet Letter,* Hawthorne imagines himself visited by two long-dead ancestors. One of these, brandishing both "his Bible and his sword," "was a soldier, legislator, judge," "ruler in the Church," and possessed "all the Puritanic traits, both good and bad"; the other, son of the first, having inherited the persecuting strain, "made himself so conspicuous in the martyrdom of the witches, that their blood may fairly be said to have left a stain upon him." Both ancestors played large determining roles in the history of their native Salem (the older evidently from the very beginning or at least, taking Hawthorne at his word, from the time when the streets numbered only one and that one was still "unworn"), and both perpetrated appalling cruelties in the performance of their official duties. Though ashamed of the nearly criminal excesses to which their religious zeal led them and offering to take their sins upon himself, Hawthorne nevertheless imagines the purpose of their visit is to ridicule him for disgracing the family line by becoming a "degenerate fellow," a mere "writer of story-books." And yet, he continues, as if he had to justify himself to them, "let them scorn me as they will, strong traits of their nature have intertwined themselves with mine." What he means is that among other things certain Puritan notions of sin, guilt, penance, and penitence found their way into his novels, as did also some of his ancestors' actual crimes, which then makes his stories criticisms as well as embodiments of Puritan spirit and sentiment.

Except for the absence of any persecutors in the Peckinpah family closet, the similarities are obvious enough: Peckinpah's family has a long history of judges and legislators who go all the way back to the inception of their native town and county, who were powerfully authoritarian, who brandished no swords but fired their fair share of rifles and carried pretty big Bibles and law books, and who played large roles in shaping local, state, and national history. Like Hawthorne, Peckinpah became the black sheep, the first to revolt against the dominant family occupation, becoming (against what the family considered better judgment) a mere teller of story-films, films that in part are by their maker's own admission criticisms, questionings, and continuations of those family conversations in which he felt the oppressive weight of that authority. Thus, obviously and equally strong traits of their nature intertwined themselves with his own, but, as with Hawthorne, only so that he may say, No!, in as much thunder as he can.

It hardly needs to be pointed out that Hawthorne's fascination with, even preference for, the remote, the exotic, and the antique all have analogues in Peckinpah. Although the gothic element appeared only sporadically in the director's films up through *The Ballad of Cable Hogue*, after that it got a fair workout in *Straw Dogs* and a thorough one in *Bring Me the Head of Alfredo Garcia*, a remarkable film whose submerged sexual tensions and guilts have little precedent in American films but are surely not unfamiliar to any readers up on their Hawthorne (or Faulkner, specifically *Sanctuary*, which once especially struck Peckinpah's fancy).* Hawthorne's obsession with individuals who are themselves obsessed with guilt, vengeance, or any other kind of all-consuming, self-destructive passion is mirrored in many of Peckinpah's characters, who are similarly afflicted, sometimes in the form of what we have elsewhere identified as the "Fred C. Dobbs" complex of paranoia (which the director gave his grimmest, it might even be said almost Hawthornesque treatment in the aforementioned *Alfredo Garcia*). Both artists also share the same interest in the processes by which history becomes myth: Hawthorne "finds" the scarlet letter itself and the story of Hester Prynne among some old, discarded, official papers in a dusty corner of the Custom House, and after retelling it informs us at the end that the "story of the scarlet letter grew into legend." Likewise, the alternation of desaturated and color images at the beginning of *The Wild Bunch* is Peckinpah's way of suggesting that the story is emerging from old newspaper accounts, and by the time the film has ended the last escapade of Pike, Dutch, Angel, and the Gorch brothers has become the stuff of legend.

Both storytellers also share a religious streak that, though narrow and set at rather an oblique slant, ran to their very cores. For Hawthorne the greatest sin, which he symbolized by hypnotism, is for one person completely to take over the soul of another. This almost always happens only after the perpetrator gains his victim's trust, so the sin is thus one of betrayal (and perhaps a form of hubris). In Peck-

---

*The mention of *Bring Me the Head of Alfredo Garcia* brings to mind a purely coincidental link between these two storytellers that has nothing to do with artistic congruence as such, but is otherwise too irresistible to let pass unnoted. In "The Custom House" Hawthorne writes about losing his position as surveyor of customs owing to a change in administrations. "If the guillotine . . . were a literal fact instead of . . . the most apt of metaphors," he observes, "the active members of the victorious party were sufficiently excited to have chopped off all our heads." Fancying that he was more secure in his office than most of his fellow Democrats, he asks, "But who can see an inch into futurity beyond his nose? My own head was the first that fell!" Getting a little playful with his metaphor, he adds, "The moment when a man's head drops off is seldom or never, I am inclined to think, precisely the most agreeable of his life": "the press had taken up my affair, and kept me, for a week or two, careering through the public prints, in my decapitated state, like Irving's Headless Horseman."

inpah, the greatest sin is always betrayal, which never cuts so deeply as when it cuts closest—from friends, family, and partners.

There are a few other important ways that these two only superficially dissimilar types may be associated. At the end of *The Scarlet Letter* Hawthorne enjoins us to "be true, be true, show your worst to the world or, if not your worst, then some symbol by which your worst may be inferred." Peckinpah once said, "In a film you lay yourself out, whoever you are."[59] There is no need to recall the pertinent scenes from all the obvious films to realize how obsessively Peckinpah endeavored to show his worst to the world. Neither the filmmaker nor the novelist was able to confess directly the guilt that tormented him, but they were both marvelously able to symbolize or otherwise allude to it in stories of extraordinary psychological depth and emotional intensity. And equally applicable to Peckinpah's films is Hawthorne's famous distinction between a romance and a novel: the letter aims "at a very minute fidelity to the probable and ordinary course of man's experience"; the former, though "it must rigidly subject itself to laws, and while it sins unpardonably, so far as it may swerve aside from the truth of the human heart," "has fairly a right to present that truth under circumstances, to a great extent, of the writer's own chosing or creation."

A complex romantic to the end, Peckinpah always presented his truths under circumstances of his own creation, answerable to few laws outside the films themselves and the artistic traditions to which they allude. He learned early all he needed to know about putting real horses onto imaginary prairies. And the truth of the human heart was for him, no less than for his great predecessor, the first and fundamental aim of storytelling. In 1975 he was asked to write a letter to his second-grade teacher, then in an old people's home. "You might be disappointed in some of the things I'm doing," he wrote her, "but my basic studies now are of the human heart and the unfortunate penchant of human beings toward violence."[60] And not long after finishing *The Wild Bunch* he told an aspiring writer who had sent him a couple of screenplays for evaluation: "I felt that you found your stories not from your own life and guts but in the silver screen of the past. You have a talent, now stop this nonsense and use it where it hurts—in your own heart."[61]

IV

Peckinpah was certainly an artist who practiced what he preached. Whatever else can be said of his films, they are a remarkable extension of the man. In them he transmuted the most important things he knew and felt and believed into some of the most beautiful works of film art ever made. Yet no talent, however individual, is *sui generis*. It has traditions that have shaped it and in turn been shaped by it, and an awareness of those traditions is as essential to a complete understanding of the individual talent as are close viewings of particular works. Peckinpah's traditions we have located in the richest, most protean American cultural heritage of them all. His sources we have charted through his personal history, his family and their history, the books and plays he read and studied, the films he watched, and, most important of all, the experience he acquired along the way. In the course of analyzing his work, we have met his characters, traveled the landscapes in which they lived and died, and retold their stories.

A desire to unify our cultural experience is natural enough and requires only that we exercise some caution, restraint, and judgment so that we may recognize when significant similarities blur into meaningless generalities, at which point we must be prepared to shift perspectives—say, by cutting from long-shot to closeup, then halfway back again so that we may conclude at medium distance. Nobody has recognized anything in Peckinpah's work that wasn't transformed into something authentically his own by the time it got there; and like them or hate them, no one mistakes his films for anybody else's. If, as Henry Cowell once said, the fabric of existence weaves itself whole, then it may be that in the end—whether due to direct influence, sociocultural osmosis, or simply that faculty which, Henry James tells us, enables the artist to fashion ells from inches—the experience of an artist's country always eventually finds its way into his personal experience, so that by telling his own story he invariably tells a story about his country.

Just how synonymous these stories are in the case of this artist is suggested by a remarkable picture that, not coincidentally, places our subject at medium distance, thereby affording the best perspective from which to take leave of him. This photograph, taken while he was making *The Ballad of Cable Hogue* in the Nevada desert and reproduced at the beginning of this chapter, speaks eloquently enough of what has gone into shaping him and of the contradictions that reside in both the man and the artist. It shows us a weathered, shirtless, almost Indian-looking man (except for the beard) astride a camera boom, his forehead wrapped in a bandana to soak up the sweat, his eyes squinting against the sun, now high above the environing desert, the setting of so many of his best films. The composition joins together man and machine, locates them in nature, and sees them enveloped in the immensity of Western space.

Studied long enough the picture begins to touch off reverberations of other pictures, the artist and the chief instrument of his art, a machine he called a piece of divinity, appearing as one integral figure, not unlike the solitary horse and rider that we are reminded of from his films. Art seems to be dissolving into life, boxes appear nestled within boxes, and we are reminded of something else: that in the right hands a camera is a window that opens at least as much into the heart and mind of the person who looks through it as it does onto the world he looks out at. If we look closely at his face, the expression we find there is, for all its intensity, not anger but something that will pass for happiness, perhaps because, sitting up there on the boom, about to look into the viewfinder, he is at work doing what he liked doing, and did, best: taking and making pictures. By now all his pictures have been made and no new ones will be taken. But this is still the best place to close a book on him—just as, focusing the lens and giving the command to action, he begins clarifying his thoughts and arranging his experiences into the sights and sounds that will become his art.

Notes

Introduction

1. Michael Sragow, "Sam Peckinpah, 1925–1984" (1985), rpt. in *Doing It Right: The Best Criticism on Sam Peckinpah's The Wild Bunch,* ed. Michael Bliss (Carbondale: Southern Illinois University Press, 1994), p. 181.

2. Kathleen Murphy, "Orbits: Sam Peckinpah: No Bleeding Heart," *Film Comment* 21, no. 2 (Mar.–Apr. 1985): 74–75.

3. Pauline Kael, "Peckinpah's Obsession" (1972), rpt. in her *For Keeps* (New York: Dutton, 1994), p. 422.

4. Quoted in David Weddle, *"If They Move . . . Kill 'Em!": The Life and Times of Sam Peckinpah* (New York: Grove Press, 1994), p. 548.

5. Sam Peckinpah to P.S., spring 1982.

6. Sam Peckinpah to P.S., spring 1983.

Chapter 1: Westerners

1. Richard Whitehall, "Talking with Peckinpah," *Sight and Sound* 38, no. 4 (Autumn 1969): 173.

2. John Cutts, "Shoot! Sam Peckinpah Talks to John Cutts," *Films and Filming* 16, no. 1 (Oct. 1969): 5.

3. Quoted in Garner Simmons, *Peckinpah: A Portrait in Montage* (Austin: University of Texas Press, 1982), p. 27.

4. Quoted in David Weddle, *"If They Move . . . Kill 'Em!": The Life and Times of Sam Peckinpah* (New York: Grove Press, 1994), p. 129.

5. Quoted in Simmons, p. 28.

6. Cutts, p. 5.

7. This and the next two quotations are from Weddle, pp. 147–48.

8. Quoted in Simmons, p. 30.

9. Jim Silke, "Wanted Sam Peckinpah Alias Dave Blassingame, Steve Judd," interview with Sam Peckinpah, *Cinema* 1, no. 4 (June–July 1962): 35.

10. Pauline Kael, "Notes on the Nihilistic Poetry of Sam Peckinpah" (1976), rpt. in her *For Keeps* (New York: Dutton, 1984), p. 668.

11. Quoted in Cecil Smith's column "The TV Scene," circa fall 1960 (a clipping is in the Peckinpah Collection, Margaret Herrick Library, Academy of Motion Picture Arts and Sciences, Beverly Hills, Calif. [hereafter, "Peckinpah Collection"]).

12. This and the next quotation are from Whitehall, pp. 173–74.

13. Patrick R. Betz to Sam Peckinpah, memo, 20 May 1960 (Peckinpah Collection).

14. James Powers, review of *The Westerner, The Hollywood Reporter,* 3 Oct. 1960, p. 9.

15. Whitehall, p. 174. Or so Peckinpah said, but a memo in his files schedules the first comedy in the fourth week, while the second episode to be aired was "School Day."

16. Several years later Gries used his teleplay as the basis for his first feature, *Will Penny,* starring Charlton Heston. For some of its length the film follows the episode in offering a realistic picture of a working cowboy's life. But Gries added a love story and transformed the hunters into a motherless family of one-dimensional crazies led by a religious-zealot father played by a bulging-eyed Donald Pleasance. In other words, the feature doesn't just lack the complexity of the original, it goes in quite the opposite direction. Despite his enthusiasm for "The Line Camp" and his friendship with Gries, Peckinpah had only a qualified admiration for the feature, and he detested the ending: "a real cop out with all that phony action" ("Sam Peckinpah Lets It All Hang Out," *Take One* 2, no. 3 [Jan.–Feb. 1969]: 20).

17. David Weddle, "'If They Move . . . Kill 'Em!': The Life and Times of Sam Peckinpah," unpublished second draft, 1991, pp. 336–38 (hereafter, "Weddle, unpublished draft").

18. Quoted in Ernest Callenbach, "A Conversation with Sam Peckinpah," *Film Quarterly* 17, no. 2 (Winter 1963–64): 5.

19. Whitehall, p. 173.

20. Garner Simmons to P.S., 1994.

21. Quoted in Aljean Harmetz, "Man Was a Killer Long Before He Served a God" (1969), rpt. in *Doing It Right: The Best Criticism on Sam Peckinpah's The Wild Bunch,* ed. Michael Bliss (Carbondale: Southern Illinois University Press, 1994), p. 173.

22. Cutts, p. 5.

23. Callenbach, p. 7.

24. Cutts, p. 5.

25. Callenbach, p. 9.

26. "*Playboy* Interview: Sam Peckinpah," *Playboy,* Aug. 1972, p. 72.

27. Sam Peckinpah to P.S., 1977.

28. This and the next two quotations are from Simmons, pp. 38–39.

29. Callenbach, p. 9.

Chapter 2: The High Country

1. Richard E. Lyons to P.S., 1976.

2. This and the next quotation are from Garner Simmons, *Peckinpah: A Portrait in Montage* (Austin: University of Texas Press, 1982), p. 43.

3. Joel McCrea to P.S., 1977.

4. Ernest Callenbach, "A Conversation with Sam Peckinpah," *Film Quarterly* 17, no. 2 (Winter 1963–64): 10.

5. Randolph Scott to P.S., 1977.

6. Quoted in Simmons, p. 44.

7. Quoted in Jan Aghed, "*Pat Garrett and Billy the Kid*," *Sight and Sound* 42, no. 2 (Spring 1973): 68. See also Colin McArthur, "Sam Peckinpah's West," *Sight and Sound* 36, no. 41 (Autumn 1967): 182.

8. John Cutts, "Shoot! Sam Peckinpah Talks to John Cutts," *Films and Filming* 16, no. 1 (Oct. 1969): 5.

9. Cutts, p. 5.

10. Callenbach, p. 10.

11. "*Playboy* Interview: Sam Peckinpah," *Playboy*, Aug. 1972, p. 72.

12. Richard Whitehall, "Talking with Peckinpah," *Sight and Sound* 38, no. 4 (Autumn 1969): 174.

13. Fern Lea Peter to P.S., 1994.

14. David Weddle, "*If They Move . . . Kill 'Em!*": *The Life and Times of Sam Peckinpah* (New York: Grove Press, 1994), p. 212.

15. Callenbach, p. 7.

16. Quoted in Paul Schrader, "Sam Peckinpah Going to Mexico" (1969), rpt. in *Doing It Right: The Best Criticism on Sam Peckinpah's The Wild Bunch*, ed. Michael Bliss (Carbondale: Southern Illinois University Press, 1994), p. 19.

17. Quoted in David Weddle, "'If They Move . . . Kill 'Em!': The Life and Times of Sam Peckinpah," unpublished second draft, 1991, pp. 381–82.

18. *Playboy* interview, p. 72.

19. Quoted in Simmons, p. 17.

20. Quoted in Schrader, p. 25.

21. McArthur calls it "judicial rather than humane" (p. 182).

22. *Playboy* interview, p. 74.

Chapter 3: The *Dundee* Story

1. Or so Peckinpah liked to tell it. Lyons's recollection was that only he was in attendance at the screening, while the director waited elsewhere.

2. Richard E. Lyons to P.S., 1976.

3. Quoted in Garner Simmons, *Peckinpah: A Portrait in Montage* (Austin: University of Texas Press, 1982), p. 52.

4. *Playboy* Interview: Sam Peckinpah," *Playboy*, Aug. 1972, p. 74.

5. William Goldman, *Adventures in the Screen Trade: A Personal View of Hollywood and Screenwriting* (New York: Warner Books, 1983), p. 70.

6. John Cutts, "Shoot! Sam Peckinpah Talks to John Cutts," *Films and Filming* 16, no. 1 (Oct. 1969): 6.

7. Cutts, p. 6.

8. Quoted in Garner Simmons, "Sam Peckinpah's Television Work," *Film Heritage* 10, no. 2 (Winter 1974–75): 11.

9. Quoted in David Weddle, "*If They Move . . . Kill 'Em!*": *The Life and Times of Sam Peckinpah* (New York: Grove Press, 1994), p. 182.

10. Cutts, p. 8.

11. Cutts, p. 6.

12. This and the next two quotations are from Sam Peckinpah to Harry Julian Fink, letter, 13 Sept. 1963 (Peckinpah Collection, Margaret Herrick

Library, Academy of Motion Picture Arts and Sciences, Beverly Hills, Calif. [hereafter, "Peckinpah Collection"]).

13. Cutts, p. 6.

14. Quoted in Weddle, p. 235.

15. Cutts, p. 6.

16. *Dialogue on Film: Charlton Heston, Jack Nicholson*, no. 1 (Beverly Hills: American Film Institute, 1972), p. 12. Unless otherwise noted, all subsequent remarks by Heston come from this interview.

17. Richard Whitehall, "Talking with Peckinpah," *Sight and Sound* 38, no. 4 (Autumn 1969): 175.

18. This and the next quotation are from Cutts, p. 6.

19. Jim Kitses, *Horizons West: Anthony Mann, Budd Boetticher, Sam Peckinpah: Studies in Authorship within the Western* (Bloomington: Indiana University Press, 1969), pp. 139–40. Kitses's book contains a detailed description of what was and was not filmed and also of what was filmed and then removed.

20. Cutts, p. 6.

21. *Playboy* interview, p. 74.

22. "Sam Peckinpah Lets It All Hang Out," interview with Sam Peckinpah, *Take One* 2, no. 3 (Jan.–Feb. 1969): 20.

23. Charlton Heston, *The Actor's Life* (New York: E. P. Dutton, 1978), p. 190.

24. Quoted in Marvin Kupfer, "Director of Violent Movies Opposes Killing, He Says," *Pittsburgh Press*, 5 May 1972, p. 12.

25. As a matter of record, the following discrepancies between fact and film may be worth noting. First, there were no prison garrisons for rebel captives as far west as New Mexico, nor were there any posts with Confederate volunteers as far south as even the northern borders of Texas and New Mexico. Second, while there were some problems of adjustment, most of the evidence suggests that Confederate volunteers were loyal and skilled soldiers, and in the judgment of their Union officers they were more reliable than the local recruits and volunteers (which, as the film correctly shows, were often taken from the ranks of thieves, cutthroats, and renegades). Third, the film's Sierra Charriba, who seems to be based on Geronimo, is Apache, which may be anachronistic. Although there was Apache raiding in the Southwestern states throughout the Civil War, the action the galvanized Yankees saw was confined to areas north of Texas and New Mexico; it primarily involved the Cheyenne, Sioux, Kiowa, and other plains Indians, not the Apaches, who were involved several years after the Civil War was over. Fourth, the film is on the right track regarding Dundee's Southern background. It was not uncommon during the Civil War to station Union officers of Southern birth or background in the West, precisely so that they could avoid the conflicts of interest the Civil War posed for them. The film's complexity would be increased if this were shown to be among the reasons Dundee's superiors stationed him out West; and the sheer stupidity of his disregard for the rules in this instance would be intensified if it were brought out that among the reasons the galvanized Yankees were confined to the plains is precisely so that additional conflicts of interest could be avoided. (Pertinent historical

texts are: D. Alexander Brown, *The Galvanized Yankees* [Urbana: University of Illinois Press, 1963]; Arlen L. Fowler, *The Black Infantry in the West, 1869–1891* [Westport, Conn.: Greenwood, 1971]; and William H. Leckie, *The Buffalo Soldiers: A Narrative of the Negro Cavalry in the West* [Norman: University of Oklahoma Press, 1967].)

26. Sam Peckinpah to Mike Frankovitch, Arthur Kramer, and Jerry Bresler, memo, 3 Sept. 1964 (Peckinpah Collection).

27. Cutts, p. 6.

28. Sam Peckinpah to Bob Woods, letter, 26 Oct. 1973 (Peckinpah Collection).

29. Quoted in Weddle, p. 233.

30. Kitses, p. 146. Kitses constructs the best argument for *Major Dundee* as a metaphoric treatment of the Civil War and beyond that of a country in search of an identity.

31. Quoted in Weddle, p. 250.

32. Stephen Farber, "Peckinpah's Return," review of *The Wild Bunch* and interview with Sam Peckinpah (1969), rpt. in *Doing It Right: The Best Criticism on Sam Peckinpah's The Wild Bunch,* ed. Michael Bliss (Carbondale: Southern Illinois University Press, 1994), pp. 8–9.

33. Stanley Kauffmann, review of *Major Dundee, New Republic,* 17 Apr. 1965, p. 40. Kauffmann's review is actually very appreciative—it is one of the few favorable American reviews the film received—and understandably registers mystification with some of the discontinuities.

Chapter 4: The Farmer and the Farmer's Wife

1. David Weddle, *"If They Move . . . Kill 'Em!": The Life and Times of Sam Peckinpah* (New York: Grove Press, 1994), p. 257.

2. Stephen Farber, "Peckinpah's Return," review of *The Wild Bunch* and interview with Sam Peckinpah (1969), rpt. in *Doing It Right: The Best Criticism on Sam Peckinpah's The Wild Bunch,* ed. Michael Bliss (Carbondale: Southern Illinois University Press, 1994), p. 7.

3. John Cutts, "Shoot! Sam Peckinpah Talks to John Cutts," *Films and Filming* 16, no. 1 (Oct. 1969): 6.

4. This and the next three quotations are from Sam Peckinpah to Robert Weitman (Head of Production, MGM), letter, 7 Dec. 1964, pp. 1, 7 (Peckinpah Collection, Margaret Herrick Library, Academy of Motion Picture Arts and Sciences, Beverly Hills, Calif. [hereafter, "Peckinpah Collection"]).

5. If anyone were to average the combined overages against the combined budgets of all Peckinpah's films, the percentage would be not only relatively small and rather the norm at the time for the kinds of pictures he was making, but also a tiny fraction of what has since become typical.

6. Pauline Kael, *Reeling* (Boston: Little, Brown, 1976), p. 331.

7. Cutts, p. 8.

8. "Sam Peckinpah Lets It All Hang Out," interview with Sam Peckinpah, *Take One* 2, no. 3 (Jan.–Feb. 1969): 20.

9. Clipping, circa 1965, in the Peckinpah Collection.

10. "*Playboy* Interview: Sam Peckinpah," *Playboy*, Aug. 1972, p. 74.

11. Daniel Melnick to P.S., 1995.

12. Quoted in *Sam Peckinpah's West: A Study of the Filmmaker*, produced and directed by Joel Reisner and Bruce Kane for KPFK radio's Tenth Anniversary Celebration, broadcast 21 July 1969 (hereafter, "*Sam Peckinpah's West*, KPFK"). A cassette transfer is on file in the Peckinpah Collection.

13. Daniel Melnick to P.S., 1995.

14. Quoted in Weddle, p. 285.

15. *Sam Peckinpah's West*, KPFK.

16. Daniel Melnick to P.S., 1995; Porter's remarks as quoted in *Sam Peckinpah's West*, KPFK.

17. Daniel Melnick to P.S., 1995.

18. This and subsequent quotations of Peckinpah's marginalia come from his copies of the novel and Porter's essay, which are in the Peckinpah Collection.

19. Quoted in Aljean Harmetz, "Man Was a Killer Long Before He Served a God" (1969), rpt. in *Doing It Right*, p. 173.

20. Quoted in Weddle, p. 18.

21. Quoted in Weddle, pp. 21–22.

22. Fern Lea Peter to P.S., 1994.

23. Quoted in P. F. Kluge, "Director Sam Peckinpah: What Price Violence?" *Life*, 11 Aug. 1972, p. 52.

24. Quoted in David Weddle, "'If They Move . . . Kill 'Em!': The Life and Times of Sam Peckinpah," unpublished second draft, 1991, p. 63 (hereafter, "Weddle, unpublished draft").

25. *Playboy* interview, p. 72.

26. *Playboy* interview, p. 72; and Richard Whitehall, "Talking with Peckinpah," *Sight and Sound* 38, no. 4 (Autumn 1969): 173.

27. Fern Lea Peter to P.S., 1995.

28. *Playboy* interview, p. 72.

29. Fern Lea Peter to P.S., 1995.

30. Fern Lea Peter to P.S., 1995.

31. Quoted in Weddle, p. 187.

32. Quoted in Weddle, unpublished draft, p. 221.

33. Fern Lea Peter to P.S., 1995.

34. Quoted in Kluge, p. 52.

35. Quoted in Weddle, unpublished draft, p. 368.

36. Fern Lea Peter quoted in Weddle, p. 195.

37. See, for example, "The Squaw Man" (Peckinpah Collection).

38. Sam Peckinpah to David Peckinpah, letter, 19 Aug. 1960 (Peckinpah Collection).

39. Quoted in Simmons, p. 34.

40. Weddle, p. 114.

41. Quoted in Weddle, p. 32.

42. This and the next two quotations are from Simmons, pp. 13–14.

43. Quoted in Weddle, p. 164.

44. Fern Lea Peter to P.S., 1995.

45. Quoted in Weddle, p. 42.

46. Denver Peckinpah, quoted in Simmons, p. 11.

47. Quoted in Weddle, p. 37.

48. Quoted in Weddle, p. 37.

49. James Hamilton, "The Judge and His Brother," *South Dakota Review* 29, no. 1 (Spring 1991): 76–94. This lovely essay reveals Denver to be as colorful and fascinating a character as his more well-known brother.

50. This and the next two quotations are from James Hamilton to P.S., letter, 22 Mar. 1995.

51. Sam Peckinpah to P.S., 1978.

52. Quoted in Weddle, unpublished draft, p. 363.

53. *Playboy* interview, p. 72.

54. David S. ("Sam") Peckinpah, "An Analysis of the Method Used in Producing and Directing a One Act Play for the Stage and for a Closed Circuit Television Broadcast" (Master's thesis, University of Southern California, Los Angeles, 1954), pp. 10–11. Both the written portion of the thesis project and a kinescope of the film, *Portrait of a Madonna*, are in the Doheny Memorial Library at the university.

55. Peckinpah, master's thesis, p. 11.

56. Weddle, p. 538.

57. See Weddle, p. 294.

Chapter 5: Men without Women

1. Robert Culp, "Sam Peckinpah, the Storyteller and *The Wild Bunch*" (1970), rpt. in *Doing It Right: The Best Criticism on Sam Peckinpah's The Wild Bunch,* ed. Michael Bliss (Carbondale: Southern Illinois University Press, 1994), p. 5.

2. Sam Peckinpah to P.S., 1977. Unless otherwise noted, all subsequent remarks by Peckinpah in this essay come from this source. For more on the differences between the Green and Peckinpah scripts, see Garner Simmons, *Peckinpah: A Portrait in Montage* (Austin: University of Texas Press, 1982), pp. 82–83, 99; and David Weddle, *"If They Move . . . Kill 'Em!": The Life and Times of Sam Peckinpah* (New York: Grove Press, 1994), pp. 307–18.

3. This and the next quotation are from Joel Reisner and Bruce Kane, "Sam Peckinpah," *Action: Directors Guild of America* 2, no. 3 (May–June 1970): 25.

4. Quoted in Paul Schrader, "Sam Peckinpah Going to Mexico" (1969), rpt. in *Doing It Right,* p. 22.

5. Quoted in Vincent Canby, "Which Version Did You See?" *New York Times,* 20 July 1969, sec. D, p. 7. Unless otherwise noted, all remarks by Feldman or Canby come from this source.

6. Richard Whitehall, "Talking with Peckinpah," *Sight and Sound* 38, no. 4 (Autumn 1969): 175.

7. Jay Cocks, review of *Straw Dogs* and profile on Sam Peckinpah, *Time*, 20 Dec. 1971, p. 87.

8. Quoted in Schrader, p. 22.

9. Because the European prints were originally in 70mm, some confusion has arisen over the years to the effect that if *The Wild Bunch* isn't shown in 70, it can't be the complete version. This is mistaken. The designations 70mm and 35mm refer only to the width of stock on which a film is shot or projected. In 1969 the only way stereophonic sound could be played back was by way of a magnetic stripe physically attached to the print. Hence any film that was dubbed in stereo, as *The Wild Bunch* was, *whether shot in 70mm or not,* had to be printed on the larger stock to accommodate the mag-stripe down the side. Projection in 70 still requires a mag-stripe, but stereo has for years been routinely played back in 35 thanks to such developments as SRD, THX, and various other matrixing systems, to say nothing of the new digital formats like DTS. There is thus no longer any necessity for projecting in 70 the films not shot in 70, and there is even some disadvantage, as the smaller format must be blown up to the larger. This means that most 70mm prints are enlarged dupes; and, technically speaking, let alone aesthetically, no dupe is better than no dupe at all.

10. Whitehall, p. 175.

11. "Sam Peckinpah Lets It All Hang Out," interview with Sam Peckinpah, *Take One* 2, no. 3 (Jan.–Feb. 1969): 19.

12. Gill Dennis to P.S., 1995; see also Weddle, pp. 370–71.

13. Phil Feldman to Sam Peckinpah, memo, 14 May 1969.

14. John Cutts, "Shoot! Sam Peckinpah Talks to John Cutts," *Films and Filming* 16, no. 1 (Oct. 1969): 8.

15. Stephen Farber, "Peckinpah's Return," review of *The Wild Bunch* and interview with Sam Peckinpah (1969), rpt. in *Doing It Right*, p. 39.

16. Phil Feldman to Sam Peckinpah, letter, 21 July 1969 (Peckinpah Collection, Margaret Herrick Library, Academy of Motion Picture Arts and Sciences, Beverly Hills, Calif., [hereafter, "Peckinpah Collection"]).

17. Winfred Blevins, "The Artistic Vision of Director Sam Peckinpah," *Show* 2, no. 1 (Mar. 1972): 38.

18. Grover Lewis, "Sam Peckinpah in Mexico," *Rolling Stone*, 12 Oct. 1972, p. 46.

19. Culp, p. 9.

20. Sam Peckinpah to Phil Feldman, letter, 24 May 1969 (Peckinpah Collection).

21. See, for example, reviews by Gary Reber, *Widescreen Review* 4, no. 6 (Nov.–Dec. 1995): 122; and Edward Buscombe, *Sight and Sound* 5, no. 10 (Oct. 1995): 62.

22. *Take One* interview, p. 19.

23. Sam Peckinpah to Phil Feldman, letter, 24 May 1969 (Peckinpah Collection).

24. In order to suggest a town in transition, Peckinpah gave it two names: signs in the background and later references in the film indicate it is in the process of changing its name from San Rafael to Starbuck.

25. Sam Peckinpah to Phil Feldman, memo, 23 May 1969 (Peckinpah Collection).

26. Ron Shelton, "The Operatic Perversity of the Last Great Western," *American Film* 14, no. 6 (Apr. 1989): 18–20.

27. Farber, p. 39.

28. Stanley Kauffmann, review of *The Wild Bunch* (1969), rpt. in his *Figures of Light* (New York: Harper and Row, 1971), p. 181.

29. This and the next quotation are from Weddle, p. 336.

30. Sam Peckinpah to Ken Hyman, note, 27 Oct. 1967.

31. David Denby, "Violence Enshrined," *Atlantic Monthly*, Apr. 1972, pp. 118, 122.

32. Cordell Strug, "*The Wild Bunch* and the Problem of Idealist Aesthetics, or, How Long Would Peckinpah Last in Plato's Republic?" (1974), rpt. in *Doing It Right*, pp. 87–88.

33. Culp, p. 8.

34. For examples see Judith Crist, reviews of *The Wild Bunch, New York Magazine*, 30 June 1969, p. 43; and 14 July 1969, p. 57; and Arthur Knight, review of *The Wild Bunch, Saturday Review*, 5 July 1969, p. 21.

35. Kauffmann, p. 181. Apart from this and a couple of other obtuse remarks, Kauffmann's is the most astute, intelligent, and perceptive of the first reviews the film received and is very much worth reading for his observations on perspectivism.

36. "*Playboy* Interview: Sam Peckinpah," *Playboy*, Aug. 1972, p. 72.

37. Quoted in John Bryson, "The Wild Bunch in New York," *New York Magazine*, 19 Aug. 1974, p. 27.

38. Northrop Frye, *A Natural Perspective: The Development of Shakespearean Comedy and Romance* (New York: Columbia University Press, 1965), pp. 43–44.

39. This and the next quotation are from Aljean Harmetz, "Man Was a Killer Long Before He Served a God" (1969), rpt. in *Doing It Right*, p. 171.

40. Dwight MacDonald, *Dwight MacDonald on Movies* (Englewood Cliffs, N.J.: Prentice-Hall, 1969), pp. 28, 30.

41. Ernest Callenbach, "A Conversation with Sam Peckinpah," *Film Quarterly* 17, no. 2 (Winter 1963–64): 10.

42. Whitehall, p. 175.

43. Sam Peckinpah addressing a group of students at the Sam Peckinpah Retrospective, Rice University, Houston, Apr. 1984; Prof. Jerry Holt, guest host. (Perhaps not coincidentally, *The Wages of Fear* was remade in 1976 as *Sorcerer*, from a screenplay by Walon Green and directed by William Friedkin.)

44. *Playboy* interview, p. 74.

45. Quoted in Schrader, p. 22.

46. Farber, pp. 42, 45.

47. *Playboy* interview, p. 72.

48. *Take One* interview, p. 18.

49. Quoted in Dan Yergin, "Peckinpah's Progress: From Blood and Killing in the Old West to Siege and Rape in Rural Cornwall," *New York Times Magazine*, 31 Oct. 1971, p. 92.

50. Robert Warshow, "The Westerner" (1954), rpt. in *The Immediate Experience* (Garden City: Doubleday, 1962), pp. 89–106.

51. Kauffmann, p. 181.

52. Quoted in Axel Madsen, "Peckinpah in Mexico," *Sight and Sound* 38, no. 4 (Spring 1974): 91.

53. Strug, p. 88.

54. *Take One* interview, p. 20.

55. Quoted in Simmons, p. 87.

56. Quoted Reisner and Kane, p. 27.

57. Andrew Sarris, review of *The Wild Bunch*, *Village Voice*, 31 July 1969, p. 39.

58. Lucien Ballard to P.S., 1977.

59. Harmetz, p. 171; see also Whitehall, p. 173.

60. Leslie A. Fiedler, *Love and Death in the American Novel*, rev. ed. (New York: Stein and Day, 1960, 1966), p. 390.

61. Richard Chase, *The American Novel and Its Traditions* (Garden City: Doubleday, 1957), pp. 7, 1.

62. D. H. Lawrence, *Studies in Classic American Literature* (1923; rpt. New York: Viking, 1964), p. 83.

Chapter 6: The World Elsewhere

1. In the first chapter of his *The American Novel and Its Traditions* (Garden City: Doubleday, 1957), Richard Chase provides a fine, telescopic essay on this important, difficult issue.

2. "Peckinpah Hits 'Butchery,'" *Variety*, 4 Mar. 1970, pp. 5, 26. See also, "Which Peckinpah Cut Is Unreeling?" *Variety*, 11 Mar. 1970, p. 6.

3. Jacob Brackman, review of *The Ballad of Cable Hogue*, *Esquire*, June 1970, 68.

4. Sam Peckinpah to P.S., 1980.

5. Quoted in Tom Milne, review of *The Ballad of Cable Hogue*, *Sight and Sound* 41, no. 1 (Winter 1971–72): 50. John Crawford and Edmund Penney wrote the original script and received sole screen credit; and Peckinpah said that although he "did some work . . . the credits stand as they do" (Sam Peckinpah to P.S., 1977). However, according to Lucien Ballard (the director of photography), Peckinpah did a lot of rewriting on the set; and Stella Stevens, who plays Hildy, says that Peckinpah reconceived the part for her as soon as she was signed. There may also have been, as with *Ride the High Country*, an arbitration by the Writers Guild, for early advertisements in the trade papers give Peckinpah a second-position writing credit in the billing block.

6. Richard Whitehall, "Talking with Peckinpah," *Sight and Sound* 38, no. 4 (Autumn 1969): 175.

7. *Film World*, interview with Sam Peckinpah, 1970, p. 89 (no additional publication information available but a copy of the interview is in the Peckinpah Collection, Margaret Herrick Library, Academy of Motion Picture Arts and Sciences, Beverly Hills, Calif.).

8. Pauline Kael, *Kiss Kiss Bang Bang* (New York: Bantam Books, 1969), p. 455.

9. Jay Cocks, review of *Straw Dogs, Time*, 20 Dec. 1971, p. 85.

10. See, for examples, David Denby, "Violence Enshrined," *Atlantic Monthly*, Apr. 1972, pp. 118–22, and "Men without Women, Women without Men," in *Film 73/74: An Anthology by the National Society of Film Critics*, ed. Jay Cocks and David Denby (New York: Bobbs-Merrill, 1974), pp. 168–76; Molly Haskell, *From Reverence to Rape: The Treatment of Women in the Movies* (New York: Holt, Rinehart, and Winston, 1974), pp. 363–64; Pauline Kael, *Deeper into Movies* (Boston: Little, Brown, 1973), pp. 393–99; and Michael Korda, review of *Pat Garrett and Billy the Kid*, in *Film 73/74*, pp. 118–19.

11. "*Playboy* Interview: Sam Peckinpah," *Playboy*, Aug. 1972, p. 70.

12. Richard Poirier, *A World Elsewhere: The Place of Style in American Literature* (New York: Oxford University Press, 1966). The quotations from Poirier in this paragraph are from pp. 6–8, 16.

13. *Playboy* interview, p. 74.

14. Poirier, p. 17.

15. Max Evans, *Sam Peckinpah: Master of Violence* (Vermillion, N.D.: Dakota Press), p. 72.

16. Quoted in Aljean Harmetz, "Man Was a Killer Long Before He Served a God" (1969), rpt. in *Doing It Right: The Best Criticism on Sam Peckinpah's The Wild Bunch*, ed. Michael Bliss (Carbondale: Southern Illinois University Press, 1994), p. 173.

17. Poirier, p. 7.

18. Northrop Frye, *The Anatomy of Criticism* (New York: Atheneum, 1968), p. 140.

19. This and the next quotation are from Poirier, pp. 14–15.

20. Pauline Kael, *For Keeps* (New York: Dutton, 1994), p. 422.

21. Northrop Frye, *A Natural Perspective: The Development of Shakespearean Comedy and Romance* (New York: Columbia University Press, 1965), p. 58.

22. Kenneth R. Brown, "Reality Inside-Out: *The Ballad of Cable Hogue*," *Film Heritage* 6, no. 1 (Fall 1970): 1.

23. Quoted in Joel Reisner and Bruce Kane, "Sam Peckinpah," *Action: Directors Guild of America* 5, no. 3 (May–June 1970): 25.

24. Milne, p. 51.

25. Frye, p. 158.

26. Frye, p. 45.

27. Brown, p. 30.

28. R. W. B. Lewis, *The American Adam: Innocence, Tragedy, and Tradition in the Nineteenth Century* (Chicago: University of Chicago Press, 1955). The three quotations that follow are from pp. 5–8.

29. Leo Marx, *The Machine in the Garden: Technology and the Pastoral Ideal in America* (New York: Oxford University Press, 1964), pp. 34–72.

30. Joseph Morgenstern, review of *The Ballad of Cable Hogue, Newsweek*, 23 Mar. 1970, p. 105.

31. Kael, *For Keeps*, p. 147.

32. Philip Young, "Fallen from Time: Rip Van Winkle," *Three Bags Full:*

Essays in American Fiction (New York: Harcourt Brace Jovanovich, 1972), p. 230.

33. Northrop Frye, introduction to *The Tempest* in *William Shakespeare: The Complete Works,* ed. Alfred Harbage (Baltimore: Penguin Books, 1969), p. 1371.

Chapter 7: Two Killers Elite

1. *Film World,* interview with Sam Peckinpah, 1970, p. 89 (no additional publication information available but a copy of the interview is in the Peckinpah Collection, Margaret Herrick Library, Academy of Motion Picture Arts and Sciences, Beverly Hills, Calif., [hereafter, "Peckinpah Collection"]).

2. "Sam Peckinpah Lets It All Hang Out," interview with Sam Peckinpah, *Take One* 2, no. 3 (Jan.–Feb. 1969): 18.

3. Quoted in Jay Cocks, review of *Pat Garrett and Billy the Kid, Time,* 11 June 1973, p. 70.

4. This account of the making of *Pat Garrett and Billy the Kid* is based on interviews conducted by the author with Gordon Carroll (1977), Garth Craven (1977), Jerry Fielding (1977), Daniel Melnick (1995), Sam Peckinpah (1977–78), Garner Simmons (1994–95), Roger Spottiswoode (1977), David Weddle (1994–95), and Robert Wolfe (1977). Unless otherwise noted, all quotations and attributions come from these interviews.

5. Quoted in Jan Aghed, "*Pat Garrett and Billy the Kid,*" *Sight and Sound* 42, no. 2 (Spring 1973): 68.

6. Quoted in David Weddle, *"If They Move . . . Kill 'Em!": The Life and Times of Sam Peckinpah* (New York: Grove Press, 1994), p. 471.

7. Quoted in F. Anthony Macklin, review of *Pat Garrett and Billy the Kid, Film Heritage* 10, no. 2 (Winter 1974–75): 35.

8. Bud Hulburd, who did the special effects on *The Wild Bunch,* visited the set and contracted the flu, dying from it shortly after he returned to the States.

9. This and the next quotation are from Weddle, p. 472.

10. For more on this, see Garner Simmons, *Peckinpah: A Portrait in Montage* (Austin: University of Texas Press, 1982), pp. 169–88.

11. Quoted in Weddle, p. 456.

12. The method of escape—Billy finds a sixgun in the jail's outhouse—is based on one of two stories told by people who were there. The other is that he managed to slip his small hands out of his handcuffs and grab a rifle. (Several witnesses said they saw him slip out of his cuffs many times, often right before his jailers' faces, laughing as he did so.) Although historians remain in dispute as to which story is true, they generally accept the validity of one or the other.

13. Peckinpah wants to make a point of irony: Garrett is sacrificed to the very same forces of "civilization" and "progress" for which he had made himself the instrument twenty-seven years earlier by hiring out to them to bring in the Kid. Given Peckinpah's themes, this is perfectly legitimate artistic li-

cense. All the same, since the murder of Garrett remains one of the most hotly debated and generally confusing incidents in the history of the Old West, the disparities between the film and those aspects of the case about which there is some consensus among historians may be worth noting. First, whereas the real Garrett was shot in the back of the head while urinating behind the buggy in which he had been riding, the film's Garrett is shot as he reaches for his rifle while still seated in the buggy. Second, there is no hard evidence to link the crime with the so-called Santa Fe Ring, the collusion of politicians, businessmen, investors, and some cattlemen believed to have helped arrange the manhunt for Billy the Kid. History abounds in conspiracy theories, and some recent historians have called into question the very existence of any such ring. (It is, however, thoroughly entrenched in the folklore that has grown up around Garrett, the Kid, and the Lincoln County cattle wars; and that folklore claims a large share of Peckinpah's interest in these materials.) Third and last, John W. Poe had nothing whatsoever to do with the murder of Garrett; and, contrary to what the film shows, the relationship between him and Garrett at the time of the manhunt seems to have been amicable. (Probably the most accurate, well-researched, and generally reliable account of Garrett's life and the incidents with which the film deals is Leon C. Metz's excellent biography, *Pat Garrett: The Story of a Western Lawman* [Norman: University of Oklahoma Press, 1974].)

14. Aghed, p. 67.

15. Quoted in Chet Flippo, "Dylan Meets the Durango Kid: Kristofferson and Dylan in Mexico," *Rolling Stone*, 15 Mar. 1973, p. 46.

16. Rudolph Wurlitzer, introduction to *Pat Garrett and Billy the Kid*, Signet Film Series (New York: New American Library, 1973), p. viii. All references to the "original script" or "Wurlitzer's original" or "Wurlitzer's version" are to this publication, which Wurlitzer describes as "a compromise between the first versions and the final, shooting script." Several shooting scripts, with various dates and changes, are available in the Peckinpah Collection.

17. Wurlitzer, pp. v–viii; see also his remarks in Aghed, p. 67.

18. Quoted in Simmons, p. 171.

19. Quoted in Aljean Harmetz, "*Pat Garrett and Billy the Kid:* What You See on the Screen . . . and What You Don't See," *New York Times*, 17 June 1973, sec. D, p. 13.

20. Roger Spottiswoode to P.S., 1977; see also Joseph Leydon, "James Coburn: His Life and 'Hard Times,'" *Take One* 4, no. 12 (July–Aug. 1974): 8.

21. Quoted in Harmetz, p. 13.

22. See, for example, Peter Biskind, "*Pat Garrett and Billy the Kid*," *Film Heritage* 9, no. 2 (Winter 1973–74): 8; and Philip Strick, review of *Pat Garrett and Billy the Kid*, *Sight and Sound* 42, no. 4 (Autumn 1973): 232. Alongside Jay Cocks's review in *Time*, Strick's superb essay is easily the best appreciation the film received at the time of its release and remains one of the most intelligent and insightful commentaries yet written on this difficult, problematic film.

23. The year of Garrett's death was actually 1908, but for unknown rea-

sons the date was got wrong in the title card that opens the prologue: "Near Las Cruces, New Mexico, 1909."

24. Leydon, p. 7.

25. David Denby, "Men with Women, Women without Men," *Film 73/74: An Anthology by the National Society of Film Critics,* ed. Jay Cocks and David Denby (New York: Bobbs-Merrill, 1974), p. 171.

26. Peckinpah later said of Alias, "He's a printer, worked on a newspaper, so I thought people might figure that he was a writer, and a source of some of the legends," adding, "in a script I wrote for Disney, I had a kind of troubadour guitar player, who follows the main character around, building the legend. And then, of course, Arthur Penn used the same thing in *The Left-Handed Gun*" (Sam Peckinpah addressing a group of students at the Sam Peckinpah Retrospective, Rice University, Houston, Apr. 1984, Prof. Jerry Holt, guest host).

27. See, for examples, Biskind, p. 3; and Arthur G. Pettit, "Nightmare and Nostalgia: The Cinema West of Sam Peckinpah," *Western Humanities Review* 29, no. 2 (Spring 1975): 113–14.

28. "*Playboy* Interview: Sam Peckinpah," *Playboy,* Aug. 1972, p. 73.

29. Grover Lewis, "Sam Peckinpah in Mexico: Over-learning with *El Jefe,*" *Rolling Stone,* 12 October 1972, pp. 40–47.

30. Weddle, p. 482.

31. This print is now part of the Peckinpah Collection.

32. Daniel Melnick to P.S., 1995.

33. See Michael Bliss, *Justified Lives: Morality and Narrative in the Films of Sam Peckinpah* (Carbondale: Southern Illinois University Press, 1993), pp. 217–31. Bliss conducts the most ardent and detailed justification for keeping all of the additional material; but doing so forces him to disregard or relegate to lesser importance all considerations of pace, tempo, timing, clarity, focus, and narrative and dramatic concision.

34. Michael Sragow to P.S., 1995.

35. This and the next two quotations are from Weddle, pp. 476–79.

36. Quoted in Weddle, p. 490.

37. Michael Sragow, "Sam Peckinpah, 1925–1984" (1985), rpt. in *Doing It Right: The Best Criticism on Sam Peckinpah's The Wild Bunch,* ed. Michael Bliss (Carbondale: Southern Illinois University Press, 1994), p. 181.

38. Sam Peckinpah to Frank Burke, letter, 25 June 1982 (Peckinpah Collection).

39. Quoted in Simmons, p. 67.

Chapter 8: The Masculine Principle in American Fiction and Film

1. Emerson may be said to bring a new convention to the jeremiad, as he doesn't stop with the invidious comparison of past and present, nor does he wish for a return to bygone days (he is usually quite aware that the past

he is invoking is a mythical, imaginative, or at least a highly selective one), but goes on to predict an optimistic future.

2. Leslie A. Fiedler, *Love and Death in the American Novel*, rev. ed. (New York: Stein and Day, 1960, 1966), p. 212.

3. This and the next quotation are from Frederick Crews, *The Sins of the Fathers: Hawthorne's Psychological Themes* (New York: Oxford University Press, 1966), p. 14.

4. Van Wyck Brooks, *The Ordeal of Mark Twain* (1923; rpt. New York: E. P. Dutton, 1970).

5. Philip Young, "'Big World Out There': *The Nick Adams Stories*," *Novel: A Forum on Fiction* 6, no. 1 (Fall 1972): 18.

6. Quoted in P. F. Kluge, "Director Sam Peckinpah: What Price Violence?" *Life*, 11 Aug. 1972, p. 52.

7. "*Playboy* Interview: Sam Peckinpah," *Playboy*, Aug. 1972, p. 192.

8. Norman Mailer, *The Armies of the Night: History as a Novel, the Novel as History* (New York: New American Library, 1968), p. 35.

9. Norman Mailer, *The Prisoner of Sex* (Boston: Little, Brown, 1971), p. 168.

10. Ernest Callenbach, "A Conversation with Sam Peckinpah," *Film Quarterly* 17, no. 2 (Winter 1963–64): 8.

11. This and the next three quotations are from Norman Mailer, *Advertisements for Myself* (1959; rpt. New York: Berkley, Windhover Edition, 1976), pp. 315, 301, 300.

12. *Playboy* interview, p. 72.

13. *Film World*, interview with Sam Peckinpah, 1970, p. 89 (no additional publication information available but a copy of the interview is in the Peckinpah Collection, Margaret Herrick Library, Academy of Motion Picture Arts and Sciences, Beverly Hills, Calif.).

14. Mailer, *Advertisements*, p. 317.

15. *Film World* interview, p. 86.

16. Quoted in Aljean Harmetz, "Man Was a Killer Long Before He Served a God" (1969), rpt. in *Doing It Right: The Best Criticism on Sam Peckinpah's The Wild Bunch*, ed. Michael Bliss (Carbondale: Southern Illinois University Press, 1994), p. 174.

17. This and the next quotation are from Mailer, *Advertisements*, pp. 300–301.

18. Crews, pp. 14–15.

19. *Film World* interview, p. 92.

20. Mailer, *Advertisements*, p. 302.

21. *Film World* interview, p. 86.

22. This and the next quotation are from D. H. Lawrence, *Studies in Classic American Literature* (1923; rpt. New York: Viking, 1964), p. 53.

23. Richard Poirier, *Norman Mailer* (New York: Viking, 1972), p. 107.

24. Quoted in Aljean Harmetz, "*Pat Garrett and Billy the Kid*: What You See on the Screen . . . and What You Don't See," *New York Times*, 17 June 1973, sec. D, p. 13.

25. *Playboy* interview, p. 74.

26. Poirier, pp. 109–10.

27. Perry Miller, *Errand into the Wilderness* (1956; rpt. New York: Harper and Row, 1964), p. 185.

28. *Playboy* interview, p. 74.

29. Quoted in Dan Yergin, "Peckinpah's Progress: From Blood and Killing in the Old West to Siege and Rape in Rural Cornwall," *New York Times Magazine,* 31 Oct. 1971, p. 92.

30. Quoted in Winfred Blevins, "The Artistic Vision of Director Sam Peckinpah," *Show* 2, no. 1 (Mar. 1972): 40.

31. Mailer, *Advertisements,* p. 332.

32. Mailer, *Armies of the Night,* p. 91.

33. Lawrence, p. 104.

34. Young, p. 19.

Chapter 9: World of Our Fathers

1. Unless otherwise noted this account of the Peckinpah and Church family histories comes from Edgar Mortimer ("Mort") Peckinpah, "Peckinpah Family History: Part 3," unpublished draft, n.d. (hereafter, "Mort Peckinpah"); Garner Simmons, *Peckinpah: A Portrait in Montage* (Austin: University of Texas Press, 1982), pp. 3–20; and David Weddle, "'If They Move . . . Kill 'Em!': The Life and Times of Sam Peckinpah," unpublished second draft, 1991, (hereafter, "Weddle, unpublished draft"); and on interviews and conversations with James H. Butler (1978), Don Levy (1978), Fern Lea and Walter Peter (1978–95), Marie Selland (1978), Garner Simmons (1994–95), Herbert M. Stahl (1977), and David Weddle (1994–95).

2. Mort Peckinpah, pp. 7–8.

3. Mort Peckinpah, p. 11.

4. Weddle, unpublished draft, p. 40.

5. William Patterson, "All Hail Father of Irrigation," *Fresno Bee,* undated newspaper article (a clipping is in the Peckinpah Collection, Margaret Herrick Library, Academy of Motion Picture Arts and Sciences, Beverly Hills, Calif. [hereafter, "Peckinpah Collection"]).

6. Richard Whitehall, "Talking with Peckinpah," *Sight and Sound* 38, no. 4 (Autumn 1969): 173.

7. The date is still often erroneously printed as 1926.

8. Lois McFarland, "Country Home Falls Victim to Passage of Time," *Fresno Bee,* 19 August 1973, p. J1.

9. Fern Lea Peter to P.S., 1995.

10. James Hamilton, "The Judge and His Brother," *South Dakota Review* 29, no. 1 (Spring 1991): 84.

11. Quoted in an unfinished documentary made by Gary Weis on the making of *The Ballad of Cable Hogue,* circa 1969.

12. Quoted in David Weddle, *"If They Move . . . Kill 'Em!": The Life and Times of Sam Peckinpah* (New York: Grove Press, 1994), p. 55.

13. Quoted in P. F. Kluge, "Director Sam Peckinpah: What Price Violence?" *Life,* 11 Aug. 1972, p. 53.

14. Quoted in John Bryson, "The Wild Bunch in New York," *New York Magazine,* 19 Aug. 1974, p. 26.

15. "*Playboy* interview: Sam Peckinpah," *Playboy,* Aug. 1972, p. 72.

16. Penelope Gilliatt, review of *The Wild Bunch, New Yorker,* 5 July 1969, p. 74.

17. This and the next two quotations are from David S. ("Sam") Peckinpah, "An Analysis of the Method Used in Producing and Directing a One Act Play for the Stage and for a Closed Circuit Television Broadcast" (Master's thesis, University of Southern California, Los Angeles, 1954), pp. 141–42. Both the written portion of the thesis project and a kinescope of the film, *Portrait of a Madonna,* are in the Doheny Memorial Library at the university.

18. This and the next quotation are from John Cutts, "Shoot! Sam Peckinpah Talks to John Cutts," *Films and Filming* 16, no. 1 (Oct. 1969): 4.

19. Fern Lea Peter to P.S., 1987.

20. Weddle, unpublished draft, p. 878.

21. Sam Peckinpah to P.S., letter, 8 Apr. 1977.

22. This and the next quotation are from Kluge, pp. 50–52.

23. Don Levy to P.S., 1978.

24. "Wanted Sam Peckinpah Alias Dave Blassingame, Steve Judd," interview with Sam Peckinpah, *Cinema* 1, no. 4 (June–July 1962): 6.

25. See Paul Schrader, "Sam Peckinpah Going to Mexico" (1969), rpt. in *Doing It Right: The Best Criticism on Sam Peckinpah's The Wild Bunch,* ed. Michael Bliss (Carbondale: Southern Illinois University Press, 1994), p. 28.

26. Reported in Schrader, p. 25. Peckinpah also admired Oscar Lewis's *Children of Sanchez,* a quasi-anthropological novel about poverty in Mexico (Jesse Graham to P.S., 1996).

27. Katy Haber to P.S., 1977.

28. Sam Peckinpah Retrospective, Rice University, Houston, Apr. 1984, Prof. Jerry Holt, guest host (hereafter, "Sam Peckinpah Retrospective").

29. The best description of the Method and its importance to American film and theater is in Steve Vineberg's superb history and critical study, *Method Actors: Three Generations of an American Acting Style* (New York: Schirmer Books, 1991).

30. Quoted in Quentin Falk, "The Two Most Beautiful People in the World on Sam Peckinpah," *Cinema/TV Today,* 15 Sept. 1973, pp. 6–7.

31. Steve Vineberg, the author of *Method Actors,* once said that the only two directors he ever felt got the best that could be got from de Havilland were Peckinpah and William Wyler (Steve Vineberg to P.S., 1995).

32. Quoted in Weddle, unpublished draft, p. 586.

33. This and the next two quotations are from Daniel Melnick to P.S., 1995.

34. Quoted in Simmons, p. 90.

35. Quoted in Weddle, p. 211.

36. Northrop Frye, *The Anatomy of Criticism* (New York: Atheneum, 1957), p. 42.

37. Quoted in Axel Madsen, "Peckinpah in from the Cold," *Sight and Sound* 36, no. 3 (Summer 1967): 123.

38. Quoted in Kluge, p. 49.

39. Garth Craven to P.S., 1985.

40. Sam Peckinpah Retrospective.

41. Quoted in Weddle, p. 355.

42. *Playboy* interview, p. 70.

43. Quoted in Max Evans, *Sam Peckinpah: Master of Violence* (Vermillion, S.D.: Dakota Press, 1972), p. 41.

44. "Mort Sahl Called Me a 1939 American," interview with Sam Peckinpah, *Film Heritage* 11, no. 4 (Summer 1976): 23.

45. See Madsen, p. 123; *Film Heritage* interview, p. 21; and *Playboy* interview, p. 74.

46. This will doubtless not deter the zealous cinematic detective, who, along with sleuths of other persuasions, may appreciate the following list, culled from several interviews Peckinpah gave during the last twenty years of his life, of films and directors that or who have most "moved, stimulated, and entertained" him at the movies: *Rashomon, The Treasure of the Sierra Madre, La Strada, Hiroshima Mon Amour, Ace in the Hole* (also called *The Big Carnival*), *Odd Man Out, Hamlet, Henry V, La Dolce Vita, On the Waterfront, Last Year at Marienbad*, the *Apu* trilogy, *Tobacco Road, A Place in the Sun, Shane, My Darling Clementine, The Hunchback of Notre Dame, Viva Zapata, Viva Villa, Forbidden Games, Los Olvidados, High Noon, The Breaking Point, The Magician, The Seventh Seal, Battle of Algiers, Bad Day at Black Rock, Bonnie and Clyde, The Left-Handed Gun, Red Desert, Blow-Up, The River,* and *Red River,* and Kurosawa, Huston, Chaplin, Ford, Bergman, Resnais, Antonioni, Fellini, Kazan, Wilder, Lean, Reed, Renoir, Curtiz, Siegel, Pontecorvo, Clouzot, Buñuel, Stevens, and Satyajit Ray.

47. This and the next quotation are from the *Playboy* interview, p. 72.

48. Jim Silke, "Wanted Sam Peckinpah Alias Dave Blassingame, Steve Judd," interview with Sam Peckinpah, *Cinema* 1, no. 4 (June–July 1962): 35.

49. *Playboy* interview, p. 72.

50. Whitehall, p. 173.

51. Cutts, p. 4.

52. Quoted in Aljean Harmetz, "Man Was a Killer Long Before He Served a God" (1969), rpt. in *Doing It Right*, p. 173.

53. "It was always Peckinpah's fantasy that there had been a Camelot for rowdy free spirits that history ruined," writes David Thomson. It is tempting to imagine what fantasy he must have been in to make such an incredible statement. When Peckinpah was feeling expansive he would occasionally say things that could be construed to mean something like that; so do some of his characters. But in his films, which is where it counts, that kind of talk functions as characterization, not as statements about history that we are expected to take literally; and when it is introduced as theme, it is ironized or otherwise made complex and ambiguous. His last Western, *Pat Garrett and Billy the Kid*, tells a story mostly set three decades before *The Wild Bunch*, and the characters still talk about the good times of even earlier days. Yet this was his grimmest vision ever. Short of writing a gloss and handing it out at

the box office, it is difficult to know what more Peckinpah could have done to get across a point that is just precisely opposite to the one Thomson ascribes to him. (David Thomson, "Better Best Westerns," *Film Comment* 26, no. 2 [Mar.–Apr. 1990]: 5–13.)

54. This and the next three quotations are from the *Playboy* interview, pp. 65, 72, 192.

55. *Film Heritage* interview, p. 23.

56. This and the next three quotations are from the *Playboy* interview, pp. 74, 192.

57. Reported in "Press Violent about Film's Violence: Prod Sam Peckinpah Following '*Bunch*,'" *Variety*, 2 July 1969, p. 15.

58. Simmons, p. 9.

59. Quoted in Dan Yergin, "Peckinpah's Progress: From Blood and Killing in the Old West to Siege and Rape in Rural Cornwall," *New York Times Magazine*, 31 Oct. 1971, p. 92.

60. Sam Peckinpah to Wilhelmina Wenzel, letter, 11 Feb. 1975 (Peckinpah Collection).

61. Sam Peckinpah to Colin McArthur, letter, 16 Nov. 1970 (Peckinpah Collection).

Sources: Bibliographic Notes, Filmography, and Videography

Bibliographic Notes

The endnotes to this book cite all information necessary to locate the sources. Of the numerous books on Peckinpah the most valuable is David Weddle's richly informative and insightful biography, *"If They Move, Kill 'Em": The Life and Times of Sam Peckinpah* (Grove Press, 1994), which strikes an ideal balance between sympathy and candor. Though now unfortunately out of print, Garner Simmons's excellent career study, *Peckinpah: A Portrait in Montage* (University of Texas Press, 1982), is by no means superseded, with enlightening accounts of how Peckinpah worked with his casts and crews. None of the several critical studies is absolutely comprehensive, but Michael Bliss's commendable *Justified Lives: Morality and Narrative in the Films of Sam Peckinpah* (Southern Illinois University Press, 1993) stands alone in covering all fourteen of the feature films. Bliss has also put together an excellent anthology, *Doing It Right: The Best Criticism on Sam Peckinpah's The Wild Bunch* (Southern Illinois University Press, 1994), which contains important essays by Robert Culp, Paul Schrader, and Michael Sragow, among others. In preparation by Bliss and Weddle is an enthusiastically anticipated book of photographs from *The Wild Bunch* (from Southern Illinois University Press).

By far the largest holding of Peckinpah materials is to be found in the Peckinpah Collection at the Margaret Herrick Library, the Academy of Motion Picture Arts and Sciences, Beverly Hills, California. Everything seems to be here: scripts, correspondence, notes, memos, clippings, memorabilia, audio tapes, photographs, production reports, schedules, and trivia. Also on file is the much longer first draft of David Weddle's manuscript for his biography, which contains nearly as much additional information of value as went into the published book, and all of his interview tapes (some five hundred hours' worth) and notes.

Television

Just about all of Peckinpah's television scripts are in the Peckinpah Collection. The listing of Peckinpah's television credits that immediately follows is based in part on two previous sources: Garner Simmons's dissertation, "The Cinema of Sam Peckinpah and the American Western: A Study of the Interrelationship between an Auteur/Director and the Genre in which He Works" (Northwestern University, 1975), and David Weddle's filmography in the October 1995 issue of *Sight and Sound*. Only scripts that actually went into production and were aired are included here. The Peckinpah Collection contains numerous others that were never produced or even sold, and many treatments and outlines that never made it to script form. Unless otherwise noted, episodes are thirty minutes in length, film, and black-and-white.

Between 1956 and 1960 Peckinpah wrote freelance—sometimes alone, sometimes in collaboration—for several series, all of them Westerns.

> *Gunsmoke:* eleven teleplays adapted from *Gunsmoke* radio plays by John Meston, titled "The Queue," "Yorky," "Cooter," "How to Die for Nothing," "The Guitar," "The Round Up," "Legal Revenge," "Poor Pearl," "Jealousy," "How to Kill a Woman," and "Dirt."
>
> *20th Century Fox Hour:* "End of a Gun" (one hour).
>
> *Boots and Saddles:* "The Captain."
>
> *Tales of Wells Fargo:* "Apache Gold."
>
> *Tombstone Territory:* "Johnny Ringo's Last Ride."
>
> *Man without a Gun:* "The Kidder."
>
> *Broken Arrow:* "The Teacher," "The Knife Fighter," "The Assassin," and "The Transfer" (which Peckinpah directed).
>
> *Klondike:* "Klondike Fever" (series pilot, which Peckinpah directed) and "Swoger's Mill."

The Rifleman. 1958–59.

> "The Sharpshooter." Series pilot written by Peckinpah for *Dick Powell's Zane Grey Theater* (from a rejected script he wrote for *Gunsmoke*), directed by Arnold Laven. Starring Chuck Conners as the title character, Lucas McCain, and Johnny Crawford as his son, Mark. With R. G. Armstrong, Dennis Hopper, and Lief Erickson.
>
> "The Marshal." Written and directed by Peckinpah (from a story by Peckinpah and Jack Gariss). With Paul Fix, R. G. Armstrong, James Drury, and Warren Oates.
>
> "The Home Ranch." Written by Peckinpah, directed by Arnold Laven.
>
> "The Boarding House." Written by Jack Curtis and Peckinpah, directed by Peckinpah. With Katy Jurado.
>
> "The Money Gun." Written by Bruce Geller and Peckinpah, directed by Peckinpah. With John Dehner.
>
> "The Baby Sitter." Written by Jack Curtis and Peckinpah, directed by Peckinpah. With John Dehner.

Dick Powell's Zane Grey Theatre. 1959.

> "Trouble at Treces Cruces." Written and directed by Peckinpah. Became pilot for *The Westerner*. With Brian Keith and Neville Brand.
>
> "Miss Jenny." Written by Peckinpah and Robert Heverly, directed by Peckinpah. With Vera Miles and Ben Cooper.
>
> "Lonesome Road." Written by Peckinpah and Jack Curtis, directed by Peckinpah. With Edmond O'Brien.

The Westerner. 1960. Series created and produced by Peckinpah. Starring
Brien Keith as the title character, Dave Blassingame. The list is in the order
shot, with air date following the title; all episodes were first broadcast in
1960.
"The Old Man." 25 November. Directed by Andre de Toth, written by
Peckinpah. With Sam Jaffe.
"School Day." 7 October. Directed by Andre de Toth, written by Peckinpah
and Robert Heverly.
"Mrs. Kennedy." 28 October. Directed by Bernard Kowalski, written by
Peckinpah and John Dunkel.
"Brown." 21 October. Directed by Peckinpah, written by Bruce Geller.
With John Dehner as Burgundy Smith.
"Going Home." 16 December. Directed by Elliot Silverstein, written by
Jack Curtis.
"The Courting of Libby." 11 November. Directed by Peckinpah, written
by Bruce Geller. With John Dehner and Joan O'Brien.
"Jeff." 30 September. Directed by Peckinpah, written by Robert Heverly
and Peckinpah. With Diana Millay, Geoffrey Toone, and Warren Oates.
"The Line Camp." 9 December. Written and directed by Tom Gries. With
Robert Culp, Slim Pickens, and Karl Swenson.
"*Dos Piños.*" 4 November. Directed by Donald McDougall, written by E.
Jack Neuman.
"The Treasure." 18 November. Directed by Ted Post, written by Cyril
Hume.
"Hand on the Gun." 23 December. Directed by Peckinpah, written by
Bruce Geller. With Michael Ansara and Ben Cooper.
"Ghost of a Chance." 2 December. Directed by Bruce Geller, written by
Milton Gelman. With Katy Jurado and Joseph Wiseman.
"The Painting." 30 December. Directed by Peckinpah, written by Bruce
Geller. With John Dehner and Madlyn Rhue.
Pericles on 31st Street. 1962. Directed by Peckinpah, written by Harry Mark
Petrakis and Peckinpah, for *The Dick Powell Show.* With Theodore Bikel,
Carroll O'Connor, Arthur O'Connell, and Strother Martin. (One hour.)
The Losers. 1962. Directed by Peckinpah, written by Bruce Geller and Peck-
inpah, for *The Dick Powell Theatre.* With Lee Marvin, Keenan Wynn, Rose-
mary Clooney, and Dub Taylor. (One hour.)
Noon Wine. 1966. Directed and written by Peckinpah (from Katherine Anne
Porter's short novel of the same title), produced by Daniel Melnick for
ABC Stage 67. With Jason Robards (Royal Earle Thompson), Olivia de
Havilland (Ellie Thompson), Per Oscarsson (Mr. Helton), Theodore Bikel
(Homer T. Hatch), Ben Johnson (Sheriff Darbee), L. Q. Jones (Mr. Mc-
Clellan), Robert Emhardt (Mr. Burleigh), Steve Sanders (Arthur), Peter
Robbins (Herbert), Jill Andre (Mrs. McClellan). (One hour, color, vid-
eotape and film.)
That Lady Is My Wife. 1966. Directed by Peckinpah, written by Halstead Welles
(from a story by Jack Laird) for *Bob Hope's Chrysler Theater.* With Jean Sim-

mons, Bradford Dillman, Alex Cord, and Begonia Palacios. (One hour, color.)

Films

The Deadly Companions. 1961. A Carousel Production, released by Pathé-America. Color, CinemaScope and Panavision. Running time: 90 minutes.
Crew: Director: Sam Peckinpah. *Producer:* Charles B. FitzSimons. *Screenplay:* A. S. Fleischman. *Cinematography:* William H. Clothier. *Music:* Marlin Skiles. *Song:* "A Dream of Love," by Marlin Skiles and FitzSimons. *Editor:* Stanley E. Rabjohn. *Special Effects:* Dave Kohler. *Sound:* Gordon Sawyer and Robert J. Callen. *Production Manager:* Lee Lukather. *Wardrobe:* Frank Beetson Sr. and Sheila O'Brien. *Makeup:* James Barker. *Hairstyles:* Fae Smyth.
Cast: Kit Tilden: Maureen O'Hara. *Yellowleg:* Brian Keith. *Billy:* Steve Cochran. *Turk:* Chill Wills. *Parson:* Strother Martin. *Doctor:* Will Wright. *Cal:* Jim O'Hara. *Mayor:* Peter O'Crotty. *Mead:* Billy Vaughan. *Gambler:* Robert Sheldon. *Gambler:* John Hamilton. *Bartender:* Hank Gobble. *Indian:* Buck Sharpe.

Ride the High Country. 1962. A Metro-Goldwyn-Mayer Production. Color, CinemaScope. Running time: 94 minutes.
Crew: Director: Sam Peckinpah. *Producer:* Richard E. Lyons. *Screenplay:* N. B. Stone Jr. *Cinematography:* Lucien Ballard. *Music:* George Bassman. *Art Direction:* George W. Davis and Leroy Coleman. *Set Decoration:* Henry Grace and Otto Siegel. *Editor:* Frank Santillo. *Color Consultant:* Charles K. Hagedon. *Recording Supervisor:* Franklin Milton. *Hairstyles:* May Keats. *Makeup:* William Tuttle. *Assistant Director:* Hal Polaire.
Cast: Steve Judd: Joel McCrea. *Gil Westrum:* Randolph Scott. *Elsa Knudsen:* Mariette Hartley. *Heck Longtree:* Ron Starr. *Judge Tolliver:* Edgar Buchanan. *Joshua Knudsen:* R. G. Armstrong. *Kate:* Jenie Jackson. *Billy Hammond:* James Drury. *Sylvus Hammond:* L. Q. Jones. *Elder Hammond:* John Anderson. *Jimmy Hammond:* John Davis Chandler. *Henry Hammond:* Warren Oates. *Saloon Girl:* Carmen Phillips.

Major Dundee. 1965. A Jerry Bresler Production for Columbia Pictures. Color, Panavision. Running time: 134 minutes.
Crew: Director: Sam Peckinpah. *Producer:* Jerry Bresler. *Second-unit Director:* Cliff Lyons. *Screenplay:* Harry Julian Fink, Oscar Saul, and Sam Peckinpah, based on an original story by Fink. *Music:* Daniele Amfitheatrof. *Title Song:* "Major Dundee March," by Amfitheatrof and Ned Washington, sung by Mitch Miller's Sing Along Gang. *Editors:* William A. Lyon, Don Starling, and Howard Kunin. *Art Direction:* Al Ybarra. *Special Effects:* August Lohman. *Costumes:* Tom Dawson. *Sound:* Charles J. Rice and James Z. Flaster. *Assistant Producer:* Rick Rosenberg. *Production Manager:* Francisco Day. *Assistant Directors:* Floyd Joyer and John Veitch.
Cast: Major Amos Dundee: Charlton Heston. *Captain Ben Tyreen:* Richard Harris. *Samuel Potts:* James Coburn. *Lieutenant Graham:* Jim Hutton. *Tim Ryan:*

Michael Anderson Jr. *Teresa Santiago:* Senta Berger. *Sergeant Gomez:* Mario Adorf. *Aesop:* Brock Peters. *O. W. Hadley:* Warren Oates. *Sergeant Chillum:* Ben Johnson. *Reverend Dahlstrom:* R. G. Armstrong. *Arthur Hadley:* L. Q. Jones. *Wiley:* Slim Pickens. *Captain Waller:* Karl Swenson. *Sierra Charriba:* Michael Pate. *Jimmy Lee Benteen:* John Davis Chandler. *Priam:* Dub Taylor. *Captain Jacques Tremaine:* Albert Carrier. *Riago:* Jose Carlos Ruiz. *Melinche:* Aurora Clavel. *Linda:* Begonia Palacios. *Dr. Aguilar:* Enrique Lucero. *Old Apache:* Francisco Reyguera.

The Wild Bunch. 1969. A Phil Feldman Production for Warner Brothers–Seven Arts. Color, CinemaScope and Panavision. Running time: 145 minutes (1995 restoration).
Crew: Director: Sam Peckinpah. *Producer:* Phil Feldman. *Second-unit Director:* Buzz Henry. *Screenplay:* Walon Green and Sam Peckinpah, based on an original story by Green and Roy N. Sickner. *Cinematography:* Lucien Ballard. *Music:* Jerry Fielding. *Music Supervision:* Sonny Burke. *Art Direction:* Edward Carrere. *Editor:* Louis Lombardo. *Associate Editor:* Robert L. Wolfe. *Special Effects:* Bud Hulburd. *Sound:* Robert J. Miller. *Wardrobe:* Gordon Dawson. *Makeup:* Al Greenway. *Associate Producer:* Roy N. Sickner. *Production Manager:* William Faralla. *Assistant Directors:* Cliff Coleman and Fred Gammon. *Script Supervisor:* Crayton Smith.
Cast: Pike Bishop: William Holden. *Dutch Engstrom:* Ernest Borgnine. *Deke Thornton:* Robert Ryan. *Old Sykes:* Edmond O'Brien. *Lyle Gorch:* Warren Oates. *Tector Gorch:* Ben Johnson. *Angel:* Jaime Sanchez. *Mapache:* Emilio Fernandez. *Coffer:* Strother Martin. *TC:* L. Q. Jones. *Pat Harrigan:* Albert Dekker. *Crazy Lee:* Bo Hopkins. *Mayor Wainscoat:* Dub Taylor. *Zamorra:* Jorge Russek. *Herrera:* Alfonso Arau. *Don Jose:* Chano Urueta. *Teresa:* Sonia Amelio. *Aurora:* Aurora Clavel. *Elsa:* Elsa Cardenas. *German Army Officer:* Fernando Wagner.

The Ballad of Cable Hogue. 1970. A Phil Feldman Production for Warner Brothers Pictures. Color. Running time: 121 minutes.
Crew: Director: Sam Peckinpah. *Producer:* Sam Peckinpah. *Executive Producer:* Phil Feldman. *Coproducer:* William Faralla. *Screenplay:* John Crawford and Edmund Penney. *Cinematography:* Lucien Ballard. *Editors:* Frank Santillo and Louis Lombardo. *Art Director:* Leroy Coleman. *Music:* Jerry Goldsmith. *Songs:* "Tomorrow Is the Song I Sing," music by Goldsmith and lyrics by Richard Gillis; "Butterfly Mornings" and "Wait for Me, Sunrise," music and lyrics by Gillis. *Orchestrations:* Arthur Morton. *Music Supervision:* Sonny Burke. *Special Effects:* Bud Hulburd. *Unit Production Manager:* Dink Templeton. *Dialogue Supervisor:* Frank Kowalski. *Wardrobe:* Robert Fletcher. *Titles:* Latigo Productions. *Assistant Director:* John Guadioso. *Makeup:* Gary Liddiard and Al Fleming. *Hair Stylist:* Kathy Blondell. *Set Decorator:* Jack Mills.
Cast: Cable Hogue: Jason Robards. *Hildy:* Stella Stevens. *Joshua:* David Warner. *Bowen:* Strother Martin. *Taggart:* L. Q. Jones. *Ben:* Slim Pickens. *Cushing:* Peter Whitney. *Quittner:* R. G. Armstrong. *Clete:* Gene Evans. *Jenson:* Wil-

liam Mims. *Claudia:* Susan O'Connell. *Mrs. Jensen:* Kathleen Freeman. *Powell:* Vaughn Taylor. *William:* Felix Nelson. *Webb:* Max Evans.

Pat Garrett and Billy the Kid. 1973. A Gordon Carroll-Sam Peckinpah Production for Metro-Goldwyn-Mayer. Color, Panavision. Running times: 124 minutes (preview), 106 minutes (original theatrical release), 122 minutes (Turner).

Crew: Director: Sam Peckinpah. *Producer:* Gordon Carroll. *Screenplay:* Rudolph Wurlitzer. *Cinematography:* John Coquillon. *Editors:* Roger Spottiswoode, Garth Craven, Robert L. Wolfe, Richard Halsey, David Berlatsky, and Tony de Zarraga. *Art Director:* Ted Haworth. *Set Director:* Ray Moyer. *Music:* Bob Dylan. *Songs:* "Billy" and "Knockin' on Heaven's Door," music and lyrics by Dylan. *Sound:* Charles M. Wilborn and Harry W. Tetrick. *Special Visual Effects:* A. J. Lohman. *Wardrobe:* Michael Butler. *Makeup:* Jack P. Wilson. *Production Managers:* Jim Henderling and Alfonsa Sanchez. *Second-unit Photography:* Gabriel Torres G. *Assistant Directors:* Newton Arnold, Lawrence J. Powell, and Jesus Marin Bello.

Cast: Pat Garrett: James Coburn. *Billy the Kid:* Kris Kristofferson. *Alias:* Bob Dylan. *Governor Lew Wallace:* Jason Robards. *Sheriff Kip McKinney:* Richard Jaeckel. *Mrs. Baker:* Katy Jurado. *Sheriff Baker:* Slim Pickens. *Lemuel:* Chill Wills. *Poe:* John Beck. *Maria:* Rita Coolidge. *Deputy Ollinger:* R. G. Armstrong. *Eno:* Luke Askew. *Holly:* Richard Bright. *J. W. Bell:* Matt Clark. *Howland:* Jack Dodson. *Alamosa Bill:* Jack Elam. *Paco:* Emilio Fernandez. *Pete Maxwell:* Paul Fix. *Black Harris:* L. Q. Jones. *Silva:* Jorge Russek. *Bowdre:* Charlie Martin. *Luke:* Harry Dean Stanton. *Mrs. Horrell:* Claudia Bryar. *Norris:* John Chandler. *Denver:* Mike Mikler. *Ida Garrett:* Aurora Clavel. *Ruthie Lee:* Rutanya Alda. *Rupert:* Walter Kelley. *Tom O'Folliard:* Rudolph Wurlitzer. *Mr. Horrell:* Gene Evans. *Beaver:* Donnie Fritts. *Sackett:* Don Levy. *Will:* Sam Peckinpah.

Home Video

Most of Peckinpah's television work is unavailable in any format except in syndicated reruns of old series like *Gunsmoke* from its half-hour years, *The Rifleman,* and *The Westerner.* All the Western films, however, are available in both laserdisc and VHS tape presentations. In the list that follows label and catalog number are given; unless otherwise noted sound is monophonic; "pan-and-scan" indicates a full-screen—i.e., television—transfer, as opposed to the wider aspect-ratio of the theatrical releases. But even a widescreen (aka letterbox) transfer does not necessarily guarantee that the apsect-ratio of the theatrical release has been accurately preserved; all discrepancies are noted. Laserdisc and VHS presentations are not necessarily made from the same print; when they are, laserdiscs are superior to VHS tapes in visual reproduction and far superior in sonic reproduction.

Gunsmoke. The half-hour episodes, including all those written by Peckinpah, are regularly shown in syndication under the series title *Marshal Dillon.*

Columbia House has also announced plans to release early episodes on video tape.

The Rifleman. Nuventures Video. Four Peckinpah episodes ("The Sharpshooter," "The Marshal," "The Home Ranch," and "The Baby Sitter") in excellent transfers on two VHS tapes. Now out of print and out of stock, copies may be available on the second-hand market.

The Deadly Companions. New World Video. Image Entertainment. Laserdisc ID6911NW: faded print, pan-and-scan, dismal effort. Star Maker Entertainment VHS SOSTM080045: like the laserdisc.

Ride the High Country. MGM/UA Home Video. Laserdisc 102223: faded print, widescreen but incorrect aspect-ratio (i.e., extreme sides of image cropped), distorted soundtrack, and literally missing frames in famous final shot to achieve jump cut director never intended; includes theatrical trailer. A disgrace on every conceivable level (even the jacket art is ugly), with no apparent excuse: pristine new prints were widely shown in Los Angeles in the late 1980s. VHS 600850: okay print, pan-and-scan.

Major Dundee. Columbia TriStar Home Video. Laserdisc 10456 (2 discs): superb transfer from excellent print, widescreen, theatrical trailer: film looks better here than in any of extant theatrical prints shown at festivals and revivals during last thirty years. One incidental oddity: jacket front has photograph of Peter O'Toole (sometime drinking buddy of director's but never in one of his films). VHS 60046: different print (much inferior to laserdisc), pan-and-scan.

The Wild Bunch. Warner Home Video. Laserdisc CAV 14035 (6 discs), deluxe boxed set: Warners went through a nightmare retiming the print for the 1995 restoration. Though much money was spent and it is claimed that the original negative was used, the release prints emerged unsatisfactory in several ways: some scenes are too dark (e.g., the famous "silver rings" scene); here and there tans, beiges, flesh tones, and whites are pale or washed out; the color spectrum throughout has less richness, nuance, depth, and variety than the original. But at least timing improves as the film goes along; in the second half it is very good, with even Lucien Ballard's blue skies appearing in something like their storied splendor. In all of this, the 70mm prints suffer rather more than those in 35mm. To place these criticisms in some perspective, nothing is anywhere so deficient as to impair enjoyment or appreciation of the film; and the comparisons here are made against the highest possible standard: the technical finish of the original 1969 Technicolor prints. Peckinpah and Feldman put the lab through hell to get these right, calling for an unprecedented sixteen answer prints (two to four is the norm). (Nor were they being mere perfectionists in their demands: the director's final cut contained over 3,600 shot-to-shot edits, more than any other color film made up to that time—possibly ever. Many shots in the opening and closing gunfights are only frames long, which complicates the timing process enormously.)

Warners also refurbished the original stereophonic dub for the 1995 restoration, and that has been managed to perfection. Steven C. Brown,

an archivist and film editor, spent weeks scrupulously gathering together and preparing the disparate sound units for the chief mixer, Robert
Litt, and his colleague, Elliot Tyson. It is thanks to their meticulousness
(especially Litt's as a dialogue mixer) that the film has never sounded
better, with dialogue, background lines, atmosphere, and effects emerging with unprecedented clarity. This is one of the great dubs in the history of film, and at last the magnitude of its achievement is fully evident.

Whatever the problems of the release prints, Warner Home Video has
accomplished a minor miracle in the transfer to laserdisc. Using the 1969
prints as a guide and all the new digital technology available for visual
restoration, Warners' video technicians, headed by Ned Price, with Gregg
Garvin doing the telecine, have come up with a transfer that for overall
color balance and timing is far more faithful to the film as it looked in
1969 than is any of the 1995 prints. The stereo soundtrack of the laserdisc is in both matrixed surround and the new, all-discrete AC-3 format.

As of this writing, the deluxe package is scheduled for release in the
fall of 1996 and is to include: (1) Theatrical trailers of all seven Peckinpah
films for Warners and MGM/UA. (2) A short documentary featuring
never-before-released footage of Peckinpah directing the film, with reminiscences by family, friends, and colleagues. (3) A compact disc of Jerry
Fielding's music score, prepared from the original four-track master tapes
by the music archivist Nick Redman. This is the first time the complete,
original score in stereo has ever been available on the home market (a
1969 soundtrack LP was of selections only and not of performances actually used on the soundtrack). Also included are a couple of cues never
used in the film. (4) A booklet—edited and designed by Trevor Wills-
mer—of essays by noted Peckinpah critics and scholars, and related material, including interviews with the director, Fielding, and Ken Hyman.
In sum, for once the rubric "deluxe" looks as if it might really mean something.

Laserdisc CLV 14034 (2 discs): in release since fall 1995, this is essentially of same technical quality as deluxe but without extras (i.e., additional
trailers, booklet, CD, and CAV format). VHA 140340: stereophonic sound
and widescreen transfer, all okay within limitations of tape format, but visual and audio quality nowhere near level of laserdisc. However, not far
off what 70mm restoration prints look like without transfer enhancements
that make laserdisc superior.

The Ballad of Cable Hogue. Warner Home Video. Laserdisc 11298 A/B: superb
transfer from very good print, pan-and-scan (though because original is
1:85, rather than widescreen, this less damaging than it might be). VHS
tape: good transfer from what appears to be same print.

Pat Garrett and Billy the Kid. MGM/UA. Laserdisc ML102238 (2 discs): superb
transfer from gorgeous print, widescreen, theatrical trailer. Billed as "director's cut," but missing one scene. VHS 201567: same print, pan-and-
scan.

Acknowledgments

A revision compounds old debts and brings new ones. As before the critic's principal critic was David Morrell, than whom he could ask for none more scrupulous and supportive. The shade of Alexander C. Kern's influence remains undiminished, as does Alan Axelrod's, and both are deeply appreciated anew. With respect to the revision alone I extend the greatest thanks—feeble word beside the immensity of my debts—to David Weddle, Peckinpah's best biographer, and Garner Simmons, the first chronicler of his career. The generosity of both men with their time, research, and permission to quote from their published work was quite literally boundless, as were their enthusiasm and encouragement for a new edition of this book. Equal thanks is extended to Fern Lea Peter, who made herself always available for my many probings about the often troubled household she and her brother grew up in. I am especially grateful for her trust in sharing some memories that were not happily recalled. It goes without saying, though it must be said, that all interpretations, inferences, and conclusions about Peckinpah and his work that I've drawn from the materials these three persons provided or the conversations we've had are entirely my responsibility, not theirs.

I've been compelled—happily, challengingly, rewardingly—by this artist for over a quarter century now. Although the main ideas here are my own, throughout the years many people—friends, family, colleagues, associates, students—have contributed much to my thinking. In addition to those already mentioned, the following list is ventured (not without some trepidation for fear of leaving off an important name or two): Robert Becker; Henry Binder; Susan Flynn; Bill Franke; Ann E. Gilmor; Andrea Heiss; Cyrus Nowrasteh; Charles Phillips; Joan C. Searles; Michael Sragow; my father, Harry Seydor; my mother, Rose Seydor; and my brother, Michael Seydor. Herschel Parker and Ron Gottesman were supportive colleagues during a difficult period. It was the enthusiasm of Michael Bliss that provided me with the first opportunity for a revision that became this full-scale reconsideration.

To those who granted interviews or made themselves available for questions I am grateful for their patience, candor, and trust: Lucien Ballard, James H. Butler, Gordon Carroll, Garth Craven, Kip Dellinger, Laurie Dellinger, Gill Dennis, Jerry Fielding, Norma Fink, Jesse Graham, James Hamilton, Walter Kelley, Don Levy, Richard E. Lyons, Joel McCrea, Daniel Melnick,

Sharon Peckinpah, Walter Peter, Randolph Scott, Marie Selland, Jim Silke, Roger Spottiswoode, Herbert M. Stahl, and Robert Wolfe.

To Kristen Peckinpah I owe many thanks for trusting me with *carte blanche* access, including copying privileges, to the Peckinpah Collection in the Margaret Herrick Library at the Academy of Motion Picture Arts and Sciences, where Valentin Almendarez, Collections Archivist, and his wonderful staff were unfailingly helpful, especially Howard Prouty and Faye Thompson. Numerous others also assisted with various aspects of the research, such as acquiring scripts, films, tapes, stills, articles, and other materials: Leith Adams, Dan Einstein, Ray Faiola, Mark Ferrara, Jerry Holt, Don Hyde, Richard T. Jameson, Kathleen Murphy, Jeff Slater, and Dennis Vellucci.

All family photographs of Peckinpah and his parents are used through the courtesy of Kristen Peckinpah. Fern Lea Peter provided the photograph of her brother used on the jacket front and for the frontispiece. Stills from *The Wild Bunch* and *The Ballad of Cable Hogue* are reprinted with the permission of Warner Brothers. Richard M. Kolbet of the University of Iowa and David H. Malone of the University of Southern California both made funds available to rent films in the days before the proliferation of home video. Four Star International lent several episodes of *The Westerner.*

The University of Illinois Press—this time in the persons of Ann Lowry, Theresa Sears, and especially Carol Bolton Betts—remains, as before, a writer's dream of a publisher: considerate, thorough, dedicated, best of all enthusiastic.

Despite extraordinary obligations both professional and scholastic, Danielle Egerer somehow managed to lighten a burdensome year with an enthusiasm, grace, and love that are beyond valuation, and provided also the continuing delight of companionship with someone who was experiencing Peckinpah's films for the first time.

I save for last the acknowledgment of my greatest debt, which is to the memory of Sam Peckinpah. It is reliably reported that Peckinpah was well disposed toward the first edition of this book, because as a work of criticism it dealt centrally with his films, not with him. I have perforce included more biographical material this time around, but only to the end of shedding further light on his relationship to these films as works of art or trying to understand why those that fail do so. In either case the original purpose remains now as then to study and articulate my feelings about a group of films that have moved me more than any in my experience.

Index

PAUL SEYDOR was educated in literature, journalism, and American studies at the Pennsylvania State University and at the University of Iowa, where he received his Ph.D. in American Civilization. He has taught literature, film, and American studies at the University of Iowa and the University of Southern California. He has written on film and music for *Sight and Sound, Quarterly Review of Film Studies, Film Society Review, The Perfect Vision,* and *The Absolute Sound.* Since 1983 he has been a freelance film editor; his credits include *Cobb, Tin Cup, White Men Can't Jump, The Program, Major League II, Shadow over China, Turner and Hooch, Time Flies When You're Alive,* and *The Best of Times.* Seydor still occasionally writes and guest lectures on film. He lives in Los Angeles.